McSWEENEY'S 45

HITCHCOCK *and* BRADBURY FISTFIGHT *in* HEAVEN

INTERNS & VOLUNTEERS: Taylor Yeomans, Nolan Boomer, Alex Bauer, Zack Grossenbacher, Frances Cannon, Erica Plumlee, Jessica McHugh, Tyler Doyle, Taylor Wallau, Shoshana Akabas, Nate Rogers, Amanda Arnold, Harriet Dwyer, Louisa Dunnigan, Sally Weathers, Aralyn Beaumont, Noah Pisner, Paolo Yumol, Ian Delaney, Valerie Snow, Yannic Dosenbach, Laura Ceron Melo, Ilaria Varriale, Jess Bergman, Lara Sichi, Will Gray, Alec Joyner, Madison Wetzell, Olivia Judge. ALSO HELPING: Andi Winnette, Casey Jarman, Sam Riley, Rachel Khong, Clara Sankey, Brian McMullen, Sunra Thompson, Brian Christian, Ruby Perez. WEBSITE: Chris Monks. SUPPORT: Jordan Karnes. OUTREACH: Isaac Fitzgerald. ART DIRECTOR: Dan McKinley. COPY EDITOR: Will Georgantas. PUBLISHER: Laura Howard. ASSOCIATE EDITOR: Annie Wyman. MANAGING EDITOR: Daniel Gumbiner. EXECUTIVE EDITOR: Jordan Bass. EDITOR: Dave Eggers.

Cover and interior art by Tavis Coburn. Author portraits by Pat Kinsella.
Printed in Michigan at Thomson-Shore Printers.

DEAR MCSWEENEY'S,

To the extent that science fiction has a reputation as a predictive literature, it is undeserved. To laud science fiction for its predictive quality is to fire a shotgun at the side of a barn, draw a target around the blast center, and declare your excellent marksmanship. SF has made innumerable predictions, and it would be a surprise if some of them *hadn't* come true.

What SF does—even when the author isn't aware of it—is expose the deep-seated aspirations and fears about technologies running through our culture. These fears and hopes are often so diffuse that it's impossible to put your finger on them, but by making them the center of a speculative parable about the future, an SF writer can surface them and make them explicit.

When you have a sore throat, you go to the doctor and she pokes a swab at the back of your throat and cultures what she finds there in agar on a petri dish. What grows there over the weekend is not an extrapolation of your body's future and it's not a prediction. Instead, it's a cartoonish world in a bottle, in which a single fact about your body—the gunk growing in your throat—becomes the lone, totalizing element.

Science fiction writers pluck one technology (or a few) out of the wider world and put them into a petri dish. This is neither prediction, nor is it extrapolation. Rather, it is a diagnostic tool that renders vivid the truth of the present.

By telling us about the present, science fiction ends up having an intimate relationship with the future. It inspires, it warns. It uses a simplistic kind of "extrapolation-lite" (but not any kind of rigorous, scientifically testable process) to make its world feel realistic enough to slide an emotional truth past your defenses and into your limbic system.

In many prose narratives, we get a running monologue from inside the heads of other people. This is as science fictional as anything in any novel. In life, we only have direct access to one internal monologue—our own. But the illusion that we are directly experiencing the interiority of other people is a powerful tool for creating empathy. An SF novel puts us into psychic contact with denizens of a hyperdistilled version of our own world, and tells us how their present feels—something we could only learn otherwise by waiting for the future to arrive and then asking hindsight what the present used to mean. A petri dish is a cheap, disposable way of asking questions about your body; a science fiction story does the same with your present.

This is valuable.

CORY DOCTOROW
LONDON, ENGLAND

DEAR MCSWEENEY'S,
Yesterday we made the first leg of the drive home to Chattanooga after vacationing with family in northern Iowa. Our stopover city was St. Louis: eleven hours' drive time, factoring in lunch and dinner. The kids unsheathed various iDevices while my husband, who was driving, turned on the radio. I took out a pen and notepad and Charles Baxter's *Burning Down the House* and a galley of a novel I was reviewing. Also Chekhov.

Here we are, then: six of us in a twelve-year-old Suburban in mid-July. It's 92 degrees, and we haven't even gotten out of Iowa. The rear AC works all the time; the front AC, sometimes. Today it's making a whirring sound—Coke machine refusing a dollar bill. Condensation drips onto the tops of my feet. Bless you, tiny intermittent droplets.

Somewhere near Cedar Rapids I open the Baxter and start reading one of the essays, "The Donald

Barthelme Blues." Four pages in I feel a bit nauseous. Roll down window. Worse. Reading in a car in hot weather with unpredictable AC is a bad idea.

The iDevice, though—not so bad! Facebook posts are short, pithy! Plus it's been two hours since I checked email. And here you are, *McSweeney's*, with your upcoming Bradbury/Hitchcock fistfight issue. Will I write a letter, something to do with genre: sci-fi, horror, detective?

"Genre?" Me, of the Baxter/ Chekhov/review assignment?

I don't think so.

The recline feature on my chair hasn't worked since 2004. I lean my face against the window to try to nap. Hot cheek. In a little while my fifteen-year old son, Keaton, speaks.

Keaton: Mom. Mom mom mom. Are you asleep? Hey Mom. What's *bulwark* mean?

Me: A wall for protection. Like a seawall.

K: Yeah, that works. (pause) How about *inimical*?

Me: Hostile.

K: *Miasma*?

Me: Something like fog. Read the sentence.

K: "Mighty battlefleets cross the daemon-infested miasma of the warp, the only route between distant stars, their way lit by the Astronomican, the psychic manifestation…"

Me (turning around): What is that?

Keaton holds up a black text-book-sized book called *Deathwatch*. The second *t* is an inverted sword. On the cover is—what? A man-machine, a machine-man? It looks like a blue Transformer with a gold eagle on its chest. It wields an enormous weapon, a sword/chainsaw hybrid. Its stance is somehow both threatening and regal.

K: It's, you know, Warhammer? Space Marines?

Me: …

K: It's a race of genetically altered super soldiers. They're human to start with, but they get recruited from across the galaxy to train to become Space Marines. The Chapters recruit them young, I guess when they're, like, eight years old, or maybe it's ten, whatever, but they have to go through a surgical process where the Apothecaries replace their organs with genetically modified super organs so they become, like, indestructible. Even if they get blown up—say if their legs or arms get blown off—they just stick them in these things called Dreadnaughts and keep on using them. They use

them up because they're so trained and valuable. And there's Chaplains who watch over their spiritual side, to make sure they don't freak out and turn bad. Their goal is to protect the Imperium from the Tyranid Menace and heretics and mutants.

There's pictures, he says, handing me the book.

I flip through. Some of these creatures are obviously bad. Anything resembling a lamprey in the mouth region = bad for sure. Lizard skin seems to indicate badness. Exposed teeth, also bad, though it's harder to tell because some of the creatures with exposed teeth don't have lizard skin. Metal exteriors are extremely confusing.

Me: How can you tell which ones are good?

K: You have to look at the symbols and structure of their armor. See the skull and crossbones? That's the Marines' mark.

Me: The poison symbol is good?

K: That's a stereotype, about a skull being bad. Skulls aren't good or bad, they're *badass*.

Me: Do the doctors replace their brains?

K: Apothecaries. No. But their training removes fear. I mean, pain comes from fear. If you don't fear pain you won't feel it.

McKenna (daughter, seventeen,

taking Eastern religions as elective, saving up for senior trip to India): That's totally Buddhist.

K: No way. Buddhists have to, like, *meditate* to get rid of fear? They don't get *operations*?

My daughter is already typing into her phone. She reads from Wikipedia—the Four Noble Truths, the existence of suffering originating in craving, the Eightfold Path—and she reads the list of the various realms of rebirth, including the cold and hot Narakas, or hells. In one of them the ground is made of hot iron. Beings in this realm are attacked the minute they begin to fear harm. In another realm, black lines are drawn on the body—guides for the hell guards who will cut along the lines with fiery saws. I'm thinking: sword/chainsaw hybrid.

I'm thinking this all sounds pretty genre.

I go back to my Baxter essay.

"The more bizarre the object, the more Barthelme seems to like it. There is a pleasant sideshow quality, a circus element, to the spectacle of desire. It generates dwarfs and witches (*Snow White*), a son manqué (eight feet tall and wearing 'a serape woven out of two hundred transistor radios' in "The Dolt"), monsters, and impossibly beautiful women…

there are the zombies, spouting their death-in-life clichés…"

"The Dolt"—one of my favorite science fiction stories.

You win, *McSweeney's*.

Yours,

JAMIE QUATRO
SOMEWHERE BETWEEN
CEDAR RAPIDS AND ST. LOUIS

DEAR MCSWEENEY'S,

In fifth grade, for Christmas, I gave my teacher a mason jar full of neon-green ectoplasm dotted with plastic spiders. Her desk was festooned with glittery gift bags, beribboned boxes, a fruit basket padded with cotton balls meant to look like snow. I did not wrap the mason jar, so Mrs. Hen knew what she was getting, but still she asked me, "What is it?"

"It's a jar full of ectoplasm." I said this proudly. "With spiders." At home, on my bedside table, I kept my own jar, and every night I would hold the goo up to my lamp and make it glow, rotating it in my hands, studying the dark matter speckling it. I considered it pretty much the coolest thing ever, right up there with my *Tales from the Crypt* comic collection and the poster on my door of an alien tearing through a door.

Mrs. Hen picked up the jar, tipped it at an angle that matched her cocked head, and together we shared a quiet moment as the ectoplasm oozed and found a new shape. A bubble burped from its bottom. "It's so..." Mrs. Hen said, and that's all she said, because the bell rang and she stood from her desk while I scurried to mine.

If the bell did not ring, if that moment in time had extended itself another few seconds, what might Mrs. Hen have said? It's so... extraordinary? Beautiful? Arousing?

I'd like to think so. I'd like to think she still has the jar on display, maybe in some prized location, the fireplace mantel, say, or the center of her dining room table. But I know better. I know, in all likelihood, she would have said, "different."

The jar was *different*. I was *different*. This is a word I hear often in the Midwest—in response to a film, a book, a spicy dish of food. It's their meek way of saying, "Not good, weird, abnormal."

My father said something similar when I handed him my first short story, written when I was in eighth grade on a wheezy computer that required two pages of typed commands before it would boot up properly.

"What's this?" he said.

"A story. I wrote it."

"For class?"

"No, just because."

"You want me to proofread it?"

"No. Just read it."

He did, and when he handed it back a few minutes later, he said, "It was different."

I asked him what he meant and he heaved his shoulders in a shrug. "I don't really know what to say."

Maybe he was put off by the rhymed verse. Or the story line about a boy with magical powers entering a new middle school, where was bullied, labeled a freak, and ultimately hurled off a cliff to splatter against some rocks below.

Sometimes people ask about my parents. As if I grew up in a cobwebby Victorian with bats in the attic and chainsaws in the basement. As if I were a product of them, like Eddie Munster or Pugsley Addams. But this is not the case.

If I am a product of anyone, it is Ray Bradbury, Shirley Jackson, Peter Straub, Octavia Butler, Stephen King, Richard Matheson. Whether parents or gods, they are legion, storytellers with marred minds that begat altered realities more compelling and somehow truer than life. I read them in the poorly lit corners of libraries and I read them in bed when storms boomed outside, sometimes spending more of my day dreaming in a book than engaging with the world. Their pages were like holographic chambers full of dragons, ghosts, and aliens, creatures that became my reality, rewiring my brain to celebrate and anticipate the fantastic.

When hiking in the woods, I would strike a tree with a stick three times and tell my sister that was how you called Bigfoot. When playing on the beach, I imagined the long tuberous seaweed as the tentacles of a kraken. When eating at a restaurant, the waiters and the chef became cannibals who in back kept a storage locker full of bodies from which they hacked steaks and chops.

You can imagine my surprise, the day I stepped into my first creative writing workshop, when the instructor handed out the syllabus and read through the course requirements and told us, "No genre."

I threw up my hand and asked what he meant.

"No vampires, no trolls, no robots."

My hand shot up again and I asked, in complete earnestness, "But what else is there?"

He never answered my question.

It was a crime, yes, that up to that point I had never read, let alone heard of, Raymond Carver, Flannery O'Connor, Alice Munro, Tobias Wolff, James Baldwin. But so was it a crime that in the semester to follow we never, not once, discussed writers like Ray Bradbury, Brian Evenson, Kelly Link, Neil Gaiman, Elizabeth Hand, Raymond Chandler—those who might be labeled genre, a filthy word. They were too... *different*.

And when I page through literary journals, I don't see nearly enough *different*.

I would like to propose an aesthetic barometer, *McSweeney's*. Let's call it the Exploding Helicopter clause. If a story does not contain an exploding helicopter, you won't publish it, no matter how pretty its sentences and orgasmic its epiphany might be. The exploding helicopter is an inclusive term that may refer, but is not limited to, giant sharks, robots with lasers for eyes, pirates, poltergeists, were-kittens, demons, slow zombies, fast zombies, talking unicorns, probe-wielding Martians, sexy vampires, barbarians in hairy underwear, and all forms of apocalyptic and postapocalyptic mayhem.

I trust that you will be on board. You are, after all, kind of *different*.

Big bad love,

BENJAMIN PERCY
NORTHFIELD, MN

DEAR MCSWEENEY'S,

Have you ever confessed that you like Michael Crichton, only to receive one of those knowing grins, as if by saying you like Michael Crichton you really mean that you don't like Michael Crichton, when in fact you couldn't be clearer?

Maybe it's just me. And maybe the skepticism is understandable, even warranted. After all, Crichton's characters usually have less depth than his jacket embossings. He describes the human heart like a befuddled parent explaining how an air conditioner works to a small child. His climate-change naysaying is a regrettable coda to a career spent dramatizing the unforeseen consequences of technological progress. But when he's on his game, he achieves the near impossible, crafting techno-thrillers so momentous they zoom right past their shortcomings.

Let me backtrack. I first crossed paths with the Crichtonian oeuvre one summer when I worked as a caddy. I must have been fifteen or sixteen years old. I'd never before been in a country club, or on a golf course, but the caddy master— seriously, that was the title on his business cards—wasn't particularly eagle-eyed. Each morning I arrived to the caddy shack, put my name

on the daily sign-up sheet, and waited around for five hours or so, until my name was called out from a tinny speaker that rattled like a can of loose change when the caddy master spoke. Those long stretches of morning went infinitely quicker with M.C. for company.

That summer I tore through *Congo*, *The Andromeda Strain*, *Terminal Man*, *Sphere*, *Jurassic Park*, *The Lost World*, *The Great Train Robbery*, *Eaters of the Dead*, *Rising Sun*, and *Airframe*. Until then, my extracurricular reading life generally consisted of R.L. Stine's *Fear Street* series. Crichton's ecotone, wherein genius met hubris, was significantly more frightening than stories of ski trips with overprivileged, under-parented high school students (viz. *Ski Weekend, Fear Street No. 10*). The urgent need to know what would happen next kept me sneaking pages on the fairways and reading long into the night.

Recently I re-reread *Timeline*, one of Crichton's deep cuts (if a writer who could sell the film rights to his shopping list can be said to have deep cuts). It tells the story of a few modern-day medievalists sent back to a fourteenth-century French town in a parallel universe. Their universe-hopping time machine breaks down, but luckily the medievalists are hip to fourteenth-century customs. Plus they have sweet sword-fighting skills. Meanwhile in the present, their colleagues joust with a tech company in boardroom battles that neatly echo the brutality of court politics. Spoiler alert: their billion-dollar technology wasn't developed solely to expand our understanding of Franco-Plantagenet relations. Instead, there's a CEO two hounds shy of being Montgomery Burns with hidden plans for time-travel adventure tourism (guess he hasn't read *Jurassic Park*).

Like Crichton's best work, it's a modern-day *Frankenstein*. It takes the heady predicament of an invention outgrowing the inventor's capacity for moral wisdom, and serves it up with crowd-pleasing panache. Its architecture is as meticulously crafted as the Gothic cathedrals populating its pages, and those pages turn with forceful velocity.

Michael Crichton's books were the starting point for me as an adult reader, the first substantial forays into literature's multiverse. Without them I may not have pursued reading far enough down the rabbit hole to one day look back with genuine affection. A novel doesn't need to be Great to be great. A novel doesn't need to be revolutionary to be life-changing for one reader.

And that reader hopes Michael Crichton is well, in whatever parallel universe he rests.

ANTHONY MARRA
OAKLAND, CA

CORY DOCTOROW (*craphound.com*) *is a science fiction author, activist, journalist, and blogger—the co-editor of Boing Boing and the author of the bestselling novel* Little Brother. *His latest young adult novel is* Homeland; *his latest novel for adults is* Rapture of the Nerds.

JAMIE QUATRO *is the author of the story collection* I Want To Show You More. *She is a contributing editor at* Oxford American *and lives in Lookout Mountain, Georgia.*

For BENJAMIN PERCY's *bio, please see page 425.*

ANTHONY MARRA *is the author of* A Constellation of Vital Phenomena. *He lives in Oakland and teaches at Stanford University.*

INTRODUCTION

T he genesis of this issue was simple. A few years ago, at a used book sale, I came across a collection edited by Alfred Hitchcock called *Stories* Not *for the Nervous*. I think I paid $2 for it.

I hadn't known that Hitchcock had edited books like these, but in his time, they were many and many were bestsellers. There were nearly sixty collections in all—from 1957 to 1986—all featuring the kind of stories you'd expect Hitchcock to like—suspenseful, strange, and often darkly funny.

I read *Stories* Not *for the Nervous* with no expectations, no information, no pre-judgments—and because I'd only paid $2 for it, I didn't even care so much if it was any good. But it was very good, and the stories held up fantastically well, despite the half-century that had elapsed between this volume's initial publication and the used book sale where I found it.

When I read "Dune Roller," a haunting and searingly vivid story that takes place in the oft-forgotten dunes of Lake Michigan, I couldn't believe I hadn't heard of it before. (I later found out that a few film adaptations had been made from it, though they aren't well-known now.) That story alone—it's more of a novella—made the collection a richly rewarding find. But there was so much more. Lucille Fletcher's classic radio drama "Sorry, Wrong Number," which went on to become a film starring Barbara Stanwyck and Burt Lancaster, was electric on the page and has, I think, held up better than the movie. And then there was Fredric Brown's creepy and fourth-wall-breaking "Don't Look Behind You," the last story in the collection and, I think, one of the creepiest things I've ever read.

When I finished the book, immediately I had the thought that Michael Chabon had many years ago, when he edited his *Mammoth Treasury of Thrilling Tales* for McSweeney's—that is, that so-called genre fiction can be highly literary while also managing something that literary fiction sometimes forgets: having something happen. Having a plot. And I thought then that it might be time to do another issue of McSweeney's celebrating this sort of fiction, maybe even including some of these stories themselves.

But we didn't. Or rather, we talked about reissuing some of the stories, or even the whole collection, and then we didn't. Other things happened instead.

Then, about six months ago, another book crossed my path—Ray Bradbury's *Timeless Stories for Today and Tomorrow*. Again, I'd bought an old copy for cheap—this time thirty cents—and read the stories inside with the particular plain happiness of knowing that the book might be hopelessly dated, not so good, or, even better, that I might find something extraordinary. I did, many times. The strange twist of Bradbury's collection is that amid the lesser-known names, there are some canonical writers—Steinbeck, Kafka, Cheever—who one wouldn't expect to find in a collection of stories that lean toward the fantastical. Who knew Steinbeck could be so darkly funny? Who knew Cheever could write speculative fiction? Who is this Sidney Carroll, author of the magisterial "None Before Me"? Who is this J.C. Furnas, writer of the Lynchian "Laocoön Complex"?

Finally a workable idea presented itself: why not combine some of the best of Hitchcock's findings with Bradbury's, and have them duke it out? Instantly a title seemed obvious: *Hitchcock and Bradbury Fistfight in Heaven*, inspired by Sherman Alexie's *The Lone Ranger and Tonto Fistfight in Heaven*. It was coming together. So we wrote to Sherman, asking for his blessing, and he said, "This sounds way cool." Then we asked Tavis Coburn to produce some kind of rendering of the two men struggling in the afterlife, and he made the astounding image you see on this book's cover.

We were almost finished with all this when a final thought occurred to the editors here, and that was to include, among the lost-and-found stories, some contemporary work that fit into the same spirit. We feel very lucky that fantastic new work by Benjamin Percy, China Miéville, E. Lily Yu, and Brian Evenson appeared within our narrow window, and we feel sure that Bradbury and Hitchcock would approve. So we hope you enjoy these stories—really enjoy, in a pure, amateur-reader way, a page-turning way that still might upend your thinking about the world—and that you might look further into the catalog of some of the authors herein. Whatever you do, make sure you read "Don't Look Behind You" last.

—DAVE EGGERS

FROM THE INTRODUCTION TO
TIMELESS STORIES FOR TODAY AND TOMORROW

This anthology was collected for three reasons: to locate stories by authors who rarely write fantasy; to find stories heretofore not used in other fantasy anthologies; and, most important of all, to publish stories of quality.

It is not enough to say that I like the enclosed narratives and hope you like and are stimulated by them. It falls to an editor to explain how and why he came to the decisions that resulted in such a book as this. What you have here, indirectly, is not only the literary ability and entertainment provided by many fine writers, but a pattern of my own thinking as evinced through my selections.

I have always believed that Life itself is more than fantastic. Therefore, most of these stories simply illustrate how fantastic life is. Life, to the believer *or* the agnostic, is a pretty wonderful affair. I mean wonderful in the sense of true wonder, awful in the sense of awe, stressing the *im* in impossible. It is truly a miracle that we are here at all, to sleep, to rise, to down quick breakfasts and run for trains and be on time or late, as Fate decides.

A child, realizing this, finds something magnificent in the whorls on his fingertips. As adults we soon transfer our attentions from our hands to our bodies to other people's bodies and circumstances and sooner or later we fall in love and *that* is a pretty strange business, too, another wonderful, awful, sometimes unbelievable business. But no matter how old we get there should always be that sense of living on the margin of impossibility. Hence, this book, in which many people discover the margin, or the precipice, or whatever you, personally, wish to call it. Some people are frightened by it, some are elated, but I believe the sense of the impossible can be used to sharpen our senses to what we are doing and where, if anywhere, we are going. We have all had moments such as The First Day I Discovered I Was Really Alive, at the age of ten. Or The First Day I Finally Realized That Someday I Must Die, at the age of fifteen. We have all walked in meadows on certain afternoons and suddenly been so keenly aware of living that we have felt a very real and deep gratitude for this chance to live. We have seen sunsets so beautiful that there is no talking of them, caused by a million interactions of events in the atmosphere, in the light, in the dust particles, and in the hidden theater of the mind. We have all felt ourselves participants of a precious privilege given to us by a God, of whatever shape or size you prefer, on the best birthday of all, the day each of us was born.

True, the greater part of life is a real and nasty business, with more failures than successes, more illness than health. Many of us quit early and threaten to drop out of the game. But give us another afternoon in a field, or a certain rain in the air outside the office window, or an hour of night when we wake to find the house asleep in moonlight, surrounded by our families, and we are set to go on again. An occasional breather, a refresher, a bit of luck, a happy meeting, can make us cling once more to this soiled small bit of existence with a ferocity that borders on and surpasses insanity. Gripe as we may, criticize as we must, when the hour comes to leave the stage, when our particular scene ends and the curtain is dropping, most of us regret that we can't stay on for at least another act.

This book, I hope, will be *your* refresher. This book, I hope, will show you that for all its reality, life is still a fantasy. For it is not only what life does in the material world that counts, but how each mind sees what is done that makes the fantasy complete. We are two billion worlds on a world here, each of us sees a different elephant; instead of seven blind men on the road to Delhi, we are multitudes of the seeing who do not see because each of us is himself. The miracle is not that we have done so much with our world, but that we ever did anything.

I believe that many of the stories in this collection, directly or indirectly, will prove once again the essential mystery in everything, no matter what or how we know of it. Scientists freely admit that they don't really know what electricity or gravity are, or why light rays travel as fast as they do, or what color is or what keeps the atom together or why the sun *really* shines. In all probability they won't ever know, for there is a certain place in any discussion of any one thing in existence where knowledge ends and the Great Vacuum extends on out into infinity. We haven't the faintest idea how order is kept in the womb and why, time after time, with amazing persistence and regularity, cells form through mammalian, and even fishlike stages, to form eyes, lips, ears, hands, fingernails, a human being. These seem to be the Unknowables. We can theorize, check reactions against each other, and thus build a fairly solvent, agreeable civilization, one that won't fly apart too suddenly, we hope. But we live by approximations and shadows of reality. We don't even know the real Why that makes water boil at a certain temperature. Luckily, we have accumulated a vast storehouse of knowledge as to How things occur. With what few pitiful sense organs we have, and the brains given us, we have "made do." But the world and the universe are still a fantasy and a mystery.

These stories, by making a fantasy of a fantasy, by showing us the unreality of reality, remind us of and entertain us with our precarious state of equilibrium. The fact is that as we get older the wonders and awes seem to fade a trifle. All of us work ourselves into our own little phonograph record existence, play the same tune each day, with perhaps a fox-trot arrangement on Saturday and a hymnal of same on Sunday. This is the safe, sane, sure little path we must all take if we are to live on this world. In habit there is comfort, in routine there is satisfaction. Only occasionally, as years pass, do the sunsets, the awes, wonders, and beauties break through our shells. So, now and then, we must remind ourselves of the wondrous and the delightful. Some of us sit down and write fantasies. Others, like yourself, read them.

A man who is unfamiliar with the mores of his own civilization is usually enlightened and refocused by a journey through some foreign country such as Mexico where he sees his own customs through the Looking Glass, brought into an astonishing clarity so they suddenly become ridiculous or understandable, or both. So a passenger through the lands of fantasy contained in this book should return, freshened and clear of eye to his normal existence. If this book achieves only one purpose, causes you to appreciate the stuff that holds you together, gives you an awareness of life that you may have lost somewhere between childhood and here, it will have done more than enough.

John Cheever's "The Enormous Radio" provides us with an insight into human nature rarely achieved in any fiction form. Here, fantasy provides us with a nice long sugar tongs with which to sort over, pick up, shake and examine the anthill of existence. To have shown Mr. Cheever's people's secret selves in a more formal, more regularly constructed story would have taken a clumsier omniscient device; the writer would have had to indulge in flitting from mind to mind at a party or used memory and flashback, neither of which could have achieved the single purpose Mr. Cheever attains here. It is a stroke of simple genius for Mr. Cheever to cut all the omniscient trappings away with one machine, this radio that hears all that goes on in an apartment house. The entire story is filtered and refined through this one touch of fantasy and, like the other stories in this volume, escapes that hackneyed label "escape literature" by being a "return." For it is a going back of the mirror and gazing out at life when it comes to preen before the reader. Fantasy enables us to look at life, sometimes, far more easily and recognizably, than the most real of realistic stories. Certainly nobody can accuse Mr. Cheever of not having created recognizable people in his tale.

"Night Flight," by Josephine W. Johnson, is much more than mere wish fulfillment and the fantasy of flying everyone has indulged in. Miss Johnson has used one imaginative element to show us the true shape of loneliness in a warring world. Again, a human emotion is clarified and re-delineated by one tiny bright crystal of fantasy which accepts the common light of the sun and throws a rainbow on the printed page.

None of the enclosed stories take themselves so seriously that they become sociological ramrods or walking symbols of political beliefs or disbeliefs. When fantasy in any of its forms starts preaching, the miracle finds itself endangered. Most of these stories try to say what they have to say of life with a gentle breath so as not to melt the pattern of the snowflake you hold in your hand. Each author has wisely chosen between writing tracts and entertainment. You'll find no pamphleteering here.

Fortunately for the equilibrium of this book, I have included a number of stories that do *not* prove anything about the mystery of life or the fantasy of existence at all, but are just wonderful good fun like Steinbeck's delightful "Saint Katy the Virgin." Good humorous fantasy is a rare thing to come by, perhaps because the atmosphere of fantasy is such that too flip or cocky an attitude can destroy any illusion the writer is trying to achieve. Steinbeck seems to have skirted this danger more than successfully, I'm sure you will agree.

So it seems I have come to the place where I must stop talking. A learned philosopher was once asked his opinion of Pragmatism and replied: "Let me talk for an hour and then I'll know." That is exactly what I have done here. I am grateful for the fine opportunity given me in putting this anthology together, for it has enabled me to think about fantasy-in-the-whole as I have never thought before.

I am no glib theorist or literary technician capable of diagramming these stories for you in great sweeps of logic and detail. And, the good Lord knows, the scientific method and I are only nodding acquaintances. I have had nothing but my emotions to go on, and what little I've learned in a few short years of writing in the field itself. It is all too easy for an emotionalist to go astray in the eyes of the scientific; and surely this is no handbook for the mathematician or the chemist or the specialist in physics. Somehow, though, I am compensated by allowing myself to believe that while the scientific man can tell you the exact size, location, pulse, musculature, and color of the heart, we emotionalists can find and touch it quicker.

Here then is an anthology of fantasy that makes reality real and says things that needed to be said about the human situation. May it entertain you and may it, once again, prove that fantasy, when well written, bears one of the most honorable names in literature.

—RAY BRADBURY

A BRIEF MESSAGE FROM OUR SPONSOR

There are those who will argue that my title, *Stories* Not *for the Nervous*, could apply to any of the various tomes of terror, sagas of suspense, or groupings of grue which I have, from time to time, fathered together for the delectation of my readers. And indeed the point is well taken.

For I am not a man to cater to the nervous. If you are in the habit of chewing your fingernails, jumping from your chair when a door slams, or swooning when someone playfully shouts "Boo!" in your ear, I have only two words of advice—pass on.

If, however, you have nerves which are under good control, nerves which are pleasantly tickled by a touch of terror or agreeably stimulated by a *soupçon* of suspense, then I invite you to join me.

Take a seat, any seat, and start wherever you wish. Break for an intermission whenever you choose and return when you are ready. Informality rules in your enjoyment of this smorgasbord of stories. There is, I think, something for every taste.

Except, that is, for the nervous.

And now my sixty seconds are up.

—ALFRED HITCHCOCK

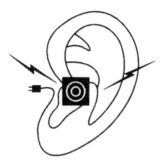

THE SOUND MACHINE

ROALD DAHL

{SELECTED BY RAY BRADBURY}

It was a hot summer evening and Klausner walked quickly through the front gate and around the side of the house and into the garden at the back. He went on down the garden until he came to a wooden shed and he unlocked the door, went inside, and closed the door behind him.

The interior of the shed was an unpainted room. Against one wall, on the left, there was a long wooden workbench, and on it, among a littering of wires and batteries and small sharp tools, there stood a black box about three feet long, the shape of a child's coffin.

Klausner moved across the room to the box. The top of the box was open, and he bent down and began to poke and peer inside it among a mass of different-colored wires and silver tubes. He picked up a piece of paper that lay beside the box, studied it carefully, put it down, peered inside the box, and started running his fingers along the wires, tugging gently at them to test the connections, glancing back at the paper, then into the box, then at the paper again, checking each wire. He did this for perhaps an hour.

Then he put a hand around to the front of the box where there were three dials, and he began to twiddle them, watching at the same time the movement of the mechanism inside the box. All the while he kept speaking softly to himself, nodding his head, smiling sometimes, his hands always moving, the fingers moving swiftly, deftly, inside the box, his mouth twisting into curious shapes when a thing was delicate or difficult to do, speaking to himself, saying, "Yes... Yes... And now this one... Yes... Yes... But is this right?... Is it—where's my diagram?... Ah, yes... Of course... Yes, yes... That's right... And now... Good... Yes... Yes, yes, yes." His concentration was intense; his movements were quick; there was an air of urgency about the way he worked, of breathlessness, of strong suppressed excitement.

Suddenly he heard footsteps on the gravel path outside and he straightened and turned swiftly as the door opened and a tall man came in. It was Scott. It was only Scott, the Doctor.

"Well, well, well,'" the Doctor said. "So this is where you hide yourself in the evenings."

"Hullo, Scott," Klausner said.

"I happened to be passing," the Doctor told him, "so I dropped in to see how you were. There was no one in the house, so I came down here. How's that throat of yours been behaving?"

"It's all right. It's fine."

"Now I'm here I might as well have a look at it."

"Please don't trouble. I'm quite cured. I'm fine."

The Doctor began to feel the tension in the room. He looked at the black box on the bench; then he looked at the man. "You've got your hat on," he said.

"Oh, have I?" Klausner reached up, removed the hat, and put it on the bench.

The Doctor came up closer and bent down to look into the box. "What's this?" he said. "Making a radio?"

"No. Just fooling around."

"It's got rather complicated-looking innards."

"Yes." Klausner seemed tense and distracted.

"What is it?" the Doctor asked. "It's rather a frightening-looking thing, isn't it?"

"It's just an idea."

"Yes?"

"It has to do with sound, that's all."

"Good heavens, man! Don't you get enough of that sort of thing all day in your work?"

"I like sound."

"So it seems." The Doctor went to the door, turned, and said, "Well, I won't disturb you. Glad your throat's not worrying you anymore." But he kept standing there, looking at the box, intrigued by the remarkable complexity of its insides, curious to know what this strange patient of his was up to. "What's it really for?" he asked. "You've made me inquisitive."

Klausner looked down at the box, then at the Doctor, and he reached up and began gently to scratch the lobe of his right ear. There was a pause. The Doctor stood by the door, waiting, smiling.

"All right, I'll tell you, if you're interested." There was another pause, and the Doctor could see that Klausner was having trouble about how to begin. He was shifting from one foot to the other, tugging at the lobe of his ear, looking at his feet, and then at last, slowly, he said, "Well, it's like this... It's... the theory is very simple, really. The human ear... You know that it can't hear everything. There are sounds that are so low-pitched or so high-pitched that it can't hear them."

"Yes," the Doctor said. "Yes."

"Well, speaking very roughly, any note so high that it has more than fifteen thousand vibrations a second—we can't hear it. Dogs have better ears than us. You know you can buy a whistle whose note is so high-pitched that you can't hear it at all. But a dog can hear it."

"Yes, I've seen one," the Doctor said.

"Of course you have. And up the scale, higher than the note of that whistle, there is another note—a vibration, if you like, but I prefer to think of it as a note. You can't hear that one either. And above that there is another and another rising right up the scale for ever and ever and ever, an endless succession of notes... an infinity of notes... there is a note—if only our ears could hear it—so high that it vibrates a million times a second... and another a million times as high as that... and on and on, higher and higher, as far as numbers go, which is... infinity... eternity... beyond the stars..."

Klausner stood next to the workbench, fluttering his hands, becoming more animated every moment. He was a small, frail man, nervous and twitchy, with always moving hands. His large head inclined toward his left shoulder, as though his neck were not quite strong enough to support it rigidly. His face was smooth and pale, almost white, and the pale-gray eyes that blinked and peered from behind a pair of thick-lensed steel spectacles were bewildered, unfocused, remote. He was a frail, nervous, twitchy little man, a moth of a man, dreamy and distracted, suddenly fluttering and animated; and now the Doctor, looking at that strange pale face and those pale-gray eyes, felt that somehow there was about this little person a quality of distance, of immense, immeasurable distance, as though the mind were far away from where the body was.

The Doctor waited for him to go on. Klausner sighed and clasped his hands tightly together. "I believe," he said, speaking more slowly now, "that there is a whole world of sound about us all the time that we cannot hear. It is possible that up there in those high-pitched, inaudible regions there is a new, exciting music being made, with subtle harmonies and fierce grinding discords, a music so powerful that it would drive us mad if only our ears were tuned to hear the sound of it. There may be anything... for all we know there may—"

"Yes," the Doctor said. "But it's not very probable."

"Why not? Why not?" Klausner pointed to a fly sitting on a small roll of copper wire on the workbench. "You see that fly? What sort of a noise is that fly making now? None—that one can hear. But for all we know the creature may be whistling like mad on a very high note, or barking or croaking or singing a song. It's got a mouth, hasn't it? It's got a throat!"

The Doctor looked at the fly and he smiled. He was still standing by the door with his hand on the doorknob. "Well," he said. "So you're going to check up on that?"

"Some time ago," Klausner said, "I made a simple instrument that proved to me the existence of many odd, inaudible sounds. Often I have sat and watched the needle of my instrument recording the presence of sound vibrations in the air when I myself could hear nothing. And *those* are the sounds I want to listen to. I want to know where they come from and who or what is making them."

"And that machine on the table, there," the Doctor said, "is that going to allow you to hear these noises?"

"It may. Who knows? So far, I've had no luck. But I've made some changes in it, and tonight I'm ready for another trial. This machine," he said, touching it with his hands, "is designed to pick up sound vibrations that are too high-pitched for reception by the human ear and to convert them to a scale of audible tones. I tune it in, almost like a radio."

"How d'you mean?"

"It isn't complicated. Say I wish to listen to the squeak of a bat. That's a fairly high-pitched sound—about thirty thousand vibrations a second. The average human ear can't quite hear it. Now, if there were a bat flying around this room and I tuned in to thirty thousand on my machine, I would hear the squeaking of that bat very clearly. I would even hear the correct note—F sharp, or B flat, or whatever it might be— but merely at a much *lower pitch*. Don't you understand?"

The Doctor looked at the long, black coffin-box. "And you're going to try it tonight?"

"Yes."

"Well, I wish you luck." He glanced at his watch. "My goodness!" he said. "I must fly. Goodbye, and thank you for telling me. I must call again sometime and find out what happened." The Doctor went out and closed the door behind him.

For a while longer, Klausner fussed about with the wires in the black box; then he straightened up and, in a soft, excited whisper, said, "Now we'll try again... We'll take it out into the garden this time... and then perhaps... perhaps... the reception will be better. Lift it up now... carefully... Oh, my God, it's heavy!" He carried the box to the door, found that he couldn't open the door without putting it down, carried it back, put it on the bench, opened the door, and then carried it with some difficulty into the garden. He placed the box carefully on a small wooden table that stood on the lawn. He returned to the shed and fetched a pair of earphones. He plugged the wire connections from the earphones into the machine and put the earphones over his ears. The movements of his hands were quick and precise. He was excited, and breathed loudly and quickly through his mouth. He kept on talking to himself with little words of comfort and encouragement, as though he were afraid—afraid that the machine might not work and afraid also of what might happen if it did.

He stood there in the garden beside the wooden table, so pale, small, and thin that he looked like an ancient, consumptive, bespectacled child. The sun had gone down. There was no wind, no sound at all. From where he stood, he could see over a low fence into the next garden, and there was a woman walking down the garden with a flower basket on her arm. He watched her for a while without thinking about her at all. Then he turned to the box on the table and pressed a switch on its front. He put his left hand on the volume control and his right hand on the knob that moved a needle across a large central dial, like the wavelength dial of a radio. The dial was marked with many numbers, in a series of bands, starting at 15,000 and going on up to 1,000,000.

And now he was bending forward over the machine. His head was cocked to one side in a tense, listening attitude. His right hand was beginning to turn the knob. The needle was traveling slowly across the dial, so slowly that he could hardly see it move, and in the earphones he could hear a faint, spasmodic crackling.

Behind this crackling sound, he could hear a distant humming tone, which was the noise of the machine itself, but that was all. As he listened, he became conscious of a curious sensation, a feeling that his ears were stretching out away from his head, that each ear was connected to his head by a thin, stiff wire, like a tentacle, and that the wires were lengthening, that the ears were going up and up toward a secret and forbidden territory, a dangerous, ultrasonic region where ears had never been before and had no right to be.

The little needle crept slowly across the dial, and suddenly he heard a shriek, a frightful piercing shriek, and he jumped and dropped his hands, catching hold of the edge of the table. He stared around him as if expecting to see the person who had shrieked. There was no one in sight except the woman in the garden next door, and it was certainly not she. She was bending down, cutting yellow roses and putting them in her basket.

Again it came—a throatless, inhuman shriek, sharp and short, very clear and cold. The note itself possessed a minor, metallic quality that he had never heard before. Klausner looked around him, searching instinctively for the source of the noise. The woman next door was the only living thing in sight. He saw her reach down, take a rose stem in the fingers of one hand and snip the stem with a pair of scissors. Again he heard the scream.

It came at the exact moment when the rose stem was cut.

At this point, the woman straightened up, put the scissors in the basket with the roses, and turned to walk away.

"Mrs. Saunders!" Klausner shouted, and his voice was high and shrill with excitement. "Oh, Mrs. Saunders!"

The woman looked around, and she saw her neighbor standing on his lawn—a fantastic, arm-waving little person with a pair of earphones on his head—calling to her in a voice so high and loud that she became alarmed.

"Cut another one! Please cut another one quickly!"

She stood still, staring at him. "Why, Mr. Klausner," she said, "what's the matter?"

"Please do as I ask," he said. "Cut just one more rose!"

Mrs. Saunders had always believed her neighbor to be a rather peculiar person; now it seemed... it seemed that he had gone completely crazy. She wondered whether she should run into the house and fetch her husband. No, she thought. No, he's harmless. I'll just humor him. "Certainly, Mr. Klausner, if you like," she said. She took her scissors from the basket, bent down, and snipped another rose.

Again Klausner heard that frightful throatless shriek in the earphones; again it came at the exact moment the rose stem was cut. He took off the earphones and ran to the fence that separated the two gardens. "All right," he said. "That's enough. No more. Please, no more."

The woman stood there holding the yellow rose that she had just cut, looking at him.

"I'm going to tell you something, Mrs. Saunders," he said, "something that you won't believe." He put his hands on the top of the fence and peered at her intently through his thick spectacles. "You have, this evening, cut a basketful of roses. You have, with a sharp pair of scissors, cut through he stems of living things and each rose that you cut screamed in the most terrible way. Did you know that, Mrs. Saunders?"

"No," she said. "I certainly didn't know that."

"It happens to be true," he said. He was breathing rather rapidly, but he was trying to control his excitement. "I heard them shrieking. Each time you cut one I heard the cry of pain. A very high-pitched sound, approximately one hundred and thirty-two thousand vibrations a second. You couldn't possibly have heard it yourself. But I heard it."

"Did you really, Mr. Klausner?" She decided she would make a dash for the house in about five seconds.

"You might say," he went on, "that a rosebush has no nervous system to feel with, no throat to cry with. You'd be right. It hasn't. Not like ours, anyway. But *how do you know, Mrs. Saunders*"—and here he leaned far over the fence and spoke in a fierce whisper—"*how do you know* that a rosebush doesn't feel as much pain when someone cuts its stem in two as you would feel if someone cut your wrist off with a garden shears? *How do you know that?* It's alive, isn't it?"

"Yes, Mr. Klausner. Oh, yes—and good night," and quickly she turned and ran up the garden to her house. Klausner went back to the table. He put on the earphones and stood for a while listening. He could still hear the faint spasmodic crackling sound and the humming noise of the machine. But nothing more. Slowly he bent down and took hold of a small white daisy growing on the lawn. He took it between thumb and forefinger and slowly pulled it upward and sideways until the stem broke.

From the moment that he started pulling to the moment when the stem broke, he heard—he distinctly heard in the earphones—a faint, high-pitched cry, curiously inanimate. He took another daisy and did it again. Once more he heard the cry, but he wasn't so sure now that it expressed pain. No, it wasn't pain; it was surprise. Or was it? It didn't really express any of the feelings or emotions known to a human being. It was just crying, a neutral, stony cry—a single, emotionless note, expressing nothing. It had been the same with the roses. He had been wrong in calling it a cry of pain. A flower probably didn't feel pain. It felt something else which we didn't know about—something called toin or spurl or plinuckment, or anything you like.

He stood up and removed the earphones. It was getting dark and he could see pricks of light shining in the windows of the dark houses all around him. Carefully, he picked up the black box from the table, carried it into the shed, and put it on the workbench. Then he went out, locked the door behind him, and walked up to the house.

The next morning, Klausner was up as soon as it was light. He dressed and went straight to the shed. He picked the machine up and carried it outside, clasping it to his chest with both hands, walking unsteadily under its weight. He went past the house, out through the front gate, and across the road to the park. There he paused and looked around him; then he went on until he came to a large tree, a beech tree, and placed the machine on the ground, close to the trunk of the tree. Quickly he went back to the house and got an axe from the coal cellar and carried it across the road into the park. He put the axe on the ground beside the tree.

Then he looked around him again, peering nervously through his thick glasses in every direction. There was no one about. It was six in the morning.

He put the earphones on his head and switched on the machine. He listened for a moment to the faint familiar humming sound; then he picked up the axe, took a stance with his legs wide apart, and swung the axe as hard as he could at the base of the tree trunk. The blade cut deep into the wood and stuck there, and at the instant of impact he heard a most extraordinary noise in the earphones. It was a new noise, unlike any he had heard before—a harsh, noteless, enormous noise, a growling, low-pitched, screaming sound, not quick and short like the noise of the roses, but drawn out, like a sob, lasting for fully a minute, loudest at the moment when the axe struck, fading gradually, fainter and fainter, until it was gone.

Klausner stared in horror at the place where the blade of the axe had sunk into the woodflesh of the tree; then gently, he took the axe handle, worked the blade loose, and threw the thing on the ground. With his fingers he touched the gash that the axe had made in the wood, feeling the edges of it, trying to press them together to close this wound, and he kept saying, "Tree... oh, tree... I am sorry... I am so sorry... but it will heal... It will heal fine..."

For a while he stood there with his hands upon the trunk of the great tree; then suddenly he turned away and hurried off out of the park, across the road, through the front gate, and back into his house. He went to the telephone, consulted the book, dialed a number, and waited. He held the receiver tightly in his left hand and tapped the table impatiently with his right. He heard the telephone buzzing at the other end, and then the click of a lifted receiver and a man's voice, a sleepy voice, saying, "Hullo. Yes?"

"Dr. Scott?" he said.

"Yes. Speaking."

"Dr. Scott. You must come at once—quickly please."

"Who is it speaking?"

"Klausner here, and you remember what I told you last night about my experiments with sound and how I hoped I might—"

"Yes, yes of course, but what's the matter? Are you ill?"

"No, I'm not ill, but—"

"It's half past six in the morning," said the Doctor, "and you call me, but you are not ill."

"Please come. Come quickly. I want someone to hear it. It's driving me mad! I can't believe it..."

The Doctor heard the frantic, almost hysterical note in the man's voice, the same note he was used to hearing in the voices of people who called up and said, "There's been an accident. Come quickly." He said slowly, "You really want me to get out of bed and come over now?"

"Yes, now. At once please."

"All right then, I'll come."

Klausner sat down beside the telephone and waited. He tried to remember what the shriek of the tree had sounded like, but he couldn't. He could remember only that it had made him feel sick with horror. He tried to imagine what sort of noise a human would make if he had to stand anchored to the ground while someone deliberately swung a small sharp thing at his leg so that the blade cut in deep and wedged itself in the cut. Same sort of noise perhaps? No. Quite different. The noise of the tree was worse than any known human noise, because of that frightening, toneless, throatless quality. He began to wonder about other living things, and he thought immediately of a field of wheat, a field of wheat standing up straight and yellow and alive, with the mower going through it, cutting the stems, five hundred stems a second, every second. Oh, my God, what would the noise be like? Five hundred wheat plants screaming together, and every second another five hundred being cut and screaming and no, he thought, no I do not want to go to a wheat field with my machine. I would never eat bread after that. But what about potatoes and cabbages and carrots and onions? And what about apples? Ah, no! Apples are all right. They fall off naturally when they are ripe. Apples are all right if you let them fall off instead of tearing them from the tree branch. But not vegetables. Not a potato for example. A potato would surely shriek; so would a carrot and an onion and a cabbage...

He heard the click of the front-gate latch and he jumped up and went out and saw the tall doctor coming down the path, his little black bag in hand.

"Well," the Doctor said. "Well, what's all the trouble?"

"Come with me, Doctor. I want you to hear it. I called you because you're the only one I've told. It's over the road in the park. Will you come now?"

The Doctor looked at him. He seemed calmer now. There was no sign of madness or hysteria; he was merely disturbed and excited. "All right, I'll come," the Doctor said. They went across the road, into the park, and Klausner led the way to the great beech tree at the foot of which stood the long, black coffin-box of the machine—and the axe.

"Why did you bring the machine out here?" asked the Doctor.

"I wanted a tree. There aren't any big trees in the garden."

"And why the axe?"

"You'll see in a moment. But now please put on these earphones and listen. Listen carefully and tell me afterward precisely what you hear. I want to make quite sure…"

The Doctor smiled and took the earphones, which he put over his ears.

Klausner bent down and flicked the switch on the panel of the machine; then he picked up the axe and took his stance with his legs apart, ready to swing. For a moment, he paused. "Can you hear anything?" he said to the Doctor.

"Can I what?"

"Can you *hear* anything?"

"Just a humming noise."

Klausner stood there with the axe in his hands, trying to bring himself to swing, but the thought of the noise that the tree would make made him pause again.

"What are you waiting for?" the Doctor asked.

"Nothing," Klausner answered, and then he lifted the axe and swung it at the tree; and as he swung, he thought he felt, he could swear he felt a movement of the ground on which he stood. He felt a slight shifting of the earth beneath his feet, as though the roots of the tree were moving underneath the soil, but it was too late to check the blow, and the axe blade struck the tree and wedged deep into the wood. At that moment, high overhead, there was the cracking sound of wood splintering and the swishing sound of leaves brushing against other leaves and they both looked up and the Doctor cried, "Watch out! Run, man! Quickly, run!"

The Doctor had ripped off the earphones and was running away fast, but Klausner stood spellbound, staring up at the great branch, sixty feet long at least, that was bending slowly downward, breaking and cracking and splintering at its thickest point, just where it joined the main trunk of the tree. The branch came crashing down, and Klausner leapt just in time. It fell upon the machine and smashed it into pieces.

"Great heavens!" shouted the Doctor as he came running back. "That was a near one! I thought it had got you!"

Klausner was staring at the tree. His large head was leaning to one side and upon his smooth white face there was a tense, horrified expression. Slowly he walked up to the tree and gently he pried the blade loose from the trunk.

"Did you hear it?" he said, turning to the Doctor. His voice was barely audible.

The Doctor was still out of breath from the running and the excitement. "Hear what?"

"In the earphones. Did you hear anything when the axe struck?"

The Doctor began to rub the back of his neck. "Well," he said, "as a matter of fact..." He paused and frowned and bit his lower lip. "No, I'm not sure. I couldn't be sure. I don't suppose I had the earphones on for more than a second after the axe struck."

"Yes, yes, but what did you hear?"

"I don't know," the Doctor said. "I don't know what I heard. Probably the noise of the branch breaking." He was speaking rapidly, rather irritably.

"What did it sound like?" Klausner leaned forward slightly, staring hard at the Doctor. "Exactly what did it sound like?"

"Oh hell!" the Doctor said. "I really don't know. I was more interested in getting out of the way. Let's leave it."

"Dr. Scott, *what—did—it—sound—like?*"

"For God's sake, how could I tell, what with half the tree falling on me and having to run for my life?" The Doctor certainly seemed nervous. Klausner had sensed it now. He stood quite still, staring at the Doctor, and for fully half a minute he didn't speak. The Doctor moved his feet, shrugged his shoulders, and half turned to go. "Well," he said, "we'd better get back."

"Look," said the little man, and now his smooth white face became suddenly suffused with color. "Look," he said, "you stitch this up." He pointed to the last gash the axe had made in the tree trunk. "You stitch this up quickly."

"Don't be silly," the Doctor said.

"You do as I say. Stitch it up." Klausner was gripping the axe handle and he spoke softly, in a curious, almost threatening tone.

"Don't be silly," the Doctor said. "I can't stitch through wood. Come on. Let's get back."

"So you can't stitch through wood?"

"No, of course not."

"Have you got any iodine in your bag?"

"Yes, of course."

"Then paint the cut with iodine. It'll sting, but that can't be helped."

"Now, look," the Doctor said, and again he turned as if to go. "Let's not be ridiculous. Let's get back to the house and then…"

"*Paint—the—cut—with—iodine.*"

The Doctor hesitated. He saw Klausner's hands tightening on the handle of the axe. He decided that his only alternative was to run away fast, and he certainly wasn't going to do that.

"All right," he said. "I'll paint it with iodine."

He got his black bag, which was lying on the grass about ten yards away, opened it, and took out a bottle of iodine and some cotton wool. He went up to the tree trunk, uncorked the bottle, tipped some of the iodine onto the cotton wool, bent down, and began to dab it into the cut. He kept one eye on Klausner, who was standing motionless with the axe in his hands, watching the Doctor.

"Make sure you get it right in."

"Yes," the Doctor said.

"Now do the other one, the one just above it!"

The Doctor did as he was told. "There you are," he said. "It's done."

He straightened up and surveyed his work in a very serious manner. "That should do nicely."

Klausner came closer and gravely examined the two wounds.

"Yes," he said, nodding his huge head slowly up and down. "Yes, yes, yes, that will do nicely." He stepped back a pace. "You'll come and look at them tomorrow?"

"Oh, yes," the Doctor said. "Of course."

"And put some more iodine on?"

"If necessary, yes."

"Thank you, Doctor," Klausner said, and he nodded his head again and he dropped the axe and all at once he smiled, a wild, excited smile, and quickly the Doctor went over to him and gently he took him by the arm and he said, "Come on, we must go now," and suddenly they were walking away, the two of them, walking silently, rather hurriedly, across the park, over the road, back to the house.

NIGHT FLIGHT

JOSEPHINE W. JOHNSON

{SELECTED BY RAY BRADBURY}

Beating slowly, a little wearily back across the long Kansas pastures, Joe thought it all over and decided it was good. Almost the real thing. He thought of her face when she had finally seen him sitting there on the bed, and forgot the creeping ache in his arms as he shot on forward. Only five hundred miles to go, but the air had the warning cold of dawn.

He smiled a little to himself. God, the things that a woman thought of to do before she let herself go to bed! And the nightgowns she wore when he wasn't there!—long-sleeved cotton, with buttons down the front. She'd looked like a cute little shoebox in it. And the ironing, ironing, ironing, while he'd paced up and down half wild, and she'd stood there mashing down a tablecloth, pleating up a skirt, looking straight at him and not knowing he was there. Then she'd just sighed and folded up in a chair and taken off her shoes. He'd noticed how little her feet looked in the damp stockings with three runs up the side.

Then she'd got up and gone to the icebox and made herself a little sandwich of bread and butter and a slice of cold sweet potato, and drunk some milk straight out of the bottle, and wiped her mouth on her sleeve. It had made him hungry and he'd almost reached over her shoulder and grabbed a cold slice of ham, but remembered Polocheck's warning just in time: "Don't eat, Joe. Don't drink. You might ground yourself coming back. It has happened." He had shaken his head in an ominous and warning way, and in his silence Joe read some unspeakable fate.

Then Charlotte had puttered and puttered and puttered. Washing her stockings and hanging them first in one place and then in another, and brushing her lovely, thick black hair and looking at herself in the mirror to see how much bigger she'd got round the waist, and then just standing there like a kid making faces at herself and whispering.

He loved her so much he thought his heart would crack, and then he thought he would let loose and crack her too if she didn't quit dawdling.

Then, finally, she'd turned out the lights and sat down on the bed facing west, and looked out at the moon and spoken his name once or twice, and that was all the praying she seemed to do; and then she'd gone to sleep and found him there.

"Jesus!" Joe said quietly to the Kansas prairies, "she was sure surprised!"

It hadn't taken as much explaining as he'd expected. Apparently she had thought of it too and wanted him to teach her how. But he'd said no, he wasn't going to have her flying around at night, and besides, his bunk wasn't very big, and for God's sake suppose they had a night alarm and inspection. "This isn't like the Mexican army, baby," he'd said. "It's for adults only, and all of those adults male."

She had thought him wonderful to have learned so quickly, and since she pointed it out he realized it *was* pretty wonderful, come to think of it. This was only Monday, and Sunday morning Polocheck had told him of his dream. "...And in the dream I ran from these dogs—but I see no reason why I ran. I could have flown." He looked at Joe and slowly lifted his glass of beer. "I often fly."

"Home?"

"Home to Czechoslovakia." He looked calmly into Joe's grinning eyes. "Tonight when it is dark I will teach you how." He raised a round, warning hand above his glass: "Hush." His blue eyes glittered behind his glasses: "We want no *more* fliers. The nights are wide and peaceful now."

Joe had leaned forward and whispered behind his hand: "When?"

"Eight o'clock."

"Do many know?"

"Some."

"Who?"

Josef's eyes had twinkled. "You would be surprised."

"Okay," Joe said.

It had been a bad morning. He wanted to forget it. Even acting like nuts out in the middle of the desert in a madman's prank was preferable to remembering. "It wasn't so much that it happened to me," he growled into her warm and patient ear, "but that it could happen at all! The fool—the damn young fool!" He reenacted the scene. The Major's office, young pudgy Major Lewis whose wife once offered Joe a bag of peanuts and who summered in New England and early-autumned in New York. It had all been trivial and hasty. The matter of a desk. The desk drawer stuck, and the Major wanted another desk and he knew where another was. He wanted it moved in, and his own desk moved out, and he needed a truck and about five men and he started writing out communications all over the place. Joe had been standing there and listening and finally he said: "Why don't you just have the desk drawer fixed?" Somewhere along the line he had put in a "sir."

And the Major had turned with his vapid young face suddenly interesting with hate, and shouted: "Who spoke to you? Wait till you're spoken to, soldier!"

Well, that was that. But it was there like a ten-word brand.

"...And then I just went out with Josef, and he showed me how..."

"You learned so quickly, darling!" She had looked at him with love and adoration. Sometimes Charlotte got God and Joe confused.

He laughed and hugged her and muttered that it was something that any fool could do. He told her how it had felt, his spirit slipping quietly between the beds, shuffling out into the moonlit desert... He had paused and taken in the incomparable beauty of this early autumn night. South the wide snow-streaked peaks, beautiful and barren in the white moonlight. The clean icy air poured down his lungs. All round him the silent tarboard barracks and the sand, sleeping in the great white flooded light. The army trucks huddled row on row like shrouded beasts.

Quietly Joe had lifted one long arm and then the other. He whirled them round like a ship's propeller, and felt the blood race through his veins. "Contact," he whispered, grinning.

Then, warmed up, he had started taxiing across the sand, his long mountain legs casting wild shadows from the moon. He aimed for the eastern fence and planned to take off and soar above the spiked wire in a gesture of derision. But halfway down the road he slowed down suddenly and crouched. By shadowy sound his spirit's sensitive ears detected another traveler, and he whirled and flattened against a barracks building. From a door of the officers' quarters a short and heavy form came striding, and paused in the open moonlight. Major Lewis hesitated, reconnoitered, and seeing only the dry, unspeaking sand, the bright expressionless autumn moon, seemed satisfied. Over his face came a silly, expectant look, and his mouth opened and shut like a toad devouring flies. After a few minutes Joe realized that the Major was singing as he flailed his arms and warmed up for the flight: "*From the desert I come to thee*," he was singing, "*On a stallion shod with fire...*"

"Oh, my God," Joe muttered. "Oh, my God."

Then the Major was running, beating his arms in perfect form, and heading for the gate with terrific speed. Breathless, Joe watched him and saw him suddenly leap, click his heels together, and soar upward with a roar like a little four-engine bomber. The perfect takeoff of long practice.

Joe sighed with envy and slid out from the shadow. "Bastard," he murmured. "Bastard!"

Then his eyes filled with a deep and cynical scorn. The Major had shot like a bullet westward and not toward the high towers of Manhattan, which seemed an odd thing for a man whose wife never went farther westward than Hot Springs, Virginia.

"*From the desert I come to thee*," Joe whinnied derisively, "*On a stallion shod with fire...*" He stamped his big feet in the sand. "Did I speak to you?" he muttered fiercely. "Wait till you're spoken to, soldier!"

A flame of intolerable hate flared up in him and then he remembered it was growing late, and started to run, forgetting the Major and concentrating with all his might on Polocheck's lesson and his warnings:

"*Flail those arms. Pick up the feet. Then jump—so—leap. Beat. Beat. Right, left, together: beat.*" He felt himself soaring upward in a wild rush, clearing the barrack fence and heading like a comet for the sky.

"Watch you level off!" Polocheck had warned him. "Once I forgot. My God, the stars!"

He had leveled off then and flown eastward in the moonlight. Brownsville, Indiana, here I come! Below him the dry autumn fields of Colorado, the bony creek beds twisting whitely, the forms of sleeping cattle soaked in moonlight. The cold pure air whistled by his ears. It was an extraordinary and exhilarating experience. He felt as though he had been doing it all his life, and wanted to try a nosedive. Just for the hell of it.

Josef was too cautious: "Keep level," he'd said. "Don't fuss round. You got to go fast." But Indiana wasn't Europe, and Joe turned down his right hand, raised his left, and bore down with a mighty rush. The cattle lifted up stricken faces and poured over the pastures, their wet hooves glittering. Joe grinned and swept on eastward.

*   *   *

Above the Solomon River he had hit an air pocket and dropped downward with a sickening rush, but recovered himself and pulled up again, beating his way above the cold scaly water, the river smell chilling his throat.

Sometimes he thought he saw other forms far off, dim wing-shapes of soldiers passing, but was not sure. Not till he pulled past Topeka, lights burning like a handful of embers on a plain, did he meet another nocturnal flier close enough to speak. Here he was overtaken by a young Negro sergeant bound for Carolina and traveling fast. Joe acknowledged his coming with a right-arm sweep and motioned as though to shake his hand. "Cold, Sergeant?"

"Cold!"

"Been at this flying long?"

"Learned last week. Been home every night since." He laughed as at something secret and very pleasant.

"First flight for me," Joe said. "I don't know how it'll be. Not sure of all the rules."

The sergeant laughed. "Me neither." He winged in closer. "You learn something new every time. Las' night I landed late and I walked up the backyard after my wife was asleep—she can't see you till she sleeps—and the lights were all out, only a bright moon so you could see everything white, and the moonflowers hanging on the fence. Well, I walk up and past that old broken swing the kids still use, and suddenly I stop. I'm not kidding you: I stopped like a man shot dead. And there, sitting down on the swing, scuffing his boots and looking all out of joint, was the mortal soul of my First Lieutenant!"

He laughed very loudly, and after a moment of uncertainty Joe laughed too.

"He couldn't get in!" the sergeant gloated. "That's one of the things you learn. She never thought about *him*. She didn't never know he was there!"

Joe took an exulting leap. "What'd you do?"

The sergeant shrugged. "Jus' let him swing. A man's got a right to dream, I guess. He was gone when I come out again. Only a scuff place under the swing." He laughed again.

They flew on for a minute in silence, and then they saw the lights of St. Louis and the sluggish, silvery mud of the Mississippi. "Here's where I leave you, brother," the sergeant said. "Take it slow and easy. Don't eat. Don't drink. And a long night to you!" He was gone, winging darkly southward, and soon lost in the shadows.

Not long now for Joe. Fly east, young man. Familiar hills and farm-lands going under, but he could not see them well in the night. "I was sure afraid," he told Charlotte. "I thought I'd pass over and land in Brooklyn! 'You'll know,' Josef kept telling me, but I got the jitters. No map, no compass—how'd I know Brownsville from Ashtabula?"

"How did you know?" Charlotte whispered.

He held her hand and laughed. There had been no question about his finding her. He had flown lower and lower, peering at highways and little billboards and the silent, impassive roofs of towns. Suddenly he realized that he was gliding slowly downward as in the grip of a thick, receding tide. "I just knew," he said.

Now, crossing the Kansas border and beating on, he knew he would find the camp all right, not by any love-gravity of the heart, but because it was so damn big that he could not miss it.

He felt calm and happy. Tomorrow was tomorrow, and to hell with yesterday. He saw the white, shining, snow-cold peaks and the canyoned towns. And then the camp stretched out far below him. There wasn't much time, but he circled slowly above it, hunting hawklike for signs of some living thing on the outskirts of the plain. Then he saw what he was seeking.

A mile westward from the camp, a small fat form, like a two-legged dusty beetle, scurried across the sand.

Leisurely, heartlessly, like a falcon over a wounded hare, Joe circled nearer and lower. He knew the Major's odd hummocky run. "He ate too much, and he drank too much, and a lot of other things too much, and he foundered all right," he thought. *"On the wings of the desert, I come to thee!"* Joe sang in a loud, sweet voice. He swooped low, and the wind of his swooping swept the Major's hat from his round, blond head. It gleamed like a moonflower opening wide in the pale gray desert air. "Get a horse, Bud!" Joe shouted coarsely. "Get a horse!"

Then happily Joe soared upward with firm, triumphant strokes and plummeted swiftly toward the barracks, taking care to avoid the soul of Josef, returning in haste from Europe, the dawn like a white Gestapo at his heels.

DUNE ROLLER

JULIAN MAY

{SELECTED BY ALFRED HITCHCOCK}

There were only two who saw the meteor fall into Lake Michigan, long ago. One was a Pottawatomie brave hunting rabbits among the dunes on the shore; he saw the fire-streak arc down over the water and was afraid, because it was an omen of ill favor when the stars left the heaven and drowned themselves in the Great Water. The other who saw was a sturgeon who snapped greedily at the meteor as it fell—quite reduced in size by now—to the bottom of the freshwater sea. The big fish took it into his mouth and then spat it out again in disdain. It was not good to eat. The meteor drifted down through the cold black water and disappeared. The sturgeon swam away, and presently, he died...

Dr. Ian Thorne squatted beside a shore pool and netted things. Under the sun of late July, the lake waves were sparkling deep blue far out, and glass-clear as they broke over the sandbar into Dr. Thorne's pool.

A squadron of whirligig beetles surfaced warily and came toward him, leading little v-shaped shadow wakes along the tan sand bottom. A back-swimmer rowed delicately out of a green cloud of algae and snooped around a centigrade thermometer suspended in the water from a drift-wood twig.

3:00 p.m., wrote Dr. Thorne in a large, stained notebook. *Air temp 32, water temp*—he leaned over to get a better look at the thermometer and the back-swimmer fled—*28. Wind, light variable; wave action, diminishing. Absence of drifted specimens.* He dated a fresh sheet of paper, headed it *Fourteenth Day*, and began the bug count.

He scribbled earnestly in the sun, a pleasant-faced man of thirty or so. He wore a Hawaiian shirt and shorts of a delicious magenta color, decorated with most unbotanical green hibiscus. An old baseball cap was on his head.

He skirted the four-by-six pool on the bar side and noted that the sand was continuing to pile up. It would not be long before the pool was stagnant, and each day brought new and fascinating changes in its population. *Gyrinidae, Hydrophilidae*, a *Carixa* hiding in the rubbish on the other end. Some kind of larvae beside a piece of waterlogged board; he'd better take a specimen or two of that. *L. intacta* sunning itself smugly on the thermometer.

The back-swimmer, its confidence returned, worked its little oars and zigzagged in and out of the trash. *N. undulata*, wrote Dr. Thorne.

When the count was finished, he took a collecting bottle from the fishing creel hanging over his shoulder and maneuvered a few of the larvae into it, using the handle of the net to herd them into position.

And then he noticed that in the clear, algae-free end of the pool, something flashed with a light more golden than that of mere sun on water. He reached out the net to stir the loose sand away.

It was not a pebble or a piece of chipped glass as he had supposed; instead, he fished out a small, droplike object shaped like a marble with a tail. It was a beautiful little thing of pellucid amber color, with tiny gold flecks and streaks running through it. Sunlight glanced off its smooth sides, which were surprisingly free of the surface scratches that are the inevitable patina of flotsam in the sand-scoured dunes.

He tapped the bottom of the net until the drop fell into an empty collecting bottle and admired it for a minute. It would be a pretty addition to his collection of Useless Miscellanea. He might put it in a little bottle between the tooled brass yak bell and the six-inch copper sulfate crystal.

He was collecting his equipment and getting ready to leave when the boat came. It swept up out of the north and nosed in among the sandbars offshore, a dignified, forty-foot Matthews cruiser named *Carlin*, which belonged to his friend, Kirk MacInnes.

"'Hoy, Mac!" Dr. Thorne yelled cordially. "Look out for the new bar the storm brought in!"

A figure on the flying bridge of the boat waved briefly and howled something unintelligible around a pipe clamped in its teeth. The cruiser swung about and the mutter of her motors died gently. She lay rocking in the little waves a few hundred feet offshore. After a short pause a yellow rubber raft dropped over the stern.

Good old Mac, thought Thorne. The little ex-engineer with that Skye terrier moustache and the magnificent boat visited him regularly, bringing the mail and his copy of the *Biological Review*, or bottled goods of a chemistry designed to prevent isolated scientists from catching cold. He was a frequent and welcome visitor, but he had always come alone.

Previous to this.

"Well, well," said Dr. Thorne, and then looked again.

The girl was sitting in the stern of the raft while MacInnes paddled deftly, and as they drew closer Thorne saw that her hair was dark and curly. She wore a spotless white playsuit, and a deep blue handkerchief was knotted loosely around her throat. She was looking at him, and for the first time he had qualms about the Hawaiian shorts.

The yellow flank of the raft grated on the stony beach. MacInnes, sixty and grizzled, a venerable briar between his teeth, climbed out and wrung Thorne's hand.

"Brought you a visitor this time, Ian. Real company. Jeanne, this gentleman in the shorts and fishing creel is Dr. Ian Thorne, the distinguished writer and lecturer. He writes books about dune ecology, whatever that is. Ian, my niece, Miss Wright."

Thorne murmured politely. Why, that old scoundrel. That sly old dog. But she was pretty, all right.

"How engaging," smiled the girl. "An ecologist with a leer."

Dr. Thorne's face abruptly attempted to adopt the protective coloration of his shorts. He said, "We're really not bad fellows at heart, Miss Wright. It's the fresh air that gives us the pointed ears."

"I see," she said, in a tone that made Thorne wonder just how much she saw. "Were you collecting specimens here today, Dr. Thorne?"

"Not exactly. You see, I'm preparing a chapter on the ecology of beach pool associations, and this little pool here is my guinea pig. The sandbar on the lakeside will grow until the pool is completely cut off. As its stagnation increases, progressive forms of plant and animal life will inhabit it—algae, beetles, larvae, and so forth. If we have calm weather for the next few weeks, I can get an excellent cross section of the plant-animal societies which develop in this type of an environment. The chapter on the pool is one in a book I'm doing on ecological studies of the Michigan State dunes."

"All you have to do is charge him up," MacInnes remarked, yawning largely, "and he's on the air for the rest of the day." He pulled the raft up onto the sand and took out a flat package. "I brought you a present, if you are interested."

"What is it? The mail?"

"Something a heck of a lot more digestible. A brace of sirloins.

I persuaded Jeanne to come along today to do them up for us. I've tasted your cooking."

"I can burn a chop as well as the next man," Thorne protested with dignity. "But I think I'll concede the point. I was finished here. Shall we go right down to the shack? I live just down the shore, Miss Wright, in a place perched on top of a sand dune. It's rugged but it's home."

MacInnes chuckled and led the way along the firm damp sand near the water's edge.

In some places the tree-crowned dunes seemed to come down almost to the beach level. Juniper and pines and heavy undergrowth were the only things holding the vast creeping monster which are the traveling dunes. Without their green chains, they swept over farms and forests, leaving dead trees and silver-scoured boards in their wake.

The three of them cut inland and circled a great narrow-necked valley which widened out among the high sand hills. It was a barren, eerie place of sharp, wind-abraded stumps and silent white spaces.

"A sand blow," said Thorne. "The winds do it. Those dunes at the end of the valley in there are moving. See the dead trees? The hills buried them years ago and then moved on and left these skeletons. These were probably young oaks."

"Poor things," said the girl, as they moved on.

Then the dismal blow was gone, and green hills with scarcely a show of sand towered over them. At the top of the largest stood Thorne's lodge, its rustic exterior blending inconspicuously into the conifers and maples which surrounded it on three sides. The front of the house was banked with yew and prostrate juniper for sand control.

A stairway of hewn logs came down the slope of the dune. At its foot stood a wooden bench, a bright green pump, and an old ship's bell on a pole.

"A dunes doorbell!" Jeanne exclaimed, seizing the rope.

"Nobody home yet," Thorne laughed, "but that's the shack up there."

"Yeah," said MacInnes sourly. "And a hundred and thirty-three steps to the top."

Later, they sat in comfortable rattan chairs on the porch while Thorne manipulated siphon and glasses.

"You really underestimate yourself, Dr. Thorne," the girl said. "This is no shack, it's a real home. A lodge in the pines."

"Be it ever so humble," he smiled. "I came up here to buy a two-by-four cabin to park my typewriter and microscopes in, and a guy wished this young chalet off on me."

"The view is magnificent. You can see for miles."

"But when the wind blows a gale off the lake, you think the house is going to be carried away! It's just the thing for my work, though. No neighbors, not many picnickers, not even a decent road. I have to drive my jeep down the beach for a couple of miles before I can hit the cow path leading to the county trunk. No telephones, either. And I have my own little generating plant out back, or there wouldn't be any electricity."

"No phone?" Jeanne frowned. "But Uncle Kirk says he talks to you every day. I don't understand."

"Come out here," he invited mysteriously. "I'll show you something."

He led the way to a tiny room with huge windows which lay just off the living room. Radio equipment stood on a desk and lined the walls. A large plaster model of a grasshopper squatting on the transmitter rack wore a pair of headphones.

"Ham radio used to be my hobby when I was a kid," he said, "and now it keeps me in touch with the outside world. I met Mac over the air long before I ever saw him in the flesh. You must have seen his station at home. And I think he even has a little low-power rig in the cruiser."

"I've seen that. Do you mean he can talk to you any time he wants to?"

"Well, it's not like the telephone," Thorne admitted. "The other fellow has to be listening for you on your frequency. But your uncle and I keep a regular schedule every evening and sometimes in the morning.

And hams in other parts of the country are very obliging in letting me talk to my friends and colleagues. It works out nicely all the way around."

"Uncle Kirk had represented you as a sort of scientific anchorite," she said, lifting a microphone and running her fingers over the smooth chrome. "But I'm beginning to think he was wrong."

"Maybe," he said quietly. "Maybe not. I manage to get along. The station is a big help in overcoming the isolation, but—there are other things. Shall we be getting back to the drinks?"

She put down the microphone and looked at him oddly. "If you like. Thank you for showing me your station."

"Think nothing of it. If you're ever in a jam, just howl for W8-Dog-Zed-Victor on ten meters."

"All right," she said to him. "If I ever am." She turned and walked out of the door.

The casual remark he had been about to make died on his lips, and suddenly all the loneliness of his life in the dunes loomed up around him like the barren walls of the sand blow. And he was standing there with the dead trees all around and the living green forever out of reach...

"This Scotch tastes like iodine," said MacInnes from the porch.

Thorne left the little room and closed the door behind him. "It's the only alcohol in the house, unless you want to try my specimen pickle," said Thorne, dropping back into his chair. "As for the flavor—you should know. You brought the bottle over yourself last week."

The girl took Thorne's creel and began to arrange the bottles in a row on the table. Algae, beetles, and some horrid little things that squirmed when she shook them. Ugh.

"What's this?" she asked curiously, holding up the bottle with the amber drop.

"Something I found in my beach pool this afternoon. I don't know what it is. Rock crystal, perhaps, or somebody's drowned jewelry."

"I think it's rather pretty," she said admiringly. "It reminds me of something, with that little tail. I know—Prince Rupert drops. They look just like this, only they're a bit smaller and have an air bubble in them. When you crack the little tail off them, the whole drop flies to powder." She shrugged vaguely. "Strain, or something. I never saw one that had color like this, though. It's almost like a piece of Venetian glass."

"Keep it, if you like," Thorne offered.

MacInnes poured himself another finger and thumb of Scotch and scrupulously added two drops of soda. In the center of the table, the small amber eye winked faintly in the sunlight.

Tommy Dittberner liked to walk down the shore after dinner and watch the sand toads play. There were hundreds of them that came out to feed as soon as dusk fell—little silvery-gray creatures with big jewel eyes that swam in the mirror of the water or sat quietly on his hand when he caught them. There were all sizes, from big fellows over four inches long to tiny ones that could perch comfortably on his thumbnail.

Tommy came to Port Grand every August and lived in a resort near the town. He knew he was not supposed to go too far from the cottage, but it seemed to him that there were always more and bigger toads just a little farther down the shore.

He would go just down to that sand spit, that was all. Well, maybe to that piece of driftwood down there. He wasn't lost, like his mother said he would be if he went too far. He knew where he was; he was almost to the Bug Man's house.

He was funny. He lived by himself and never talked to anyone—at least that's what the kids said. But Tommy wasn't too sure about that. Once last week the Bug Man and a pretty lady with black hair had been hiking in the dunes near Tommy's cottage and Tommy had seen him kiss her. Boy, that had been something to tell the kids!

Here was the driftwood, and it was getting dark. He had been gone since six o'clock, and if he didn't get home, Mom was going to give it to him, all right.

The toads were thicker than ever, and he had to walk carefully to avoid stepping on any of them. Suddenly he saw one lying in the sand down near the water's edge. It was on its back and kicked feebly. He knelt down and peered closely at it.

"Sick," he decided, prodding it with a finger. The animal winced from his touch, and its eyes were filmed with pain. But it wasn't dead yet.

He picked it up carefully in both hands and scrambled over the top of the low shore dune to the foot of the great hill where the Bug Man lived.

Thorne opened the door to stare astonished at the little boy and wondered whether or not to laugh. Sweat from the exertion of climbing the one hundred and thirty-three steps had trickled down from his hair, making little stripes of cleanness on the side of his face. His T-shirt had parted company from the belt of his jeans. He held out the toad in front of him.

"There's this here toad I found," he gasped breathlessly. "I think it's sick."

Without a word, Thorne opened the door and motioned the boy in. They went into the workroom together.

"Can you fix it up, mister?" asked the boy.

"Now, I'll have to see what's wrong first. You go wash your face in the kitchen and take a Coke out of the icebox while I look it over."

He stretched it out on the table for examination. The abdomen was swollen and discolored, and even as he watched it the swelling movement of the floor of its mouth faltered and stopped, and the animal did not move again.

"It's dead, ain't it?" said a voice behind Thorne.

"I'm afraid so, sonny. It must have been nearly dead when you found it."

The boy nodded gravely. He looked at it silently for a moment, then said: "What was the matter with it, mister?"

"I could tell if I dissected it. You know what that is, don't you?" The boy shook his head. "Well, sometimes by looking inside of the sick thing that has died, you can find out what was wrong. Would you like to watch me do it?"

"I guess so."

Scalpel and dissecting needle flashed under the table light. Thorne worked quickly, glancing at the boy now and then out of the corner of his eye. The instruments clicked within the redness of the incision and parted the oddly darkened and twisted organs.

Thorne stared. Then he arose and smiled kindly at the young face before him. "It died of cessation of cardiac activity, young fellow. I think you'd better be heading for home now. It's getting dark and your mother will be worried about you. You wouldn't want her to think anything had happened to you, would you? I didn't think so. A big boy like you doesn't worry his mother."

"What's a cardiac?" asked the boy, looking back over his shoulder at the toad as Thorne led him out.

"Means 'pertaining to the heart,'" said Thorne. "Say, I'll tell you what. We'll drive home in my jeep. Would you like that?"

"I guess so."

The screen door slammed behind them. The kid would forget the toad quickly enough, Thorne told himself. He couldn't have seen what was inside it anyway.

In the lodge later, under the single little light, Thorne preserved the body of the toad in alcohol. Beside him on the table gleamed the two tiny amber drops with tails he had removed from the seared and ruptured remains of the toad's stomach.

*　　*　　*

The marine chronometer on the wall of Thorne's amateur station read five fifteen. His receiver said to him:

"I have to sign off now. The missus is hollering up that she wants me to see to the windows before supper. I'll look for you tomorrow. This is W8GB over to W8DVZ, and W8GB is out and clear. Good night, Thorne."

Thorne said, "Good night, Mac. W8DVZ out and clear," and let the power die in his tubes.

He lit a cigarette and stood looking out of the window. In the blue sky over the lake hung a single, giant white thunderhead; it was like a marble spray billow, ponderous and sullen. The rising wind slipped whistling through the stiff branches of the evergreen trees on the dune, and dimly, through the glass, he could hear the sound of the waves.

He moped around inadequately after supper and waited for something to happen. He typed up the day's notes, tidied the workroom, tried to read a magazine, and then thought about Jeanne. She was a sweet kid, but he didn't love her. She didn't understand.

The sand walls seemed to be going up around him again. He wasn't among the dead trees—he was one of them, rooted in the sand with the living greenness stripped from his heart.

Oh, what the hell. The magazine flew across the room and disappeared behind the couch in a flutter of white pages.

He stormed into the workroom, bumped the shelves, and set the specimens in their bottles swaying sadly to and fro. In the second bottle from the end, right-hand side, was a toad. In the third were two small amber drops with tails, whose label said only:

YOU TELL ME — 8/5/57

Interest stirred. Now, there was a funny thing. He had almost forgotten. The beads, it would seem, had been the cause of the toad's death. They had evidently affected the stomach and the surrounding tissues before they had had a chance to pass through the digestive tract. Fast work. He picked up the second bottle and moved it gently. The pale little thing inside rotated until the incision, with all the twisted organs plainly visible inside, faced him. Willy Seppel would have liked to see this; too bad he was across the state in Ann Arbor.

Idly, Thorne toyed with the idea of sending the pair of drops to his old friend. They were unusual looking—he could leave the label on, write a cryptic note, and fix Seppel's clock for putting the minnows in his larvae pail on their last field trip together.

If he hurried, he could get the drops off tonight. There was a train from Port Grand in forty-five minutes. As for the storm, it was still a long way off; he doubted that it would break before nightfall. And the activity would do him good.

He found a small box and prepared it for the mails. Where was that book of stamps? The letter to Seppel: he slipped a sheet of paper into the typewriter and tapped rapidly. String—where was the string? Ah, here it was in the magazine rack. Now a slicker, and be sure the windows and doors are locked.

His jeep was in a shed at the bottom of the dune, protected by a thick scrub of cottonwood and cedar. Since there was no door, Thorne had merely to reverse gears, shoot out, swing around, and roar over the improvised stone drive to the hard, wet sand of the beach. Five miles down the shore was an overgrown but still usable wagon trail which led to the highway.

The clouds were closing ranks in the west as Dr. Thorne and his jeep disappeared over the crest of a tall dune.

Mr. Gimpy Zandbergen, gentleman of leisure, late of the high sea and presently of the open road, was going home. During a long and motley life, Mr. Zandbergen had wandered far from his native lakes to sail on more boisterous waters; but now his days as an oiler were over, and there came into his heart a nostalgic desire to see the fruit boats ship out of Port Grand once more. Since he possessed neither the money for a bus ticket home, nor the ambition to work to obtain it, he pursued his way via freight cars and such rides as he was able to hook from kindly disposed truck drivers.

His last ride had carried him to a point on the shore highway some miles south of his goal, at which he had regrettably disputed the intrinsic worth of the Detroit Tigers and had been invited to continue his journey on foot. But Mr. Zandbergen was a simple soul, so he merely shrugged his shoulders, fortified himself from the bottle in his pocket, and trudged along.

It was hot, though, as only Michigan in August can be, and the sun baked the concrete and reflected off the sand hills at the side of the road. He paused, pulled a blue bandanna handkerchief from his pocket, and mopped his balding head under his cap. He thought longingly of the cool dune path which he knew lay on the other side of the forest, toward the lake.

It had been a long time, but he knew he remembered it. It would lead to Port Grand and the fruit boats, and would be refreshingly cool.

When the storm came, Mr. Zandbergen was distinctly put out. He had not seen the gathering storm through the thick branches, and when the sky darkened, he assumed that it was merely one of the common summer sun showers and hoped for a quick clearing.

He was disturbed when the big drops continued to pelt down among the oak trees. He was annoyed as his path led him out between the smaller and less sheltering evergreens. He swore as the path ended high on a scrubby hill.

Lightning cut the black clouds and Mr. Zandbergen broke into a lope. He had taken the wrong turning, he knew that now. But he recognized this shore. He dimly remembered a driftwood shanty which lay near an old wagon road somewhere around here. If he made that, he might not get too wet after all.

He could see the lake now. The wind was raging and tearing at the waves, whipping the once placid waters of Michigan into black fury. Mr. Zandbergen shuddered in the driving rain and fled headlong down a dune. Great crashes of thunder deafened him and he could hardly see. Where was that road?

A huge sheet of lightning lit the sky as he struggled to the top of the next dune. There it was! The road was down there! And trees, and the shanty, too.

He went diagonally across the dune in gigantic leaps, dodging the storm-wracked trees and bushes. The wind lulled, then blasted the branches down ferociously, catching him a stinging blow across the face. He tripped, and with an agonized howl began to roll straight down the bare face of the sand hill. He landed in a prickly juniper hedge and lay, whimpering and cursing weakly, while the rain and wind pounded him.

The greenery ripped from the trees stung into him viciously as he tried to rise, gave up, and tried again. On the black beach several hundred feet away, waves leaped and stretched into the sky.

Then came another lull and a light appeared out in the lake. It rose and fell in the surf and in a few moments the flattened and horrified little man on the shore could see what it was. A solemn thunderclap drowned out his scream of terror.

Shouting wordless things, he stumbled swaying to his feet and clawed through the bushes to fall out onto the road. It saw him! He was sure it saw him! He struggled along on his knees in the sand for a short distance before he fell for the last time.

The wind shrilled again in the trees, but the fury of the storm had finally passed. The rain fell down steadily now on the sodden sand dunes, and dripped off the cottonwood branches onto the quiet form of Mr. Zandbergen, who would not see the fruit boats go out again after all.

*   *   *

The sheriff was a conversational man. "Now I've lived on the lake for forty years," he said to Thorne, "but never—*never* did I see a storm like today's. No sir!" He turned to his subordinate standing beside him. "Regular typhoon, eh, Sam? I guess we won't be forgetting that one in a hurry."

Dr. Thorne, at any rate, would not forget it. He could still hear in his mind the thunder as it had rolled away off over the dunes, and see the flaring white cones of his headlights cutting out his way through the rain. He had gone slowly over the sliding wet sand of the wagon road on the way home, but even at that he had almost missed seeing it. He remembered how he had thought it was a fallen branch at first, and how he got out of the car then and stood in the rain looking at it before he wrapped his slicker around it and drove back to town.

And now the rain had stopped at last, and the office of the Port Grand physician who was the county medical examiner was neat, dim, and stuffy with the smell of pharmaceuticals and wet raincoats. Over the other homely odors hung the stench of burnt flesh.

Snip, went the physician's bandage shears through charred cloth. Thorne lit a cigarette and inhaled, but the sharp, sickening other smell remained in his nostrils.

"According to his Seamen's International card, he was George Zand-bergen of Port Grand," said the sheriff to Sam, who carefully transcribed this information in his notebook. To Thorne he said, "Did you know him, mister?"

Thorne shook his head.

"I remember him, Peter," said the physician, experimentally deter-mining the stiffness of the dead fingers before him. "Appendicitis in 1946. Left town after that. I think he used to be an oiler on the *Josephine Temple* in the fruit fleet. I'll have a file on him around somewhere."

"Get that, Sam," said the sheriff. He turned to Thorne, standing awkwardly at the foot of the examination table. "We'll have to have your story for the record, of course. I hope this won't take too long. Start at the beginning, please."

Gulping down his nervousness and revulsion, Thorne told of returning from town about nine o'clock and finding the corpse of a man lying in the middle of a deserted side road. Dr. Thorne recalled puzzling at the condition of the body, for although it had been storming heavily at the time, portions of the body had been burned quite black. Thorne had found something at the scene also, but failing to see that it had any connection with the matters at hand, prudently kept his discovery to himself. The sheriff would hardly be interested in it, he told himself, but nevertheless he hoped that the bulge it made in his pocket wasn't too noticeable.

Officer Sam Stern made the last little tipped-v that stood for a period in his transcription and looked nervously about him. His chief peered approvingly—even if uncomprehendingly—at the notes and then said:

"How does it look, doctor?"

"Third-degree burns on fifty percent of the body area, seared to the bone in some parts of the face and about the right scapula. How did you say he was lying when you found him, Mr. Thorne?"

"In an unnatural kind of sprawled position, on the right side."

The physician yawned, rummaged in a cabinet, and produced a sheet with which he covered the charred body. "Pretty obvious, Peter, with these burns and all. Verdict is accidental death. The poor devil was struck by lightning. Time of death was about eight p.m." He tucked the sheet securely around the head. "That lightning's pretty odd stuff, now. Can blow the soles off a man's shoes without scratching him, or generate enough heat to melt metal. You never know what tricks it's going to play. Take this guy here: one side of him's broiled black and the other's not even singed. Well, you never know, do you?"

He picked up his phone and conversed briefly with the local

undertaking parlor. When negotiations for the disposition of the unfortunate Mr. Zandbergen had been completed, he replaced the receiver and shuffled toward the door. Thorne could see that he had bedroom slippers on underneath his rubbers.

"You can finish up tomorrow, Peter," he resumed. "My wife was kinda peeved at me coming out this way. You know how women are, ha-ha. Good night to you, Mr. Thorne. I think there's an old overcoat in that closet I could let you take. You'll be wanting to send yours to the cleaners."

There was a genial guffaw from the sheriff. "We won't keep you any longer tonight, Mr. Thorne. Just let me know how I can get in touch with you."

"Through Kirk MacInnes on River Road," said Thorne. "He'll be glad to contact me through his amateur station." He edged through the door into the quiet night. The sheriff came close behind.

"So you're a ham, eh?" he said warmly. "Well, can you tie that! I used to have a ticket myself in the old days."

Polite noises. How about that? Kindred souls. Sorry about all this sloppy business, old man. Tough luck you had to be the one to find him. Really nothing, old man. *Why* didn't he stop talking? The weight in Thorne's pocket seemed to grow.

"You know, I'll be dropping in to see your rig some one of these days if you don't mind. I'll bet you could use a little company out there in the dunes, eh?"

No, why should he mind? Delighted, old man. Any time at all.

The thing in his pocket seemed to sag to his ankles. It would rip the pocket and fall out. And it had bits of charred cloth on it. Why didn't they go? They couldn't possibly suspect that he hadn't—

Oh, yes, he was on ten meters. Phone. Oh, the sheriff had done c.w. on 180? Well, wasn't that nice.

They walked to the cars under the big old elm trees that lined the comfortable street. A few stars came out and down where the street dead-ended into the river, they could see lights moving toward the deepwater channel that connected the river with the lake.

"Well, good night, Sheriff," Thorne said. "Good night, Mr. Stern. I hope next time we'll meet under more pleasant circumstances."

"Good night, Mr. Thorne," said Sam, who was thoroughly bored with talk he didn't understand, and anxious to get home to his wife and baby.

The police got into their car and drove off. Thorne sat quietly behind the wheel of the jeep until he was sure they were gone, then gingerly removed the weight from his pocket and unwrapped the handkerchief that covered it.

This one was the size of a closed fist and irregular in shape. He had found it flattened under the black char that had once been a man's shoulder, glowing with a bright yellow light in its heart. It looked the same as the three small drops he had previously seen, but he saw that what he had mistaken for golden flecks inside of it was really a fine network of metallic threads which formed a web apparently imbedded a few centimeters below the thing's surface.

The damn thing, he thought. There was something funny about it, all right.

Around him, the lights of the quiet houses were going out one by one. It was eleven o'clock. A few wet patches still glistened on the street under the lamps, and a boat motor on the river pulsed, then stilled.

Thorne looked around him quickly, then got out of the car and laid the thing on the curb. The wet leaves in the gutter below it reflected yellow faintly.

It was funny that a mere matter of shape could change his feeling toward it so radically. The smaller drops had been rather beautiful in their droplike mystery, but this one, although it was made of the same wonderful stuff, had none of the beauty. The irregular cavity in its side that would fit a human shoulder blade made it a thing sinister; the dried blood and ashes made it monstrous.

He took a tire iron out of the tool kit and tapped the glowing thing experimentally. It was certainly stronger than it looked, at any rate. When harder taps failed to crack it, he raised the iron and brought it down with all his strength. The tool bounced, skidded, and chipped the concrete curbstone, but the thing flew undamaged into the gutter.

Thorne bent down and poked it incredulously. And suddenly, with a cry of agony, he dropped the tire iron. It was hot! The tool arced down and lay sizzling sullenly among the little drops of water that still clung to the grass blades. His hand—he clenched his teeth to keep from crying out.

But the glowing thing in the gutter was not hot. Steam rose from the iron in the grass, but the little rivulets bathing the glowing thing were cool. He seemed to remember something, but then the shocked numbness coining over his hand took his attention and he forgot it again.

Down among the leaves and trash, the thing that was not shattered by the strength of Dr. Thorne grew, momentarily, more golden; and with a deliberate, liquid ripple the ugly bulges on its surface smoothed and it assumed the perfect drop shape of its predecessors.

200000 AU PLUS PLENTY WATTS. TELL ME PRETTY MAIDEN
ARE THERE ANY MORE AT HOME LIKE YOU? ARRIVE NOON
THURSDAY. LOVE. SEPPEL.

"You think you're pretty smart, don't you?" said Thorne.

"Yep," said Willy Seppel smugly, smirking around the edge of his beer. He put down the glass and the smirk expanded to a grin. "Smart enough to see what those drops were that you sent me for a gag. That was a great little trick of yours, you know. I was all set to throw them out after reading that note of yours. The only thing that saved them was Archie Deck. He thought they might be Prince Rupert drops and tried to crack the tails off with a file."

"Aha," said Dr. Thorne.

Seppel looked at him with bright, blue, innocent eyes. He was a large, pink-faced, elegantly dressed man with an eagle-beak nose and a crown of fine blond hair.

"You don't have to look at me like that," said Thorne. "I've been able to find out a little bit more about them myself."

"Tell me," said the pink face complacently.

"They generate heat. And I found out the same way as Archie Deck probably did." He gestured with one bandaged hand. "Only I managed it the hard way." He swept up the empty glasses and beer bottles with a crash and disappeared into the kitchen. His voice continued distantly:

"I found those two I sent you inside the stomach of a toad. Or at least what was left of the stomach of a toad. Look in the lab room, the big shelf; second bottle from the end on the right-hand side."

Wiping his good hand on his trousers, he returned to Seppel, who stood looking thoughtfully into the toad's bottle. "It ate the drops," Thorne said shortly.

"Mm—yes," he mused. "The digestive juices might very possibly be able to—"

"Come on, Willy. What is it?"

"You were almost right when you said it generated heat," Willy said. "I brought one of them here to show you." He left the room and returned in a minute with a large cowhide briefcase.

"This thing's in a couple of pieces," Seppel apologized. "You'll have to wait until I set it up. Have you got a step-down transformer?"

Thorne nodded and fetched it from the bookcase.

"Now, this little drop here may look like a bead, but it has some singular properties." He removed the thing from a box which had been heavily sealed and padded, and set it in a nest of gray, woolly stuff in the middle of the table.

"It gives off long infrared, mostly stacked up around two hundred thousand Angstroms. But their energy is way out of proportion from what you'd expect from the equation. This little gadget is something Deck and I rigged up to measure it crudely. Essentially, it's a TC130X couple hooked up to a spring gun. You put the drop in here, regulate the tension of the spring, and firing the gun releases this rod which delivers the drop an appropriate smack." His fingers with their immaculately groomed nails worked deftly. "We don't get a controlled measurement, of course, but it'll show you what I mean... Where do you hide your outlets?"

"Behind the fish tank. Be careful not to disconnect the aerator."

"The screen on that end will show you the energy output. Watch now."

The horizontal green line on the little gray screen bucked at the firing of the spring, then exploded into an oscillating fence of spikes.

"Mad, isn't it?" remarked Dr. Thorne. "Hit it again, but lower the tension of the spring."

If anything, the spikes were even higher.

"The smack-energy ratio isn't proportional," said Seppel. "Sometimes a little nudge will set it off like a rocket. And again, after we tapped it for a week at Ann Arbor figuring out what it was, it showed a tendency to sulk and wouldn't perform at all after a while."

"The energy output," Thorne said. "It's really quite small, isn't it?"

"Yes, but still surprising for an object this size." He removed the drop from the device and put it back into its little box. "We think that glowing heart has something to do with it. And those gold threads—they are gold, you know—come in there too. Old Camestres, the Medalist himself, was visiting the University, and he says that glow is something that'll have the physicists crawling the walls."

"Oh, come now," said Dr. Thorne broadly.

"You just wait," said Seppel. "We haven't done the analysis yet, but we expect great things. The glow," he added, "isn't hard radiation, if that's what you're thinking."

Willy was proud of it, Thorne thought. It was really his discovery after all, not Thorne's, and Seppel, who found challenge and stimulation in the oddest places, had hit the heights with the little golden drops.

But Thorne was remembering a larger drop, the size of a man's fist, and the charred body of a dead man.

"I found another specimen," he said, turning to a drawer in the work-table. "A larger one." He took out Mr. Zandbergen's drop.

"This is wonderful!" Seppel cried. "It's almost the size of a grapefruit! Now we can—"

Thorne cut him off gently. "I want to tell you about this one. Then I'll turn it over to you. When I first found it, it was irregularly shaped. Lumpy. Ugly. It's smooth now, just like the others, but it changed right before my eyes. It just seemed to run fluid, then coalesce again into the drop shape. And there's something else."

He told Seppel about the attempt to crack the thing and the abrupt heating of the tire iron.

"Yes, that could be," Seppel decided. "It's easily possible that a larger specimen such as this one could cause a metal object near it to become perceptibly warm. Infrared rays aren't hot in themselves, but when they penetrate a material their wavelength is increased and the energy released heats the material. In the case of the tire iron, the conductivity of the metal was greater than that of your hand, and you felt the warm iron before the skin itself was affected."

"The iron wasn't warm, Willy. It was damn hot. And in a matter of seconds."

Seppel shook his head. "I don't know what to say. It's the funniest thing I've ever run across."

"The dead man who lay down on it didn't think it was funny," said Thorne.

"You don't think this little thing killed him, do you? He was charred to a cinder all along one side of him. Do you know what kind of infrared could do a thing like that? None."

"I didn't say I thought *this* one killed him," said Thorne, with a cue that Seppel chose to ignore. "I just said the body was right on top of it."

"Too wild for me," said Seppel. He got up, stretched leisurely, and glanced at the clock. "And anyhow, it's sack time. We can worry about it tomorrow, eh?"

Thorne had to smile. Good old Willy. No little glowing monster was going to keep *him* from his sleep.

"We'll put grapefruit back in the drawer," Seppel suggested, "have ourselves a snack, and go to bed."

"Wouldn't the big one be better off in a pail of ice?" asked Thorne, half laughingly.

"If it did decide to give out, it would probably melt the pail before it melted the ice. And besides," he added with dapper complacency, "they never radiate unless they're disturbed."

In the dream, there was sand all around him. He was in it, buried up to his neck. There was a sun overhead that was gold and transparent, and a wind that never seemed to reach his feverish face threw up little whirls of yellow sand.

Sometimes the familiar face of a woman was there. He cried her name and she was gone. And after that, he forgot her, for small shapeless things gamboled out on the sand into the sunlight, only to be burnt black as the rays struck them...

For the fifth time that night, it seemed, Thorne awoke, his eyes staring widely into the darkness. He cursed at himself and turned the perspiration-soaked pillow over, pummeling it into a semblance of plumpness. Seppel lay beside him, snoring gently.

Somewhere in the lodge a timber creaked, and he felt the fear come back again, and saw the black, huddled heap lying before his headlights, and felt the pain renewed in his slowly healing hand. Of the dream, strangely enough, there was no memory at all.

Only the fear.

But why should he be afraid? There was nothing out there. Nothing out there at all.

But the heap in the road. Lightning. *But the little one had burned.* So what? *The little one was too small to burn a man seriously.* I know that. *He was burned.* Lightning, you silly fool! *He was burned!* Shut up. *One of them burned him.* Shut up! Shut up! *There's another one out there tonight.*

No. Nothing out there at all.

Nothing but the dunes and the lake. Nothing.

The wind squalls strummed the pine branches out there, and swirls of sand borne up the bluff from the beach below tickled faintly at the window. The waves of Michigan were roaring out there—but there was nothing else.

Finally, he was able to sleep.

It was nearly dawn when he woke again, but this time he was on guard and alert as he lowered his bare feet softly to the floor. His hand closed over the barrel of a flashlight on the chest of drawers, and he moved noiselessly so that he would not wake the sleeper beside him.

He tiptoed slowly through the workroom and the living room. Something was on the porch.

As he came through the doors, he said sharply: "Who's there?"

An odor of burned wood hit his nostrils. He exclaimed shortly under his breath and shone the light down near the sill of the outside door. There was a round black hole in the door, smoking and glowing faintly around the edges.

He raced back into the workroom and pulled out the drawer that had held the grapefruit-sized drop. It was empty, and a hole gaped in the bottom of it. The hard wood was still burning slowly.

He yanked out the drawer, put it in the kitchen sink, and turned on the water. Then he filled a pan and soaked the hole in the door thoroughly.

They never radiate unless they're disturbed! That was a laugh. Not only had it radiated, but it had somehow focused the radiation. Dr. Thorne was no physicist, but he began to wonder whether the meter had told the whole story of the little glowing drop.

He unlocked the door and slid out into the night. Below the stair was a small, almost imperceptible track in the sand. He followed it down the ridge of the dune, lost it momentarily in a patch of scrub, then found it again in the undisturbed expanse of the sand blow.

He went down into the silent valley, the bobbing yellow light from his flash throwing the tiny track into high relief. When he reached the center of the bowl, he stopped among the long shadows of the gaunt spiky trees.

There was another track in the sand, meeting and merging with the little one. And the track was three feet wide.

He followed it as if in a dream to the crest of the first low shore dune and stood on its summit among the sharp grass and wild grape. The moon's crescent was low over the water and orange. He saw the track go down the slope and disappear into the waves which were swirling in a new depression in the sand.

The wind whipped his pajama shirt about his back as he stood there and knew that he was afraid of that track in the sand, and that no lightning had killed the little tramp.

It was not until he had locked the door of the lodge behind him that he realized he had run all the way back.

Friday was a quiet day in the dunes country, but the police did receive three minor complaints. A farmer charged that someone had not only made off with and eaten three of his best laying hens, but had burned the feathers and bones and left them right in the chicken yard. The Ottawa

County Highway Commission wanted to know who was building fires in the middle of their asphalt roads and plastering the landscape with hot tar. And a maiden lady complained that the artists in the local summer colony must be holding Wild Orgies again from the looks of the lights she had seen over there at three a.m.

Dr. Thorne bent down over the tracks in the sand. It certainly looked to him as though the big one had been waiting for Mr. Zandbergen's drop.

Seppel said, "Get out of the way there," and snapped his Graflex. "These sand tracks won't last long in the winds around here. And I frankly tell you that if I hadn't seen it with my own eyes, I would never have believed it." He circled the point of conjunction, laid his fountain pen beside it for size reference, and the Graflex flashed again.

"We'll want the door, too," he said, putting the camera aside and scrawling in his notebook.

Thorne howled.

"Well, just the part with the hole in it then," Seppel conceded. "Did you find out where the large track came from?"

"I tracked it to the woods. The ground there is too soft and boggy to hold a wide track like that, and I finally lost it."

Seppel struggled to his feet and retrieved his coat, which he had hung for safety's sake on the white peg branch of a skeleton tree. "Just imagine the size of an object which would make a three-foot track in soft sand!" he exclaimed. "And to think it's been in the lake for heaven knows how long and this is the first time it's come into evidence!"

"I wouldn't be too sure about that—about this being the first time, I mean. There have been some funny old stories told along these shores. I heard one myself from my grandmother when I was about twelve. About the dune roller that was bigger than a schooner and lived in the caves at the bottom of the lake. It came out every hundred years and rolled through the dune forest, leaving a strip of bare sand behind it where it had eaten the vegetation. They said it looked for a man, and when it found one, it would stop rolling and sink back into the lake."

"Great Caesar," said Seppel solemnly. "I can see it now—the great glowing globe lurking deep in the caverns where the sun never shines and there is no life except a few diatoms drifting in the motionless waters."

Thorne gaped at his friend for a minute, and then spied a suspicious twinkle in one blue eye.

"This is no laughing matter, you Sunday supplementist!" he said sharply.

"Hmp," said Willy Seppel, and brushed a few grains of sand from the sleeve of his handsome suit.

It was late when Miss Jeanne Wright got out of the movie in Muskegon— so late that she barely had time to do the shopping which had, ostensibly, been her reason for taking *Carlin* out. "You just can't buy decent dresses in Port Grand, Uncle Kirk," she had pleaded, and he really wouldn't mind if she took the boat, would he? MacInnes had growled indulgently from the depths of his new panadaptor and said he certainly did, confound it, and what was the matter with using the car? But he had tossed her the keys just the same.

The streetlights of the city were going on when, laden with bundles, she finally hailed a cab and drove to the yacht basin. It was a beautiful evening, with soft-glowing stars in a sky that was still red-purple in the west. *Carlin* slipped majestically out among the anchored craft into Muskegon Lake.

A bonfire blazed cheerfully on the shore and singing voices from some beach party floated melodiously out over the water. They shouted a jocular greeting to *Carlin* and Jeanne blew a hail to them with the air horn. Her heart was light as she led the cruiser through the channel into the lake and headed for home.

A secretive smile danced on her lips, and she thought kindly about a certain stern-faced young biologist. He was a strange man, occasionally even rude in an unintentional sort of way, and preoccupied with such dreary things as plant cycles and environmental adaptations. But he had walked with her in the dunes one day and changed for a little while, and kissed her once, very gently, on the lips. And after that she had known what she wanted.

He would be sitting in his workroom now, looking over the day's bugs and not thinking of her at all. Or perhaps he would be talking to her uncle over the radio.

She hummed dreamily to herself. The cruiser's speed increased to twenty, and it rocked momentarily in a trough, setting the little good-luck charm hung up over the wheel to bobbing like a pendulum. Ian had given that to her. She loved it because of that.

After a while she turned on the shortwave receiver that sat on one of the lockers in the deckhouse and listened to Ian and her uncle.

"I have a colleague of mine out from Ann Arbor," Thorne was saying. "About that amber drop we found. Remember my telling you about it? I gave one to Jeanne for a souvenir. My friend is a biophysicist and thinks the drops are a great scientific discovery. His name is Willy Seppel. Say something, Willy."

"Gambusia," said Seppel, recalling the minnows in the larvae pail.

Jeanne listened absently. Ian was telling how the drops gave off hot light when they were disturbed. How he thought there might be bigger drops around that could really grind out the energy 40db. above S9. (What in the world did *that* mean?) Thorne and this Willy person would look for the bigger drops.

"Is it really hot?" Jeanne wondered, staring curiously at the pendant drop, swinging above the binnacle in its miniature silver basket. It didn't seem to be. But then Ian had said the little ones didn't radiate very much. Only enough to tickle a something-or-other.

Far out in the lake, the lights of an ore boat twinkled. She passed the little village of Lake Harbor and put out a bit farther from shore. There would be no more towns now until Port Grand.

Over the radio, her Uncle Kirk's voice, homely and kind, was describing the great things in store for the new panadaptor. Ian would put in a comment here and there, but she noticed that he sounded tired, poor darling.

Cleanly, powerfully, *Carlin* sliced through the waves, pursuing the shadow of herself. The shadow was long and very black. A boat with a searchlight, thought Jeanne, and looked astern.

It was there, riding high in the dark, choppy water: a great glowing globe of phosphorescence not twenty yards off the stern. It was coming after her, rapidly overtaking the cruiser.

She screamed then, and when the thing came on, she opened the throttle and attempted to outmaneuver it. But the great glowing monster would pause while she veered and spiraled, then overtake her easily when she tried to run away. The motors of the Matthews throbbed in the hull beneath her feet as she tried to urge them to a speed they were never meant for.

The thing was drawing closer. She could see trails of water streaming from it. What was it? What would it do if it caught her?

Bigger ones! Her eyes turned with horror to the tiny drop on its silver chain. Its glow was the perfect miniature of the monstrous thing in the water behind her. She sobbed as she wrenched *Carlin*'s wheel from side to side in hysterical frenzy. Across the cabin, the quiet voice of Ian was telling MacInnes how to rig the panadaptor as a frequency monitor.

Ian!

And if you're ever in a jam...

With tears streaming down her cheeks she set the automatic pilot and fumbled with the little amateur transmitter that had been built into the locker. She had seen her uncle use it only once. That turned it on, she thought, but how did she know it was set right? Or did you set these things?

The little panel wore three switches, two knobs, a dial, and a little red light. Naturally Kirk MacInnes had not labeled the controls of an instrument he had built himself. The panel was innocent of any such clutterment.

Carlin tore through the night. The glowing thing was less than fifteen yards behind.

Jeanne wept wildly and the placid voices over the receiver spoke sympathetically of the ruining of Thorne's beach pool by the storm.

Oh, those knobs and switches! This one, then this one, she thought. No—that wouldn't be right. The transmitter might not even be on the air at all. Or she might be in some part of the band where Ian and her uncle would fail to hear her. But what was she supposed to do? And she couldn't read this funny tuning scale.

"I've got a swell mobile VFO in *Carlin*," said MacInnes.

"What's VFO?" said Seppel.

"In Mac's case, it means Very Frequently Offband."

Laughter.

Oh, what difference would it make? What could he do to help her? The brilliance of the huge thing was lighting up the water for yards around.

The calm voices floated from the receiver and the globe drew closer than it had ever been.

She clawed at the stand-by switch of the radio and suddenly her sobs and the beat of the engines were the only sounds in the deckhouse. She would try. That was all. She would try to reach Ian and pray that her uncle had left the transmitter set to the correct frequency.

"Ian!" she cried, then remembered to press the button on the side of the little hand microphone. Forcing back her tears, she said, "Ian, Ian— can you hear me?"

Trembling, her hand touched the receiver.

"Jeanne!" the sound burst into the deckhouse. "Is that you? What are you doing?"

"It's after me, Ian!" she screamed. "A glowing sphere fifteen feet high! It's chasing the boat!"

"The boat," came MacInnes's voice numbly. "She took it to Muskegon."

"Jeanne! Listen to me. I don't know whether this will do any good, but you must try. You must do exactly as I say. Do you hear me?"

"I hear you. Ian! That thing is almost on top of the boat!"

"Listen. Listen to me, darling. You have that little amber drop somewhere in the boat. Do you remember? The little amber drop I gave you. Get it. Take it and throw it overboard. Throw it as far as you can. The amber drop! Now tell me if you heard me."

"Yes. I hear you. The drop..."

The drop. It danced on its little silver chain and the light in its core was bright and pulsating and warm. She tore it from its place over the wheel and groped back to the open cockpit of the cruiser. She clung for a full minute to the canopy stanchion, blinded by the golden light.

And then the small drop arced brightly over the water, even as a meteor had, many centuries past.

The light reflecting off the walls painted a flat, clinical white, was full of blurred, fuzzy forms. They might have been almost anything, Thorne thought. And he shuddered as he thought of what they might have been. A table, for instance, with a burden that was sprawled and made black all along one side.

Without moving his head or changing his expression he squeezed his eyes shut very slowly and opened them again. But it was not the medical examiner's office. It was the waiting room of the little local hospital, and Willy Seppel was sitting beside him on the leather couch. Through the open window behind lowered blinds, a clovery night breeze stirred, parting the smoke that filled the room and turning a page of the magazine that Seppel was staring at.

A young man of twenty-five or so sat across the room from them and ate prodigious quantities of Lifesavers. "My wife," he had grinned nervously at them. "Our first."

The persons in the waiting room could see through the open door to a room at the end of the hall. People in white would periodically enter and leave this room, but another, grimmer group which had entered nearly an hour ago had not come out.

"Willy, I'm going nuts," Thorne burst out at last. "What are they doing in there? You'd think they'd at least let me know—let me see her."

"Easy. It'll be any minute now." He proffered a gold cigarette case, but Thorne shook his head. "Why don't you lie back and try to relax?" Seppel said. "You've been crouching there staring at the floor until your eyes look like a pair of burned-out bulbs. What good do you think you're going to do her in that kind of shape?"

Thorne sank back and lay with the back of his hand shading his eyes. If he could have been there when they brought her in! But it takes time to find where an unmanned boat has drifted. Time while he sat before his receiver with nothing to do but wait. The hands of the clock had wound around to one a.m. before the call finally came and he knew she was saved.

It was three thirty now. MacInnes and his wife were in there with her. He looked despairingly down the white corridor, and waited.

The sound of her voice, made broken and breathless with weeping, rose again in his mind. She had said the thing was fifteen feet high. The big one itself. And it could have—

This wouldn't do at all. The memory of his dream the previous night stood out in his mind with horrible clarity. The bright golden sun and the little burned things. But infrared doesn't burn. The bright golden sun.

"Sun," said Dr. Thorne to himself, very quietly.

"Mm'mm?" said Seppel.

"Sun," he repeated firmly. "Willy, do you always think the same way?"

"Nope."

"If I hit you, how do you think?"

"Mad," said Seppel, with a winning smile.

"But if you figure the best way to sneak out of here without being seen, how do you think?"

"Rationally."

"I've been thinking about the drops again. You know, we've got a pretty serious discrepancy in the so-called properties of the things. We've proved the infrared emission, but infrared doesn't sear flesh."

"That's what I've been trying to tell you," said Seppel, with patience.

"Nonetheless, I'm convinced that the big one Jeanne saw is the thing that did in the tramp. Now what if the energy emitted is not always infrared? What if the infrared is a sort of involuntary result of the blows we gave the drop, while ordinarily when it's aroused it gives off another wavelength? Say something in the visible with a lot of energy, that that drop shape could focus into a beam."

Seppel didn't say a thing.

Silence precipitated heavily. The young man in the chair opposite them shifted his position and stared at them with gaping awe. Scientists!

There was a starchy swish and a nurse appeared in the doorway. Thorne started to his feet. "Can we—"

"Mr. De Angelo," she beckoned coolly. "It's a boy. Will you follow me, please?"

The young man gave a joyous, inarticulate cry and rushed out of the room.

Thorne dropped back. "Ye gods," he muttered.

"You've really got it bad, haven't you?" Seppel marveled.

"Oh, Willy, shut up. You know I'm only interested in her because of the thing that chased her. And wipe that look off your face. Between you and MacInnes a man doesn't have a chance."

Seppel looked slightly hurt.

"I'm sorry," Thorne apologized briefly. He walked around the room.

The young man with the new son had been so anxious to leave that he had forgotten his Lifesavers. Thorne ate one. It was wintergreen. He hated wintergreen.

Seppel yawned delicately, then leaned forward and glanced out the door. "Someone's coming," he warned softly.

A tall man in a uniform of summer tans had left the room at the end of the corridor and walked purposefully toward the waiting room.

Seppel rose to his feet as the man entered the room. He said: "Good evening—or rather, good morning. Is there something I can do?"

"My name is Cunningham, commander of the Coast Guard cutter *Manistique*. Are you Mr. Ian Thorne?"

"My name is Seppel. This is Mr. Thorne. Won't you sit down?"

"Thanks, I will." To Thorne, who stood with his hands rudely clasped behind his back, he said briskly: "Mr. Thorne, at nine this evening your amateur station contacted our base with information that the cruiser *Carlin* was in difficulty off the mainland somewhere between Port Grand and Muskegon."

"It wasn't me, it was Kirk MacInnes." Thorne was not interested in brisk, nautical gentlemen.

"We found the cruiser drifting, out of gas, some seven miles off the Port Grand light. Miss Wright, the operator of the craft, was found lying unconscious on the cockpit floor. I've just seen her—"

"How is she?" Thorne cut in.

"The doctors say she is suffering from shock, but other than that, they can't find a thing wrong with her. Now what I'd like to know—"

"Is she conscious? Has she been able to talk?"

"She's very weak and what she says makes no sense. I thought perhaps you might be able to help us on that score."

Thorne looked at the Coast Guardsman narrowly. "We were conversing with her over the radio, when she suddenly seemed to become disturbed and evidently fainted."

"Didn't MacInnes tell you anything?" asked Seppel.

"No."

"Quiet, Willy," Thorne said.

"She seemed to be trying to tell us that someone was chasing her," Cunningham persisted. "Are you sure she said nothing in her talk with you that could give us a hint of the trouble?"

"I knew there was something wrong from the sound of her voice. That's all. When she didn't answer, Mr. MacInnes radioed the Coast Guard."

"And we found her after a four-hour search. That young lady was very lucky that she ran out of gas. Her automatic pilot had the cruiser headed straight out into the middle of the lake."

"There was—nothing else on the water near her?"

"The lake was empty." Cunningham paused, then said casually, "Was there something you expected us to find, Dr. Thorne?"

"Certainly not. I was just wondering."

"I see." The officer got to his feet. "I don't mind telling you gentlemen that I think there's something you're not letting me know. My job is done, and it's true that legally I have no business questioning you at all. But my business *is* keeping the waterways safe. The young lady in the room down the hall didn't faint from nervous exhaustion or hunger. Something scared the hell out of her out there on the lake. If you know what it was, I wish you'd tell me!"

"Have you ever read any science fiction, Commander Cunningham?" Seppel asked, toying with his gold cigarette case. Rather belatedly, he said, "Cigarette?"

The Coast Guardsman took one with suspicious thanks. "Are you trying to tell me that the little green Martians have put outboards on their rocket ships and are chasing the pleasure craft on our lake?"

Thorne said harshly: "What Dr. Seppel means is this. We have reason to believe that a highly unusual occurrence was responsible for tonight's unpleasantness. I don't like to mince words, Commander. I think I *do* know what was out there last night, but I'm not going to tell you. I can't begin to prove my suspicions, and I have a rather intense aversion to being laughed at."

"I have no intention of laughing, Mr. Thorne. But if you have information relative to marine safety, let me remind you that you have an obligation to report it to the proper authorities."

"Proper authorities are not notorious for their sympathy. They'd laugh in my face. No, thank you, Commander. Until I have proof, I say nothing."

The door at the end of the corridor opened once more, and closed softly. Kirk MacInnes and his wife came down toward the waiting room. Thorne started up.

"She wants to see you, son," MacInnes said tiredly. "She's a little stronger now, and she asked for you. I'm taking Ellen back home. This has been pretty raw for her."

"I'm all right," his wife said stiffly. She clutched a damp, tightly balled lace handkerchief, but her features were immobile.

"Will Jeanne be all right?" Thorne asked brokenly.

"She'll be fine," said MacInnes, clapping him on the back. "Now get down there and see her before those medics decide she can't have any more visitors."

"I'm there now. And—thanks, Mac." He disappeared down the corridor. The engineer and his wife left quietly.

"Thorne is a good man," Seppel said, "even if he is a trifle muleheaded." His bright blue eyes looked humorously into the half-angry face of the Coast Guard officer. He laughed, moved over on the leather couch, and said: "Sit down here, Commander. Have another cigarette. Have a Lifesaver. I'm going to tell you a singular story."

*　　*　　*

It was shortly before lunchtime in Thorne's dune lodge, but the bubbling beaker on the range that Willy Seppel was stirring exuded a decidedly unappetizing aroma. Pungent, acidic in an organic kind of way, with noisome and revolting overtones, the fumes finally brought indignant remarks from Thorne.

"Look," he said, peering in the doorway, and holding his nose. "I'm the last one to criticize another man's cooking, but will you tell me what in heaven's name that is?"

"Oh, just a bit of digestive juice," said Seppel cheerily, turning off the gas and removing the beaker with a pair of potholders. He carried his foul-steaming container into the workroom. Thorne fled before him.

"I suppose I'd better not ask where you got it," he said, from the sanctuary of the radio room.

"Don't be silly," said Seppel. "I merely raided your enzymes and warmed up a batch. Just an idea."

He took the little drop out of its container and set it on the table beside the beaker. "I thought since digestive juice provoked it into emitting once, it might do it again." Thorne regarded him dubiously.

"I only wish," Seppel went on to say, "that the grapefruit-sized one hadn't escaped." He set the drop in a loop of plastic and dipped it into the brew.

"Take it easy with that one, Willy. It's the only link we have with the big one."

"So you think they can communicate, too," said Seppel without looking up.

"I don't know whether it's communication or sympathetic vibration or the call of the wild. But that thing did follow Jeanne because of the little drop in the boat, and it disappeared when it got what it wanted. The grapefruit heard mama, too, and got away. I'll bet if that little one had been strong enough to get through your fancy insulation, it would have disappeared along with the other one."

"And the two tracks merged into one," said Seppel, testing the soaked drop in the thermocouple. Nothing happened. "As the rustic detective was heard to remark, 'They was two sets o' footsteps leadin' to the scene of the crime, and only one set leadin' away.' I wonder what kind of a molecular bond that transparent envelope has?" He felt the drop with his finger, shrugged, and put it back into the juice.

"The big globe killed the tramp, if my idea is correct," said Thorne. "He must have seen the thing coming out of the lake, turned to beat it, and fell on his face. And I think he picked exactly the wrong place to fall."

"On grapefruit," Seppel agreed. "All mama wanted to do was to pick up her offspring. She couldn't help it if there was a body in the way."

"But she killed just the same," said Thorne. "Those old dune roller stories hint that she may have done it before." He fished the miniature drop out of the liquid and looked into its yellow heart meditatively.

"And Willy," he said abstractedly, "unless something is done soon, she'll do it again."

During the days that followed, Dr. Thorne went about his work with quiet preoccupation; and this in itself was enough to make Seppel more than a little suspicious. He rarely mentioned the drops, although he visited Jeanne every day, carrying sheaves of flowers and boxes of candy and fruit. Seppel went along on these pilgrimages for the ride, but almost always tactfully declined visiting the sickroom and hiked out instead to the Coast Guard station for a parley with his new ally, Commander Cunningham.

Anxiety furrowed Seppel's pink forehead as he paced up and down the officer's quarters. "He's got something up his sleeve," he maintained. "He goes off in the jeep in the morning and doesn't come back until noon. When I ask him where he's been, he says he just went into town to see Jeanne. But visiting hours are from two to four! If he doesn't go to the hospital, where does he go?"

Cunningham shrugged, and picked up a folded newspaper that lay on the table. "Have you seen this, Willy? It might explain a few things."

Mystified, Seppel read aloud: "'We pay CASH for certain unusual minerals. Highest prices, free pickup. Samples wanted are round, semi-transparent, amber colored with metallic veining. HURRY! Write today, Box 236, Port Grand, Michigan.'"

Seppel stared aghast.

"I take it you weren't acquainted with this," the officer said. He walked to the window and looked down at a fruiter steaming through the channel. "Do you know what he plans to do?"

"No, but I know what I'd do. There's some kind of an attraction between the big globe and the drops—a force that draws the little ones home to mama when they get her call. We found that out with a drop at Thorne's lodge. But that attraction is so great that it works the other way too. Little Miss Wright told you that. If the drops can't come, if we hold them back, mama comes after her children. That's what Thorne will probably count on."

It was Cunningham's turn to stare. "You mean he'll use the drops from the ad for *bait*?"

Seppel said gently: "What's a man to do, Rob? He can't let it go free. The fellow that finds the monster has three choices: he can run home and hide under the bed, and pretend he didn't see it at all, he can try to inform the proper authorities, or he can attempt to dispose of the monster himself. Thorne knows nobody will believe his dune roller story so he just doesn't waste time convincing people."

Cunningham turned abruptly from the window and said violently: "You aren't going to start on me too, are you, Willy? Sure. Here I am, one slightly used but still serviceable authority. I believe your damn dune roller yarn for some reason or other. But it doesn't do any good. I'd earn the biggest haw-haw from here to the Straits of Mackinac if I tried to initiate an official search for a round glowing thing fifteen feet high.

The world won't unite simply because Michigan has itself a monster, you know. And what can I do, even if I take the *Manistique* out? Maybe Ian Thorne knows how to catch monsters, but I certainly don't."

"You want to let him go on, I suppose," Seppel said. He added a trifle wistfully, "I hate to see him get his hide fried off when he's just beginning to think about settling down."

"You watch him. That's all. And let me know when you think he's going to pull something. I'll do everything I can." He glanced at his watch. "I have to get out of here now, Willy. Keep your eyes open. All *we* can do is wait."

"And that," said Seppel, with dark doubt shading his pleasant voice, "seems to be all there is to say."

The drops glowed on the kitchen table. "Seven!" said Ian Thorne triumphantly. "How do they look to you, Willy? From the size of a pea to a tennis ball. Seven little devil eyes."

"What are you going to do with them?" asked Seppel. He wore an old lab apron over his trousers and wiped the breakfast dishes. It was very early in the morning.

"Just a little experiment. I got a bright idea the other day while I was visiting Jeanne. You can have the drops after I'm finished if you like, but I want to try this thing out first."

"I wish you'd let me help you."

"No, Willy."

"Cunningham believes you, too," Seppel went on recklessly. "Why don't you tell us what you're going to do?"

"No." He scooped the drops into a Bakelite box. "I'll be gone most of the day. I have some collecting to do out in the dunes."

He vanished into the bedroom and came out wearing hiking boots and a heavy leather jacket. An empty knapsack dangled over his arm. He put the Bakelite box into the buckled pouch on the outside of the sack, and took a paper packet from the sink and stuffed it into his back pocket.

"Oops! Almost forgot my collecting bottles," he laughed, and went into the radio room.

Seppel put down the dish towel and stepped softly after him. There were no collecting bottles in the radio room. He was just in time to see Thorne drop a handful of little metal cylinders and a black six-inch gadget into the knapsack.

Thorne did not seem at all abashed to find Seppel standing there. He brushed past and went out the kitchen door.

"So long, Willy. Keep the home fires burning. Send out the posse if I'm not back before dark." The screen door slammed.

After waiting a minute, Seppel grabbed up the binoculars from the china shelf and glided silently through the sandy yard, past the generator building to the path that led down the side of the dune to the shed where the jeep was kept.

The early-morning mist still curled around the trees and settled in the hollows, and a distant birdcall echoed down on the forest floor. At a bend in the steep path, Seppel caught a glimpse of Thorne's broad back dappled by the pale sun rising through the fog.

The path turned sharply and cut off diagonally down the dune toward the shed. Instead of continuing, Seppel stepped off the path, and treading cautiously, circled across through the woods to arrive at a point on the slope directly above the garage. Then he removed his apron, spread it on the twiggy, dew-wet ground, and stretched out among the bushes, bringing his binoculars to bear on the man below.

Thorne removed a small wooden crate from the rear of the jeep. It bore the red-stenciled inscription:

G.B. VANDER VREES & SONS — HIGHWAY CONSTRUCTION

There were other words, too, but Thorne stood in the way of Seppel's vision. He quickly transferred the contents of the crate to his knapsack, and with a single look around him, set off down the dune trail that ran through the forest, parallel to the lakeshore.

As soon as Thorne was out of sight, Willy Seppel scrambled heavily to his feet and went back up the path to the lodge. There he addressed some intense words to the microphone of the amateur station, an operation which would have been frowned upon by the FCC, which discourages the use of such equipment by unlicensed persons.

He would have maintained his disinterest and scientific detachment if he had been asked about it, but the truth was that Dr. Ian Thorne deeply loved the dunes. He had lived in them during his childhood, grown up and gone away, and come back to find them substantially the same. He recalled that had surprised him a little. You expected the dunes to change; they were like a person, though only one who has known the heights and swamps of them can explain the curious sleeping vitality of the sands under the forest. Things with a smaller life than the dunes would flutter and creep and stalk boldly through them until you might think of them as dead and tame. But Dr. Thorne had seen the traveling dunes shifting restlessly before the winds and felt a kinship with the great never-lasting hills.

The path he strolled along was an old friend. He had pursued the invertebrate citizens of the forest along its meandering length, waded in the marshy inter-dunal pools which it carefully skirted, and had itched from encounters with the poison ivy that festooned the trunks and shrubs beside it.

The path wound along the shore for a good five miles—horizontally, at least—and he did not hurry. The knapsack was too heavy, for one thing, and the still air was warming slowly as the sun rose up through the pines and oak trees. An insect chirred sleepily in a gorge on his right, and as if at some prearranged signal, an excursion of mosquitoes bobbed out to worry the back of his neck.

The path took him through a clearing in the sand covered with patches of dusty, green grass and scarlet Indian weed. On the lee side of a great bare dune at the edge of the clearing stood a single, short cotton-wood, half buried in the sand. But the tree had grown upward to escape, modifying its lower branches into roots. The tree was one of the few forms of life that defied the dunes—by growing with them—and its branches were brave and green.

Thoughtfully, Thorne passed on again into the dimmer depths of the forest.

It was nearly noon when he reached the foot of a cluster of sand dunes, the principal peak of which rose some hundred and fifty feet above the floor of the woods. It was the highest point for many miles along the shore, and its name was Mount Scott. The path circled its eastern slope and then continued on, but Thorne stepped off onto the faintly defined, spiderweb-laced trail leading to the summit.

The going was rough. Thorn-apple branches probed after his eyes, and as the ascent grew steeper, sudden shifts in the dirty sand under his feet brought him to his knees. The tree roots across the path had partially blocked the sand, forming crude natural steps in the lower reaches of the dune; but as he climbed higher, the trees were left behind while the sand grew cleaner and hotter, and the wild grape, creeper, and ubiqui-tous poison ivy became the prevalent greenery.

He was winded and perspiring when he finally stood on the peak of the dune. He glanced briefly about him and selected a spot partially shaded by a scrub juniper as his campsite. He sat down, shucked the knapsack and his heavy jacket, and lit a cigarette.

The hills below rolled away in gentle, green waves toward the farm-lands and orchards in the east and the brilliant blue lake in the west. He could see the spires of the town of Port Grand poking out of the haze a few miles down the shore, and some white sails appeared off the promontory that hid the entrance to the river harbor.

He turned his attention to Mount Scott itself. The summit of the dune was really composed of two shallow humps, with a depression on the lakeward side in which Thorne had made his camp. Below this, a sheer, fairly clean slope of sand swept down to the low tangle of woods which lay between him and the shore.

He looked cautiously in the knapsack and removed the seven small drops, grouping them in a circle on the white sand of the lake slope. After that, he retreated to his hollow and settled down as comfortably as he could.

The paper packet in his pocket yielded three ham-and-pickle sandwiches, slightly soggy, which he consumed leisurely. A short foray around the peak brought dessert in the form of a handful of late blueberries. After his meal he employed himself at length with the contents of the knapsack. When the job was finally done, he sat down under the juniper tree and began to wait.

The shade of the tree diminished, disappeared as the sun climbed higher, and then reappeared on the other side of the tree, leaving Thorne with the sun in his face and a monumental thirst. The blueberries, unfortunately, were all gone.

At last, at four p.m., the largest drop began to move.

It rolled slowly out of the shallow hole in the sand that cupped it and moved down the hill. Thorne watched it roll *up* a small pile of sand that blocked its path and disappear into the woods at the foot of the hill.

At 4:57 one of the smaller drops followed in the track of the first. It had a little trouble when it came to the pile of sand—which was one of several strung across the face of the dune—but it negotiated the obstacle at last and disappeared.

Just as the sun was beginning to redden the water, a third drop began its descent. Quietly, Thorne rose and replaced it in its hole. The faint gleam within it might have grown a bit brighter when he interfered, but perhaps it was only the reflection of the sun.

The five remaining drops were grouped in a horseshoe, downward pointing, and the drop whose elopement had just been foiled reposed at the end of one prong. A few minutes later, the larger drop at the other prong attempted to roll down the hill. Thorne put it back and rapped sharply on each of the others with his cigarette lighter, tamping them down further into the sand. He was strained forward alertly now, with his eyes on the strip of forest below. The sun slipped grudgingly behind the flat lake, and a tang of pine washed up the slope. The drops did not move again.

With the departure of the sun, the glow in the heart of each alien thing leaped higher and higher, until the string of them was like a softly glowing corona in the sand—a strange earthbound constellation.

But their glow was not beauty, Thorne reminded himself. It was death. Death had dwelt in their great, glowing mother who had already called two of her incredible children home. Death that rolled seeking through the lake and the dune forest...

His cigarette end made a dimmer eye in the dusk than the glow of the drops. There was still enough light to see by—the sky was red around him and the dune forest was silent.

He wondered idly what long forgotten power had strewn the drops along the shore. They were not terrestrial, he was almost sure of that. Perhaps they had been a meteor that had exploded over the lake, and the life of the great thing—if it was life—had been patiently gathering up its scattered substance ever since, assimilating the fragments during its long rests at the bottom of the lake.

From the size of it, it must have been growing for hundreds of years, collecting a drop of itself here and there, from roadbeds and sand dunes and farmyards, responding to those who imprudently hindered it with the only defense it knew.

And now he was to destroy it. It had killed a man. Perhaps before this, even, men had found the drops attractive and carelessly put them in their pockets... and the dune roller sought a man. It had killed the little tramp, and almost killed Jeanne. He couldn't take a chance of letting it go again.

The image of Jeanne rose in his mind. The memory of the time they had walked down the winding forest path, and of a twig caught in her sandal. She had had grains of sand on her tanned arms, and a bright yellow flower stuck crazily in one dark curl. She had laughed when he plumped her down on the moss-soft root of an old oak and took the twig out, but she had not laughed when he kissed her.

Around him, the forest was still.

A cold breath whispered along his skin. The forest was still. Not a bird, not an insect, not an animal noise. The forest was still.

He felt like yelling at it: *Come on out, you!* Come out and chase me like you chased her!

He fingered the stud of the little black instrument in his hand. He would show it. Let it dare to come out.

Come out!

It came.

He had never dreamed it would be so big.

It had made no noise at all. In a fascination of horror he watched it roll to the foot of the tall dune. It vanished among the trees, but a warm yellow radiance lit the undersides of the fluttering leaves as it moved beneath them. The light blazed as it emerged from the brush and came straight toward him, rolling up the hill.

The small drops pulsed in their sandy snares and he gave each one a savage rap. As if it, too, shared the insult, the great globe flared, then subsided sullenly. But its ponderous ascent was alarmingly rapid.

He could not take his eyes away from it. The smaller drops were rocks, were mere bits of oddly glowing crystal; but this great thing before him seemed the most beautiful and the most terrible thing he had ever seen in his life. And it was alive. No man could have looked upon it and said that it was not alive. The brilliant golden heart in it swelled and blazed upon the golden veining that closed it in.

There were noises now from the winding path in the forest below, and the twinkling pinpoint lights of men. But Thorne did not hear them, nor see any light except the great one before him. He could not move. Sweat stood out on his face and the instinct to flee dissolved into terror that folded his legs like boneless things. He half crouched on hands and knees and stared... and stared.

The thing was closer now, nearly up to the line of sand humps that Thorne had worked so hard on. He had to get away. There was no more time. He forced his paralyzed hands and feet to tear into the loose sand at the side of the depression and pull him up. He had to get on the other side of the hill.

In the last instant, his numbed fingers pressed the stud of the little transmitter that would activate the firing caps of the neo-nitro buried in the sand.

But the monster must have realized, somehow. Because he felt— when he flung himself out over the peak with the deep red sky around him—a searing, mounting pain that started on the inside and flooded outward. He rolled unconscious over the far side of the hill just as the five solemn detonations blasted the golden glowing globe to bits.

There were white, gauzy circles around the place where his eyes looked out. He was vaguely surprised to see six people with the eyes—three sets of two. He made the eyes blink and the six people changed into Seppel, MacInnes, and Jeanne. He tried to raise an arm and was rewarded by a fierce jab of pain. The arm was thick and bandaged, like the rest of him.

The six—three—people had seen his eyes open and they moved closer to him. Jeanne sat down beside the bed and leaned her head close.

"I hope that's you in there," she said, and he was amazed to see there were tears in her eyes.

"How am I?" he mumbled through the bandages.

"Medium rare," said Seppel. "You doggone crazy fool."

"We almost got to the top, anyway," said MacInnes gruffly. "But you went and beat us to it."

"Had to," Thorne said painfully.

"You would," Jeanne said.

"Is it gone?" he asked. There were six people again and he felt very tired.

"Shivered to atoms," said Seppel with finality. "You should see the crater in the sand. But we'll still have small ones to study. Your ad brought in four more today. I was talking to Camestres on the phone, and he says he's sure he can swing a nice fat research grant for us as soon as you're able to get out of that bed—"

Thorne groaned.

"He says," Jeanne translated firmly, "that he's sticking to *Ecological Studies of the Michigan Dunes*, Chapter Eight. No more dune rollers, thank you."

MacInnes laughed and wagged his gray old head. "You'd better surrender, Dr. Seppel. Jeanne's got her mind made up. And one thing about her—whatever she says, she'll always be Wright."

"Don't be too sure about that," she said pertly, laying her two small hands gently on Thorne's bandaged arm. It didn't hurt a bit.

High on a dune above the lake, the moon rode high over a blackened crater in the sand. Two of the grains of sand, which gleamed in the moonlight a bit more golden than the rest, tumbled down together into a sheltered hollow to begin anew the work of three hundred years.

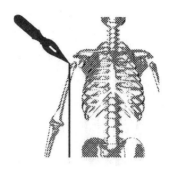

THE DESIGN

CHINA MIÉVILLE

There is a fact familiar to anyone who has worked with the dead. Do anything to a cadaver, it will do something back to you. This is not gusty spiritualism but psychology. It is true for even the gentlest interaction: actually *cutting* those quiet specimens provokes a far more serious response. One adjusts with speed, but the act never loses its taint.

This is the second time I have tried to write this document. The first, years ago, I started thus: "Now that William is dead, I am released from the concerns of his discretion." In fact I decided, to my own surprise, to extend that care beyond his passing, up to the point of mine.

Upon his arrival in Glasgow, William—a clever, ambitious, somewhat sheltered young man, but no sort of a prig—indulged with enthusiasm in all the typical carousing for which students at the medical school were notorious. He also worked hard, including at anatomy. In those days, he later told me, he handled the dead with adequate respect and interest, but little more.

The laboratory was belowground. Its frosted windows were at ceiling level, calf-high to pedestrians outside. Our class—I was not present in those early weeks, and what I describe here I do from later knowledge—would gather in groups of four around each of the cadavers and prod and probe, lifting the formalin-soaked sheets while professors issued instructions.

It was the third month of study, late, and cold (for obvious reasons the room was not heated above a minimum). Evening access to the room was permitted, on the understanding that while swotting was acceptable, actual cutting outside official hours would constitute a discourtesy to one's quartet, like underlining in a shared textbook. There were three students present that night. One of them was William.

He was sketching musculature. He prodded at a flayed limb. He rotated it to see how its inner fibres moved.

The body was that of a man in his sixties, still rangy and muscled under a certain later-life thickening. William rummaged between flexors and extensors. They had been disconnected from the tendons of the hand, and he folded them back. He uncovered a long bone curving gently in the dead man's arm.

He stopped. For many seconds, William was still, looking closely at what was beneath his fingers. He wiped away tissue, felt his fingers slide on the ulna's sausage-skin-thin casing.

On the off-white of the bone were scratches. For a moment William thought they must be the results of injury. But they were not random. No chance mishap could have caused what he saw.

The markings were a design. They were pictures.

Through a tear in the periosteum, the bone's fibrous fascia, William saw curlicues. Carved filigrees entwined the shafts of ulna and radius like the borders of an illuminated manuscript.

William looked up at the age-stained walls, at John and Harpreet at their own stations, back down at last at the bone he touched. It remained impossibly carved. He could make out rust-red lines as if through gauze.

With hands that had begun to tremble, he peeled back muscle and meat, brought more bone into the light. He traced intricate illustration. Near the wrist he uncovered images of plants, between the leaves of which, rendered in even finer lines, was the tiny figure of a man.

William was certain that until he and his classmates had taken scalpels to it, the skin of the arm had been unbroken. He leaned on the table. He loomed over the cloth-obscured face.

"You chaps," he said. Neither John nor Harpreet heard him. He had to clear his throat and repeat himself. What he heard himself say when they looked up, he later told me, astonished him. What he'd intended was to say, "Here's a queer thing—come tell me if this makes any more sense to you than it does to me." What he said, after a tiny hesitation, was, "I'm going to get knocked for six by this test. I've no idea what I'm looking at in here."

At which misleading truth his classmates grinned, insisted on their own equally shocking ignorance, and went back to work, leaving William staring into the grey arm, at the intricacies on the bone.

The dead man in his care had no tattoos, and only everyday scars. His hands suggested manual work and his knuckles that he had not been a fighter.

When one has put oneself in the frame of mind necessary for cutting, I can attest, it is hard to see a cadaver's face as a face at all. It was with effort, when he lifted the flannel, that William registered not planes of skin but features. He pulled back the lids of the eyes and tried to imagine this etched man moving in the world.

Eventually Harpreet and John left. Bourne, the porter, peered in and nodded good evening, then withdrew, leaving William alone in the presence of the mystery. He sat motionless in the cold room for a long time, as if keeping vigil. When at last he stood, he moved decisively. He took a blade and extended the cut with more finesse than he'd expected he would muster. He sluiced the nestled bone with water, and all along it found more marks.

Paisleys, cloudlike forms, waves. Here was a woman, bent, her body crisscrossed lines. William opened the man's thigh. He tugged the tremendous muscles apart to uncover the femur—there is no profit in being gentle with the dead—and looking up at him from within the leg was an eye scratched onto the bone.

Two cuts to the chest, like martyrs' wounds. On the ribs to one side was a scene of sailing; on the other, abstract shapes.

William cleaned his hands. He listened to the occasional footsteps that came and went outside.

There were no anatomy classes for another two days, but any of his three cadaver-sharers might come in at any time. He later said he knew he had no moral right to do what he decided to do, that the design was his only contingently, that it had not been vouchsafed to him. I have never in fact believed he was quite sure he was unchosen.

"Late one for you tonight," Bourne said when William at last signed out.

"Indeed," William said. "Exam coming up." He was shaking. He blinked and smiled, not very successfully, and headed into the chilly dark.

Perhaps two hours later he was back. He wore drab, featureless clothes, a hat low on his head. He pushed a compost-filled barrow taken with agonizing silence from the garden of his lodgings. There were not many hours until dawn. William glanced at the rear of the houses that overlooked him. They were unlit. He knelt on the pavement outside and tugged open the window he had left unlatched.

Reaching into the darkness, where the dead lay, he extracted the bag of chemicals and tools he'd tied to the frame. He braced himself, leaning against the wall. He groped for the ends of the winding sheets he had coiled into ropes. They stretched from where he had secured them to the worktop below, and to the results of his long, unpleasant work.

William had no expertise. It must have been a bad business. With the help of the textbooks in the cutting room, in agonies, terrified of interruption, he had, as quickly as he could and with clumsy care, dismembered the body.

One slip now and his burdens would slam down with a din like the dead stamping. Bourne would come rushing. Part by part William pulled the body out by its own shroud.

At last he sat back in the alley, gasping. His shirt was damp with sweat, and with preserving fluid soaked through the wrappings. He reeked. He arranged the swaddled components in his wheelbarrow, smothered them in compost. He buried his dead. Hoping he looked like an early-rising workman, he lifted the handles and walked away.

It would not be until late the following day that William's crime was discovered. Two students, alone in the room, found that the body at their station was not the one on which they had hitherto been working.

William had considered various ways to spread confusion, including desecrating every cadaver (a notion he instantly rejected). In the end, he simply rearranged all their gurneys, wheeling them all to new positions, and leaving his own, now empty, discreetly by the wall.

It was effective. It took Johnson and Hirsch almost half an hour to find their specimen, in the corner where William had left it. When they did, at first they simply assumed they'd forgotten some explanatory announcement, and recommenced working on it. Uneasy at last, they finally reported the situation, but it was hours again after they did so that the porters, rolling their eyes at what seemed a prank, tried to return every cadaver to its designated place, and realised that one was missing.

William's pressing need was for a hiding place. His heart clamouring in his chest, he had pushed the barrow into an unsalubrious quarter of the city, haunted by a sudden wish that his dead man was whole and unbroken.

The night was nearly gone when he found the tenements he remembered. They were, for the length of four or five buildings, empty, broken-windowed and fire-damaged. It was the work of minutes to pry open a rear door and push in through clutter and rubbish. He passed a noisome chamber used by tramps and local boys to relieve themselves. The smell was revolting and, William hoped, offputting to other intruders. He hauled his burden up the stairs and laid it down.

He tried to sit it up, in its pieces, in a body shape, shoulders to the wall. He hoped the chemicals would keep rats away. Not one part of the flesh was visible. The thing regarded him with its filthy-cloth-obscured face. William watched it back, his stomach fluttering.

He imagined how the sun would rise, how at a certain point its rays would crawl across the shroud and the dead man, cross from one side of him to the other, and how he would not move at all under that light.

I was present when the dean, Dr. Kelly, thundered about the heinous act that had been committed. It was my first, dramatic day. I'd transferred from my previous place of studies to Glasgow in a rush of instructions and hurried plans. What I arrived to was that outraged speech.

There were police constables in the room. When we were dismissed, and I was shuffling out among a group of young men politely introducing themselves, I saw a porter call four fellows from the crowd to where the officers were waiting.

"Who are they?" I said.

"The chaps whose body's toddled off," someone said. "Hauled before His Nibs and Scotland's finest." He shuddered theatrically.

It was helpful to William to hear how aggrieved by the questioning were his innocent colleagues. His own denials of knowledge could approximate theirs. He'd discarded the clothes he'd worn that night. Mrs. Malley's wheelbarrow was at the bottom of a canal. That William was not discovered then does not make this a story of the incompetence of the police.

"So, come on, then," said Mills, a phlegmatic young Yorkshireman who was to fall in France in 1940. "Who has a theory?"

We took turns speculating on what had happened to the cadaver. We mooted theft, ghostliness, complicated games. William had joined us in the pub by then, and his own flight of fancy was that the man had woken up, realized he wasn't dead, shrugged, and gone home. Mine— my classmates encouraged the new boy to play—was that they were all victims of a hex operating on their memories, that there had never been any such corpse as the one they remembered.

The newly bodiless quartet was dispersed—"like the tribes of bloody Israel," according to Adenborough—among their peers. I was also assigned a place, so five of the anatomy stations became five-man teams. William complained exactly sufficiently about this disruption.

The disappearing body quickly became shorthand. Anything lost was considered pocketed by our ambulatory corpse on its way home. Unexpected noises in corridors were the incompetent creepings of the revenant. William took part in such joshing no more and no less than anyone else.

*   *   *

Under a stretch of houses overlooking a railway cut, William found store-rooms where local shops kept surplus wares. He peered into a grimy window. A train passed. A little girl playing in the gutter looked up from her doll.

The owner of the room, an aging tough, agreed to a price. William impressed upon his landlord the need for discretion and privacy, hinting that he might be working with dangerous chemicals. The man obviously assumed this would be some cottage industry in liquor or narcotics. William allowed the impression.

"Can you keep the local lads out?" William said.

"They'll mind me."

When William crept back to the old house for the bundled parts, he was afraid the police would be waiting for him. But there was only the stained cloth and the flesh within. The moon spotlit the floor a little to one side of the remains: incompetent stagecraft.

William took three awful night walks to his new laboratory. He brought the torso in a suitcase. Then two legs; then both arms and the head, in a hiker's backpack. Treated as they were, his burdens did not smell of rot, but they did not smell good.

Did anyone, in those days, notice how tired he was? Did his work slip, his marks suffer? I think not. We were all working hard, all exhausted. His secret researches meant William was absent sometimes, but that was hardly unusual. We'd always cover for each other—"Oh, Bryce is down with fever, sir." It was second nature. The professors were game enough, drily wishing absentees recovery.

I had got to know William a little by then. He was not the centre of any social group, but neither was I.

One night, while we were among Bradley's guests (Bradley was a braggart, but for his club we indulged him), attention turned to me.

"But what was it happened?" Leadwith kept saying. He was a good fellow, without malice, but he was rather in his cups. "How'd you end up here in the middle of term in such a fearful rush? You were at Durham, weren't you?" He chortled. "Was it a girl? Why *Glasgow?*"

I responded vaguely and jocularly, but he wouldn't let it lie. "No, really, do tell, Gerald," he said. He was staring. I avoided looking at anyone in particular. "What was it brought you up here?"

"Come now, Charles," someone said, but the chaps were interested, too, and I think pleased that someone was gauche enough to ask such questions. The knave at the feast is a blessed exoneration for better-behaved diners.

William spoke.

"Charles," he said. "You're being a bore. Gerald doesn't want to talk about this. It's a poor show that you won't let it go."

In the silence that followed, William was the only person who did not seem embarrassed. "You would say that," someone said feebly, "gallivanting off with some secret fancy all the time." But William said, "And is it not my right to gallivant exactly as much as I wish?"

He smiled. A few people laughed. Conversation moved on. Leadwith came and found me and muttered, "I'm sorry, old man, I'm an ass." Of course I told him not to give it another thought.

William and I left together, our hands jammed in our pockets, huddled against the cold. We didn't speak much. He did not even say anything along the lines of "Old Leadwith can put his foot in it." When we reached my rooms, we paused under a street lamp and he met my eyes. After a moment he clapped me on the shoulder and walked off in the fog.

A revolting rancidity was setting in to the remains, preservative or no. *Dermestes maculatus* would have turned up their beetle noses. Acid would have damaged the bone. In his newfound workroom, with the small window painted over and the door padlocked, William proceeded by the only methods available to him.

He cut for hours, excising grey flesh and piling offcuts in a covered pail. He dipped a handkerchief in dilute cologne and fastened it around his face. Larger bones he separated by knife; he did not try to do so with the smaller, the digits, the fiddly metatarsals.

How many times he wished for a larger stove! He boiled as large a tub of water as he could, and into it he placed the head. The room grew horribly hot. No matter how scientific and dispassionate one's mindset, to look into a bubbling stockpot and see the flash of eyes looking up when tumbling water lets them, eyes one ought, one realises, to have removed against such glances, to be treated to a sneer as the heat pulls back what remains of lips, is desperate.

The liquid thickened. In an action revoltingly like cooking, William scooped out the lifting flesh with a slotted spoon. He could not stop himself from retching.

He smoked and studied as well as he could while he waited, which was not well. He added water to the stove. It was much later, at the other end of the night, by the time he at last fished in the pot with tongs. What he brought out made him gasp and fumble. It fell back into the water, splashing him with scalding drops and human particulate as he clapped a trembling hand to his mouth.

William tried again. The head steamed. The distended eggy sacs the eyes had become stared in an awful manner. He took them out. He could see bone through the parting flesh.

William peeled off the remains of the face. He cleaned the skull down. The brain would necessitate creative cerebrectomy, Egyptian style, perhaps, through the nose. For now he held out his prize and met its empty gaze.

It was marked by lines in the same dark red he remembered from within the arm. Stained not by lampblack but by the endless passage of blood.

On one side of the frontal bone was a tall ship. It bore unknown cargo on an intricate sea. Over the left eye was a knot of lines that might have been a submerged beast following that vessel. The maxila: a jungle. Thickets of ivy in beaux arts curves, boughs teeming with squirrels, birds of paradise courting in the greenery.

The sphenoid swarmed with animals. On the zygoma were cogs of some shaded machine. On the temporal bone were clouds. There were weapons on the parietal; on the mandible, monkeys and fruit. Surrounding the nasal cavity were marks like those made by a calligrapher breaking in a new pen.

The display had been obscured by blood and skin. Life had been necessary to finish this piece—years of blood-flow to colour the lines, years of growth to pull the skeleton into the right configuration. How had the design looked when the man was six years old? When he was ten, and seventeen?

William ran his fingers over the voyaging ship. He could feel the lines scratched in the still-cooling bone.

Of course I asked more than once about the body that had gone missing immediately before my arrival. Such curiosity on my part was perfectly understandable. What had it looked like? I asked. Where had it been cut? Joking aside, what *did* people think might have happened?

I asked those whose specimen it had been. "I'm afraid I have not even the idlest speculation," said Sanders. "I don't even *like* anatomy," he said, as if that were relevant. Adenborough and Parish offered no more insight.

When I addressed my questions to William he was affable enough, but quiet, not at all forthcoming. I could not but note his guarded reaction. It left me more crestfallen than I wanted to admit. By then I was not indifferent to his preferences.

*   *   *

The cadavers we used were assiduously anonymised, but let us not be naïve: with sufficient money, time, and energy, William could have uncovered the identity of his. But he could not think how to protect himself if he pursued that route. He decided, with a gladness that bewildered him, that he would not seek to learn the name of the man on whose remains he worked.

My own cadaver was near William's new station. During classes, I watched to see his oddly intent interventions. When we removed several inches from the tops of our specimens' scalps, William went from station to station, examining each unmarked skull. His expression might have been one of disappointment or relief.

The little girl he had seen playing near his makeshift lab seemed excluded from the company of others of her age. She was often there in the shadow of a wall, always alone but for her rough toy, with its unravelling mouth and grubby dress. She would watch William come and go with the frank suspicion of the very young.

William steeled himself. He cooked down the meat of the feet and the hands so long that it crumbled when he pushed out the tiny bones. These he set carefully in place on a sheet he'd painted with a rough human outline. In its head-circle was the skull. William put down scaphoid, capitate, triquetral, and lunate, the phalanges of the fingers an undone puzzle.

Each piece, even the very smallest, was illustrated.

He kept water boiling, softened tough flesh, wiped clots of it from ulna, from vertebra after vertebra, ribs and hips. He laid down a disaggregated etched man, impatient to see what he'd found within the flesh.

*   *   *

William and I were visiting a small maritime museum. I performed repeated astonishment at that fact. "Not that I'm not delighted," I kept saying, "but how did I end up here?"

"Mind games is how," William said. "I bend all to my will."

I asked him about his family. When he spoke of his father, that affable clerk, William conjured him for me with rueful dislike. For his mother he expressed affection, and a pity he tried to disguise. His sister was a teacher, his brother an importer of goods, and of them he had nothing to say.

I read aloud vainglorious descriptions of Glasgow's shipyards. Not without sarcasm, I admired a little model clipper, some once-majestic such and such, et cetera.

I stopped at the sight of William staring at a cabinet of scrimshaw. Etchings of ship life, sea monsters, homilies on whale tooth and bone.

"That one's American, I believe," he said of a filigreed narwhal tusk. There was no note to say so.

"Are you an expert?" I managed at last to say. "At whose knee have you been investigating such things?"

"We all have interests," he said. "I don't doubt you have your own hidden depths, Gerald."

I didn't reply. When we left we deposited thank-you coins in the establishment's donations box and wry remarks in its guest book.

"When you arrived," William said after a long silence, "you must have felt like you'd stumbled into some secret society."

"How so?"

"Oh, I don't know. What with all of us already knowing each other. Sometimes one can't help feeling one's blundered into something as an outsider."

"Well, thank you very much," I said. "I rather thought I wasn't doing badly."

"Oh, hush," he said. "I'm talking in general terms, as well you know.

I suppose I'm saying that that feeling hits one more often than one might think. Walk into *any* room with *any* people already in it, that'll do it. No matter how charmingly they try to bring you up to speed. Let alone coming up here as abruptly as you did." He did not meet my eye. "About which of course I am terribly curious, though Leadwith remains an ass."

He saw me open my mouth to speak, and he saw me close it again without a word. He cleared his throat. "I suspect that sense of *not being in on something* is more or less the human condition," he said.

"I suppose," I said.

"And on rare occasions," he said, "there might actually be something to it. One stumbles into something to which one shouldn't have been privy. I wonder what sort of efforts those who *are* in the know might go to in response."

He looked, in that moment, rather heartbreakingly boyish and forlorn. For a while neither of us spoke.

"Is everything all right?" I said.

"Oh," he said, "I was going to ask the same of you." I said nothing. "Pay me no mind."

"If something's been going on…" I said it hesitantly, as if fearful that he might tell me something *had*, and what it was.

"Pay me no mind."

It was done. The bones were clean. They were laid down in a jigsaw man.

Winter was waning. William sluiced his drains with acid.

He had taken a long way to his room that day, unable to shake the feeling that he was being followed. Now he dried the skeleton, brushed the bones gently. He rotated the humerus, tracing the voyage of some Sindbad-like figure through various lands. He wanted to make it glow.

He hesitated, scribbled something in a notebook and tore out the page, then opened his door and looked at the girl playing with her doll.

She stood guardedly under his gaze. "Hullo," he said. "Would you like to earn a shilling?"

The girl answered at last, in so strong a local accent that William could not but laugh. He could understand barely a word.

"You know Mr. Murray?" They knew him there. "Give him this. He'll give you beeswax. Bring it here and I'll give you the shilling."

The child took the paper and ran off in the right direction. For all he knew, that was the last he would ever see of her. William sat on his step, closed the door and leaned back on it, and smoked in the sunlight.

When the girl did return holding a big jar, he cheered her and raised his hands. She rewarded him with his beeswax and a remarkable smile.

She said something. When he understood that she was asking him "whit he had in there," he said, "I can't tell you," and she turned and walked away instantly, without a word, without wheedling. Her lack of surprise that her hopes would be dashed horrified him. He called her back.

William's were now the pleasures of polishing. One by one he made the etched bones shine. The skull gleamed. Scapula, sternum, tib and fib. On the left patella, a rising sun: on the right a crescent moon with a wolf face. The dead man had kneeled on pagan signs.

"I don't mind telling you," William said to me later, "it made me weep to see it all, like that, at last." *This is something to be parsed*, he thought as he tracked the illustrations, sought a route, a journey on the ship he had seen. Arm leg leg arm head, around the rib cage, perhaps? A hero's journey?

"Do you know what this is?" William said.

The girl stared at the marked nugget he held. Is it, she ventured, a biscuit? "It's called a sacrum," he said. "I have one. And so will you when you've finished growing. But d'you see?" Flags in a breeze, blowing left to right across the bone. Mountains, a forest. The child regarded it gravely. Did he draw that? No, he told her. He told her that something or someone else had done so.

He let her run her fingers along the patterns. It was no longer only he who had seen this thing and he was glad. He put it in her memory. He told her that this had been underneath a man's skin.

"You can imagine where that leaves a chap like me," he said. "A free-thinker, I might once have called myself, though that's hardly anything like so dashing a label as once it was. It's a rum thing for the likes of me, because who else could have put these here, eh?" His voice went low. "God is a scrimshander."

The girl did not look at him nor he at her.

"Who *was* this man?" he said. "Did he know? Of how many is he one? I wonder about some brotherhood—sisterhood, too, I've no reason to doubt. Some siblinghood of the lovingly carved."

The house creaked. William glanced up. There was a new tenant above, whose motions made him wary, whose step he imagined he recognised.

"No one could say it isn't done exquisitely," he said. "But here's the thing. Isn't there something a little *haphazard* about it?"

If there was a story in the design, William could not decode it. He could make no narrative sense of the men and monkeys, women and nightjars, the stars, monsters furred and feathered, machines, clocks, the hunt conducted with flintlocks, the giraffe pasha on a stone throne, cities with onion domes above clouds, knots like those on Celtic graves. William made the girl laugh at the beasts on the mandible.

"In some illuminated manuscripts," he said, "you can tell why images are where they are relative to the text. And there are others in which whatever riotous assembly's at the edges would probably have been more or less the same whatever the subject matter." There was another sound from above, a creak like someone lowering himself to a hole. This time William was too deep in thought to notice. The girl, however, heard. She looked up startled as William continued. "For a while I thought that's what I was looking at here. Essentially…" He hesitated. "Doodles. If of a most splendid kind. Marginalia. But."

William pointed at curlicues in the crook of a rib. "See these marks," he said. "They change very specifically. They grow *curvier*. What starts at one end of the bone as a set of relatively simple lines becomes virtuoso.

"You see that sort of thing all over. Developments. The same figure here"—one shin—"and here"—the side of the skull—"but with far more finesse above. There are plenty of these *improvements*."

"I think what are on these bones are experiments. Studies, references, preparations, the testing out of ideas. This skeleton's been used to loosen up the wrist. Before the artist turns to the real project. Which will be who knows what? Not this man, and perhaps not Man at all."

William looked at a paint-covered window. It glowed from the light outside. He spoke quickly. "Perhaps in twenty years, some Norwegian ship'll land, shall we say, a blue whale. And as the crew flense it, Gunnar Gunnarson will point: there, on an exposed corner of that great skull, will be carved a human figure. Life-sized. Perfect. Crosshatched more delicately even than the real thing. And there at last, under *that* flesh, will be the piece all this has been leading up to. And it'll be so beautiful. And it'll tell so astonishing a story. What would you say to that?" He smiled at the girl. "Scratched in the bones of a whale."

The girl regarded him. "Our friend here?" he said. "And who knows who else?" He raised his hands at the door, at everyone in Glasgow. "Rough sketches, every one. What's been done to this chap is what you do to such scraps when you're done. You throw them away. So here we are." He smiled again and his eyes filled. "In a waste bin."

He was too agitated for even an adult observer easily to follow, let alone the girl. He stared at the bones.

"If we were to look under my skin or yours, what do you think we might find? There can't be too many such people—one would have heard.

But I find I can't believe him unique. How many of us are scribbled on?

"I've considered, of course I have, uncovering a few inches." He tapped his own shin. "But do you know? I find I cannot bear to discover if I am, *or* if I'm not."

William raised a finger to his lips. The girl, solemn thing, copied him. She glanced at the ceiling again, but the noises from above had stopped. "If those who wear the design know they do," he said, "whether they know why or what it portends, they obviously go to some lengths to avoid attention. Which would make *this* fellow here a serious oversight on their part. Who knows who they might send, what they might do to someone like me, who chanced on the knowledge? Best to keep what we know hush-hush. In case they're a bad lot.

"After all, it's always possible that the artist isn't God, but the other party."

The girl tried to steal a vertebra. William fished it out of her pocket in mock astonishment, as if chancing upon it like a fossil on a beach. "This is a wonderful specimen," he said. "I must have this." He told her he would buy it from her and gave her another shilling.

She paused at the door. "No' a whale," she said. "A wee mouse."

"Yes. Yes!" William was delighted. "Why not?"

He watched her go. It might indeed be that rather than submerging to biblical deeps, the work for which this man was a draft scampered for crumbs. That one day a cat would catch it, and crunch down on filigree illustration so fine, so exquisite, it might only have been made out with microscopy of the mouse's bones.

*   *   *

Given her age and situation, it seemed reasonable to assume that anything the girl might report would not be listened to. Later, though, hoping to move on to a new phase of life, I felt I had to seek, at considerable effort, the young woman she was by then. I did not know her name, and knew there was only a negligible chance that she remembered what she had seen. Nonetheless, after reflection, I became anxious at the thought that she might disclose any recollections she did have to some other interested persons, or indeed to any but me, and what attention that might bring.

William had grown paler even than the Scottish sky would warrant, and he was losing weight. I watched him scuttle into lectures late, strewing papers like a figure from a *Punch* cartoon.

"Can I speak candidly?" I asked him.

"Where do you stand on God?" he interrupted. His voice was strained. He spoke too quickly, as he had to the girl.

"On the crown of his celestial pate," I said. It raised the desired smile, if fleetingly. "I come from what you might call nonconformist stock," I said with care. "Am I a believer? I don't detain myself with theology most of the time. But beliefs aren't only in the brainpan: they're in the body. We're all issued beliefs and instructions by our backgrounds. Some implicit, some explicit." I gave him a glance. "We're all given orders."

He was noticeably startled that I'd said such a thing. As was I. I was under some pressure, at the time.

"Of course, whether we obey those old injunctions or not is another matter," I continued in a rush. "Sometimes we might surprise ourselves. Obedience comes with risks, just as disobedience does, and it seems one only risks what one is willing to lose. The chaps are all worried about you, you know. I'm worried about you."

"It's good of them," William said. He cleared his throat. "Really there's no need."

"Nonsense," I said. He was startled, but I would not make light of it. "Whatever you're up to, it's putting you in harm's way. William, you *must* stop."

He looked at me with those exhausted eyes and struggled to formulate something. "As regards Yahweh," he said, "and related phenomena, perhaps *understanding's* overrated. Some of us are observers by nature, not philosophers. What do you think?"

"I think," I said slowly, in as light a tone as I could muster, "that I shall enjoy being a surgeon." I looked away. "I've been won over by this knife-handed tinkering. One's often surprised by what one ends up caring for."

"Quite," he said. I did not meet his eye. Eventually his attention shifted from me. I could almost see it go, back through the tenement streets by routes I could have walked, back to the secret that he had still not told me. I knew—I could tell—that he felt pursued.

The moment came. A typical grey day, a typical wind gusting in the alleys of that resilient city. It irked William ever after that he never knew what he had done to provoke suspicion, nor who it was who had given him up.

He was in his makeshift laboratory with his bone journals, administering to the camera with which he inexpertly captured only strange and gloomy underlit images of the design. He would not risk buying the discretion of a professional photographer. There was a knock.

At the door were two officers of the law and a porter from the medical school. They gained entry easily enough while William remonstrated weakly. He stepped into the street as they investigated. He waited for them. Locals gathered. The little girl was not among them, but William's landlord was. He looked up, above William's head, into the upstairs window. He looked stricken with guilt. That this, William thought, had befallen his tenant under his supposed protection. When he had the man's attention William gave him a nod of reassurance.

Over the years of our association I saw William perform many other laudable acts. I saw him save lives, of course; I saw him put frightened people at their ease in ways I assure you not every doctor bothers to do. But it was the homely scale of that unspoken intervention that struck me. That he not only took a moment but that moment, of his own undoing, to reassure a man he barely knew. It was difficult, to feel such admiration and yet be unable to express it.

On the floor by the skeleton were a small drill, tiny screws, adhesive paste and wire. William had been boring minute holes in the bones. "I wouldn't leave it all in bits," William said to the porter. He held his hand up to indicate a brace like a gallows, from which he had intended the skeleton ultimately to hang. "Oh please, please," he said. The constables bundled up the bones more roughly than he could bear.

To William's astonishment, he was hauled in front of the university authorities rather than the police. Seven old men, provosts and heads of department and so forth, flapped their gowns and bellowed harsh questions. William was thinking about his parents, he told me later, about his imminent expulsion. He was thinking about the discards of a scrimshander. "And about you," he added to me.

"What possible macabre pleasure," Dr. Kelly demanded, "would you derive from making such carvings?"

"Oh." William was startled. "I didn't," he started to say. "That wasn't me. That skeleton..." He stopped, seeing the dean's expression.

"This is a grisly business," Kelly said, William told me, *fiercely*. "Moral your artistic proclivities are not, nor fitting for a physician, though I won't deny the skill in them. They are, I will say it, unnatural. Now. Where did you procure your materials?"

William stared at him. "You would not end," Kelly said slowly, "what has so far been a promising career with *illegality*, I am sure. So—where did you get those bones?" And William, open-mouthed, took what he had been offered.

"I bought them, sir," he said at last, firmly. "For my art." He raised a hand and made a little etching motion. The dean sat back. The look on his face was one of relief.

•

William's landlady told us that his rent was paid to the end of the following month, but that he had disappeared. Most of the class believed him sent down. Even I heard nothing from him. But two weeks after his questioning, utterly unexpectedly to almost everyone there, though not to me, William slipped quietly into the hall after a lecture had started.

The great wave of astonishment was muted by Professor Serge's wrathful glance. Just once, after we had settled down, William looked up and found me. He gave me a huge smile, and held up a finger in assurance that he would explain.

After the lecture we all crowded around and clapped him on the back and demanded to hear the story. He grinned. "Oh, you know," he said. "I was a silly ass. Got my wrist slapped. What did I miss?" and so on.

Out of earshot of the others he said to me, "They caught me fiddling around with stuff I shouldn't have been. They found me with bones, and—"

"Human bones?"

"Absolutely human bones." We stared at each other. "And they must've suspected where they came from. But for reasons I can't fathom, I think someone put in a word, and… Well, I got a stern warning, my bones got confiscated, and here I am promising to be a good boy until the end of my professional life." He gave an unhappy laugh.

"I do realise, old man," I said, in a voice that perhaps shook a little, "that this isn't the whole story." He laughed again. "You once in a rather civilised fashion insisted that it was permissible for a chap to not hold forth about things he didn't want to. Well." I gave him a bow.

Indeed, he did not speak of these events to me again for a long time. And yet I never thought this would be the last I would hear on the matter.

I graduated respectably, William well. We found work in South London, Oxford, Leeds, London again. William got a position in Swansea, where he remained for two years, before moving to a hospital on the south coast. I took work in Durham.

"I can't believe it," William said. It was, I insisted, not so very far.

"It most certainly is." He raised his voice. "You don't even like *talking* about that place. You may feel duty-bound to revisit whatever sordid past you have there"—William, though angry, still did not pry—"but Durham doesn't agree with you. I'm the one who meets you off the train all gaunt and harrowed."

"I'm not thrilled by the prospect," I allowed, "but don't exaggerate. In every life one must dot and cross."

We were five years into our careers when a conference at Glasgow was announced with a remit broad enough that most chaps from our year could attend. It became a reunion. It was a pleasure seeing everyone again, socialising with some of our old teachers, now colleagues. Five years, I know, is nothing: it is impossible now not to be amused at the nostalgia we felt.

There was—perhaps still is—a tiny medical museum in one wing of the quad. "Come on," I said to William the day we were to leave. "Let's." I suspect it is evident in what direction this story is heading.

The two rooms were jumbles of cases, charming in their way. Old surgical artifacts, dioramas of medical history. Sunlight slanted in, not particularly usefully.

I turned a corner and stopped. "What is it?" William saw my expression. He rushed to the case when he saw what I had found.

It was not a whole skeleton that dangled inside: only the skull, the shoulders and rib cage, the right arm and hand, and the humerus of the left. Everything below the fourteenth vertebra was missing. The bones had been polished. The design was vividly clear. I stared at the maritime scenes, the gargoyles, plants and patterns, the lines that looked like lines for the joy of lines.

He put his hands on the glass. "That's quite something..." William started to say at last, and I said "Don't."

ORIGIN UNKNOWN, the label read. ARTIST UNKNOWN.

I looked at the skull. "William," I said, "when you were suspended, as you can probably imagine, there were all manner of rumours..."

"All right," he said. "I'll tell you." He stepped toward it. "That's it. The body you heard so much about. For a moment I wondered if it might be *another*, but that's it. Or what's left of it. What did they *do?*" he breathed. "*Look* at it..."

"How did it get here?" I said.

"*Here* here?" he said, pointing right at it, "or *here* here?" He circled his finger to indicate the world. "I don't know. And I think it would not be sensible for me to pursue such enquiries." He spoke with odd formality. "If there are those who know how it got here, I should avoid their company." He looked at me. "But you and I will talk."

I came south. He looked me over when I alighted: I had lost weight. We bicycled to the downs and contentedly munched sandwiches in a basin of clay. It was an unusually hot afternoon. One of those days all slowly ambling bumblebees and honeysuckle and so forth, at which the English country-side, when it puts its mind to it, excels, and quite unlike any summer day anywhere else. Calm and still and lovely, but never without a sense of some-thing impending. The sort of day one misses even as one experiences it.

"So how are you getting on up there?" William said tightly.

"Muddling through," I said. "It won't be for much longer." He nodded.

"I'm sure," William said at last, "I could say what you chaps thought happened, in Glasgow." He took a bite of bread, a puff of cigarette, a swig of cider. "But I can't scrimshaw, Gerald. Not a notion how." He gave me quite a smile. "It's a queer thing to know your colleagues think you a thief of corpses for necromantic art. Who narrowly escaped gaol..."

"Not everyone," I told him. "Some of us..."

He waved his hand to hush me. "I didn't carve it, but I did take the bloody body," he said. And as the light grew slowly thick and the shadows long he told me all of it, his story, that I have, with a few omissions and a few amendments, outlined here.

It was obvious he could tell I believed every word he said. I could see his relief at my lack of doubt. Only his description of the body's early nights in the tenements elicited some shock from me.

We had a hair-raising time of it cycling back to the station in time for our train.

I was privileged to work with William for many years after that. I even ran one of his charities for a time after his death. I was not good at it, but I wanted to do my best for him.

It was after the war, when his initial coolness toward the new National Health Service metamorphosed into enthusiasm, that William's career blossomed. He was not a political man, but through his work in teaching hospitals in the 1950s he became committed to what is now called "social medicine." It was for his efforts in this field that he was ultimately granted an OBE. He took great interest in pedagogy: he was a good teacher, though one who was easily sidetracked. His name is now attached to a surgical technique, an honour he would have pooh-poohed, and that I think would have delighted him.

William was provocative on medical ethics. Not only did he support a presumed-consent model of organ donation, but he insisted that without explicit instructions to the contrary, everyone should be considered to have offered up their bodies to medical science. "William," I would scold, "that is ridiculous. You don't mean it."

"Certainly I do." It was one of those arguments that people who've shared a lot for a long time are happy to perform in company. "You're going to put me on the slab when *I* go," he would insist. "So I can keep an eye on the class." For all his joshing, he took the principle seriously. Not only did he sign his own body over, but he harangued his friends, insisted it was the duty of all doctors to make the same gesture. He went on at me in particular, of course, until at last I gave in and signed the form in front of him.

I once mooted returning to Glasgow together, to look again at the exhibit. "It won't achieve anything," William told me firmly.

"You know," I said carefully. "*I* could do some sort of investigation into what happened. *You* might be in an awkward position, but I—"

"Gerald," he said. "I don't want you to draw attention to yourself. I don't want *anyone* connected to whatever it is I stumbled on looking for me. Or for you."

I nodded and looked away, remembering his young interlocutor. "Perhaps," I said, "it's just as well someone sent the police to your workshop. Before any other authorities could track you down."

Whenever I watched him operate, I noticed William's close observation of the bones. Perhaps he thought lightning might strike twice, or perhaps that it had not been random lightning the first time, but a message, for him. "There are days," he said to me more than once, "when everyone I see looks like a candidate. As if the world is full of designs."

It would not have been hard to check William's own bones. I put it to him. I tapped his knee. "A little anaesthetic?" I said, and he looked at me curiously. He mumbled a platitude about God refusing to prove His own existence. I think certainty either way would still have been excruciating to him, as he had admitted to the girl it would be, years before.

None of us has to obey instructions. I consider my own existence proof of that. So much of life is cobbled together when plans go awry. That is often where happiness comes from.

As soon as I was able, I wound up my loose ends in Durham and, eager for change, came permanently south. William and I moved in to a house we could not really afford.

More than once in those early years one or the other of us would go off for a few days, without much explanation. I did so after that day on the downs. At other times it was William who disappeared, to return in a contemplative mood.

We were always scrupulously respectful of each other's secrets. I did not discuss his trips with him, but it took only a cursory search to find Scottish papers and ticket stubs to Glasgow among his things, for all his stern words to me about that destination. Only once did he ever make mention of any such journey. Years later, after two days' absence, William cleared his throat and poured himself some tea and said, "It's gone."

I eventually said, "They change their exhibitions, museums, from time to time." That was that.

Perhaps on my own returns, William sought evidence as I did. He must have been disappointed if so: I was more careful than he, and never one for mementos or trophies, even after successful searches. He would find no telltale tickets, no scribbled directions through Glasgow tenements, no old rag doll with fraying lips.

Very much later, when it became impossible to ignore the fact that William was dying, he began to speak about the design again. It was my task, by then, to let him talk of anything he wished. I am proud of how I did so, no matter if he ruminated in those last days on topics of which I wished he would not speak: on discarded drafts; on how it was the police got word of his researches and found him; on his inability to ever find the girl again. Elaborate theories about the design, not without surprising insights. Hardest of all, his own death.

At the very end, when he could barely move or see, he whispered to me, "Let Glasgow have me. Why not, eh? You never know, Gerald." Then urgently: "Oh, but, oh, but I wish, I do, I wish, I wish."

I knew he longed for certainty, even as he purported to abjure it, to be part of something, but still it was very hard to hear this.

And so I gave him my hand as he wheezed in the bed, and he held it, and I whispered and put my other hand around his and clasped it. He squeezed back.

But though I was gentle I did not let up the pressure. William opened his eyes as I pressed his fingers into mine. I pressed his fingers so he could feel the bones beneath my thin old skin. I did not speak and neither did he. He did not speak ever again. He watched me and his eyes grew wider with something other than surprise and at the sight of them I had to close my own.

William's body was delivered to our long-haired student descendants, as he had wished.

That final pedagogic task uncovered nothing unusual. A few years later, when his demonstrations were done, his body was released. It rests now in a lovely cemetery, as close to those downs as we could arrange.

I sat alone in the kitchen, in a world in which beautiful, elegantly wrought secrets lie hidden less than an inch from sight. I sat in my pyjamas drinking tea among those bones, and I told William in his absence that I was sorry he was at best a bystander. I told him I was sorry he'd never been able to find his young confidante, for vindication, to know again that someone other than he had seen the full design uncovered, released.

I'm sad as I approach my own death, but I am tired of so missing whom I miss. I am tired of secrets.

The skeleton will not appear again, in that museum or anywhere. The only person other than me in whom William ever confided will never speak of it. But for this document, which it is an immense relief to write, the story would end with me.

All the arrangements are taken care of. I'm touched at the thought of friends coming to a service for me. I would tell them not to bother, but I know they will and that it will be for them.

It is not a pleasant thing to break a promise to the dead, but I must urgently draw attention to the updated instructions about my funeral and remains, the version of the document I changed after William's death. Glasgow Medical School will now receive a larger monetary bequest than it expected, in lieu of the cadaver previously promised. My plot, in the same cemetery as William's, was paid for long ago, but I will not be using it. Instead, I ask that my ashes be scattered on William's grave.

Perhaps mice will run over us, William and me, with designs beneath their fur. How glad William would have been to know with certainty that a few of his theories were correct! That in the darkest parts of the sea the bones of great fish and whales are scrawled on. That the sky is full of birds taking their designs heavenward.

I should warn whoever grants my last request that the ashes from cremation are coarser than those from any fireplace or cigarettes. No need for alarm at the sight of that distinctive bone grit on the grass where my William lies. A little coastal wind and I shall dissipate. One rainfall, and I will, you have my word, sink toward him, out of sight.

THE LAOCOÖN COMPLEX

J.C. FURNAS

It was on January 26, 1937, that John Howard Simms first found a snake in his bath.

Half lying, half sitting in the tub, he was considering whether he would turn off the warm water when it reached his armpits or wait till it was up to his neck. As he balanced the exertion of lifting his feet to the faucet against his pleasure in the creeping warmth of the rising water, something wriggled beneath his right hip—wriggled convulsively and indignantly like a fish on the end of a line. Simms reared himself clear and snatched behind him. His clawing fingers closed on something tubular and vigorous; he leaped from the tub and found himself dripping and trembling and gripping a writhing green snake in his right hand. It never occurred to him to be incredulous about it. The snake was as solid and corporeal as the hand that held it.

Moving with gasping speed, he hurled the snake back into the tub and stood glaring at it, unconsciously wringing and wiping his hand.

His frantic haste had spattered water over the whole room. Stunned or dead, the snake floated passively on the surface of the water. Its weary length peacefully undulated on the small waves and tidal sloshing in the tub. Simms felt no desire to probe into the matter of where it had come from. He merely stood and stared, while his trembling slowly left him; and, although he knew there was no one else in the apartment, something moved him to close the bathroom door with a bang.

Presently it became evident that the snake was still alive. Its undulations began to run counter to those of the water until it was swimming lazily, even lifting its head an inch or so above the surface. Simms was relieved to see that it had survived rough treatment.

Yet he did want to get rid of it. He could use the fire tongs; but the snake was a good four feet long and might coil up to touch his hands; very possibly it was poisonous; and he could not endure the notion of again coming into contact with that writhing vigor. Perhaps he could wash it down the drain, as if it were so much dirt. Gingerly he opened the outlet and was relieved again when the water level began visibly to sink.

Seemingly unconscious of any change, the snake floated serenely until its belly was aground. Then, moving its head cautiously from side to side, it crawled through the soapy scum to the outlet. Too late Simms realized that its flat head and plump middle were much too large to go through the holes in the metal cap over the drain. But the snake, investigating the situation with a grave air of businesslike concern, astounded him by sticking its head into the central hole—which was certainly much too small—and crawling deliberately through, inch by inch. When about six inches of tail were left, it seemed to encounter difficulties farther down. Having resisted an impulse to drag it out again, Simms shortly had the satisfaction of seeing the tail wriggle in triumph and disappear.

He ran to his kitchenette and boiled several panfuls of water which he poured down the drain with a vague faith in boiling water for getting rid of any sort of hostile pest from bacteria up. Then he rubbed himself down and dressed and went out for his breakfast, concerned because he was going to be half an hour late at the office.

He was not on sociable enough terms with any of his associates at the office to tell them about his strange morning. He was tempted to confide in the stenographer who took his dictation, but reflected in time that such a story going the rounds might gain him a reputation for eccentricity. The obscure pride which he sometimes felt in being the wheel horse of the correspondence department had often served him as counterweight in just this fashion. After work and his solitary dinner, however, he found himself unwilling to spend his customary quiet evening with the newspaper. Instead he went to a movie; moreover, he neglected to wash or brush his teeth before going to bed because he did not care to enter the bathroom.

But in the morning he had to shave and he told himself, while lathering his face, that it was childish—and unhygienic—to forswear bathing because of a strange accident. It was a bright morning; a streak of sunshine across the tub cheerfully illuminated the running water. No sign of a snake—nothing out of the way except a stray scrap of paper which he carefully removed before getting in. As he lay back gratefully in the warm water, he realized that he was completely relaxed for the first time in twenty-four hours. Almost in that instant he felt the same electric wriggling under his hip.

This time he leaped from the water without investigating, scarcely frightened at all but feeling abused because he could not bathe in peace. It was outrageous that four feet of anomalous reptile should again be floating in his bath with its head daintily raised above the water. In a passion of pettish anger, he opened the drain and witnessed the same scene—the subsiding water, the snake's good-natured acceptance of the situation, and the horrid unreasonableness of its disappearing into a hole much too small for its girth.

A crafty longing for revenge came over him. With complete disregard for office hours, he filled the tub again, got in, lay back, and got out in still hotter anger at the now familiar sign that the visitor had returned. He had carefully watched the outlet and was certain that it had not crawled back; yet, to all appearances, it was the same snake. He got the fire tongs and seized its head with the purpose of holding it under water until it drowned. But its convulsive thrashings under such treatment made him ill; there was unendurable terror in the drops of water which showered on his face and shoulders as he leaned over to the work. He might have persevered, however, if it had not occurred to him that perhaps snakes could not be drowned. It would be better to kill it instantaneously.

He had long owned a revolver, purchased as a spiritual precaution against robbery. As he took it from its place in the bureau drawer under his socks, he wondered if the superannuated cartridges would fire. They still looked grim and deadly; he took careful aim with the edge of the tub for rest and shot the snake's head off cleanly. The noise of the report in the narrow bathroom deafened him; yet he was even more sharply aware of the snake's convulsive thrashings.

Such a blast should have alarmed everyone in the house. But there were no poundings on the door, no footsteps on the stairs. He waited for only a few minutes before going back to the tub and observing with satisfaction that the snake, its head mangled and hanging, was floating on water, quite dead.

His mind was made up. With the aid of the tongs, he coiled the snake neatly into a hatbox, dressed, and went out with the box under his arm. This matter was going to be looked into. Where to go and what to do puzzled him until he remembered that doctors know everything.

At the hospital they wrote a great deal of pointless information about him on a form and let him get as far as the word *snakes* before calling two orderlies. Simms was annoyed to see that ALCOHOLICS was written on the door of the office to which they took him with elaborate precautions.

The doctor, looking inquisitively at the hatbox, also let him speak a good while without interruption. When Simms reached the second appearance of the snake, however, he raised his hand.

"How many drinks do you usually have a day?" he asked, with a weary suggestion of routine in his voice.

"I don't drink at all," Simms answered shortly, outraged by this confirmation of the sign on the door.

"Now come," said the doctor, "I can't waste my time on you if you won't be frank."

"I don't just see snakes," said Simms, reflecting that, after all, the doctor was well justified in being skeptical, "I feel 'em—kill 'em." He opened the hatbox and dumped the snake—which he could still not bear to touch—on the doctor's desk. Water and blood oozed from its mangled head on to the green blotter. The doctor started back in amazement.

"I shot that one this morning," said Simms, almost in apology.

The doctor picked up a paper cutter and stirred the body. Then, becoming bolder, he prodded it and held it up, limp and resigned, like a cat lifted by the middle.

"It's real!" he said indignantly.

"They're all real," answered Simms, going on with the story of the morning's battle. The doctor listened in reflective silence and then began to ask questions about his patient's private life: where did he work? how long had he been there? was he generally in good health? and so forth. Then, politely asking permission beforehand, he phoned Simms's office and checked up the story.

"This isn't my line," the doctor finally said, after pondering a long while with his fascinated eyes on the snake. "Better give the psychiatrists a chance at you, I think. Go and see—" and he named a great man. "Wait a moment!" He telephoned the head of the hospital and, having first convinced him that he had not gone mad himself, persuaded him to phone the great man and lay the case before him. Within ten minutes, Simms was assured the great man was deeply interested and would see Simms at half past ten.

There was something to being a unique case, Simms decided, on his way uptown. The Sunday sections of the newspapers, which he read religiously, had long been full of this Dr. Eisenmark, with particular emphasis on his uncompromising feuds with brother psychiatrists. Under ordinary circumstances, Simms could have become acquainted with international celebrities only through the papers. And yet here he was on his way to a personal interview with the greatest man he would probably ever meet in his life, with an entrée assured, his passport coiled in a hatbox under his arm. He treated himself to the luxury of a cab the whole way.

Two women, plump and well dressed, got off at the same floor in the hotel and went ahead of him into Dr. Eisenmark's office. Simms marched intrepidly forward, said: "Mr. Simms—Polyphonic Hospital—half past ten." Door after door opened before him until he was in the great man's presence.

Dr. Eisenmark was ugly. His arms hung apelike from his stooped shoulders and swayed loosely as he paced the floor and inspected his subject. For a moment his gaze rested malevolently on the hatbox and Simms felt a passing pity for the dead snake. He looked square into Simms's face and Simms's cheeks and jaws were suffused with the incipient sweat of embarrassment. But when he spoke, his voice was completely reassuring, in spite of a thick German accent, all the more so because it came on the heels of so much silent intimidation.

His opening remarks were a strange combination of rudeness and brusque courtesy. He suspected Simms and his snake of being an elaborate hoax and said so. On the other hand, he pointed out, there was often much interest to be found in the psychopathic aspects of elaborate hoaxes. He regarded Simms's keeping the appointment as primary evidence of good faith and was glad to see him. And if Mr. Simms did not mind, they would proceed at once to business. The first thing would be Mr. Simms's story, told without reservations and as directly as possible.

During his narrative, Simms astonished himself with his own pithy eloquence. He told it three times as well as he had at the hospital and ended with a touch of genuine drama, producing the incontrovertible evidence with proud and confident solicitude. There was a gleam of affection in his eye as he displayed the snake, for it was all that stood between him and being accused of bad faith or lunacy.

Dr. Eisenmark nodded an accompaniment to the story, at first perfunctory, then vigorous, and finally, with narrowed eyes and bared teeth, he began to furnish exclamation points to the narrative with hissing repetitions of "*Kolossal!*" If Simms had been an actor, he would have been tempted to take a bow.

"You will take another bath—here—now," Dr. Eisenmark said. "I shall go with you and see." He flung open a door and stood aside for Simms to pass through, observing him so narrowly all the while that Simms already felt naked. He badly needed the reassurance of seeing his faithful snake sprawled in the middle of the carpet, a pathetic thread of substance between him and the truth.

"You take your bath warm?" asked Dr. Eisenmark, turning on the faucets with his hairy hands. "Undress!" As Simms took off his coat and vest, the psychiatrist sat himself on a corner of the washbasin and lighted a cigarette. "You see," he said, "I do not promise to think you a liar if there are no snakes now; but if there should be snakes now, ach, what trouble would we save!"

"Not snakes," said Simms, "only one." His hands were trembling as he slipped his undershirt over his head, and he was shaking from head to foot as he stepped into the warm water.

"Come," said the psychiatrist, "I have seen ladies by the dozen giving birth to babies with more calm."

Simms sat shivering in the water with his hands round his knees. The psychiatrist came and peered into the tub.

"So," he said. "Where is this snake?"

"They don't come till I lie down," Simms mumbled.

"Lie down!" said the psychiatrist. Simms lay down and then leaped from the tub with a scream, almost knocking the great man down. When he recovered his composure, he was dripping in a corner and watching Dr. Eisenmark's effort to lay hands on a four-foot green snake which was lashing the surface of the water in vigorous efforts to escape.

"*Wunderschön!*" he was hissing to himself. "*Ach, mein Schatz, mein Liebling, du lebst!*"

There was a final struggle and the psychiatrist rose out of the tub, soaked to the waist but clutching his prey in his hands. One fist held it firmly just below the head so that its fangs were useless. His exultant eye spied a wicker hamper for dirty towels; in a panic of panting triumph, he popped the snake within and secured the rattan hasp. Then he came to Simms, threw his ape's arms round him, and kissed him soundly.

"I am famous now," he said brokenly, "but I shall be more famous, and you—you will be famous with me. We must talk—I must ask you crazy questions—you must tell me so many things. Come!"

"But your other patients?" Simms asked, overcome by diffidence.

"It is good for them to wait," said the psychiatrist, throwing him a towel. "It stimulates their egos. *Schnell!*"

It was late afternoon and the street lamps were lighted when Simms left Dr. Eisenmark and decided he had better walk home even though his knees were still trembling beneath him. He felt as if someone had applied a stomach pump at the base of his brain. His taste in moving pictures and light fiction, his feelings toward his landlord and his opinions on the heavyweight situation had all passed in review. He had told of things he had not thought of for years, particularly in connection with snakes; he had remembered the most unaccountable details of past trivialities; he suspected that he had remembered a great deal which had never happened, but the psychiatrist had seemed to entertain no doubts.

"What do you think?" he had asked at the end, while Eisenmark stood in the gathering gloom, clasping and unclasping his hands.

"I think—so much," the great man said soberly, "but it is not for you to think or to know of thoughts. I must do much also. You must come back tomorrow—at two o'clock. And do not bathe. I shall bathe you here."

Safely at home, Simms phoned his office to tell them he was sick and indefinitely in a doctor's hands. It was not entirely a lie, of course; he found himself pondering with unaccustomed subtlety the real meaning of the word *sick*. If inconvenient abnormalities all came under that head, he could lay claim to being sick with a vengeance. Anyway he had every right to a bit of private illness on any pretext; what good was a record of ten years' faithful service if you couldn't lay off now and again?

He spent the evening in the public library, reading about snakes, not only anacondas and boa constrictors and cobras, for his was not a romantic curiosity, but also about garter snakes and black snakes, beneficent vermin which have been known to be companionable. From the moment he had seen the last arrival struggling in the doctor's grip, he had lost much of his loathing for the snake family. The man was so triumphant and the reptile so harassed; and the next morning, when he saw the scar left by the bullet in the bottom of the bathtub, he was a trifle ashamed of himself for having attacked his guest in such an unsportsmanlike way. After all, it might have been more his doing than the snake's that it had been there. Such, at least, was the implication of some of the psychiatrist's questions.

It is not strange, then, that he spent his morning in the snake house of the zoo. Here were many of the genera and species he had been reading about, heavily coiled in long glass cases or restlessly exercising themselves in flickering rhythms. Even so he was disappointed; these had nothing of the irreconcilable vigor of his own snakes. They were caged and did not seem to mind very much. Only one large boa digesting evilly with unblinking eyes, obscenely conscious of the lump in back of his head which represented a rabbit swallowed whole, appealed to Simms's new sensibility. He felt sure that these fifteen feet of gorged malevolence could be irritable and thrash round in its cage.

At two o'clock Dr. Eisenmark welcomed Simms with a jubilant warmth that made him stare. He also felt inclined to stare at the doctor's companion, a sharp-faced man who was introduced as Dr. Harvey, curator of reptiles in the very zoo that Simms had been visiting. Scalpels and forceps were spread over the desk.

"You see," said Dr. Eisenmark, "I have been forced to seek consultation. I know nothing of snakes. But my good friend here who has spent the morning with me, he knows them like his ten fingers. We have been violent with our friend of yesterday—" and he produced a huge corkboard on which, pegged down, flayed, and opened up like a half-made necktie, Simms beheld the snake that had been confined in the hamper. Simms felt ill; only yesterday it had been uncompromisingly alive.

"I do not think my friend will regret the hours he has spent with me," the psychiatrist went on. "It has been in-interesting, *ach*, so interesting. Even to me who knows nothing of snakes. But you must tell him—I do not know the language."

The curator of reptiles spoke at some length while Simms stared at the dissected wreck on the board. This snake, it appeared, belonged to no known species or variety. But that was its mildest eccentricity. Its anatomical features were scientifically fantastic: "Its fangs," said the curator, "are built like dog teeth and its scales attached like fish scales. Then I dissected—and I found, Mr. Simms, that beyond a rudimentary alimentary canal and a vaguely differentiated brain and spinal cord, it has no internal organs at all. No subsidiary nerves—no reproductive system—no muscles—how it managed to move and live I could not imagine, and yet Eisenmark told me it was uncommonly vigorous." There was a melancholy fear in his eyes as he gazed at the dissected specimen. "I don't like it—I don't like it at all," he said, and reached for his hat.

Dr. Eisenmark laughed.

"He does not understand!" he told Simms. "He does not understand any better than you did, even less if possible!" He turned on the curator ferociously. "Do you not see? It is just the kind of snake a man who knew nothing about snakes would imagine."

"Don't go over that again," said the curator. "I want to forget about it." And he left without another word, forestalling thanks by his haste, the picture of a man bewildered beyond endurance.

When the door banged, the psychiatrist burst into a roar of laughter.

"The real man of science!" he said. "Shut up in his own specialty and afraid to look out of it. He knows the little snakes, but you must not tell him there is a whole world outside!" Then he reverted to the suppressed excitement of the preceding evening. "*Ach!*" he went on, "do you know what we have found? I suspect—I guess—and the stupid expert tells me I am right. There—" he indicated the corkboard and its horrid display— "there is the death of the old science! Not for nothing have I kept my mind open. Einstein! A trifler with paper and pencil! Newton! Mendel! Darwin! All fools running in a circle: We break through—we—"

"I don't understand anything," said Simms drearily. "What have you proved!"

The psychiatrist panted in disgust and shook a hairy finger in his face.

"We prove," he said, "that you—you, an insignificant young man—" Simms winced—"can think matter into existence. And that is not all— that you can organize it into moving, living flesh, that you can make life. *Himmel*, do not stare at me so! Here is the flesh you have made—it was alive—do I not know?"

"But I didn't want to make snakes," said Simms. "I had nothing to do with it. They just came."

"My friend," said the psychiatrist, "if you do not stop being foolish, I shall send you to my colleagues who will try to tell you that your snakes are libidinous symbols and insult your grandmother. They will call your trouble the Laocoön complex and ask you questions for three years until you become self-conscious about the way you get your hair cut. Why do I take time to tell you what you mean to the world? You did not think snakes as you think eggs for breakfast—but yesterday I see you are a man who cannot fall in love, who does his work like a blind horse in a mine, who is alive only because he cannot help breathing—who likes warm water because it is flexible and alive as he is not. *Ach*, I tell you it was fear and horror you wanted—fear and horror that was alive, more alive than the cinema and little books about murder. And you tell me you did not make these snakes when you have made them without knowing it because it is fear and horror you need! *Dummkopf!*"

As he looked at Simms's pale face, a glint of humor crept into his voice.

"But I shall take care of you," he went on, obviously striving to collect himself. "You come to me not like a guinea pig for experiment but as a patient to be cured. You will make me a snake in the presence of eminent witness and then I shall cure you. Then, if you are wise, you will go murder a nice girl and run away and enlist in the Frenchman Foreign Legion and try to live a little."

Simms gaped at him and hung his head.

"So," said the psychiatrist, in a kindlier voice, "I am not polite. But it is my business to speak strongly. You will come back tomorrow and we will talk about the witnesses and the demonstration."

Incapable of saying a word, Simms gulped and went out. Out of his new scientific significance he had gotten nothing but an uncomfortably bloated feeling. Now that he was out of Dr. Eisenmark's hearing, he repeated to himself again and again that he had not wanted snakes, they just came; and, nuisance that they had been, it was all nothing compared to the scale of the troubles they had brought upon him. He shrank pitifully from the prospect of taking such a momentous bath in the presence of bearded, pretentious witnesses. He should have said nothing to anyone and disposed of his snakes unaided, or even let them stay. It might have been hasty to decide that they were hostile; it seemed inconceivable that they should be, now that he had seen yesterday's specimen in such pathetic *dishabille.*

When he got home, he went straight to the bathroom and stared at the scar in the bottom of the bathtub. He recalled the agonized care with which he had aimed the revolver and the cataclysmic reverberations of the explosion when he fired. Trying to kill the snake would be the last thing he would consider doing in his new frame of mind. Perhaps it was because the psychiatrist had put the notion in his head, but there was now something attractive and satisfying about that convulsive wriggling which made every fiber tingle throughout the brute's whole length. With as casual an air as he could manage, he turned on the hot water and began to undress.

The bath was quite cold when the cleaning woman found him on the bathroom floor the next morning. He had got as far as the medicine cabinet before he lost consciousness, and a tiny bottle of a popular disinfectant proved that he had not lost his man-in-the-street faith in first aid. The curator had been right; the fangs of Simms's snakes were poisonous.

The green snake the woman found in the tub was still swimming gallantly with its head raised above the water. Its remarkable powers of endurance can be attributed only to the fact that Simms had inclined to believe that snakes could not be drowned.

THE PEDESTRIAN

RAY BRADBURY

To enter out into that silence that was the city at eight o'clock of a misty evening in November, to put your feet upon that buckling concrete walk, to step over grassy seams and make your way, hands in pockets, through the silences, that was what Mr. Leonard Mead most dearly loved to do. He would stand upon the corner of an intersection and peer down long moonlit avenues of sidewalk in four directions, deciding which way to go, but it really made no difference; he was alone in this world of A.D. 2131, or as good as alone, and with a final decision made, a path selected, he would stride off sending patterns of frosty air before him like the smoke of a cigar.

Sometimes he would walk for hours and miles and return only at midnight to his house. And on his way he would see the cottages and homes with their dark windows, and it was not unequal to walking through a graveyard, because only the faintest glimmers of firefly light appeared in flickers behind the windows. Sudden gray phantoms seemed to manifest themselves upon inner room walls where a curtain was still undrawn against the night, or there were whisperings and murmurs where a window in a tomblike building was still open.

Mr. Leonard Mead would pause, cock his head, listen, look, and march on, his feet making no noise on the lumpy walk. For a long while now the sidewalks had been vanishing under flowers and grass. In ten years of walking by night or day, for thousands of miles, he had never met another person walking, not one in all that time.

He now wore sneakers when strolling at night, because the dogs in intermittent squads would parallel his journey with barkings if he wore hard heels, and light might click on and faces appear, and an entire street be startled by the passing of a lone figure, himself, in the early November evening.

On this particular evening he began his journey in a westerly direction, toward the hidden sea. There was a good crystal frost in the air; it cut the nose going in and made the lungs blaze like a Christmas tree inside; you could feel the cold light going on and off, all the branches filled with invisible snow. He listened to the faint push of his soft shoes through autumn leaves with satisfaction, and whistled a cold quiet whistle between his teeth, occasionally picking up a leaf as he passed, examining its skeletal pattern in the infrequent lamplights as he went on, smelling its rusty smell.

"Hello, in there," he whispered to every house on every side as he moved. "What's up tonight on Channel 4, Channel 7, Channel 9? Where are the cowboys rushing, and do I see the United States Cavalry over the next hill to the rescue?"

The street was silent and long and empty, with only his shadow moving like the shadow of a hawk in mid-country. If he closed his eyes and stood very still, frozen, he imagined himself upon the center of a plain, a wintry windless Arizona country with no house in a thousand miles, and only dry riverbeds, the streets, for company.

"What is it now?" he asked the houses, noticing his wristwatch. "Eight-thirty p.m. Time for a dozen assorted murders? A quiz? A revue? A comedian falling off the stage?"

Was that a murmur of laughter from within a moon-white house? He hesitated, but went on when nothing more happened. He stumbled over a particularly uneven section of walk as he came to a cloverleaf intersection which stood silent where two main highways crossed the town. During the day it was a thunderous surge of cars, the gas stations open, a great insect rustling and ceaseless jockeying for position as the scarab beetles, a faint incense puttering from their exhausts, skimmed homeward to the far horizons. But now these highways too were like streams in a dry season, all stone and bed and moon radiance.

He turned back on a side street, circling around toward his home. He was within a block of his destination when the lone car turned a corner quite suddenly and flashed a fierce white cone of light upon him. He stood entranced, not unlike a night moth, stunned by the illumination and then drawn toward it.

A metallic voice called to him:

"Stand still. Stay where you are! Don't move!"

He halted.

"Put up your hands."

"But—" he said.

"Your hands! Or we'll shoot!"

The police, of course, but what a rare, incredible thing: in a city of three million, there was only one police car left. Ever since a year ago, 2130, the election year, the force had been cut down from three cars to one. Crime was ebbing; there was no need now for the police, save for this one lone car wandering and wandering the empty streets.

"Your name?" said the police car in a metallic whisper. He couldn't see the men in it for the bright light in his eyes.

"Leonard Mead," he said.

"Speak up!"

"Leonard Mead!"

"Business or profession?"

"I guess you'd call me a writer."

"No profession," said the police car, as if talking to itself. The light held him fixed like a museum specimen, needle thrust through chest.

"You might say that," said Mr. Mead. He hadn't written in years. Magazines and books didn't sell anymore. Everything went on in the tomblike houses at night now, he thought, continuing his fancy. The tombs, ill-lit by television light, where the people sat like the dead, the gray or multicolored lights touching their expressionless faces but never really touching *them*.

"No profession," said the phonograph voice, hissing. "What are you doing out?"

"Walking," said Leonard Mead.

"Walking!"

"Just walking," he said, simply, but his face felt cold.

"Walking, just walking, walking?"

"Yes, sir."

"Walking where? For what?"

"Walking for air. Walking to *see*."

"Your address!"

"Eleven South St. James Street."

"And there is air *in* your house, you have an air *conditioner*, Mr. Mead?"

"Yes."

"And you have a viewing screen in your house to see with?"

"No."

"No?" There was a crackling quiet that in itself was an accusation.

"Are you married, Mr. Mead?"

"No."

"Not married," said the police voice behind the fiery beam. The moon was high and clear among the stars and the houses were gray and silent.

"Nobody wanted me," said Leonard Mead, with a smile.

"Don't speak unless you're spoken to!"

Leonard Mead waited in the cold night.

"Just walking, Mr. Mead?"

"Yes."

"But you haven't explained for what purpose."

"I explained: for air and to see, and just to walk."

"Have you done this often?"

"Every night for years."

The police car sat in the center of the street with its radio throat faintly humming.

"Well, Mr. Mead," it said.

"Is that all?" he asked politely.

"Yes," said the voice. "Here." There was a sight, a pop. The back door of the police car sprang wide. "Get in."

"Wait a minute, I haven't done anything!"

"Get in."

"I protest!"

"Mr. Mead."

He walked like a man suddenly drunk. As he passed the front window of the car he looked in. As he had expected, there was no one in the front seat, no one in the car at all.

"Get in."

He put his hand to the door and peered into the backseat, which was a little cell, a little black jail with bars. It smelled of riveted steel. It smelled of harsh antiseptic; it smelled too clean and hard and metallic. There was nothing soft there.

"Now if you had a wife to give you an alibi," said the iron voice. "But—"

"Where are you taking me?"

The car hesitated, or rather gave a faint whirring click, as if information, somewhere, was dropping card by punch-slotted card under electric eyes. "To the Psychiatric Center for Research on Regressive Tendencies."

He got in. The door shut with a soft thud. The police car rolled through the night avenues, flashing its dim lights ahead.

They passed one house on one street a moment later, one house in an entire city of houses that were dark, but this one particular house had all its electric lights brightly lit, every window a loud yellow illumination, square and warm in the cool darkness.

"That's *my* house," said Leonard Mead.

No one answered him.

The car moved down the empty riverbed streets and off away, leaving the empty streets with the empty sidewalks, and no sound and no motion all the rest of the chill November night.

SORRY, WRONG NUMBER

LUCILLE FLETCHER and ALLAN ULLMAN

{SELECTED BY ALFRED HITCHCOCK}

She reached for the telephone on the night table once more, spinning the dial with unnecessary force. The light from the bed lamp—the only light glowing in the darkened room—caught in flashing pinpoints the jewels on her moving hand. On her face, softly beautiful in the flattering half light beyond the lamp's white circle, a frown of annoyance matched her swift, overenergetic manipulation of the clicking dial.

The dialing completed, she sat tensely for a moment, feeling the uncomfortable strain on her back from sitting unsupported in the bed. Then the pulsing of the busy signal squawked in her ear and she slammed the phone back into place, saying aloud, "It can't be. It can't be."

She flounced back against the piled pillows, closing her eyes, shutting out the shadows of the room and the rectangle of hazy night she could have seen through the open window. As she lay there on top of the thin, summer coverlet, she could feel the evening breeze lightly fingering the folds of her nightgown. She could still hear the night sounds floating up from the river and from the streets three stories below.

In a fury of concentration she considered the aggravation that was making that hour one of torment. Where *was* the man? What was keeping him? Why had he picked this night of all nights to leave her alone, to vanish without a call, without word of any kind? That was not like him. Not like him at all. He knew only too well the effect such behavior might have on her. And on him, too. It was unbelievable that he'd deliberately provoke the kind of scene that had nearly done for her once or twice in the past. But if his absence now was not deliberate— what then? Had he been hurt? How unlikely that he'd been hurt without someone notifying her instantly!

There were other aggravations, all stemming from the larger aggravation of his unexplained absence. There was the matter of the telephone. In many ways that was the most infuriating thing of all—the telephone. She'd been ringing and ringing his office for more than a half hour. Or at least she'd tried to ring his office. Each time she'd dialed the number she'd got a busy signal. Not a "don't answer," which would have been a little more reassuring. But a busy signal. If he was there—and obviously someone was there—was it possible that he'd be on the telephone for a full half hour? Possible? Yes. Probable? No.

She ran over in her mind the things he might be doing, resolutely facing *all* the things he might be doing. Perhaps at last the impediments of illness—her illness—had cracked the reservoir of his patience. He had never seemed to mind the ever-lengthening periods in which she had been unable to respond to him. Although he was a man of intense passion—a vigorous, healthy animal—his self-control had always been inexhaustible. In other words, if she wanted to be plain about it, she'd never dreamed that there could be another woman—or women! But now...?

Somehow that obvious possibility didn't seem to fit the circumstances. Not after she'd driven it out in the open and examined it thoroughly. He was a cautious man. Everything he did was carefully planned and neatly executed. He'd never in a million years be so stupid—or so careless—as to brand himself in so flagrant a manner.

And the milder prospects didn't fit either. He preferred everything on a large scale to match his own boldness, the boldness perfectly reflected in his powerful, brooding good looks.

Thinking of him, she opened her eyes for a moment, glancing toward the wedding picture in its sleek frame on the night table. Dimly seen, except in the sharp clarity of her mind's eye, were her own ivory-satined magnificence and his towering, broad-shouldered, smiling presence. Nothing about him had changed, she thought. In ten years nothing had altered the clean, muscular lines of his body, or the rare, fleeting smile on his smooth, unlined face.

But she had changed. Only the utmost care controlled the little evidences that time and her now chronic invalidism left behind. Soon, unless she was able to regain her strength, to take advantage of the youth that still remained, even the utmost art would no longer conceal the deepening network of wrinkles around her eyes, the puckering at the corners of her mouth, the sagging flesh under her chin. Had he perhaps noticed something more than illness in her aversion to daylight?

She returned to his likes—the things she knew he prized. After ten years of marriage—a marriage she'd planned with almost military thoroughness—she knew perfectly well that her father's fortune had been a mighty bulwark against any restlessness on his part. He had a profound respect for that mountain of money. It was hardly to be expected that he'd ever do anything to place himself out of reach of the Cotterell millions.

That was the way she wanted things, she reminded herself. Let there be no mistake about it. She had always wanted it that way. For the practical relationship with him that now flourished gave her what she wanted most—a man who above all gave force to the illusion she had created, the illusion of a happy marriage. She was envied by her friends, and to be envied was the most desirable state of affairs life had to offer.

The consideration of her tailor-made marriage palled, and once more the irritation of unwanted solitude boiled within her. That damned telephone! There was something fishy about that telephone—about that recurrent busy signal.

It occurred to her that there might be a mechanical defect of some kind in the dialing system. She sat up, reaching for the phone, impatient with herself for having failed to think of it before. She whipped the dial around to "Operator" and waited. The intermittent purring in the phone was followed by a click and a pleasant voice saying, "Your call, please?"

"Operator," she said, "will you get me Murray Hill 3:0093?"

"You may make that call by dialing," the operator told her.

"But I can't," she said with annoyance. "That's why I called you."

"What is the trouble, madam?"

"Well, I've been dialing Murray Hill 3:0093 for the last half hour and the line is always busy. Which is too incredible."

"Murray Hill 3:0093?" the operator repeated. "I will try it for you. One moment, please."

"It's my husband's office," she said, listening to the operator dialing. "He should have been home hours ago. And I can't think what's keeping him—or why that ridiculous wire should be busy. His office is usually closed at six o'clock."

"Ringing Murray Hill 3:0093," the operator said mechanically.

Again the busy signal! The confounded, stupid, eternal busy signal. She was about to take the phone from her ear when, miraculously, the signal ended and a man said, "*Hullo?*"

"Hello!" she cried eagerly. "Mr. Stevenson, please."

Again the man said, stupidly, "*Hullo?*"

He had a deep, hoarse, thickly accented voice, a voice easily distinguished though but one word had been spoken.

She moved her mouth closer to the telephone, saying carefully, crisply,

"I want to talk to Mr. Stevenson, please. This is Mrs. Stevenson calling."

And the hoarse voice said, *"Hullo, George?"*

Crazily, out of nowhere, a second voice—flat, nasal—answered, "Speaking."

In desperation she cried, "Who's this? What number is this, please?"

"I got your message, George," the deep voice rumbled. *"Is everything okay for tonight?"*

"Yeah. Everything's okay. I am with our client now. He says the coast is clear."

It was fantastic. It was unbelievable and impossible. Icily she said, "Excuse me. What's going on here? *I'm* using this wire, if you please."

Even as she spoke she knew they could not hear her. Neither "George" nor the man with the deep voice could hear her. She'd blundered on a crossed wire. She'd have to hang up, dial the operator again, and go through the whole rigmarole once more. At least that was what she ought to do. But she couldn't. The strange men were talking, and what she heard froze her to the phone.

"Okay," the deep voice rumbled. *"Is it still at 11:15, George?"*

"11:15 is right. You got it all straight now, I hope."

"Yeah, I think so."

"Well, run it down once more so I know you got it right."

"Okay, George. At 11 o'clock the private cop makes the bar on Second Avenue for a beer. I go in the kitchen window at the back. Then I wait for a train to go over the bridge—in case her window is open and she should scream."

"Right."

"Say, I forgot to ask you, George. Is a knife okay?"

"Okay," the nasal voice of George said flatly. *"But make it quick. Our client does not wish to make her suffer long."*

"I get it, George."

"And don't forget to take the rings and bracelets—and the jewelry out of the bureau drawer," George continued. *"Our client wishes it to look like simple robbery. Simple robbery. That's very important."*

"There won't be no slipup, George. You know me."

"Yeah. Now once more..."

"Okay. When the cop knocks off for a beer I go in the back window—the kitchen, that is. Then I wait for a train. After I'm through I take the jewelry."

"Right. Now you're sure you know the address?"

"Yeah," the hoarse voice grated. *"It's—"*

Rigid with fear and excitement she pressed the phone to her ear until it hurt her temple. But at that instant the line went dead, followed in a second or two by the steady monotony of the dial tone.

She gasped in horror, crying aloud, "How awful! How unspeakably awful!" Could there be any doubt about the meaning of those queer, unemotional, businesslike remarks? A knife! A *knife*! He had said it as blandly as though it was the most ordinary thing in the world to talk of knives and open windows and women screaming.

9:35

She held the phone, staring at it, staring in horror at the cluttered night table. What had she just heard? It couldn't be—it just couldn't be. It was some trick of her imagination—a brief pause in time in which reality faded and a dream swept through the caverns of the mind. But the calm, impersonal tones of George and the man with the deep voice returned with unmistakable clarity the instant she tried to recall them. No dream ever had these sharp outlines. She *had* heard them. As sure as there was substance in that cool black instrument she held in her hand, she had heard those men. She had heard their different voices synopsizing the death of some poor woman—someone alone, unprotected, someone whose murder had been ordered as one might order the delivery of vegetables from the market.

But what could she do? For that matter, what *should* she do? She had heard all this accidentally, a mechanical slip in the telephone system. She had heard nothing that might lead directly to those awful men. Perhaps it might be best to force from her mind the remembrance of that curious conversation. But, no, there was that woman—perhaps a woman like herself, lonely and friendless—who might be warned if only there was a way. She could *not* stand idly by—she had to do something at once to ease her conscience. With shaking fingers she picked up the telephone and dialed the operator.

"Operator," she said nervously, "I've just been cut off."

"I'm sorry, madam. What number were you calling?"

"Why," she said, "it was supposed to be Murray Hill 3:0093. But it wasn't. Some wires must have been crossed, and I was cut into a wrong number and I—I've just heard the most dreadful thing—a murder—" She raised her voice imperiously. "And now I want you to get that number back for me."

"I'm sorry, madam, I do not understand."

"Oh!" she said impatiently. "I know it was a wrong number and I had no business listening, but these two men—cold-blooded fiends, they were—are going to murder somebody. Some poor innocent woman—who is all alone—in a house by a bridge. And we've got to stop them—we've got to."

"What number were you calling, madam?" the operator asked patiently.

"That doesn't matter," she snapped. 'This was a wrong number. A number you dialed yourself. And we've got to find out what it was immediately."

"But—madam—"

"Why are you so stupid?" she raged. "Look. It was obviously some little slip of the finger. I told you to try Murray Hill 3:0093 for me. You dialed it. But your finger must have slipped—and I was connected with some other number—and I could hear them but they couldn't hear me. Now, I simply fail to see why you couldn't make the same mistake again, on purpose. Couldn't you try to dial Murray Hill 3:0093 in the same sort of careless way?"

"Murray Hill 3:0093," the operator said quickly. "One moment, please."

As Leona waited, her free hand moved over the medicine bottles on the night table, picking up the tiny lace handkerchief that lay crumpled among them. She was dabbing at her forehead with it when the busy signal sounded, and the operator cut in to say, "That line is busy, madam."

In her anger she punched the side of the bed with her fist. "Operator!" she called. "Operator! You didn't try to get that wrong number at all. I asked you explicitly. And all you did was dial correctly. Now I want you to trace that call. It's your duty to trace that call!"

"One moment," said the operator pleasantly, if resignedly. "I will connect you with the Chief Operator."

"Please," she said, settling back indignantly against the pillows. Then another soothing, calmly efficient voice said, "Chief Operator," and once more she concentrated on the mouthpiece of the phone, talking with exaggerated care, her voice strained with annoyance.

"I'm an invalid, and I've just had a dreadful shock—over the tele-phone—and I'm very anxious to trace a call. It was about a murder—a terrible cold-blooded murder of some poor woman, tonight—at 11:15. You see, I was trying to reach my husband's office. I'm all alone—my maid is off and the other servants sleep out. My husband promised to be home at six—so when he didn't get home by nine I started to call him. I kept getting a busy signal. Then I thought something might be wrong with the dial and I asked the operator to try the number for me. And when she did I got on a crossed wire and heard this ghastly conver-sation between two killers. Then I was cut off again before I could find out who they were, and I thought if you could connect me again with that wrong number, or trace it, or something…"

The Chief Operator was gentle and understanding—almost

maddeningly so. She explained that only live calls could be traced. Calls that had been disconnected couldn't be, of course.

"I know they must have stopped talking by now," she said sharply. "They weren't exactly gossiping. That's why I asked your operator to try to get them back right away. You'd think a simple thing like that..."

The bitter criticism in her voice failed to ruffle the Chief Operator. "What is your reason for having this call traced, madam?"

"Reason!" she exclaimed. "Do I have to have any more reason than I've already given you? I overheard two *murderers*. The murder they were talking about is going to take place tonight—at 11:15. A woman's going to be killed—somewhere in this city..."

The Chief Operator was sympathetic—and reasonable. "I quite understand, madam," she said. "I would suggest that you turn this information over to the police. If you will dial the operator and ask..."

She hung up for an instant, then picked up the receiver, waiting for the dial tone. Fury rose within her, flushing her pale cheeks, shutting her off from everything but the feverish twirling of the dial. She heard nothing of the whispering noises of ships cutting through the black river, or the rush, rush, rush of traffic slipping steadily along the express highway that skirted the river's edge. She heard nothing of the clanking and groaning of steel on steel, of the *cluckety-cluck, cluckety-cluck* of the train's approach to the bridge. She didn't notice the trembling of the window frames in her room—the vibrations transmitted molecularly from the shivering bridge. Not until the train had reached the roaring peak of its crescendo did she hear it, and by then the operator was saying, "Your call, please?"

"Give me the police," she said, wincing as the scream of tortured steel echoed in the night and then slowly died away.

While the phone purred she became once more aware of the oppressive warmth. She touched her forehead and the damp flesh under her eyes with her handkerchief. Then a tired voice said, "Police Station.

Seventeenth Precinct. Sergeant Duffy speaking."

"This is Mrs. Stevenson—Mrs. Henry Stevenson—of 43 Sutton Place," she said. "I'm calling to report a murder..."

"*What* was that, ma'am?"

"I said I want to report a murder..."

"A *murder*, ma'am?"

"If you will only let me finish, please..."

"Yes, ma'am."

"It's a murder that hasn't been committed yet, but it's going to be... I just overheard plans for it over the telephone."

"You say you heard this over the telephone, ma'am?"

"Yes. Over a wrong number the operator gave me. I've been trying to get them to trace that number myself—but everybody is so stupid..."

"Suppose you tell me where this murder is supposed to happen, ma'am."

"It was a perfectly *definite* murder," she said witheringly, sensing the policeman's doubt. "I heard the plans distinctly. Two men were talking. They were going to murder some woman at 11:15 tonight. She lived in a house near a bridge."

"Yes, ma'am."

"And there was a private policeman on the street. He goes someplace on Second Avenue for a glass of beer and then this killer is supposed to climb in a window and murder this woman with a knife."

"Yes, ma'am."

"And there was some third man there—a client—that's what they called him—who was paying to have this—this terrible thing done. He wanted the woman's jewelry taken so it would look like a burglary."

"Yes, ma'am. Is that all, ma'am?"

"Well, it's unnerved me dreadfully—I'm not well..."

"I see. And when did all this take place, ma'am?"

"About eight minutes ago."

"And what is your name, ma'am?"

"Mrs. Henry Stevenson."

"And your address?"

"Forty-three Sutton Place. That's near a bridge. The Queensboro Bridge, you know. And we have a private patrolman on our street—and Second Avenue…"

"What was that number you were calling, ma'am?"

"Murray Hill 3:0093. But that wasn't the number I overheard. Murray Hill 3:0093 is my husband's number. I was trying to call him to find out why he hadn't come home—"

"Well," the policeman said dully, "we'll look into it, Mrs. Stevenson. We'll try to check it with the telephone company."

"But the telephone company said they couldn't check the call if the parties stopped talking. Personally I think you ought to do something far more immediate and drastic than just checking the call. By the time you track it down—they'll already have committed the murder."

"Well—we'll take care of it, lady," Duffy sighed. "Don't worry."

"But I *am* worried, officer," she complained. "You've got to do something to protect this person. I'd feel a lot safer myself—if you sent a radio car to this neighborhood."

Duffy sighed again. "Look, lady, do you know how long Second Avenue is?"

"Yes, but…"

"And do you know how many bridges there are in Manhattan?"

"Of course, but I…"

"Now what makes you think this murder is going to happen in your block, if it happens at all? Maybe it wasn't even a New York call you heard. Maybe you were cut into a long-distance line."

"I should think you'd want to try," she said bitterly. "You're supposed to be there for the protection of decent people. But when I tell you about a murder that's going to happen you talk as though I were playing some kind of prank."

"I'm sorry, lady," Duffy said calmly. "A lot of murders happen in this city. If we could stop 'em all, we would. But a clue like you've given me—well, it's vague, see? It isn't much more use than no clue at all. Now, look," he added brightly. "Maybe what you heard was one of them freak radio receptions. Maybe you somehow got hooked up with one of them crime programs. Maybe it was even coming in the window and you thought you heard it on the phone."

"No," she said coldly. "Not at all. I tell you I heard it on the telephone. Why must you be so perverse about this?"

"I want to help you if I can, lady," he assured her. "You don't think there could be something phony about this call—that maybe somebody's planning to murder you?"

She laughed, nervously. "Me? Why—of course not. That would be ridiculous. I mean—why should anybody? I don't know a soul in New York. I've only been here a few months and I see nobody except my servants and my husband."

"Well, ma'am, then there's nothing for you to worry about," he told her matter-of-factly. "And now—if you'll excuse me, ma'am, I've got some other things needing my attention. Good night, ma'am."

With an exclamation of disgust she dropped the phone back on its hook. From the night table she took a tiny vial of smelling salts, uncorked it and passed it under her nose. She inhaled the sharp fumes with relief, then replaced the stopper in the bottle, and put the bottle on the table. She returned to the pillows once more, wondering what next to do. Her anger at the casual attitude of the policeman subsided some-what. After all, it was unlikely that those men could be traced directly. But still, they should do something—they could at least have offered to send out a radio alarm of some kind, to alert the police of the city to this danger that threatened someone—no matter where.

In a little while the urgency that was born of the murder call began to blur. Not that she could put completely out of her mind the memory of that shocking conversation—or the thought of that poor, doomed woman. But her own loneliness became again the most immediately disturbing fact. It was absolutely unforgivable for Henry to have left her this way. If only she had known, she could have insisted that the maid remain.

Now everything around her began to rasp her nerves. The dimly lit room, so richly, so splendidly furnished, became a hateful cocoon from which there was no escape. The expensive array of jars and bottles, boxes and atomizers, glowing dully on the vanity against the wall reminded her only of her ebbing beauty. The plumply upholstered chaise longue, the chairs and gaily covered little benches, the daintily painted boudoir tables—all planted in ankle-deep gray carpeting that matched the walls—looked as though they had been set there by an unimaginative stagehand. The room had no life. It was a cell. The bright chintz drapes and gently moving curtains that framed the windows might as well have been iron bars. She despised the place. She despised her inability to cope with loneliness. Again she snatched up the telephone and dialed the operator.

"Operator," she said, "will you for heaven's sake ring that Murray Hill 3:0093 number again? I can't think what's keeping him so long."

This time no busy signal! Instead the purring ring continued, until the operator broke in to say, "They do not answer."

"I know," she said tartly. "I know. You don't have to tell me. I can hear it for myself." And she hung up.

Now she lay back again, glancing at the half-open door to the room, listening with that intentness with which lonely people try to draw from the surrounding quiet some sound, some evidence of movement, some sign that the emptiness is at an end. But there was nothing. Her glance fell on the night table, with its clutter of medicine bottles, its clock, its crumpled handkerchief—all grouped around the telephone. Rather absently she reached out, opening the little drawer in the night table, taking out a jeweled comb and a small hand mirror. She began combing her hair, pulling the flashing comb swiftly through it, turning her head from side to side to study it in the mirror. Satisfied that she had restored the elegance of her hairdo, she took a lipstick from the drawer, carefully refreshing the crimson arcs that slashed across her face.

Henry had never failed to show his appreciation of her beauty, she thought. Lately, perhaps, his laconic comments had become a bit less spontaneous, a bit more mechanical. Or did they seem so now in the light of his present unexplained delay? Which reminded her that his whereabouts were still the problem of the moment, the annoying situation about which something had yet to be done.

From the same night-table drawer she took a small, black-covered loose-leaf notebook. She had opened it to the letter *J* when the telephone rang. Swiftly, eagerly she snatched it up, crying musically, "Hello-o-o."

Her gaiety collapsed when she heard, "This is Long Distance. I have a person-to-person call for Mrs. Henry Stevenson. Chicago is calling."

"Yes," she said. "This is Mrs. Stevenson." And a few seconds later, "Hello, Daddy, how are you?"

"Just fine," Jim Cotterell boomed. "Just fine, Leona. And—how's my girl tonight?"

All her life Leona Stevenson had heard and resented the modified bellow with which her bull-like father customarily conducted his customarily one-sided conversations. Usually he was telling someone what to do. And usually what was done had something to do with big Jim Cotterell's personal comfort or prodigious bank account, or both. His blustering energy and blistering tongue had rolled a pill formula into one of the world's largest pharmaceutical manufacturing businesses. No chemist himself, he'd spotted the vein of pure platinum that streaked the public's passion for self-medication. Chemists—as he liked to say whenever there were no chemists present, and sometimes when there were—chemists came a dime a dozen. But good salesmen were scarce and worth their weight in gold.

Thirty years ago Jim Cotterell had bullied a corner druggist into selling him for a song the formula for a harmless, and occasionally effective, headache remedy. Today his pills, powders, and soothing syrups flowed from a dozen giant plants to every corner of the globe. He ruled this vast corporate network with an iron hand, the same hand that trembled with agitation whenever his daughter, Leona, chose to frown. It was strange about Jim and Leona, and no one knew it better than Jim and Leona.

Leona's mother, who had not survived her daughter's birth, had had a great beauty and a gentle pride. But she had been no match for the hustling demon who had swept her off her feet. Her death had been Cotterell's first defeat, and a major one at that. It had left him empty of all tenderness, of all respect for the pleasanter, less acquisitive instincts. Except in those things that concerned Leona. Leona became not so much an object of love as a kind of souvenir of love. He tended her as a lost and shivering hunter would tend a flame. And as she grew he began to be afraid. Not that the flame would consume him, but that it would die.

Leona, inheriting beauty from her mother, had within her a queer mixture of her mother's pride and her father's stubbornness. As the years went by she developed no particular strength of character from this lopsided brew. Instead she became overly shrewd, overly calculating, determined to have her own way whatever the issue. And at whoever's expense.

Jim, for reasons carefully concealed in the depths of his aggressive nature, encouraged his daughter's excesses of temperament. In some twisted manner it pleased him—or satisfied some need in him—to have this one shrine before which he might abase himself. On the surface he had excused his indulgence by attributing to Leona a delicacy of health that threatened her life. His fears in this regard had been conveniently supported by the family physician who, frankly puzzled by Leona's tantrums, had advised a policy of appeasement. The ease with which she had, in childhood, made both sword and shield of an imaginary affliction had encouraged her, until in later years a pattern of illness established itself with all the manifestations of the real thing. The memories of childhood sank below the surface of her consciousness—only the alarming physical symptoms appearing at moments of extreme stress remained. So that now, in her thirties, she believed herself hopelessly at the mercy of a weak heart. Her physician, still puzzled, thought this might be so. There were certainly plenty of indications to support his judgment. He had continued to treat her accordingly. Only when she had determined to go to New York did he suggest she consult another heart specialist.

"How's my little girl tonight?" Jim had asked.

"I'm terribly upset," she said, pouting.

"Upset?"

"Well, who wouldn't be upset?" she asked. "Wondering where Henry is, and—hearing a murder being planned right over the telephone!"

"For heaven's sake, honey, what in blue blazes are you talking about?"

"I was trying to get Henry at the office. And somehow I got on a crossed wire and I heard these two men talking about killing some woman..."

"Now wait a minute," Jim said hoarsely. "Let me get this straight. Why were you trying to get Henry at the office—at this time of night?"

"Because he simply hasn't come home. I don't know what's happened. I tried him at the office, and I kept getting a busy signal. Until these two men got on, that is."

"Really, dear," her father roared, "this thing gets my cork. This guy hasn't another responsibility in the world and he pulls a trick like this. Even if he went to that meeting in Boston, he should have..."

"Boston?" she cried. "What about Boston?"

"Didn't Henry say?" he asked. "There's a druggists' convention in Boston and in his last report Henry wrote that he was thinking about running up there. But even if he made up his mind at the last minute, he had no right to go without letting you know."

"Maybe he's tried," she said doubtfully. "Maybe he's been trying to get me at the same time I've tried to get him. If he had to catch a train he might..."

"He might, my eye! Nothing should have kept him from getting word to you."

"I know."

"Well, no need to worry, dear. I'll straighten Henry..."

"The trouble is," Leona broke in, "I can't help worrying. That phone call I heard..."

"Relax, honey. It was probably a gag—a couple of clowns. Who'd talk about a real murder over the phone?"

"It *was* real," she assured him sullenly. "And I don't feel at all right about it—alone in this house."

"Alone! You mean even your servants...?"

"Of course," she said.

"Well, if that doesn't beat... Did you call the police?"

"Certainly. They weren't much interested. It's a crazy sort of thing."

"Well, you've done all you could under the circumstances. So don't let it bother you any more, honey. And tomorrow," he added, his voice heavy with the weight of his anger, "tomorrow we'll have a little talk with Henry—wherever he is."

"All right, Dad. Good night."

"Good night," he said, "and I wish you'd come home, dammit. The place is like a morgue. I don't know why I ever let Henry talk me into... Well, take care of yourself and don't worry. I'll call you tomorrow."

Leona hung up, the faintest trace of a wry smile on her face, thinking how Henry hated those calls to, or from, his father-in-law. Not that Henry ever said anything, but his hate was something you could feel rather than see, or hear.

9:51

She was somewhat appeased by her father's concern, and by the thought of scorching retribution awaiting Henry. Nevertheless she was unable to persuade herself to relax and permit time to answer her questions. Of the ominous talk between "George" and that other knife-wielding fiend, she had done everything she could to bring it to the attention of the police. There was no reason why in all honesty she could blame herself if some tragedy occurred. Tomorrow's papers would probably reveal the end of that story—if end there was. And if some innocent soul *was* found stabbed to death, and robbed, she'd have Henry write to the newspapers, and to the Police Commissioner, and perhaps to the Mayor, disclosing the casual, disinterested manner in which the Police Department treated information of so vital a nature. Then, too, she thought, they would have to investigate a real mystery, since her testimony would prove the robbery was only a fake and that someone had hired the poor woman's murderer. Such a thing would be a sensation in the press, and her unselfish attempt to forestall the crime would certainly make headlines. Her friends in Chicago would be amazed at her daring. And she an invalid—or very nearly one.

But where was Henry? She had interrupted her thoughts several times to listen again to the tiny sounds—amplified by the raptness of her attention—that might mean someone's presence in the house. A board creaked, or a bit of paper fluttered in the gentle breeze, and for a moment she'd fancy she'd heard a step, or a human breath. Each time her heart would beat faster in anticipation; each time disappointment fed the flame of her resentment. She couldn't lie there just waiting. She could, at least, make some effort to get news of Henry.

She remembered the little black notebook and fished it out of the night-table drawer, turning again to the J's. There was an entry for a Miss Jennings, and next to it the number: Main 4:4500.

This she dialed.

*   *   *

The birdlike ladies who nested in the Elizabeth Pratt Hotel for Women were twittering madly in the main lounge. It was Bingo Night, and perched around a score of tables—bridge tables, library tables, and just plain tables borrowed from the dining room—the ladies concentrated their attention on the cards in front of them, clucking, chirruping, occasionally crowing as the numbers were called.

It was a fusty room, ancient, threadbare, smelling of old velvet and respectability. Dim and dusty paintings in enormous gilt frames hung on the fading brown walls. Overstuffed settees and chairs, separated by tables holding an assortment of pottery lamps with fringed shades, stood against the walls in stiff array. Overhead a tortured brass chandelier, on which the substitute illuminating gas cocks spoke the age of skepticism in which it had been manufactured, shed a kind of light from clusters of shaded electric bulbs. There was nothing in or about the room to disturb the illusion of the past in which most of the hotel's guests lived.

At one end of the room a large bony woman in rusty black peered through her pince-nez at the numbers she was drawing from the drum before her. As each number revealed itself to her close inspection she would cock her head on one side, look out across the lounge, and call the number in a loud, high, piercing voice. Then her thin face would crack in a smile, and she'd prepare to draw another number. The process had been going on for some time with monotonous regularity, when an unprecedented interruption threw the lady with the pince-nez completely off balance.

A wispy little woman in gray, with starched collar and cuffs, had crept into the lounge and raised a hesitant hand toward the number-caller. "H-s-s-s-t!" she said. "Miss Jennings—!"

The lady addressed, startled and outraged, glared at the intruder. "Please!" she said sharply, and began once more to select a number from the drum. But the intruder, although visibly intimidated, was not to be put off. "It's the phone," she murmured apologetically. "For, you... Miss Jennings... a Mrs. Stevenson..."

Miss Jennings, holding the cardboard slip in midair, looked sharply at the nervous little woman. "Who?" she asked, startled.

"A Mrs. Stevenson... If she's still holding on..."

Miss Jennings's eyes widened, and the pince-nez on her beak trembled. "Oh!" she cried. "Tell her I'll be right there." Then, rotating her head with its dyed black topknot toward her audience, she said excitedly, "I'm terribly sorry, ladies. I hope you won't mind. It's an urgent call from Mrs. Stevenson... You know—Mr. Cotterell's daughter... Mr. Cotterell who owns the Cotterell Company... My company..." And off she flew.

Sailing out of the lobby, past the desk behind which the switchboard was located, she called out to have Mrs. Stevenson put through to her room. This was at the end of a long, narrow corridor on the first floor—a distance she seemed to negotiate without once setting foot on the carpeted stairs or the corridor's bare boards. She unlocked her door, flung herself into the monstrous green velour chair next to her brass bedstead, and swooped up the telephone—all in one continuous motion. "Hel—hello. Hello, Mrs. Stevenson," she puffed, her beady eyes more birdlike than ever now that the pince-nez lay at the end of its silken cord in her lap. "So nice of you to call."

"I'm sorry if I disturbed you," Leona said.

"Why, not at all," Mrs. Jennings cried. "I was just participating in a bit of entertainment here at the hotel. I hope I haven't kept you waiting."

"No," Leona told her, "you haven't. I only wanted to ask you if you knew where Mr. Stevenson might be. My phone—has been busy so much this evening that I—I'm afraid he may not have been able to call me. And I'm most anxious..."

Miss Jennings clutched the phone tighter to her bony bosom. A gleam of unholy interest awoke in her eyes. This *was* exciting.

"Why, no," she said breathlessly, "I haven't any idea. It's odd that he hasn't reached home yet."

"Would he have had some reason for working late?" Leona asked.

"N-no. I don't think so. He wasn't there when I left at six."

"He wasn't?"

"No. As a matter of fact he was only there for a few minutes during the day. That was around noon. He went out with that woman then and that was the last I saw of him."

"Woman—?"

"Why, yes," Miss Jennings said, the gleam brighter than ever. "There was a woman who waited more than an hour for Mr. Stevenson to come in. Very anxious, she was."

Leona hesitated a moment. Then she asked, tremulously, "Was—was it—someone Mr. Stevenson knew? Someone who'd been there before?"

"N-n-n-no. She'd never been there before. I don't believe. And Mr. Stevenson didn't seem to—to want to recognize her. At first, that is."

"Do you remember her name, Miss Jennings?"

"It was Lord—L-O-R-D, *Mrs.* Lord. I believe her first name was Sally."

"Well, what did they do?" Leona demanded.

Miss Jennings cast her glance at the ceiling, recalling just what had happened that day.

"Mr. Stevenson seemed a bit embarrassed. I could tell he was trying to make the best of the situation, though. He told Mrs. Lord he had an appointment, and asked her if she would care to see him another day. She said, no, it was important. So Mr. Stevenson suggested that she have a bite to eat with him before his appointment. Then they went out."

"And he didn't come back at all?"

"No, Mrs. Stevenson. I left at six, as I told you, and he hadn't come back. There was only one message for him during the afternoon."

"A message? From whom?"

"Oh, it was from that Mr. Evans—the man who calls Mr. Stevenson every week. A regular pest he is, too."

"Well," Leona said falteringly, "this is all very strange. But I'm sure if it were anything important Mr. Stevenson would have told me. He's always telling me the things that happen at the office."

"Yes, Mrs. Stevenson." There was a faint, mocking smile on her face as she said it.

"Tell me," Leona continued, "did Mr. Stevenson say anything about a trip to Boston? He—he mentioned something to me…"

"Oh, that!" Miss Jennings said. "He did report to Mr. Cotterell that he might go to the convention in Boston. But if he went today—I wouldn't know."

"Well, thank, you," Leona said as brightly as she could. "Thank you very much, Miss Jennings. I won't keep you any longer."

"Thank *you*, Mrs. Stevenson. It's been a pleasure. I hope I've been helpful. Most of us in the office—well—we sort of envy you, Mrs. Stevenson. Mr. Stevenson is so devoted to you."

"Yes," Leona said, "he is—"

"I hope you liked the flowers today," Miss Jennings went on. "I thought camellias would be nice, for a change…"

"Very nice," Leona said. "Good-bye, Miss Jennings."

Miss Jennings said good-bye and hung up. She leaned back, staring contentedly at the brass ceiling fixture from which three naked bulbs sprayed light. She saw neither the harsh light nor anything else. Her eyes were turned inward, inspecting what promised to be a startling, juicy secret. She had no doubt that it was a secret, or something that had been a secret. Any simple explanation of Mr. Stevenson's strange actions she rejected at once. There had always been something a little odd about Mr. Stevenson. An atmosphere of conflict that his rugged, handsome face and reserved bearing did not dispel. He certainly spent little enough time in the office, when you came to think of it. And Miss Jennings, with her devious mind spinning along in high, was coming to think of everything.

*　　*　　*

Pale and shaken, Leona fell back against the pillows. So that *was* it! What could not happen had happened! The fool! The utter damned fool! To get himself trapped in a shoddy affair with a wench he'd known years ago. To get caught at it almost instantly. To expose the casual way he'd treated his duty to her father's company. To force upon her a choice that in one direction meant public disgrace—the shattering of her life's pleasant illusion—or in the other to live a life of private shame, forever defeated by Henry's knowledge that she no longer could destroy him. It was unthinkable! Why had all this happened tonight? Was someone trying to drive her out of her mind? Was someone—Henry perhaps—trying to bring on another heart attack? Something caught in her memory... That woman's name—Lord. She'd heard that before. Or seen it. Today. Some time today she'd come across that name. It was difficult, in her anxiety, to recall where she'd seen it. She *had* seen it, she was certain. And in an instant she remembered where. Swinging her feet off the bed she stood up, shakily at first. She walked toward her vanity table, switching on one of the lamps that stood at either end of it. Her eye fell upon the white card by the flower bowl—the card that had come with the camellias Henry had sent today. *All my love, Henry*, he had written. She snatched it up, tearing it to shreds, strewing them on the floor. She began to rummage among the litter on the vanity, until behind a row of perfume bottles she saw it—a slip of paper with a few lines on it in the maid's heavy scrawl. As she picked it up the telephone rang.

She scuttled back to the bed, the paper clutched in her hand, and picked up the phone. A man's voice—hollow, tired, elderly, with an unmistakable British accent, said, "Mr. Stevenson, please."

"He's not in," she snapped. "Who's calling?"

"This is Mr. Evans. When do you expect him? It's very urgent. I've been telephoning his office, and he doesn't seem to be there."

"I'm sure I don't know where Mr. Stevenson is," she replied. "You'd better call back later."

"In about fifteen minutes?" the man asked. "I haven't much time. I'm leaving the city at midnight."

"All right," she said. "In about fifteen minutes."

"Thank you," he murmured, "I will. And—you'll tell him that I called, please? In case he does come in? The name is Evans—E-V-A-N-S. It's very important."

Evans and his call drifted out of her mind the moment she had hung up. She moved the slip of paper she'd taken from the vanity under the light. It was headed: CALLS FOR MR. STEVENSON. Underneath were three brief entries:

3:10 p.m. Mr. Evans. Richmond 8:1112.

4:35 p.m. Mr. Evans. Richmond 8:1112.

4:50 p.m. Mrs. Lord. Jackson Heights 5:9964.

There it was. Mrs. Lord! Calling Henry right in his own home—in *her* home. It was ridiculous. There were limits to that sort of thing, and one had been reached now. She reached for the telephone, dialing the Jackson Heights number, her face frozen, jealous, hard as flint. The fingers of her free hand flickered in a nervous, silent tattoo on the edge of the bed as she waited. Then the call signal clicked off and, incongruously, a child's reedy voice said, "Hello, this is the Lord residence."

Puzzled, Leona said, "I'd like to speak to Mrs. Lord, please."

"One moment," the child said, "I'll see if she's in."

She could hear the jar as the phone was set down. Faintly a man's voice said, "Is that for me, son?" She heard the child say, "Mommy," and then there was a confused murmur of male voices, not quite near enough to the telephone to be distinguishable. She strained to listen, to recognize, if possible, the men speaking. But there was nothing familiar about either of their voices. Suddenly she tensed, grinding the phone into her ear in her desire to strengthen the sounds she heard. For distinctly she had heard the name "Stevenson" emerge from the blur of talk. And "Cotterell

Corporation"! And "Staten Island." After that someone—a woman—moved close to the phone, cautioning the child to get back into bed, saying to one of the men, "Fred—how could you? He was out on the sidewalk in his bare feet." Then there was a grating sound as the phone was picked up, and the woman said, "Hello?"

Leona's mouth had suddenly filled with cotton. She paused for a second to swallow. "Hello," she managed to say. "Mrs. Lord?"

"This is she."

"This is Mrs. Henry Stevenson, Mrs. Lord. I—I don't believe we have met—but I understand you saw my husband this afternoon?"

"Oh—why—yes," the other replied with some hesitancy.

The woman's obvious nervousness released Leona's tongue.

"Ordinarily, of course, I wouldn't dream of bothering you, Mrs. Lord," she said with heavy sarcasm. "But—as it happens—my husband hasn't come home this evening. I can't seem to locate him at all. And I thought perhaps you might give me some idea…"

"Oh—why—yes," the woman said again, faintly.

"I can't hear you, Mrs. Lord. Will you please speak up a little?"

"Certainly—I—"

"Is there anything wrong?" Leona asked icily. "You're not keeping something from me, I hope."

"Oh, no… Could I call you back?"

"Call me back? Why?"

"Because I…" The woman's voice suddenly changed from quiet desperation to an odd, strained gaiety. "It's my bridge day, you know."

"What's that?" Leona demanded. "What has bridge got to do with it? Excuse me, but I don't understand you at all, Mrs. Lord!"

"And then there's that trip to Roton Point," the woman went on idiotically.

"Look here," Leona said harshly, "are you trying to make fun of me, Mrs. Lord? Just in case you don't happen to know, I'm an invalid. I can't stand very much aggravation. Now tell me: Is my husband there with you? Is he? Tell me the truth!"

"It's three eggs separated," the woman babbled, "two measuring cups of milk, a third of a cup of shortening. Cream the shortening with a little sugar, then add a level tablespoon of flour..." For a second there was silence, then the woman whispered into the phone, "Leona... Leona... it's Sally Hunt, Leona. Remember? I'm sorry to be so ridiculous, but my husband was standing so near. I can't talk here. I'll call you back as soon as I can. Wait for me..." And she was gone.

Leona lay back in the bed, relaxing a little. She was completely bewildered by this latest revelation. How strange that Sally should reenter her life at this time!

Sally Hunt!

Sally had been in love with Henry, probably was still, although she seemed to be married and a mother. She'd been in love with him when she'd invited him to that dance at college. That was the night Leona had picked him out of the crowd. It was so long ago. But she found it easy to remember that night.

Dance music had been blasting from the phonograph perched on the Assembly Hall stage. Below, in the large room hung with banners and paper streamers, couples danced, or stood and talked, or wandered off to the refreshment table. Most of the boys looked alike—crew haircuts, baggy slacks, tweed jackets. And the girls had their own uniform—sloppy sweaters and skirts, hair worn long and knotted at the nape of the neck.

But there were two who were different.

The man dancing with Sally was certainly no college lad. His clothes matched, his hair was cut conventionally and carefully groomed, his dancing was definitely on the unimaginative, nonviolent side. He was tall, solidly knit, darkly handsome. It was easy to see from the adoring way Sally looked up at him that something more than festival spirit had brightened her glance.

There was nothing particularly revealing in the young man's face. He looked over Sally's head at the rest of the dancers with an air of indifference that came close to being patronizing.

Leona, a sophisticated, pallid beauty in black faille with her shining hair in a shoulder bob, was as noticeable in that crowd of youngsters as an ocean liner in a fleet of tugs. Everything about her was almost too obviously different. That her difference had been achieved at no small cost was plain. Girls didn't dress that way on pin money.

She watched Sally dancing for a few moments, then marched across the floor, making for Sally's partner's broad back. She tapped him on the shoulders and said, smiling, "May I cut?"

They had been startled, had stood apart, Sally bewildered, the man looking at Leona with unabashed curiosity.

"You don't mind, do you, Sally?" Leona said.

Sally recovered quickly, saying, "You've made a conquest, Henry. Congratulations."

Leona turned her languid gaze full on Sally's partner. "I'm Leona Cotterell. What's your name?"

Before he could answer, Sally swiftly introduced him. "This is Henry Stevenson, Leona."

Leona smiled, tossed her shining head gaily, and moved toward him. "Shall we dance?" she said. That was all there was to it.

They danced, and Leona had been dazzling. There had been no indifference in Henry's expression after that. He had been frankly enchanted, and though there had been nothing flashing in his talk, he had managed to convey a sense of appreciation of her charm, of the gulf that separated her from her schoolmates, that separated her, for example, from girls like Sally.

He guessed right away that her father was Jim Cotterell. "That's the kind of man I admire," he said. "Knows what he wants. Has the brains to go out and get it. Money. You can do anything with money. Someday…" And he stopped, smiling boyishly.

Leona liked his smile. It did not sprawl all over his face like the toothy contortions of some of the other boys. Rather it seemed as though candles lit in his eyes, and attractive arcs deepened at the upturned corners of his mouth. It added strength to his expression. It was a candid smile, neither naïve nor superior.

As they continued to move slowly about the floor Leona found that there were other things about this self-possessed young man that appealed to her. He made no bones about not being a college man himself.

"Too poor," he said, not smiling now. "My family's too poor. I have to help out as much as I can."

Leona picked that up smoothly. "Some of the most interesting men I know don't go to college. My father isn't a college man."

"Oh?" Henry said in amusement. "Then there's hope for me. To be successful, I mean."

"My father always says," she replied, "if a man hasn't any talent for making money, college won't knock it into him. And if he has a talent for making money, why waste time in college?"

That had pleased Henry. "Hurrah for Father!" he said.

The music stopped and Henry took his arm from her waist, dropped the hand he had been holding. "Thanks," he said. "Many thanks."

Leona smiled at him, almost mischievously. "Let's sit the next one out?"

"Now wait a minute," he said in mock horror. "What about Sally? After all, Sally's my—my escort—if she hadn't invited me…"

Leona pointed across the floor to Sally talking animatedly to a crew haircut. "Sally's taken care of, and we'll only be a few minutes. Come on out and I'll show you my car—it's a honey."

She took his hand and led him out of the hall. They crossed the moonlit lawn to the road that ran past it. Dozens of cars were parked along the curb, but one was lower and longer and twice as rakish as any of those near it.

"Isn't it *beautiful?*" she crowed. "No one's got one like it. It'll do a hundred and ten, the man said who sold it to Daddy. Daddy thought it was too much car for me, but after I saw it, there just weren't any other cars."

"It's something, all right," Henry said. "A Bugatti! Not bad! Not bad at all!"

Leona took his arm. "How'd you like to drive it?" she urged. "Just down the road a bit. No one will miss us."

He'd agreed quickly enough, and she could clearly remember now how he had loped back across the lawn to get her fur jacket and his own overcoat. In a matter of minutes they had been roaring down the road, top down, the Bugatti trembling with impatient power. The sharp winter air sliced at their faces, stirring them with tingling exhilaration. She knew now—as she thought about it—that it wasn't herself, or the outlandish car, that accounted for Henry's almost frenzied pleasure in that drive. It was what she and the throbbing car represented—not seen always from afar, not dreamed about, but here under his hand. That was why his face, as he drove, was alight. That was why he had cast aside the reserve of the dance floor.

She had sensed most of what later she knew for fact, and her mind had begun even then to scheme, to plan, to fix a pattern for the future. There was already in this brief encounter an element of certainty growing within her. She directed him to make a turn which brought them shortly to a dead end.

"Some car," he said, slowing reluctantly to a halt. "This baby can really roll. I'd like to take it out someday and turn it loose."

"You will," she answered slowly. She reached out and turned off the ignition. "Let's sit for a minute. I want to talk."

"Say," he said laughing, "I hardly know you. I'm afraid you'll have to take me home. Or must I get out and walk?"

Leona leaned back against the roadster's cushion to look at the night sky, black velvet strewn with stars, torn in one place by a cold blade of moon.

"Sally Hunt," she said, dreamily. "I'd never put the two of you together in a million years."

He turned from the wheel to face her, his arm across the back of the seat. "Why not?"

"Oh—just a feeling. I've been around a good deal. My father's taken me everywhere—abroad and so forth—and I've met a lot of people. You begin to classify people after a while—after you've traveled like that. You and Sally just aren't in the same class. You're worlds apart."

"You mean money," he said bitterly. "You mean her family's got money and I oughtn't to try to cut in on that kind of setup?"

"You're completely wrong," she said hastily. "I wasn't thinking of that at all."

"No? What then?"

"I was thinking that Sally's right for that small town you both come from. But you're different."

"I'm different, am I? You can tell all that—now?" His little laugh was derisive.

"Why not?" she asked. "Look at those kids back at the dance. College boys from nice, rich, respectable families. But you made them look like babies. And most of them will be babies all their lives."

"And me?"

"You're not a baby, Henry. Maybe you've never been a baby."

That was when he had leaned over and kissed her—roughly, expertly, long enough to start little shivers of ecstasy racing along every nerve in her body.

Then he'd settled back, looking at her like a craftsman inspecting the product of his art. "I've always wanted to kiss a million dollars," he said.

She smiled slyly. "Would you like to try for two million?"

She'd caught him off balance, forcing him to grin in spite of himself. She'd drawn his claws—for a moment, anyway—and his eyes had sparkled with amusement.

"Ouch!" he'd said, and then, "Maybe I am a little dryer behind the ears than those punks back at the dance. But it's only because I've had to make my own way so far—and not so far at that."

"You'll go far. I know you will. It's in the way you look. The way you affect other people. People like me."

His expression had grown cold and cynical again. "This is really funny," he said. "Me sitting here soaking up flattery from a girl whose millions of dollars and fur coats and Bugatti roadsters I'll never see again."

"You don't know," she said. "You don't know—anything."

"I don't get it."

"You will," she said softly, "by-and-by. Tell me about yourself, Henry. Where do you come from? Who're your people?"

He laughed cynically. "That's an easy story to tell. I come from what is usually referred to as 'the wrong side of the tracks.' My old man delivers coal when he's sober, and speeches about poverty when he's drunk. My mother would have been all right if she hadn't fallen for Father. She had some education, and wanted more. Instead she's worn herself out raising six kids, keeping them alive and out of trouble, with a roof—a leaky roof—over their heads and something or other to go in their stomachs. That's all. The American dream."

"But what about you?" she asked. "You don't look exactly as though—as though—"

"As though the seat was out of my pants? As though I broke cigarettes in half to make them last longer? No," he said, "it isn't that bad. My mother made me go to high school, instead of going to work after I'd finished the eighth grade. In high school they found out I could run fast with a football under my arm. I was big stuff. Sally Hunt took me around to meet her family—in our town the Hunts are considered pretty fancy—and her old man took a liking to me. He got me a job in the town's biggest drugstore."

"A drugstore!" she exclaimed. "Why, Henry, it's fate!"

"Sure," he grinned, accepting her sarcasm. "I thought you'd feel that way."

"Tell me more," she cried gaily. "Are we still in the same business?"

"Of course," he said. "I'm now the manager of everything except the prescription department. Local boy makes good. Good sodas, good sandwiches…"

"What about Sally?" she asked.

The brief, silly moment was gone. He hesitated, the brooding look that seemed most natural to him returning to his face.

"Sally's a good kid," he said. "We're good friends. Nothing more. Her family's been swell to me. Helped me out when things got too tough at home. But I don't know. Sometimes I feel as though…"

He wasn't looking at her now. His eyes were fixed on something distant, something as far away as the black woods beyond the fields at the far side of the road, something much farther than either of them could see.

"Yes?" she prompted gently. "As though…?"

"As though I'm trapped. As though no matter what I do—how hard I work—I'll never get what I want because I want too much."

They sat in silence. Henry offered her a cigarette, took one himself, and lit them both. His outburst seemed to have left him charged with unspoken anger. Finally he exhaled a huge plume of smoke, turned toward her with a grin on his face, and said, "You and your damned Bugatti! Let's get back to the dance."

They drove back swiftly, saying nothing until he'd parked the car and opened the door for her to step out. Then she caught his sleeve. "How'd you like to meet my father, Henry?"

"Sure," he said. "That would be fine. We have a lot in common. We're both in the drug business." He laughed, not bitterly this time, but to show her that he thought the situation quite funny.

"I mean it," she said. "I think he'd like you. Especially if I told him to. He's coming to New York next weekend and I'm going to cut classes next Saturday. Why not meet us?"

"You know," he said slowly. "Why not? What've I got to lose?"

That had been the beginning. Henry, like a restive colt, hadn't been too easy to handle at first. Pride, his independence, his knowledge that one of the richest girls in America took a special interest in him, a very special interest in him, made him suspicious. But she could wait. Henry had said that maybe he wanted too much. That was the key with which she'd unlock his heart. With the world in his grasp, his pride couldn't hold out. And when that had crumbled she'd have what she wanted.

She remembered that almost comical scene with Sally Hunt, not long after the dance. Sally had come to her room one afternoon, somewhat hesitant, but with determination clouding her pretty, usually cheerful face.

"Leona, there's something I've got to talk to you about."

Leona was bending over a couple of suitcases on her bed. She looked up at Sally, saying peevishly, "Well—say it, for goodness' sake, and get it over with. I'm leaving for Chicago in a few minutes."

Sally had stared at the floor for a moment, then abruptly lifted her eyes and leveled them at Leona. "You've been seeing a lot of Henry these past few weeks, Leona, and there's something..." She hesitated.

"Yes?" Leona was obviously scornful.

"There's something I felt—I thought—I ought to tell you."

"You said that before. And I say, out with it."

"He's not the type—to play around with, Leona. Don't play around with him anymore—please."

"And who says I'm playing around with him?" Leona wanted to know, stalking to her closet for another armful of clothes.

"Oh—Leona—he's not your kind—any more than the others…"

Leona stopped dead in her tracks. "I like your nerve…"

But Sally went on earnestly, "If you don't stop now, you'll regret it, Leona. Henry's not right for you. I've known him almost all my life. My father's helped him. My whole family has treated him almost as though he were one of us. And he's all right when one of us is near him—to sort of look after him. But he's—he's all sort of twisted up inside. He's sweet and kind and gentle—for a while, and then he has—moods. He wants things he can't get. And deep down inside of him it drives him wild. That's when he needs—us. Oh, I suppose I do love him. But the understanding is more important than the love. He isn't safe with someone who doesn't understand him. He's done things that—that would get him into all kinds of trouble if people didn't know about him."

Leona laughed recklessly. "It's a nice trick, but it'll get you nowhere, Sally. You just can't stand the competition. As a matter of fact, I think a great deal of Henry Stevenson. And I understand him. And I happen to think he's much too good for that town of yours. If I want to show him a good time, introduce him to certain people, that's my business. If I want to marry him—that's my business, too."

"Marry him!" Sally gasped. "You don't mean that. You're kidding."

Leona smiled complacently. "Is there any good reason why I shouldn't?"

Sally had folded up after that, she remembered as she stirred restlessly on the bed. There hadn't been much fight in Sally. And a lot of good it would have done her if there had been.

Fight hadn't done Jim Cotterell much good, either, although he'd struggled like a steer at branding time.

"But the fellow has nothing," Jim had said a year later, a hint of pleading in his rumbling voice. "Sure, he's a well set-up lad. But he's an ordinary kid—common as rocks—a dime a dozen. After all the money

I've spent on your education—taken you abroad—given you everything you've ever wanted—why do you want to throw yourself away?"

"I love him," Leona said clearly, staring her father in the eye.

"Rubbish!" Jim bellowed. "You're just being stubborn."

She argued with him stubbornly to establish once and for all that she wasn't being stubborn. She loved Henry. She said it repeatedly. But Jim knew better. She loved Henry the same way she'd loved that Bugatti roadster, he'd roared.

"The trouble with you," Leona blazed, "is that you don't want me to marry anybody. You only want me to stay here, and stay home—with you."

Defiance stiffened her whole body as she stood there. Jim, looking miserable, walked up and down the length of his den, his beefy face almost purple with dismay and displeasure.

"It's not true—not at all," he said, halting before her. "You know I'd give you anything in this world. I've always given you what you wanted—let you do what you wanted to do, without any thought of my own feelings. But this time it's different. Marriage is a big thing for a girl in your position. I've worked hard. I've built a big business. For me? No! First for your mother, now for you. When I die, you'll get it all. And I wouldn't want to see some dumb cluck get his hands on it just because you'd saddled yourself with him. At a time when you were too wrought up to think properly, too.

"Listen to me, honey," he went on. "You must think about this some more. Give yourself a year—say—to see if this lad wears well. See him as much as you want. And then, if you still want him…"

His reasonableness only fueled her impatience.

"You're hateful!" she cried. "Selfish and hateful. You don't care about me. You're thinking only of yourself and that hateful old business. You've taken a dislike to Henry simply because you think he'll interfere with your selfish plans. Suppose he is a country boy. What were you when you started—down there in Texas?"

She was trembling with rage. She gloated at the immediate concern that spread swiftly over Jim's face.

"Take it easy, honey," he begged. "You'll make yourself sick."

"Sick!" she shouted. "Make myself sick! You're the only one who's making me sick. You and your wonderful business and your wonderful money. You don't care if they drive me into my grave, just so they're safe and nobody takes them away from you."

She began to sob, and Jim tried to put his arm around her. She moved away from him, sinking dejectedly into a chair. "I—I don't want to talk about it anymore," she said sadly through the tears. "I don't feel very well…" And then, with furious concentration, she had managed to faint, hearing, as she approached the welcome dark, her father frantically summoning the butler.

The wedding had been a well-oiled, richly caparisoned triumph. She recalled readily the exultant, passionately possessive vibrance with which she had uttered, "I—Leona—take thee—Henry—"

And Henry's bearing had measured up to her hopes. Neither nervous— nor overly relaxed—his manner had charmed the wedding guests. Already he had begun to absorb the soothing, emollient effects of contact with endless luxury. If within himself there were any lingering doubts, any reservations, she'd quickly disperse them. For the present he carried himself perfectly, and she was proud.

Even Jim had seemed, for a few moments at least, to warm to the scene. But she knew his smiling, tired face hid much misery. Jim would never completely accept Henry. Never. No matter how hard he tried.

All of this had occupied her thoughts during the wedding and after at the breakfast in Jim's great house. To her Henry was a project under-taken, an equation to be solved. She intended to solve the equation, complete the project at any cost. In the end Jim would have to admit his mistake. The pleasure of that victory not yet won bubbled merrily in her brain as she deftly—unseen by anyone—guided Henry's hand through the maze of silverware that gleamed on the breakfast table.

During the long European honeymoon that followed she had been pleased by the unembarrassed ease with which Henry submitted to her teaching. There was no doubt that the limitless offering of luxury she made to him, coupled with her lacquered good looks and the exceptional willingness of her body, had disarmed him. He accepted her teaching with good grace, even with appreciation. If she insisted upon choosing his clothes, and the way in which he was to wear them, it was a matter for delight rather than annoyance or indifference. He seemed quick to realize how important these things really were in her world, how much more comfortable he could feel if his appearance was correct, his manner beyond reproach. And he was not unaware of the way his rugged, husky handsomeness was set off by all this careful grooming.

Leona watched him settle into a life in which the past—whatever it had been—vanished, or so she thought. It didn't really matter. The important thing was that he would in time become so entranced with the life she sketched for him that no power would ever be strong enough to challenge its values. Which was the way she wanted things to be.

A look of triumph—a smile of smug satisfaction—played over her worn and fretful features as she lay there thinking of what had happened since the night Sally Hunt introduced her to Henry.

Just then she heard a throaty blast from one of the ships in the river. The smile faded as she started up, glancing at the medicine bottles on the night table, at the clock next to them. As she did so the telephone came to life, startling her.

9:55

It was Sally.

"I'm sorry I had to be so silly and mysterious just now," she said. "I couldn't talk. I was afraid my husband would overhear me. So I found an excuse to slip out to this phone booth."

"Well," Leona said, "it certainly was odd, to say the least."

"You'll probably think the whole thing is peculiar, Leona—hearing from me after all these years. But I had to see Henry again today. I've been so terribly worried about him."

"Worried? Why, may I ask, should you be worried about Henry? I hope you'll remember, Sally, it never was much use trying to pull the wool over my eyes."

"I'm not trying to do anything—but help. This may be very serious—deadly serious for Henry. It's a little difficult to explain. I'll try to tell you as quickly as I can."

"Please do," Leona said brusquely.

"Well—Fred, my husband, is an investigator for the District Attorney's office..."

"How cozy!" Leona murmured.

"About three weeks ago he showed me a newspaper clipping about you and Henry. It was something or other from the Society page..."

"I remember."

"...and he wanted to know if that wasn't the Henry Stevenson who'd once been my beau."

"Your beau?" Leona said. "How quaint!"

"I told him it was, and Fred laughed and said, 'Well, what d'y' know.' Then he stuffed the clipping in his pocket. I asked him what was so unusual about seeing Henry's name in the paper. He just smiled and said it was a coincidence—something to do with a case he was on."

"A case!"

"Yes. He said it wasn't anything he could talk about—just a hunch.

I tried to worm some more out of him. But he started kidding me about still being in love with Henry…"

"Which, of course, you denied," Leona said sarcastically.

"Why, of course—" Sally sputtered. "What a ridiculous thing to say after all these years!"

"Do go on—"

"We were almost finished breakfast by that time. The phone rang. It was one of Fred's men—one of the men from the DA's office. I heard Fred say something about 'Stevenson' and someone who sounded like 'Harpootlian.' Fred said, 'Well, sure we'll go. Tell Harpootlian to set it up. Make it Thursday, around 10:30, at the South Ferry change booth.'"

Sally paused for a moment, and Leona blurted angrily, "Look, Sally. This is all very interesting. But can't you get to the point? Henry may be trying to call me at this very moment. Anyway, what possible connection can there be between Henry and all this rubbish about your husband?"

"I'm telling you as quickly as I can," Sally wailed. "But it's sort of complicated and I've got to tell you the whole story. I wouldn't bother you, Leona, if it wasn't important."

"Well—" Leona sighed in resignation, "what next?"

"I—I followed them—"

"You what—?"

"I followed them. That Thursday morning. I know it's hard to believe—it sounds so crazy—but I was frightened. I wanted to know what was going on. After all, I'd known Henry almost all his life. I—well—there are things about him that are rather strange. I tried to tell you once, years ago."

Leona made impatient little noises. "Really," she said. "But really—is all this necessary? If you're trying to alarm me, Sally, you might as well stop right now."

Sally's reply was even more forlorn. "Please don't be so suspicious of me," she pleaded. "I'm only telling you what happened because it may have something to do with Henry's absence tonight. I don't know for sure. But let me finish…"

"By all means," Leona said. "As quickly as you can."

"It was drizzling that morning. I was carrying an umbrella, so that it shielded my face most of the time, although I don't think that made much difference. It's not hard to follow people—especially in the rain.

"I saw Fred meet two men—one of them was Joe Harris, who works with Fred most of the time, the other was a dark, heavyset fellow with wavy white hair. I suppose he was this man, Harpootlian, Fred had mentioned.

"I waited in the distance until they had moved with the crowd toward the ferry. Then I bought a ticket and followed. It wasn't hard to keep out of sight on the ferry. I spent most of the trip in the john, anyway."

"How lovely!" Leona sneered.

"Well, it was the best place… Oh, well," Sally continued doggedly. "After they left the ferry at Staten Island they got on the train. I was right behind them. Not in the same car, of course…"

"Of course!" Leona echoed.

"…but a couple of cars away. I watched for them to get off, and when they did I did too. It was still drizzling and nobody paid any attention to me. Most people were hurrying along, anxious to get out of the rain, I imagine."

"Very observant—" Leona said.

"This place was a sort of beach colony, Leona. It looked terribly run-down and empty. The streets were all crooked and badly paved. They were covered in spots with drifts of sand. The houses were mostly shacks and right at the center of them was a boarded-up casino. After Fred and the two men had walked off toward the beach I went over to the casino and watched from a corner of the porch. I had a good view from there. And nobody was likely to notice me in the shadows."

"Really!" Leona said. "Am I really expected to…?"

"It's true! It's true!" Sally exclaimed. "I told you it would sound crazy…"

"Crazy is hardly the word…"

"There was only one person besides Fred and the two men in sight—a boy digging clams by the water's edge. The man with the white hair seemed to stop for a moment and stare at the boy, and the boy moved his head just a trifle toward something in the distance. Then he went on digging, and the men walked over to a luncheonette and went inside."

Leona, fuming with indignation, interrupted, crying, "For heaven's sake, Sally, must you go on like this? Can't you tell me what it's all about without dragging me all over Staten Island? Or are you deliberately keeping me on the phone for some other reason?"

Sally reassured her. "You've got to hear it all. Do you think I like being cooped up in this stuffy booth? The man who owns the store keeps looking over here all the time. He's angry because he wants to close up."

"Anyway," she continued, "I waited there in the drizzle for about an hour and nothing happened. Then, just as I was thinking I'd been a terrible fool for taking that awful trip, I saw something very strange. The boy who'd been digging clams stood up and stretched his arms as though he were yawning. A little while after that I heard a motorboat roaring off the shore, and soon I could see the boat speeding toward the land. When it got near it slowed down and headed for a broken-down wharf next to one of the weirdest houses in the whole place.

"I wish you could have seen that house, Leona. Old as the hills, and slightly lopsided. I suppose its foundation has been sinking for years. It's a scary-looking, scrollwork sort of place, like one of those Charles Addams houses—in the *New Yorker*, you know."

"Please," Leona said, "*will* you get to the point!"

"Well, the boat went to this wharf and a little hunchbacked man hopped out and tied it up. Then a tall, heavy, middle-aged man climbed out of the boat. He was dressed all in black except for a Panama hat, and he was carrying a briefcase under his arm. The minute he was safely off the boat the little hunchback started up the motor and raced away.

"The man in black walked down the wharf and into the old house. A moment later the clam-digger picked up his pail and shovel and started toward the luncheonette. I noticed that when he passed there he stumbled, knocking the pail of clams against the luncheonette door. It must have been a signal. He went on down the beach, and Fred and the others slipped out of the luncheonette and walked up to the old house. The man with the white hair knocked, the door opened, and in they went.

"I still don't understand any of it, Leona—who those people were, or what was happening in that house…"

"A brothel, no doubt," Leona suggested sarcastically.

"…but I know they were in there for a good half hour. When they came out, Fred was carrying that briefcase—the one the man in black had brought!"

"All right," Leona said, "Fred was carrying a briefcase. What next?"

"I don't know," Sally said feebly. "After that I had to hurry to get home—ahead of Fred, of course. But I know," she added vigorously, "that we've got to do something… before it's too late!"

Before Leona could reply, a coin clunked to the bottom of the box and the operator interrupted. Sally's five minutes were up. Leona could hear her muttering as she ransacked her purse. Finally she said, "Here it is, operator." And then, "Leona, Leona—are you still there?"

"Yes, I'm here," Leona said suspiciously. "This is all very strange, I must say."

"I know," Sally agreed. "It's very strange to me. I couldn't believe it. I couldn't connect Henry with—with the kinds of crimes Fred investigates. That's why I went to see him today—to find out the truth from him."

"And did you?" Leona asked grimly.

"I saw him—you know that—but I couldn't find out anything.

I didn't have a chance."

"But you went out with him," Leona said. "His secretary saw you."

"Yes, I went out with him. He wasn't very enthused about it either. Of course I didn't exactly expect him to jump for joy. But he was—hardly civil. He seemed terribly preoccupied. I'd known him to be that way as a boy, and it was usually when he was—well—going through some sort of conflict with himself.

"He asked me if I'd like a bite of lunch with him, and we went to the Georgian Room at the Metropolis. Almost as soon as we sat down a man named Freeman—Bill Freeman—a prosperous-looking elderly man— came over and started to talk stock market with Henry."

"Freeman?" Leona said. "I'm sure we don't know any Mr. Freeman—"

"Henry didn't seem to want to talk about it. But Mr. Freeman kept right on. I got the idea that something very serious had occurred in some stock or other that morning. Henry said, 'You've got to be wrong sometime,' and Freeman laughed and said, '*Sometime*, Stevenson? You've had more than a little tough luck, I'd say. But a man in your position can take plenty of punishment. Now me, I've got to be careful. I'm just a small potato.'

"Henry didn't eat much, and neither did I. What bothered me was that with Mr. Freeman there, talking about his troubles, I couldn't say a word. Finally we got up to go, and Freeman left. Henry and I walked into the lobby of the hotel. Henry said he was sorry, he had an appointment in a few minutes, and why didn't I call you, Leona, sometime and perhaps we could all get together. He didn't seem to mean it, though. Not really. We were standing near the entrance of a broker's branch office in the hotel, and a dried-up little man came out and called to Henry, 'Oh, Mr. Stevenson, I'd like to see you as soon as possible.' Henry turned very pale, it seemed to me, and he said to the little man, 'All right, Mr. Hanshaw, I'll be with you directly.' He said good-bye to me rather hurriedly and I watched him walk into the broker's office. On the door it said, T. F. Hanshaw, Manager."

"Well—he must—he must have said something to you," Leona sputtered. "I'm sure he didn't sit there and talk stocks and bonds—about which he knows nothing—every single solitary minute."

"Oh," Sally said, "I *did* ask him if he was happy, and how he enjoyed his work. He said, 'Fine—fine. I'm a big vice-president now. I push more buttons than anybody—except all the other vice-presidents.' He was trying to be funny, but I could tell the bitterness that he really felt. I started to ask him something about it, and that was when Mr. Freeman came over."

"I don't understand this at all." Leona's sneering skepticism was plain. "When Henry left me this morning he was quite his usual self, I assure you. We've been awfully happy for more than ten years—awfully happy. Henry hasn't had a care in the world. Daddy saw to that. And as far as his business association is concerned, I'm quite sure it's most suitable for Henry. You must have mistaken his remarks—if he made them at all. I'm still not so certain this isn't some kind of game you're trying to play with me, Sally."

Again, before Sally could reply, the operator said, brightly, "Your five minutes are up, madam. Please deposit five cents for the next five minutes."

Sally fished in her bag, saying at last, despairingly, "I haven't another nickel. I'll have to call you back when I get change." Then she added in a rush, "I only want to say—I know now—that Henry *is* in trouble. Fred's working on some kind of report tonight. The case, whatever it is, seems to be coming to a head. He's been telephoning. I've heard Henry's name over and over again. And there's somebody else in it, too—somebody named Evans."

"Your five minutes are up, madam," said the operator.

"Waldo Evans," Sally hurried on breathlessly. "I think that's the name I saw on that Staten Island house..."

"Your five minutes are *up*, madam."

10:05

As soon as Sally had hung up, Leona reached for the crumpled bit of paper on which she'd found Sally's phone number. There it was. *Mr. Evans. Richmond 8:1112.* She carefully dialed the number, surprised when the operator interrupted after a brief interval to ask, "Are you calling W. Evans, Richmond 8:1112?"

"Why, yes," Leona said apprehensively. "That's right."

"That number... has been disconnected."

She sat bolt upright in bed, laying the phone down on its cradle, staring into space—her eyes wide and bewildered. The events of this strange evening chased each other madly through her brain. Henry's absence, the killers on the telephone, Miss Jennings, Sally's crazy tale—none of it made sense. And yet, somehow, there was disaster, danger in the air. Perhaps Henry *was* in trouble. Perhaps there *were* things she'd never suspected going on. The thought that she should be alone in this nerve-racking quandary encouraged a rising tide of self-pity. Why had all this to happen tonight—the one night when she had no one—not even a servant—near her? It was too much. Entirely too much for an invalid to bear. Her lips quivering, she dialed the Long Distance Operator and placed a call for Jim Cotterell in Chicago.

The Chicago operator repeated the number, and soon Leona could hear the phone in Jim Cotterell's house ringing. Someone picked it up, and Leona called, "Hello," but she was instantly cut off. The silence angered her and she made little sounds of exasperation. Seconds went by and then the operator said smoothly, "Mr. Cotterell is not at the Lake Forest number, madam. I will try to locate him for you."

"What?" Leona asked irritably.

"I will call you back, madam," the operator replied and rang off.

Defeated by her father's habit of running off to night clubs, or all-night card games, she cast about again for someone in whom she could confide her anxiety. It was difficult—being almost a total stranger in New York—to select someone close at hand. The paucity of choice was maddening.

At last she thought of the doctor—Doctor Alexander. Just the person. He'd examined her several times. He'd made several tests, the results of which she still didn't know. She could send for him, and he'd have to come. At least she'd have someone near her for a while.

She groped for the phone, halting the action while another train rolled noisily over the bridge. It was awful—that confounded racket. How foolish, she thought, to live in a city where no one, no matter who he might be, could find peace and quiet. She thought, too, of the train the killer had mentioned (How like this one it must be!) and she shuddered. It was best not to remind herself of that horrible thing.

The noise of the train died away and she made another movement toward the telephone. It chose that moment to ring and she picked it up.

It was the man Evans. She had no difficulty in recognizing immediately the weary, hollow, cultured voice.

"Is Mr. Stevenson there?" he asked.

"No," she said. "Is this Mr. Evans?"

"Yes, Mrs. Stevenson."

She said crisply, "First of all—I want to know the truth about this Staten Island business. I've just heard about it tonight—and I'm nervous enough as it is—what with Mr. Stevenson not being here—and then getting all sorts of strange calls—including two murderers—" She broke off, mystified.

As she talked, she had become increasingly aware of a far-off, whining sound in the telephone. It came from wherever Mr. Evans was. As she listened its volume grew. It sounded like something she had heard many times before—whenever fire apparatus or police cars careened along the city streets. Nervously she called, "Are you still there, Mr. Evans?"

The sound grew louder and again she cried, "Mr. Evans—? Are you still there?"

There was no reply save the whining sound, and in despair she hung up. Immediately the phone rang.

"Hello? Mr. Evans?" she asked quickly. There was no answer. Instead she heard a rushing, grinding roar more frightening than before.

"Mr. Evans—" she called again, loudly, to be answered only by rolling thunder.

Almost hysterically she cried, "Hello! Who's there? Who's calling?" She paused a moment, then cried, "Why don't you answer me?" Again she paused. Then, as no voice arose over the mysterious din, the floodgates of hysteria broke and she screamed, "ANSWER ME!"

From far off, almost buried by the continuous roar, she heard a faint voice say, "Leona—?"

Frightened, Leona asked, "Who's *that?*"

The noise seemed to retreat now and, more distinctly, the voice said, "It's Sally. I'm phoning from a subway station. All the stores close in this neighborhood at ten o'clock. I had to speak to you, so I came down here. I've been home, Leona—since I spoke to you—and *more* has happened."

Leona, her face strained and tense, said, "This time, Sally, please get it all out, or don't bother me anymore. I've listened to just about enough tonight."

"There was a police car standing in front of the house when I got home," Sally told her in a rush. "That house on Staten Island burned down this afternoon. The police surrounded it. They captured three men. But this Evans man escaped."

"But who is Evans? What's his connection with Henry?" Leona asked.

"I still haven't found out, Leona. But I do know the whole thing has something to do with your father's company..."

"My father's company? But—that's absurd. My father called me from Chicago tonight and he never mentioned a thing."

She stopped, waiting for the noise of another train to subside. Then she continued, "Now look, let's get this thing straight. Who's been arrested? And why?"

"Three men," Sally answered. "I don't know why."

"And why do you think Henry's one of them?"

"I didn't say he was," Sally said. "I only know he's terribly involved."

Leona's exasperation grew. "Did they say he'd been arrested—or was going to be?"

"No, not exactly."

"Then—what are you talking about?" Leona asked furiously. "Why are you calling me like this? Don't you realize you're frightening me to death?"

"I know, but—"

"...first I picked up my phone and overheard two horrible murderers..."

"Murderers—!"

"...planning to kill a woman... then this creature, Evans, calls me, sounding as though he was talking from the grave... then everybody else is either busy or disconnected... and now you—for no good reason at all..."

"I'm sorry—"

"...for no good reason at all..." She paused for breath. "Are you jealous that I took him away from you? Can't you bear to see me happy?"

"Really, Leona..."

"Can't you stop telling lies and making trouble even now? I don't believe a word of it—do you hear?—not a word of it. He's innocent. He's on his way home to me—right now!"

Before she could say any more, Sally hung up.

She lay there fluttering her fingers, wondering if she had been right in allowing herself the luxury of that screaming moment. Despite everything, Sally might really know something that involved danger for Henry. But what? Money? All that talk about the stock market? It was hard to understand. She knew that no one dabbled in the market without money. Henry had no money. His salary as a vice-president of the Cotterell Company was not large, and most of it went into the household expenses he insisted on paying. His pride made him do that, just as his pride had been responsible for that silly episode of the apartment—the apartment he had wanted to rent for her when they were living with her father in Chicago. No, Henry really had nothing. It was all right for him to keep the house going. But the heavy expenses were still borne by Jim Cotterell.

She couldn't see any opportunity Henry might have had to play the financier. Even the investments Jim kept turning over to her—to reduce the death taxes that someday would be levied against his estate—were registered in her name, untouchable as far as Henry was concerned. Unless, of course, she died. If she died they'd be Henry's. Her will took care of that—and she was glad for Henry's sake. But what a morbid thought—at this time! She'd put that out of her mind at once. It was too frightening.

But there must be some reason behind Sally's outlandish tale. Unless it was pure fantasy on Sally's part. Unless Sally had some obscure, demented idea of hurting her because of the past. Suppose she had. Was she capable of concocting the story she'd just told? And if she was, why tell it on this particular night?

The mystery grew in her mind, swirling about in clouds of conjecture. Tiny, frightful suspicions blossomed and refused to die. Each hideous thought bred another, and her imagination became a screen across which flashed a succession of fiendishly logical possibilities. Suppose! Suppose! Like nightmares, their overpowering terror brought about sharp physical reaction. Her heart began to beat faster, painfully faster. In breathing she found it was only with effort that she could force the air from her lungs. Trembling, she found her handkerchief and mopped hurriedly at the clammy evidences of fright on her face. She no longer tried to understand what had happened to Henry—or what might have happened. Her concern for herself outweighed all else. The thought of chaos to come, of the toppling of her little edifice of deceit, was unbearable. She had started to rock in agony on the bed when the telephone again shrilled into action.

"Is this Plaza 9:2265?" a man asked.

"Yes, what is it?" she said shakily, almost in a whisper.

"This is Western Union. I have a message for Mrs. Henry Stevenson. Is there anyone there to receive the message?"

"This is Mrs. Stevenson."

"The telegram is as follows: 'Mrs. Henry Stevenson, 43 Sutton Place, New York, New York. Darling, terribly sorry, but decided attend Boston meeting at last minute. Stop. Taking train out. Stop. Back Sunday morning. Stop. Tried to call you but line always busy. Stop. Keep well, happy. Love. Henry.'"

10:15

Dumbfounded, she sat there, her hand moving toward her mouth in a gesture of despair. The Western Union operator wanted to know if a copy of the message was to be delivered and she said, "No, it's— not—necessary," in a faint voice and mechanically replaced the phone. Now she could hear another grinding roar from the bridge and, as in a dream, she slipped from the bed and tottered to the window. One hand on the casement, she looked out at the great Gothic outlines of the bridge silhouetted against the night. Now she could see the train, a long column of segmented light, moving wormlike onto the bridge, its clatter growing louder as it swung toward her, louder and louder and louder, then diminishing as it swung back and away. She could feel the window casement tremble under her hand. She stood there as though hypnotized. Shreds of talk drifted through her mind, *"Then I wait... until the train goes over the bridge... our client says the coast is clear... got your message, George, everything okay for tonight?... Where's Henry? Business. What business?... sometimes days have gone by when Mr. Stevenson hasn't come in... Henry is in trouble... desperate trouble... darling, terribly sorry, taking next train out... then I wait until a train goes over the bridge... then I wait until a train goes over the bridge..."*

With a moan she wrenched herself back to reality, weaving back to the bed, clutching at the impersonal coolness of the telephone. The depth of her urgency was translated into the nervous force with which she spun the dial.

Over the babble of voices in the apartment's small, bare living room a fan droned steadily, its blast directed at the telephone switchboard that lined one wall. It offered comfort to the four girls seated at the board busily working telephone plugs, pressing keys, swiftly writing down the messages that later would be relayed to the Answering Service's customers. On a couch near the open windows a fifth operator was resting. If she turned her head toward the windows she could look out on the stark fire escape, with one bedraggled geranium tilting crazily in a pot in one corner. Not being a nature lover, however, the girl lay and watched the others working out their tours of duty. At a signal, she stood up and slid into a seat at the switchboard as the other operator slid out. She slipped the tape of a suspension mouthpiece around her neck and adjusted the receiver over her hair. Her eye caught the first winking light, and she went to work, saying, "No, madam, Doctor Alexander is not in. May I take the message?"

She listened for a moment, her face a picture of alarm. "What is that, madam? No—I couldn't say... If you'll give me your name and telephone number? Yes, madam. Yes—Mrs. Stevenson. Mrs. Henry Stevenson. Plaza 9:2265. I'll certainly try to reach him."

Dr. Alexander laid his cards down, arranging them in long, neat rows with his long, neat hands.

"There you are, partner," he said, smiling across the table. "See what you can do with that."

"Perfect!"

"I thought it would be—if I understood your bidding." He turned to his hostess, who sat at his left. "Excuse me for a couple of minutes, will you, Mona? I'd like to call—"

"Of course, Philip," she said. "You know where the phone is—?"

"I'm afraid…" he said, rising.

"Right across the hall in the den. You'll see the phone on Harry's desk. Can't miss it."

"Now I remember," he said. "How stupid of me…"

Long strides took his erect figure swiftly out of the room. The two women at the bridge table involuntarily turned to watch him go. He commanded much attention from women. As a consequence he also commanded fat fees—deservedly fat, for his skill was at least the equal of his imposing personality.

As he sat now at the desk, the telephone in front of him, the lamp-light cut attractive shadows under the lean planes of his face. It was a hawklike face, vigorous, healthy, with lines deepened by time and humor at the corners of his gray eyes and around his thin lips. His hair was a thick dark shock neatly graying at the temples. He was, as so many prosaic husbands had remarked when prosaically footing the bills, an Arrow Collar medico—a screen character armed with a scalpel instead of a script. But they had to admit he was good—even though their wives often acquired a dreamy, beyond-the-horizon kind of look along with the look of health.

Mechanically he dialed the Answering Service, thinking how pleasant it would be if nothing were to disturb his evening. He was enjoying himself—a rare thing for even successful medical men.

"Doctor Alexander," he said to the girl who answered. "Anything for me—and I hope there isn't?"

"Oh—there *is*, Doctor," she told him. "A Mrs. Stevenson. Mrs. Henry Stevenson. Very ill and worried, she said. One of your heart patients, she said. She sounded kind of frantic to me."

"Anything else?" he asked.

"No, Doctor, just Mrs. Stevenson."

"Fine," he said. "I'll call Mrs. Stevenson right away."

He took a small, beautifully bound notebook from a pocket of his dinner jacket and picked out Leona's telephone number. He hesitated before dialing, thinking despairingly that this might be a bothersome call. Mrs. Stevenson was inclined to be imperious. She was also inclined to be imperious at great length, and he had no desire now to listen to her interminable elaborations of her condition. Evidently she had frightened the girl at the Answering Service, although there was little chance— Well, grin and bear it, he thought. It can't be too bad, since by this time she must know the real state of affairs.

He dialed the number.

Leona answered the phone in the instant of its first ring. Whimpering one moment, belligerent the next, she flooded his ear with her troubles.

"I'm terribly, terribly frightened," she said weakly. "My heart feels as though it had a clamp around it. The palpitation is so painful—I— I can't bear it. My lungs feel as though they'll burst if I take a deep breath. And I can't stop trembling. I can hardly hold this phone, it's so bad."

"Oh—come—come, Mrs. Stevenson," he said soothingly. "I'm sure it's not that bad. Where's your maid tonight? Can't she sit with you? I'm sure that if someone were there with you you wouldn't be suffering."

"There's no one here—no one," Leona cried. "And I'm not well. I know I'm not well. I want you to come here tonight. You're my doctor and I need you now—tonight."

"Why—I'm afraid I can't," he told her, still professionally silken.

"I'd come if I thought it was necessary—but I know that it isn't. You're just having a bad case of nerves, that's all. If you'll force yourself to relax and sit quietly for a few minutes you'll see how much better you'll feel. If you wish, take a couple of bromides. They'll help quiet your nerves."

Leona cried, "But you know I'm a sick woman. What have I been coming to you for all these months? How can you refuse to see me now, when I need you? What kind of a doctor are you, anyway?"

His jaw set grimly. This was going a bit too far, even for the rich Mrs. Stevenson. "Look here, Mrs. Stevenson," he said briskly. "Don't you think it's about time you faced this thing squarely and began to cooperate with your husband and me?"

"What are you talking about?" she asked. "What do you mean—cooperate?"

Her question took him aback. "What am I talking about? Why, Mrs. Stevenson, you know as well as I do. I explained it all to your husband—a week ago."

"My husband? You must be trying to aggravate me like all the rest of them. I assure you my husband hasn't said a word to me…"

Doctor Alexander was becoming more and more puzzled. "Surely your husband… I told him the whole story… He promised… And he hasn't said a *thing*?"

"What whole story?" Leona demanded. "What story? What is all this mystery?"

Doctor Alexander paused. This was rather confusing.

"Well, that's very, very strange indeed, Mrs. Stevenson. I discussed your case with him—completely—about ten days ago. He came to my office."

"And what did you tell him, Doctor?"

"Really, dear lady, there's hardly time to go into all that now. If you will compose yourself—get some sleep—perhaps we can discuss it tomorrow."

"You'll discuss it now—NOW! Do you hear me!" Leona shrieked.

"How do you suppose I could get through this night not knowing—wondering what kind of terrible thing is going to happen to me next? I won't hear of you..."

Doctor Alexander shrugged his shoulders, and arched a cynical eyebrow at the telephone.

"All right, Mrs. Stevenson. If you will hold the phone for one moment..."

He laid the phone on the desk and walked out of the den back to the living room. In the doorway he stopped. The hand had been played and they were waiting for him.

"I'm sorry," he told them. "I'm going to be a few minutes longer..."

"Another of your conquests, Philip?" his partner said with a shade too much gaiety in her voice.

"Of course. But I'll only be a little while. Hate to hold up the rubber this way, though."

He returned to the den. "Thank you for waiting, Mrs. Stevenson," he said.

"I hope you'll clear up this mystery at once," she demanded, sulkily. "I had no idea that my husband had been consulting you."

"He came to my office to hear my diagnosis of your condition. He told me that he had been warned by your father about your heart—that you were subject to attacks, had been since childhood. He said, in response to my questions, that you had long periods of good health, that he didn't know anything about a heart condition before he married you. Your father told him on your wedding day. It was quite a shock."

"My father is inclined to be—rather blunt."

"Your husband said that you hadn't had any attack until about a month after your return from the honeymoon. Is that right, Mrs. Stevenson?"

"Yes," she said. "I remember that. I was sorry it happened."

"Your husband told me that it had happened because he wanted to break away from your father's firm, and you wouldn't hear of it."

"I—I suppose it was that," Leona agreed. "Henry wanted—quite foolishly, of course—to get out on his own. He's impetuous that way—at times."

"According to him it was more than that, Mrs. Stevenson."

"Oh? More?"

"Yes, I believe there had been some friction with your father—hadn't there?"

"Well, yes..." she admitted grudgingly. "Henry had the idea that Dad was not giving him sufficient responsibility. A ridiculous notion."

"Your husband didn't seem to think so."

"Just the same, it was ridiculous. Why, Dad even made Henry a vice-president and gave him one of the most beautiful offices..."

"At any rate, he quarreled with your father and then with you. And you became gravely ill."

"Yes," she said. "I can't stand quarrels."

"Your husband apparently guessed that," the doctor said dryly. "He didn't care for them either—after that. He seems to be a pretty strong man—and shrewd, if I may say so. At any rate he said there were no further attacks until he surprised you with that apartment—the one he wanted you to live in."

"Oh—yes," she said. "He was very foolish. He wanted to take me away from my father's home and live in a place he had rented. Poor Henry. He knew nothing about such things. He hadn't begun to appreciate how wonderful it was living with my father, with no problems of making a home. Dad never bothered us. It was just that Henry had some silly idea about being the man of the house—like some ordinary book-keeper or salesman in the suburbs."

"You quarreled about that too, didn't you?"

"Yes," she said. "And, although I tried not to be, I was terribly sick."

"That coincides with your husband's story," Doctor Alexander said. "It made him determined not to cross you again. But you went into a decline after that, and you've got worse—he says—until now you're almost a permanent invalid. Naturally he wanted to know what to expect in the future."

"I'm sure he was upset," Leona said. "He's always watched over me. He's very much in love with me."

Doctor Alexander coughed. "I agreed with him that he hadn't any picnic. I asked him if he had ever thought of leaving you." He heard Leona gasp, and hurried on. "He looked up as though shocked. Said he hadn't considered it. I told him that in my view that was what you needed, Mrs. Stevenson. Obviously he'd been the cause of all your emotional disturbances for these past ten years. If he dropped out of the picture you might improve at once."

"That's—that's horrible of you—just horrible," she whispered tearfully.

"He thought it might kill you," the doctor went on calmly. "But of course I reassured him on that point. I told him you'd probably make a pretty frightening scene, but in the long run you'd pull out of it—as you would, I'm sure. In other words, I told him the truth, dear lady. There's nothing wrong with your heart…"

"What!"

"That's right, Mrs. Stevenson. Organically your heart is as sound as a bell."

"How can you say such a thing?" she raged. "You know I'm a sick woman…"

"It's not the kind of sickness you thought," he said. "It's in your mind."

"My *mind!* I think you're in league with—with those others to *wreck* my mind."

"Please, Mrs. Stevenson, you must be reasonable. Nobody is trying to harm you."

"They are!" she cried. "They are!"

"I'm sure I don't know what you're talking about," he said easily.

"May I suggest that you discuss this whole thing with Mr. Stevenson...?"

"Discuss it? How can I discuss it? He isn't here. I don't know where he is."

"Perhaps tomorrow will be time..."

"Oh, you..."

He could almost feel the shock as she banged the receiver back in place. The dial tone hummed in his ear for an instant. He lowered the phone partway, his hand poised over the dial on the desk. Call her back? No. He smiled cynically, shrugged his shoulders, gently replaced the phone in its cradle. As he started for the door a voice floated in from the other room. "Philip! You've been long enough, darling."

Leona—stunned, incredulous—stared at the telephone instrument, an infernal machine especially designed to torture her beyond endurance. Anger, hurt pride, doubt fought within her. It couldn't be so! Perhaps in her childhood she had exaggerated the seriousness of her illness. But now she was sick! She wasn't pretending! She was sick! She was sick! Her hand went to her heart, pressing it close where the hurt was. She took a deep breath, feeling the sharp, stabbing pain. Alexander was a fool. A brutal fool. The idea of telling her all those terrible things, suggesting that she had caused Henry any real unhappiness. Was he deliberately trying to upset her, to bring on some kind of a crisis? She'd see that he was reported to the Medical Association.

And his lies about Henry! They were lies, all right, and she'd make Henry face the doctor with them. They were lies. She was a sick woman. And Henry loved her and wanted to help her. It must be that way. It couldn't be any other way. It couldn't.

Suddenly her eyes blazed defiantly. She tossed aside the coverlet, swinging one foot to the floor, then the other. She rose to her feet, holding her breath, taking a shaky step toward the window. Her heart was beating crazily. She clutched at her breast as if she could still its fluttering with the pressure of her fingers. And once more the telephone rang!

It was too much! She toppled back upon the bed, gasping for breath, racked with the intensity of her anguish, "Liars!" she sobbed. "Liars… liars… liars!"

The phone continued to ring, and she turned her stricken face toward it, crying, "I won't talk to anybody. I hate you all!"

But the measured rings mocked her anger. Then, above the ringing she heard a familiar sound. She could feel the faint trembling of the building as another train crossed the bridge. Its closeness restored her to her senses, choked off the feverish impulses that sprang from jangled nerves. Meanwhile the phone rang and rang. She picked it up.

10:30

"Hello," she said, her voice emerging weakly, tearfully.

"Mrs. Stevenson?"

She had no difficulty this time in recognizing his voice. "Yes, Mr. Evans," she said. "This is Mrs. Stevenson."

"Has Mr. Stevenson come in yet?"

"No," she said tautly, "he hasn't. He won't be home until tomorrow." Then explosively she added, "Will you please—please, for goodness' sake, Mr. Evans, tell me what this is all about? Why are you calling him every five minutes?"

Evans said apologetically, "I'm very sorry. I haven't meant to annoy you."

"Well, you are annoying me," she cried. "I insist that you—"

"It's rather a precarious moment—for Mr. Stevenson, that is," Evans said mournfully. "I thought that if you could tell him…"

"I can't take any messages now," Leona broke in wildly. "I'm too upset…"

"I'm afraid you must try, Mrs. Stevenson. It's very important."

"What right have you...?" she started to ask.

But Evans went on imperturbably, "Please tell Mr. Stevenson that the house at 20 Dunham Terrace—that's D-U-N-H-A-M—20 Dunham Terrace—has been burned down. I burned it down this afternoon."

"*What*? What's that?" she cried, startled.

"Also—please tell Mr. Stevenson," he continued calmly, "that I do not believe Mr. Morano—the name is spelled M-O-R-A-N-O—betrayed us to the police, as Mr. Morano has already been arrested. And so it is no use trying to raise the money now."

"And—who's Morano?" Leona asked shakily.

Evans ignored her question as he had the others. "Thirdly," he said, "will you please tell Mr. Stevenson that I escaped and am now at the Manhattan address? However I do not expect to be here after midnight— and if he wishes to find me—he may call Caledonia 5:1133. Will you write that down correctly, please? Caledonia 5:1133."

"But—what is this all about?" she protested.

"And now I believe that is all," Evans said smoothly. "If you will be so good as to repeat it to me—"

"Repeat it to you! I'll do no such thing," she shrilled. "Do you realize that I'm an invalid, Mr. Evans? Dangerously ill? I—I can't stand much more of this..."

There was a touch of pity, a quality of understanding in Evans's weary voice as he said, "I am well aware of your unfortunate position, Mrs. Stevenson. In fact I've known all about you for some time."

"You know all about *me*?" Leona said furiously. "Well—I've never in my life heard of *you* before—never!"

With some deference Evans said, "I am very sorry for you, Mrs. Stevenson. But I can assure you the whole affair has not been—ah— entirely Mr. Stevenson's fault."

"For heaven's sake will you stop talking in riddles, please? What has happened?" she demanded.

"Perhaps it *would* be better to tell you," Evans said thoughtfully, "before the true facts are garbled by the—ah—police."

"The—*police*...!"

Evans paused for an instant, then said slowly, "Do you have a pencil, Mrs. Stevenson? There are names and places in what I am about to tell you that might prove helpful—if you—ah—were to write them down..."

I shall begin with the night when I first became acquainted with Mr. Stevenson (said Evans). I believe the exact date of the meeting was October 2, 1946. The place was your father's factory at Cicero, Illinois. Things had been rather busy, and I was working late in my laboratory— checking through some of the formulae records. A slight sound behind me attracted my attention and I turned to see someone staring at me through the glass pane in the door to my room. A moment later the door opened and a young man came in.

"Good evening," he said. "Late for you, isn't it?"

"Yes, Mr. Stevenson," I replied. "Necessarily so."

I explained that it was my custom to work late at night.

"I've wondered about this place," he told me, roaming about the laboratory. "First time I've had a chance to look it over."

I was pleased at this. I seldom had visitors who were interested in my work, and the opportunity to show off was, I must confess, most welcome. Since Mr. Stevenson was Mr. Cotterell's son-in-law, the visit was doubly interesting.

The laboratory was a pleasant place. I had the very best equipment with which to work, and all of it had been placed in the best possible arrangement under the batteries of fluorescent lights that gleamed from the ceilings and reflected off the softly colored wall tiles.

"Is there anything in particular I can show you?" I asked.

"No—no—just curious," he said. "Always been curious about this department. What do you do here?"

"Our work here," I said, "involves the chemistry of narcotics. Narcotics are not always the harmful things we read about. Many of them are boons to mankind when taken in the proper dosage—such as in some of the Cotterell products."

I suppose my somewhat pedantic manner amused him. He smiled at me. "Look, Evans," he said, "I've been around drugs most of my life. Now, tell me, just what goes on here?"

"Well," I replied, "in this laboratory we break down raw opium into its various alkaloids. I suppose you know that opium has twenty-four alkaloids—morphine, codeine…"

"Fine," he said, interrupting me. "Dope. Must be a lot of it in here."

"There certainly is," I agreed. "It's quite a responsibility, if I may so so, sir."

"What do you do with the various alkaloids?" he asked.

"Why, they're used in Cotterell products, of course."

"No, no," he said. "I mean, what do you do with them before they're needed by the factory? You don't just keep them around in jars on a shelf."

"Well—that's rather a secret," I told him.

"As it should be," he said. "I suppose I could ask Mr. Cotterell…"

"Nonsense," I assured him. "I was only impressing upon you how carefully we guard this information. Of course there's no reason why Mr. Cotterell's son-in-law should not know about it."

I walked over to the tiled wall facing the door and inserted a key into a small aperture just above the light switch. Part of the wall slid aside, revealing the huge safe in which our narcotic supply was kept. Mr. Stevenson seemed much impressed.

"Worry you?" he wanted to know. "Having all that human dynamite around?"

"As I said before," I assured him, "it's a responsibility, but that vault is not likely to yield to anything except the right combination."

"What I mean," he continued, "is: what about mistakes? Suppose you made a mistake in the amount that you released for one of the products. Couldn't it do a lot of harm?"

"It's most unlikely that such a thing could happen," I assured him. "Our measures are exact, and conform to the formulae involved. I've been here fifteen years, and nothing untoward has happened."

"Of course," he said with a smile. "I was just curious."

He dropped into the laboratory a few times after that—always very friendly and decent to me. I showed him the various processes in action, and he seemed to have from his years of drugstore experience a basic grasp of what was fairly complicated terminology. I was flattered that so important a figure in the company was so cordial to me.

You haven't told me anything I don't know, she thought. Henry is like that. Curious. Thorough. Makes it his business to know everything about the company. What Dad calls snooping. That's one of the things they argue about. Henry thinks Dad resents him, is trying to hold him down. He even told Doctor Alexander about it. Maybe Dad's too severe.

About a month after my first meeting with Mr. Stevenson I was outside the plant waiting for a bus to take me to my home. It was a bitter evening, with a high wind driving a cold rain almost horizontally across the city streets. My umbrella was not very much protection, as you can imagine. I was utterly miserable, waiting on that corner. But not for long. A most magnificent black sedan stopped directly in front of me, and someone called, "Evans!"

I peered through the rain and saw it was Mr. Stevenson. "Hop in," he said. "Give you a lift."

"Very kind of you," I said. "But I'd not like to trouble you. Perhaps you could help me pick up a bus farther down. I own I've no wish to stand in the rain anymore."

"Forget it," he said. "Glad to take you home. As a matter of fact, I hate driving alone."

We rolled smoothly along, and I couldn't help admiring the beauty of that automobile.

"My wife's," Mr. Stevenson said, when I mentioned it.

"I've never owned a car," I told him. "They've always seemed a bit too—well—mechanical. Personally I'd rather have a brace of spanking horses and a good carriage."

Mr. Stevenson didn't stop me, so I suppose I rattled on for quite some time about—horses. You see, I was brought up around horses. In Surrey, that is. And I suppose no one ever gets it out of his blood.

"Horses are fine creatures," I said, "so powerful—and at the same time, so gentle. I've often wished I owned hundreds of them."

At this Mr. Stevenson looked at me rather oddly. "You don't say...?"

"Yes," I assured him. "Nothing I'd like better. Like to have my own little place. Good clean stables. Plenty of pasture. And the best stock in all England."

"England?" asked Mr. Stevenson.

"Oh, yes," I replied. "I fancy every Englishman living abroad hopes to spend his old age at home. There's something that tugs at you no matter how long you've been away."

He looked at me again, with the hint of a smile on his lips. "There's nothing wrong with wanting a thing," he said. "The wrong is in not doing anything about it."

"It's easy to say that, if you'll forgive the impertinence," I said, "but not everyone can back his desire with the requisite energy—and coin of the realm. Sometimes one doesn't know what one wants until it is too late. For instance—I play a little game with myself."

"You do...?" he said with a hint of amusement.

"Yes," I replied. "I went back to England for a holiday a few years ago, and I picked out a spot near Dorking. A perfect spot. A bit of land there, all green grass and shade trees, and a beautiful brook. Horses do love a brook. Every now and then I price that place—just for the fun of it, you know—but I know I shall never be able to buy it. I do get pleasure out of planning what I'd do with the place if I could."

"You're right," Mr. Stevenson said rather cynically. "You'll never get that place working for my father-in-law."

This rather embarrassed me. "No," I admitted, "I suppose not."

Again he glanced at me, and I noticed his look at this time was a bit on the speculative side, as though he were making up his mind to tell—or not to tell—me something. What he said, finally, nearly bowled me over.

"You and I, Evans, have a lot in common."

Fantastic! she thought. *Henry and this weary old man! Why would Henry link himself with a tiresome drudge? He sounds as if he might be a little queer.*

"But—but—Mr. Stevenson, sir, what rot! I thought…"

"Don't think, Evans, unless it's about your job and about that farm in England." He said that rather grimly. For a while neither of us spoke. When we reached my house, I opened the car door to step out. Suddenly I felt his hand on my arm. "Wait a minute, Evans, I want to talk to you."

"Certainly, Mr. Stevenson," I said and closed the door.

"Evans," he began, "I've got a little idea. If it's a good one, it'll mean that place in England for you. For me, it'll mean—well, never mind what it'll mean for me. You can tell me if it's a good idea, Evans. Nobody else but you can tell me." He wasn't smiling now. There was a look on his face as black as night. His eyes were drilling into mine. His grip on my arm tightened until it was almost painful.

"What do you mean?" I asked hastily, for his manner was certainly frightening.

"I mean you can buy your way to England, or anywhere else, by just making a few mistakes."

"Mistakes?" I gasped. "I'm afraid I don't follow you."

"Mistakes," he said evenly, "in the amount of dope you put into Cotterell products. Not more, Evans—less. Much less."

"Good heavens, no," I said, trembling. "I never heard—"

"No one but you—and me—would know, Evans," he said. "You know as well as I do that those cheap nostrums would really be better for suffering humanity if there were less dope in them. Nobody— certainly not the Cotterell Company—would ever know the difference. And the dope you held out, Evans, would buy that farm you were talking about—England."

No! she cried inwardly. *It's impossible. This man is a lunatic. What's he trying to do? Who does he think will believe his ravings? To suggest that Henry would do such a thing! He's crazy. That's what he is. Crazy! But there must be something underneath all this nonsense. Henry must have had some dealings with the man. Miss Jennings mentioned that he'd called Henry several times.*

I was horrified—and fascinated. He'd struck so swiftly that I hardly could think. I wanted a bit of time to collect my wits.

"I'm not so sure it could be done as easy as all that," I said.

"What!" he said. "For a fine chemist like you it would be simple."

His flattery warmed me, I must admit. No one had ever bothered to show any appreciation or understanding of the miracles of chemistry that were so carefully produced under my direction in the Cotterell laboratory. Least of all, Mr. Cotterell himself!

"You really believe I'm a good chemist," I asked, foolishly.

"I know you're the best around," he said quickly. "I've watched you work. I've looked up your record. And I've hated seeing them pick your brains for peanuts."

I didn't know what to do. Temptation is a terrible thing, especially when what was wanted of me was so easy to do—for a good chemist. I hesitated, fumbling with the handle of the car door. But Mr. Stevenson had more to say.

"Come on—Evans, don't be a fool. I've already talked the whole thing over with someone else."

I was aghast. "Someone else?" I cried. "Good heavens, man, what folly!"

"Not folly," he said, grimly smiling. "Good sense. Someone has to sell the stuff after we get it. I wouldn't know what to do with it. Not yet—anyway. But the man I spoke to does. Name's Morano. He'll take everything we can give him—and split three ways."

Insane, she thought. *No doubt of it now. Perhaps a discharged employee whose mind has broken down. This crazy tale. Sounds like a movie.*

The cold-blooded enormity of the thing finally rang a warning bell in my mind. Had it been anyone but Mr. Stevenson, I would not have been quite so shocked. But that this handsome, powerful young man, living in the bosom of a millionaire family, could broach such a scheme was incredible.

"You—you've been pulling my leg, Mr. Stevenson," I said weakly. "Why would you—of all men—want to embroil yourself in the kind of tawdry affair you suggest? I do believe you've been testing my integrity—and I resent it, sir."

His lip curled, and the sneer on his face was not pleasant. "Evans," he said, "*you* want something—that farm. I want something, too. Money. My own money. I'm going to get it. And the sooner, the better. And the easier, the better. That's all. I want it. I get it. Now let's go up to that room of yours and talk it over."

"But wait," I pleaded. "What if we're caught?"

"We won't be," he said. "Let's go."

*   *   *

And we were not caught, Mrs. Stevenson. From the 15th of December, 1946, to the 30th of April, 1947, we were not caught. I carried out my part of the bargain, with surprising ease. It was a simple matter to substitute harmless powders and liquids for considerable quantities of morphine alkaloids. I did it at night, usually, when my staff was away. No one paid me the slightest attention. And the packages of illicit drugs I turned over to Mr. Stevenson every Friday. He, in turn, gave them to Mr. Morano. Where, I don't know. I never saw Mr. Morano at any time.

By the 30th of April I had saved nearly fifteen thousand dollars. It was incredible. It was my dream coming true. Then, one day, I received a notice from the Cotterell Company telling me that I was to be transferred to the Bayonne, New Jersey plant. Although, according to the notice, I also was to be in charge of the narcotics laboratory there, I was frightened. It seemed so unnecessary to move me to a place where I would do the same work, for the same pay. I went to see Mr. Stevenson at the first possible opportunity.

When we were safely alone in his office, I showed him my notice of transfer.

"You asked to be transferred?" he said sharply.

"No, never," I assured him. "That's why I'm rather upset about it. I'm sure something is suspected."

"Nonsense," he said. "You'd have been picked up by the police long ago if anything was wrong. This transfer must be a routine matter. I'd check on it myself, but why draw attention to it? There's nothing to worry about."

I wasn't entirely calmed by his cool assurance. Mr. Stevenson has a core of iron in his character, but not I.

"It's a sign," I said nervously, "a portent. I'm sure of it."

"A sign—of what?" he asked.

"To stop," I said. "This—this is a terrible business, Mr. Stevenson. I can't go on much longer. I'm not young, for one thing. I've almost enough money to quit now and go back to England. Perhaps I can do that after the transfer to Bayonne becomes effective."

Mr. Stevenson looked at me with that sly little smile of his. Not a very cheerful thing to behold, I assure you. "Evans," he said softly, "you'll stop when I say you stop. Let us be perfectly clear about that—when I say you stop. Not before."

He got up from his desk and walked to the door to make certain no one was within earshot. Then he came back, and sat on the edge of the desk close to my chair. He was still smiling, but his eyes were cold as ice.

"I need you, Evans, and I don't intend to let you go. Maybe you're interested in the chicken feed we've collected. But not me. I want more. A lot more, Evans, and I'm going to get it. And I think I know how to get it—fast. Faster than we've been getting it lately."

"What do you mean?" I asked.

"You've given me an idea, Evans, a big idea—the kind of idea that appeals to me. You were right when you said the transfer was a sign. It's the biggest sign you ever saw. And it's pointing right at the biggest pile of money you ever saw. When I get that pile—you can have out, Evans. It shouldn't be too long a wait—if you do as you're told."

He was talking in a low voice, but there was no mistaking his determination. His eyes were alight with a burning intensity that had something almost maniacal in it.

"Please, Mr. Stevenson," I begged, "are you sure it would be wise to carry this thing along any further? I'll admit it's been rather a simple thing so far. But aren't you permitting this initial success to topple your judgment? After all, how far can you trust Mr. Morano?"

He snorted. "Morano. A small-time gangster. He's been using us like a couple of stooges, Evans. We take all the risk, and he gets a fat share of the profits."

He got up and walked to the window, looking out over the huge plant. With his back to me, he said, "I don't see Morano in this picture anymore. No, I don't see him at all—the little chiseler." He turned to face me. "With you in Bayonne, Evans, I think Mr. Morano will have to find someone else to supply him."

I hadn't any idea what he was talking about. "It's not too easy to stop dealing with such a man as Morano, I should imagine," I said. "These men work in groups, and are generally supposed to be rather difficult— rather *physical*—about such matters."

"I'll handle Morano," he said. "When he learns that you've been transferred to Bayonne, cutting off my source of supply, he'll never give it a second thought. He's a stupid man, Evans. And his whole mob hasn't got a brain among them. He'll make no trouble."

"Now," he said, sitting down at his desk once more, "here's the setup. This narcotics racket is a big one. I've never realized how big until I saw what a small-time gunman like Morano draws down just from us. And he's dealing with others, too, don't forget. All right. We close up shop here, getting rid of Morano and his one-third cut. We start our own business out of Bayonne, peddling in New York, the richest market in the country. We'll do more business, at a larger profit, with larger shares for each of us. All you have to do is just what you've been doing right along. Except perhaps warehouse the stuff some safe place. We find another place for our—showroom. And we're in business!"

"But Mr. Stevenson," I said, "it's fantastic. Suppose, for the sake of argument, I were able to help you this way. How would you be able to— to contact the purchasers of our products? It's too risky, I tell you. It's better to stay small, and safe, than to tempt Providence."

"Look, Evans," he said, "when I was a kid, jerking sodas and wrapping up packages in a drugstore, I always managed to stash away a few compacts, bottles of perfume, all kinds of small things. There was always someone who would buy things from me, cheap, and no questions asked.

I only got caught once. And an old guy named Dodge, who liked me and knew I was poor and had to help my family, got me out of it. I got caught because I didn't watch my step—and that taught me a lesson. You can get away with anything if you're smart and watch your step. Well, Evans, I'm smart enough to establish the right connections in New York. You leave that to me. And believe me, no one will ever dream that either you or I have anything to do with the business."

Good heavens, it was insidious! She was actually beginning to believe him. He made it all seem so real. Everything fit together so neatly. But she must not, she dare not, give in to him. It could not be true. She would not let it be true.

One and a half months later we began operations on Staten Island, New York. Our headquarters were in an old house at 20 Dunham Terrace. I bought the house for Mr. Stevenson. I managed to hire a couple of local lads—not too bright, you understand—who thought I was working on a scientific project for the government. One of the lads acted as a sort of lookout for me, warning me of strangers and so forth. The other, a hunchback, kept the house fairly tidy and ran the small motor launch I bought to carry me by water to the house. Both were very loyal and very closemouthed, although I had little to fear, for nothing was kept in the house for them to see. It was only a distribution point—the "showroom" Mr. Stevenson mentioned—and the drugs were brought there from the "warehouse" and instantly disposed of.

The warehouse has been my room, the room from which I'm calling you now. It is an eminently respectable private home—my landlord is a retired minister of great simplicity. My trunk has served well as a repository for the various substances we sold. It seems unlikely that a place could have been found safer than this pleasant room.

I traveled to Staten Island several times a week, where I would be met by clients whom Mr. Stevenson sent. How he solicited them I do not know. We had a code word to identify the clients until I got to know most of them by sight. These men—and a few women—were small dealers. They bought in quantity and redistributed the products to the—ah—ultimate consumer.

You might suppose that I was banking considerable sums of money each week and you'd be correct. But apparently Mr. Stevenson was not satisfied with my progress.

Several months ago—as you know—Mr. Stevenson arrived in New York, having somehow effected his own transfer to the New York office of the Cotterell Company. His real objective, as you may surmise, was to take over the supervision of our drug sales, for he believed that the mounting volume of our little business could be further stimulated if he were close at hand. I discovered a short while after that there was a far greater urgency than merely Mr. Stevenson's desire to make as much money as quickly as he could. The truth was that Mr. Stevenson had been quietly playing the stock market, using the proceeds of his less honorable pursuit as capital. Unfortunately he was less astute in his stock-market speculations than he had been in his unlawful enterprise. He was in rather difficult straits. What was even more unfortunate was that he continued, as soon as he reached New York, to pour more of his money into futile market operations, so that every penny he got from me was turned over immediately to his brokers.

Sally! Sally had mentioned a brokerage office. And that man—Freeman or whatever his name was—commiserating with Henry over losses. This was no coincidence. Evans hadn't made this part of it up. More and more the whole story was becoming rational, terrifyingly rational. Perhaps Evans was not insane...

This was all very shocking to me, for I could see no opportunity to free myself from Mr. Stevenson's grasp. His overwhelming vanity—which was really at the root of his anxiety to succeed in a legitimate field—drove him to repeated attempts to recoup his losses. When I suggested that he stop and simply accumulate funds while our business was in such excellent shape, he would stare at me with that cold contempt I'd learned to know so well, and tell me to save my breath.

One day I asked him, "Mr. Stevenson, why do you insist upon gambling in the stock market? Surely in these days the opportunities to make substantial profits on the exchanges are limited—compared to our own business, that is."

He smiled at me queerly. "You know I want money. Not any money. But money I can show around—money that will buy me a little respect. I want lots of it. And I don't want to wait all my life for it. Okay—How can I explain the money I get from this racket? The answer is—I can't. All I can do is use it to get me going in something respectable. So I play the market. When I hit it right, nobody'll know what it cost me to start. I can tell them I saved some of the dough old man Cotterell paid me for warming the bench. Then, when I've got this thing licked, I'm rich, respectable, a smart operator—and I can tell Cotterell what he can do with his tailor-made vice-presidency."

Mr. Stevenson was, as you can see, very bitter—and very vain. His desire to be thought well of would have been perfectly natural in another young man. But another young man would have been content to work honestly toward his goal, whereas Mr. Stevenson intended to reach the goal without the work. I can moralize tonight about Mr. Stevenson's lack of morals, because—as you must now suspect—I have finally extricated myself from bondage. I do not belong to him any longer. I don't excuse my own conduct. But mine was the weakness of a hopeless old man sorely tempted. His, on the other hand, was the unhappy product of a warped, degenerate mind in a strong and beautiful body. In other words: I am a bad man—he is a dangerous one.

Fortunately—or unfortunately, depending on how you look at it—the final chapter of our story was being written even as Mr. Stevenson set about improving the sales of the drugs I was supplying. About a month ago we had a visitor.

10:40

I was to meet Mr. Stevenson at the Dunham Terrace house one evening. I arrived a bit later than usual. This time I'd come by ferry from Manhattan, and fog on the river caused some delay. I hurried up the steps of the old house, and entered the living room. Mr. Stevenson was seated in one of the rickety chairs with which the room was furnished. An oil lamp stood on the table near him, and in its light I could see his face plainly. He was white as a sheet, and that queer halting little smile of his flickered about his face. He looked at me, then looked away toward the corner of the room behind the door which I was holding open. I stepped in, closed the door—and saw the man in the corner!

He was straddling a kitchen chair, his arms folded across the chair's back. In the rather dim light of the lamp I couldn't make him out too clearly. But I knew I had never seen him before. He seemed to be a small man, carefully dressed. His oily black hair reflected the lamp's beam. He was looking at me, and what I could make out of his face was not pleasant—sharp, regular features, swarthy complexion, tiny eyes that did not blink. For a second after I'd closed the door no one spoke. Then the little man turned his head toward Mr. Stevenson. "Him?" he asked.

Mr. Stevenson said, "Him." And then to me, "Evans, meet an old friend—Morano."

The small man looked over at me. "Siddown," he said.

I sat down—with relief, I might add. The shock of this unexpected meeting had unnerved me. I was thoroughly alarmed.

"Morano is not pleased with us," Mr. Stevenson said mockingly. "He is hurt to think that we have voted him off the board of directors."

I looked anxiously at Morano to note the effect of Mr. Stevenson's gibe. If there was any, I couldn't see it. He sat there in silence, waiting for Mr. Stevenson to finish.

"I have just advised Mr. Morano that we cannot consider his application for reinstatement," Mr. Stevenson continued. "He was about to comment on this when you joined us." He put the tips of his fingers together, pursed his lips, and looked at Morano with exaggerated politeness.

Morano stared a moment longer as though making up his mind about something. Then he began to talk. His words slurred a little as he slid them out between almost motionless lips. Nevertheless I'm sure both Mr. Stevenson and myself had no difficulty in understanding them.

"Climb down," he said. "Maybe this ain't so funny. Maybe if you button up and listen you'll learn something, Stevenson. Even a very smart gentleman like you can sometimes learn something. Something like f'r instance how to keep alive." He paused for a moment.

"What kind of business you think this is? The grocery business? Anybody can open a store? Anybody can just move in and go to work? Did that fancy brain of yours tell you that, Stevenson? Like it told you to cross me up? I wouldn't know to keep an eye on you?"

"One for you," Mr. Stevenson said lazily. "I misjudged you, Morano."

"That ain't all you misjudged," Morano snapped. "If it wasn't for me you'd probably be very dead right now. Every mob in the business knows what you're doing. Or maybe you thought they didn't? You were a cinch to be knocked off as soon as they figured how to get to the professor here. They wanted him. As soon as they had him in line, so they could keep the stuff coming in, something would happen to you, Stevenson. Something very sad. But I fixed that. I got plenty friends here. So they let you alone—for only a small cut."

Mr. Stevenson was no longer smiling. "I don't think we're interested, Morano. I think we'll carry on without your help. When we have to make a deal, we'll make it direct. You've got your Chicago business. That ought to be enough."

"It's funny," Morano said, "but it ain't enough. You are being very foolish, Stevenson. I don't think you have much choice in this deal. It looks like you ain't got any choice at all."

"Which means what?"

"Which means either I move in—or I blow the whistle on this joint. It's as easy as that. I take over—now—or there ain't any business."

Mr. Stevenson sat bolt upright. "You wouldn't do that, Morano. You were in the Chicago deal yourself. You'd go down with us."

"Na—" Morano said, "nobody'll bother me. Nobody's got anything on me that would stick. I never saw you guys before in my life, see? What's more, nobody's going to know who done the singing about old man Cotterell's drug-running son-in-law. A tip like that buys plenty protection."

Then it happened.

Mr. Stevenson sprang from his chair, livid with rage, and lunged at Morano. His fist hit the little man on the side of the head, sending him reeling backward. Like a crazed animal Mr. Stevenson followed him, flinging himself on Morano, clawing at his throat as they both fell to the floor. I have no doubt he would have killed Morano then and there—all things being equal. But as I had already discovered, where Morano was concerned, nothing was equal. As the two men hit the floor, the door opened and in an instant Mr. Stevenson was standing upright, his arms locked in the grasp of a couple of Morano's men. Savage-looking desperadoes, they were, and I feared they would beat Mr. Stevenson to a pulp. But Morano said from the floor, "Leave him alone, boys. I don't want him marked up. I don't want he should have to explain anything to anybody."

Morano got up from the floor, brushing off his natty clothes, straightening his necktie. From his pocket he took a comb and carefully restored his shiny black hair to its gleaming perfection. Then he said, "Sit him in that chair—and scram."

They hustled Mr. Stevenson back to his chair. I noticed one of the men run his hands over Mr. Stevenson's clothing—searching for a weapon, I suppose. Mr. Stevenson, white and shaken, sat down and the men went out of the room. Morano walked over and stood before Mr. Stevenson. "See what I mean?" he said.

Mr. Stevenson nodded sullenly.

"Okay. Now we understand each other. No need we should get in each other's hair anymore. You do like I say, and I'll take care of you. That goes for the professor, too." He grinned evilly at me.

"Now," he went on, "from here on I run this show. We split fifty-fifty, half for me, half for the two of you. Not so good for you as before—but I got heavy expenses."

"It—it's not fair," Mr. Stevenson said weakly. "There won't be enough..."

"It's fair," Morano snapped. "It's fair because I say it's fair. If you don't like it you can always get out, just so long as the professor stays." He turned to me. "Maybe the professor would like that? A full share? The professor would not try to cross anybody—except maybe you, Stevenson."

But Morano's cocky humor didn't last very long. His cold gaze returned to Mr. Stevenson. "Now we know where we stand from here on. So there's only one more little matter to settle—a little matter of a hundred grand."

Mr. Stevenson stiffened in his chair. "A hundred grand? For what?"

"For the time between now and when you walked out on me."

"You're out of your mind," Mr. Stevenson cried. "I don't have that kind of money. I've lost every cent I made in this racket."

"That's too bad," Morano said sorrowfully. "That's really what you call too bad." Then his face froze. "You'll get it up. And you'll get it up in a month."

Mr. Stevenson paled. "You're insane, Morano. I couldn't raise that much in that time. I need a lot more time. Then maybe my wife..."

Morano said with contempt, "Your wife! You couldn't get a nickel from your wife."

"You don't understand," Mr. Stevenson said hoarsely. "She's a sick woman. She's going to die… in a little while. She's leaving me every-thing… It's in her will. Wait just a few months… That's all, I'm sure…"

"I don't wait for nobody to die—ever," Morano said, "and you don't either—if you're smart. If somebody is supposed to die—they die."

"Good God!" Mr. Stevenson cried, "I can't…"

"Never mind what you can or you can't," Morano barked. "You get that dough up in thirty days."

"But—"

"Look—" Morano grinned. "I don't want to be too hard on you, Stevenson…"

"Yes?" Mr. Stevenson asked hopefully.

"You have too much trouble, you come to me. Maybe I give you—some help."

That was on the night of July 17. I haven't seen either Mr. Morano or Mr. Stevenson since. And now—as I've already given you the final message, I believe the rest explains itself quite simply…

The phone shook in Leona's hand. Frightened tears started in her eyes. Her body felt drained and empty and she could scarcely control the trem-bling of her jaw. "Explains itself—how?" she managed to ask. "Where's my husband? Where's Mr. Stevenson now?"

"I wish I knew, Mrs. Stevenson," the weary voice replied. "Perhaps if you were to try the Caledonia number…"

"The—Caledonia—number?" she asked.

"The number I gave you in the message," he told her. "And now—if you will check it all over with me…"

"I can't," she cried, "I can't. I've forgotten."

"Then I will repeat it for you once more, Mrs. Stevenson. Point one: the house at 20 Dunham Terrace was burned down this afternoon by Mr. Evans. Point two: Mr. Evans escaped. Point three: Mr. Morano was arrested. Point four: it is not necessary to raise the money as it was not Mr. Morano who tipped off the police."

"It doesn't matter," Leona mumbled. "It doesn't matter. Just give me that Caledonia number—the one for Mr. Stevenson."

"Point five," Mr. Evans said evenly. "Point five: Mr. Evans is at the Manhattan address, but he is leaving now and may be found at Caledonia 5:1133."

"Caledonia 5:1133," Leona repeated, scrawling the number on the bit of memo paper with her lipstick.

"After midnight—" Evans said quietly. Then, with something that might have been a sigh, he added, "Thank you very much, Mrs. Stevenson. And good-bye."

After Evans had hung up, she continued to stare at the scarlet numbers streaming across the paper, as though if she took her eyes away they might disappear. Mechanically, numbly, she dialed. The first time she tried, the trembling of her fingers made her slip and she had to start over again. As she moved the dial, the tension within her mounted so that every breath was a painful effort. This time she completed the call, and after two purring rings the phone was picked up at the other end.

A man said, "Caledonia 5:1133."

Fear, fright, the approach of hysteria pitched her voice unnaturally high. "Caledonia 5:1133?" she asked. "Is Mr. Stevenson there?"

"Who, lady?"

"Mr. Stevenson. Mr. Henry Stevenson. I was told to call by—by a Mr. Evans."

"Stevenson, you say? Just a minute—I'll see." She heard the thud as he laid the phone down. Straining to listen, she could hear his departing footsteps. Then silence. The seconds slowly passed. Her heart beat wildly as though it were struggling to fly from her breast. She clenched and unclenched her free hand, squeezing until her long nails bit into the flesh of her palm. Outside a low, moaning whistle drifted up from the river, and somewhere below someone—a policeman, perhaps?—rattled wood against an iron fence.

Suddenly the man was back. "Nope. He's not here, ma'am."

"Oh," she said, "Mr. Evans said he might be expected. Could I leave a message?"

"A message? We don't take no messages here, lady." The man seemed puzzled—and a little amused. "They wouldn't do no good here, lady."

"No?" she asked. "What number is this? Who—? What am I calling?"

"Caledonia 5:1133," the man said. "The City Morgue."

Now she sat motionless in the bed, desperately trying to piece together the macabre jigsaw of that night's happenings. Out of the dreamlike chaos of shock piled on shock she began to shape the truth. And as the stark outline grew more distinct, its enormity made her shudder. That such a thing could happen to her! That such evil could have found her out!

That awful phone call, she thought. Why had she been the one to hear those terrible criminals? Why had all her calls to Henry's office—the calls before she'd asked the operator to help—been answered by a busy signal? Who had been in Henry's office, if not Henry? And if someone, no matter who, had been using the phone in Henry's office, could one end of that mysterious crossed wire have been...? No—she wouldn't think of it. She'd force it from her mind. There were other things to think about.

What about Sally's story? That Henry was involved in some land of trouble with the authorities? She had to believe that—or at least part of it—for Evans had established the truth of it. If any of it was truth, that is, and not a plot to drive her out of her mind. Suppose Evans *was* telling the truth. Henry would then be hard-pressed to find that money, that hundred thousand dollars. And he couldn't. Unless he told the whole sordid story to Jim Cotterell! Which he'd never do! She marveled at the way Henry had managed to seem so—so normal these past few weeks. And as she did, she found herself recalling Sally's talk, the talk of years ago, when Sally had tried to tell her about the strange depths of Henry's character. Sally hadn't been lying!

What then was left for Henry to do? She knew the answer, of course. She had known it ever since Evans had finished talking with her. She could no longer exclude it from her thoughts, any more than she could exclude the real meaning of those crossed telephone wires.

And as the awful realization tore at the foundation of her reason, she heard again the grinding, clanking progress of a train across the bridge. Wisps of remembered conversation now floated freely across her consciousness... *our client... Then I wait until the train goes over the bridge... in case she should scream... is a knife okay... our client... our client... she's going to die... I don't wait for nobody to die... our client... our client...*

Frantic with fear she snatched up the phone again and dialed the operator.

"Your call, please?" How smooth! How impersonal!

"Give me the police," she cried brokenly.

"Ringing the Police Department."

In a few seconds the phone was picked up. "Police Station. Seventeenth Precinct. Sergeant Duffy speaking."

"This is Mrs. Stevenson again," she said. "I called you a little while ago..."

"Yes, ma'am. Mrs. Stevenson did you say?"

"Mrs. Henry Stevenson, at 43 Sutton Place. I called you about a phone call I overheard."

"Why, yes, ma'am. I remember it very well."

"Well, I wondered what—what you'd done about it?"

"It's right here on the blotter, ma'am," Duffy said cautiously.

"But—haven't you...?"

"We'll do everything we can, ma'am. If anything happens—"

"If anything *happens?*" she echoed. "Do you mean to say a thing has to happen before you do anything?"

"I told you before, ma'am, that when the information is vague there isn't much we can do."

"But…" She paused. She *couldn't* tell him. Even though it might be true, she couldn't. For in spite of everything, it might *not* be true. And if she told now, it would be irrevocable. She could never take it back. It would be the end of her dream. She couldn't tell the police. She'd have to find another way…

"I'm sorry to trouble you," she said faintly. "I thought perhaps you might at least have sent out a radio call…"

"That's up to Headquarters," Duffy said. "We pass along the tip, and it's up to them to take care of it. So far there hasn't been a call."

"Thank you," she said. "I—I hope it's all a mistake."

She hung up, thinking fearfully of her next step. She must do something, something to protect herself in case…

A detective agency? That might be one way of getting someone to watch over her, someone who could be sworn to secrecy. She glanced at the clock on her night table. Eleven! She didn't have much time. Trembling, she dialed the operator.

"I want a detective agency," she said nervously.

"You will find all detective agencies listed in the Classified Directory, madam."

"I haven't a Classified Directory—I mean—I don't have time—to look anything up—it—it's getting late."

"I will connect you with Information."

"No!" Leona shouted angrily. "You don't care what happens to me, do you? I could die—and you wouldn't care…!"

"I beg your pardon…?"

"Give me a hospital," Leona said.

"Is there a particular hospital?"

"Any hospital!" she shouted. "Any hospital at all—do you hear?"

"One moment, please."

11:00

She waited while the phone rang, looking uneasily about the room, glancing nervously at the half-open door, the shadowy pictures on the wall, the elegant debris on her night table and vanity. Soon the ringing stopped and a woman said, "Bellevue."

Leona said, "I want the Nurses' Registry, please."

"Whom do you wish to speak to?"

"I want the Nurses' Registry. I want a trained nurse. I want to hire her immediately for the night."

"I see," the woman said. "I will transfer your call."

"Nurses' Home," another voice murmured.

"I want to hire a nurse," Leona repeated. "I need one right away. It's very important that I get one right away."

"What is the nature of the case, madam?"

"The case? Why—I—I'm an invalid—and I'm all alone—I—don't know anyone in the city—and I've just had a frightful shock—I just can't be alone tonight."

"Have you been instructed to call by one of our doctors, madam?"

"No," Leona said, her voice rising peevishly, "but I fail to see why all this—this catechizing is necessary. After all, I expect to pay this person..."

"We quite understand that, madam," the voice went on calmly. "But this is a city hospital. It isn't private. We don't send nurses on cases unless an emergency is certified by one of our staff physicians. I'd suggest that you call one of the regular Nurses' Registries."

"But I don't know any," she wailed. "I can't wait. I'm desperately in need of help."

"I'll give you a number you may call. Schuyler 2:1037. Perhaps someone there will be able to assist you."

"Schuyler 2:1037. Thank you."

Again she worked the dial, its clicking beating like little hammers in her head. The phone's ringing seemed interminable, although it was only a matter of seconds before she got her answer.

"Center Registry for Nurses. Miss Jordan speaking."

"I want to hire a nurse—at once."

"And who is this calling, please?"

"Mrs. Stevenson. Mrs. Henry Stevenson, 43 Sutton Place. And it's very urgent."

"Have you been recommended to us by a doctor, Mrs. Stevenson?"

"No," she said impatiently. "But I'm a stranger here—and I'm ill— and I've been going through the most awful night. I can't be alone any longer."

"Well," Miss Jordan said doubtfully, "nurses are very scarce now. It's most unusual to send one out unless the doctor in charge has specifically stated that it's absolutely necessary."

"But it is necessary," she pleaded. "It is. I'm a sick woman. I'm alone in this house—I don't know where my husband is—I can't reach him. And I'm terribly frightened. If someone doesn't come at once—if something isn't done, I'm afraid I'll go out of my mind."

"I see," the woman said reflectively. "Well—I'll leave a message for Miss Phillips to call you as soon as she comes in."

"Miss Phillips? And when do you expect her?"

"Sometime around 11:30 or so..."

"Eleven *thirty!*"

And then she heard the click. It was a tiny click, a click in the phone. It was a sound she thought she had heard many times before.

"What was *that*?" she cried.

"What was what, madam?"

"That—click—just now—in my telephone. As though someone had lifted the receiver off the hook of the extension downstairs…"

"I didn't hear anything, madam."

"But I did!" she gasped in a voice almost suffocated by fear. "There's someone in this house… someone downstairs in the kitchen… and they're listening to me now. They're…" Terror gripped her and she screamed, hanging up the phone with a mechanical movement.

Clutching the bedclothes in an agony of fright she concentrated on the silence around her. Suddenly she heard a quiet tapping along the floor—slowly—steadily. She started up with a shudder, eyes wild, her hand raised to her contorted face.

"Who is it?" she called frantically. "Who's there?"

She was like a creature at bay. As the tapping continued—slowly—relentlessly, she stared in horrified fascination at the door to her room—waiting—waiting. Suddenly she yelled, hoarsely, "Henry—! HENRY!"

No answer. The steady, remorseless tapping went on. She threw back the coverlet, trying to get out of the bed. But paralyzing fear sapped her strength. She stretched and strained, then collapsed against the pillows—frozen with terror—unable to move. Her wild gaze roamed the room, fastening for an instant on the half-open door, then darting past it for fear of what she might see. The sound of a roaring motor truck rolled up from the street, and looking toward the window she discovered at last the source of the tapping—the weighted window drapes stirring in the freshening breeze!

For a while she knew relief. The pounding of her heart subsided. Doctor Alexander must be right, she thought. It's sound as a bell. And suddenly she was tearfully glad. If she lived through this night, she'd never stay in bed again, never. She'd get strong as quickly as she could. But the odor of danger was everywhere. She must do something quickly. How could she escape that room!

Automatically she reached for the telephone. But in midair her hand froze. Whom should she call? Who would help her now? The silent listener somewhere in the house had heard her talking to that nurse. What chance had she of avoiding his frightful presence now?

She lay there in a mist of indecision, terror strangling her ability to sort out the teeming product of her brain. Then, as so often before, the brooding, massive silence was shattered by the telephone's sharp ring. She snatched it up quickly, clutching at any straw.

"Hello?" she said with pitiful expectancy.

The maddening, unconcerned voice of an operator greeted her. "New Haven is calling Mrs. Henry Stevenson. Is Mrs. Stevenson there?"

"Yes," Leona cried, adding with sinking heart. "But I haven't any time now... call back later. I can't talk—"

"I have a person-to-person call for Mrs. Henry Stevenson from Mr. Henry Stevenson. You do not wish to accept the call, madam?"

Thunderstruck, Leona asked, *"Mr. Henry Stevenson...?"* Almost in tears, she said, "Did you say—Mr.?—from New Haven?"

"Do you wish to accept the call, madam?"

And now the fantastic hope grew that it was all a lie—a terrible dream. Nothing so awful could have been conceived by the man whose life she had shared for so long. Yet she knew it wasn't a dream. If there was only some other answer to the whole thing—! Well, at least she could ask Henry to call the police. That would bring things out in the open.

"Yes... I'll... accept it," she said.

She waited tensely, hovering, breathless. She heard the Long Distance Operator's little ring, and then, "Go ahead, New Haven."

11:05

The railroad station in New Haven was a lonely place so late at night. The few people who walked about, or sat idly on benches, were mere specks in its vastness. Footsteps clicked on the stone floors and echoed to the high ceilings. There was an emptiness that could almost be felt, a strange unreality—as though the station, drained of its daytime bustle, slumbered through the night.

Under a huge clock a row of telephone booths extended along the wall, all save one dark and empty. Beside the door of the occupied booth stood a handsome valise—a pigskin affair, with the initials H.S. neatly stamped in gold near its center lock. In the lighted booth Henry Stevenson waited to talk with his wife.

He was hatless. Under unruly brown hair his face was heavily handsome—an attractive face with wide-set, thickly lashed eyes, straight fleshy nose, powerfully molded mouth and jaw. As he stood there staring at the telephone, his expression was one of grimness and determination. He looked like a young man who knew very well what he was doing, knew that what he was doing must be done.

At last he heard the Long Distance Operator say, "Go ahead, New Haven."

"Hello. That you, darling?" he asked quietly.

"*Henry*! Henry, where *are* you?" He could almost feel her clutching at him over all those miles.

"Why—I'm on my way to Boston, dear. I stopped off in New Haven. Didn't you get my wire?"

"Yes. I—I got it... But—but I don't understand—"

"Nothing to understand, dear. I couldn't reach you before. Your line was busy so often. I thought I'd call now and see how you were. I was sorry—about leaving so unexpectedly—but I knew you'd be all right."

"I'm *not* all right—I'm..." she began wildly. "There's someone in this house right now—I'm sure of it."

An ugly, malevolent light gleamed for an instant in his eyes. His nostrils flared, and he drew in his breath sharply.

"Nonsense, dear. How could there be?" he said. "You're not there alone?"

"Of course I am," she replied, whining. "I'm all alone. Who else could be here? You gave Larsen the night off..."

"So I did," he admitted gravely.

"And you promised to be home at six sharp."

"Did I?" he asked innocently. "I don't remember."

"You most certainly did," she said. "And I've been alone here for hours. I've been getting all kinds of horrible phone calls that I don't understand... and Henry... I want you to call the police... do you hear me?... Tell them to come here at once."

He wondered at the panic in her voice. She was really frightened. Yet—it didn't make sense. What could she know? He could understand it if she were only irritated—Leona had an oversized capacity for irritation. But this kind of fear was another thing. "Now Leona," he said crisply. "No need to be so nervous."

"*Nervous!*"

"You know you're perfectly safe in that house. Larsen certainly must have locked the doors before she left."

"I know," she said weakly, "But—I heard—someone—someone pick up the phone in the kitchen. I'm sure I did."

"Nonsense," he said. "The house is locked. There's that private patrolman. And the telephone's right by your bed. What's more, you're in the heart of New York City, Leona. Safest place in the world."

"I'd feel better if you'd call the police, Henry. I called them. They wouldn't pay any attention to me." She started to sob in self-pity.

"Look," he said, "I'm in New Haven. If I call from here, the police'll think I'm crazy. Why the police, anyway? Maybe if you call Doctor Alexander?"

String it out, he thought, glancing at his watch. Let her run on—a few more minutes. What could she do then? He was smiling now, a queer half smile that transformed his brooding face into a mask of glowering evil. Shifting his position in the booth, he glanced casually out of the door for an instant, then turned back toward the phone. He had scarcely noticed the burly, white-haired man with dark skin and the large liquid eyes lounging a few paces from the booth.

But what was this Leona was saying?

"Henry! What do you know about a man named Evans?"

"Evans?" he asked, taken by surprise.

"Yes," she said. "Waldo Evans."

"Never heard the name in my life, Leona. What makes you ask?"

"He called me up—tonight—I had a long talk with him... about *you*!"

11:10

The huge man with the white hair and the dark, permanently sad face had moved just far enough away from the booth to be out of sight of its occupant. Otherwise he might have noticed Henry grow pale as death— the pallor pointing up the defiant set of his jaw. But the man was not interested in Henry's telephone call. He was only interested in Henry. He waited patiently, observing the line of booths, absently fingering the badge in his pocket.

"About me!" Henry said as naturally as possible. "What could he have had to say about me?"

"He told me some terrible things. Some of it sounded... insane. But there were parts that sounded true..."

"A crackpot," Henry said. "You mustn't listen to every crackpot who calls. Now, just try and forget it..."

"He told me—you'd been stealing dope from Daddy's company. Is that true?"

Henry snorted. "True? Now see here, Leona, I'm a little hurt that you even bother to tax me with that kind of rot. You must have had a bad dream..."

"Dream!" she shrilled. "I haven't been dreaming, Henry. He left some kind of message for you. He said to tell you that the house on Staten Island had been burned down—and that the police knew everything. He said someone named Morano had been arrested..."

"What!" Henry snapped. "What was that you said?"

"And—I—I'd never have believed him—except there was that Mrs. Lord—you remember—Sally Hunt—and she told me the same things."

There was a silence for a second, and Leona called, "Are you still there—Henry?"

He wet his lips. "Yes," he said. "Yes, I'm here."

"They said you were a criminal," she babbled, "a desperate man... And Evans said—you—you—you wanted me—to die!"

"I—" he started to say, but there was no stopping the flood.

"That money—Henry—the hundred thousand dollars. Why didn't you ask me for it? I'd have got it for you—gladly—if I'd only known."

"Forget it," he muttered.

"Is it too late?" she cried. "I'll get it for you now—if it isn't too late."

"It's all right," he said. "Forget it."

Now the tears that had been threatening streamed down her face. Her voice was hoarse and strangled.

"I didn't mean to be so awful to you, Henry," she said. "I—only did it—because—I loved you. I guess I was afraid you didn't really love me. I was afraid—afraid you'd run away—and leave me all alone..."

11:11

Henry remembered now the man he had seen standing near the booth. He looked through the door and, seeing no one, cautiously opened it to get a broader view. The man was there, not far away. He was watching the booths. Henry shut the door. He called into the phone.

"Leona?"

"Yes."

"Leona, there's something you've got to do."

"Will you forgive me—first, Henry?" she sobbed. "Will you?"

"For God's sake," he said brutally, "will you stop that nonsense and listen to me?"

"All—right," she whispered.

"Now do just as I say, will you? I want you to get out of bed..."

"I—I can't," she moaned. "I can't."

"You've got to," he commanded. "You've got to get out of that bed—and walk out of that room. Go into the front bedroom. Get to the window and scream—scream out into the street."

He waited, tense, fighting the fear within him. He heard her breathing heavily into the phone.

"I can't!" she mumbled piteously. "I can't move, Henry. I'm too frightened. I've tried and tried. But I can't move."

"Keep trying," he urged. "Don't you know I'll burn if you don't... I'll..."

"Burn!" she shrieked. "What...?"

"You've got to move, Leona. Try again. If you don't you've only got three more minutes to live!"

11:12

"What...?" There was a terrible gagging in her voice.

"Don't talk anymore, Leona." His own voice broke with fear. Sweat poured over his body. He leaned heavily against the wall of the booth to take the strain away from his shaking knees. "Don't talk. Get out of that bed. You've got to. It's all true, Leona. All of it, you hear me. I'm in pretty deep. I was desperate—I even tried—tonight I arranged—to have you..."

"Henry!" A great wail of terror tore from her lips. "Henry! There's someone—coming up the stairs!"

"Get out," he shouted madly. "Get out of that bed. Walk, Leona."

"I *can't.*"

"You must! You must!"

"Henry!" she cried again. "Henry! Save me! *Save* me!"

No longer able to control himself—the awful certainty of his fate and hers sapping the last remnant of courage—he shivered all over. "Please, Leona," he cried, "they'll get me—they'll *know*—they'll find out from Morano."

And then, through the telephone, he heard a sound—faintly—a sound that might have been a train grinding across the bridge. And above it Leona's bloodcurdling scream, "*Henry!*"

11:15

For one fleeting moment after her scream she clutched the telephone. Then she threw it back on its hook. Her eyes glazed with unspeakable fright, her heart hammering mercilessly, she heard the onrush of the pounding train. Gasping and gagging she tried to drag herself off the bed. But she might have been bound with bands of steel. She couldn't move. Louder and louder, rending the black stillness, came the train, until there was nothing in the flight but its thundering roar. Nothing could be heard above it. Not even her last, terrible sigh.

The train passed, and in the room there was no sound except a coarse breathing—a stealthy movement away from the bed.

Suddenly the phone began to ring. Rubber shoes shuffled softly across the floor. A hand in a bloodstained glove reached down and lifted the instrument from its base. Henry's voice, trembling with desperate hope, floated up, "Leona! LEONA!"

There was a pause. Then a deep, guttural voice said, "Sorry, wrong number..."

11:16

THE DUST

BRIAN EVENSON

I

A few days after they arrived, the baffles started to clog. They had expected the baffles to clog—that wasn't a surprise. Grimur had been trained to unclog them, and now he trained one of the men. Trained Orvar, in fact: with a skeleton crew, just enough of them to prepare for the arrival of the full contingent three months later if the site proved productive, there was little at the moment for Orvar to do.

At first Orvar protested. As head of security, cleaning baffles was not part of his job description. Grimur just stared patiently, with his pale, steady eyes, and waited, impassive, for Orvar's protestations to run down. When they did, Grimur simply opened the contracts file, called Orvar's up, and appended a clause assigning him the cleaning of the baffles. Then he turned the screen toward Orvar for his thumbprint.

"Supposing I refuse?" asked Orvar.

"You won't," said Grimur.

Orvar looked uncomfortable. "You could clean them," he said. "You know how to do it already."

Grimur shook his head. "I have other things to do," he said. "You don't. Not yet."

That wasn't entirely true, Orvar thought. Though there were only seven men, not counting himself and Grimur, there had already been a fight, a drunken one. It had nearly cost a man an eye. Orvar had broken it up, separated the men, but there was no brig yet—that would come later, after the arrival of the next vessel. For now, all they had was the space that would become a brig: three doorless, unreinforced walls, exposed ductwork. There was no way to hold someone in.

So he had had to improvise. He had chained the uninjured man, Jansen, to the rock drill halfway down the shaft and left him bellowing there to grow sober. The other man, Wilkinson, he'd restrained with nylon cord before closing the cut above his eye with suture tape. When he was done, he propped him up against the wall in what would one day be the brig.

"What gives you the right?" the man complained in an uneven slur.

"What gives me the right?" repeated Orvar, surprised. "This is my job."

But Wilkinson wasn't listening. He had already passed out.

Orvar stared at the screen for another moment and then pressed his thumb against the scanner, just as he and Grimur had always known he would. Grimur nodded once, curtly, then stood.

"Come on, then," he said.

They clambered through the partially built complex, past the workers' bunkroom, around the piles of boxes and through the stacks of paneling, to arrive at the system that brought in the unbreathable air from outside and scrubbed it. There was, Orvar felt, always a bad taste to the air afterward, a taint to it. He had been feeling lightheaded. If he ran or otherwise exerted himself, as he had when breaking up the fight, his head throbbed.

Some of the particulate matter was so fine that it passed through the filters and baffles, Grimur was telling him. That was the problem with the filters, he said: they had not been designed for this environment.

He showed Orvar how to close the baffles and shut the filtration down, and then how to remove the filters and clear them. When he took one out Orvar could see the sides of the channel coated in a thin layer of dust. Grimur banged the filter softly against the metal wall, and a haze of dust arose and floated in the air. The cloud stayed there, motionless. Orvar could see it, but when he passed his hand through it he felt nothing. When he drew his hand back, though, it had taken on a faint sheen.

"Ideally," Grimur said, "we'd do this in a contained space. But we haven't built one yet."

Orvar nodded. "Only the necessities," he said.

Grimur pointed at the remaining filters. "I'll leave you to do the others. Clean them and slide them back in, then turn the system on. Put your hand up here," he said, and pointed to the first vent in the ductwork above. "If you feel air pushing out, then all is as it should be."

"And if I don't?"

"Then take the filters out and clean them again."

It was not a hard job. There was, to be truthful, nothing to it, and it gave Orvar something to do. He'd been languishing, he realized. Cleaning the filters helped him pass the time.

There had been no more fights. When he'd unchained Jansen, the man had been sheepish and embarrassed. He'd asked immediately how Wilkinson was.

"He lost an eye," said Orvar initially, but when he saw Wilkinson's pained expression he decided to drop it. "Or could have, anyway," he said. "No more fighting."

As for Wilkinson, when Orvar had asked what he'd said to set Jansen off, he'd just shrugged. He'd been so drunk he didn't even remember the fight. He had been surprised to awaken tied up. Why, Wilkinson wanted to know, had Jansen attacked him?

"I always liked him," Wilkinson said. "I thought he liked me too."

"He does like you," said Orvar. "And how do you know that you weren't the one attacking him?"

"Was I?" asked Wilkinson.

Orvar didn't know. "You didn't lose an eye," Orvar told him. "You probably won't even have a scar." And then he made him promise to be careful the next time he drank.

So, no more fights, but more and more dust in the filters. He banged them out twice daily; sometimes, especially first thing in the morning, he would have to knock them against the wall repeatedly before he'd feel a healthy current of air flowing from the vent. After a week or so, even the airflow from the just-cleaned vents seemed to be growing weaker. Or was he just imagining it?

Working hours were lonely, with half the crew drilling in the shaft and the other half analyzing and sorting samples in the makeshift space that might one day be a lab. For now they made do with a series of plastic sheets tacked to the ductwork above to form a rough square enclosure, sheets that did little to keep out the dust that now seemed to be every-where. It was on them all, a kind of pollenlike layer that made their skin gray. Every night Orvar would use enough of his water ration to dampen a cloth in order to wipe his body down, but the dust seemed to be on him again immediately. It wasn't gritty or grimy; he could hardly feel it. But there was still the nagging awareness of it being there, on him, on everything.

Find anything? he'd ask each man at some point in the day, sometimes more than once. They always shook their heads. The site was not, or at least not yet, productive. They had another month, perhaps, to make it so, before the company would have to decide whether to dispatch their reinforcements or simply send a vessel to retrieve them.

Sometimes Orvar would go to watch the progress being made in the shaft, the men shouting at one another over the noise of the rock drill. He would stand at the entrance, feeling the rumble in his legs, and then he would turn and go back.

At other times he would go to the office, the only room in the complex that qualified as finished. It was sparsely furnished—computer system, communications console, a series of control panels regulating the temperature of the complex, monitoring the environment, or perhaps just in stasis, awaiting the arrival of the machinery they would monitor. There was the single metal desk, foldable but nonetheless solid, and a set of metal folding chairs, all stacked against the wall except for the one Orvar habitually used. Grimur's chair was different, an upholstered and wheeled thing that despite the vessel's space restrictions he'd managed to fit in. Behind it, near the wall, was a bedroll. Grimur slept alone in here, rather than in the bunkroom.

Grimur always seemed to be busy, though what he was doing was hard for Orvar to say. He suspected Grimur had even less to do than he did, yet the man was always at his computer, always typing. He often kept his hands poised over the keys while they spoke.

He would ask Orvar how he was, then nod in acknowledgment no matter how Orvar answered. He would ask about the men, and nod there as well.

"No more fighting?" he might say, one eyebrow raised. And Orvar would explain that no, everything seemed to be going well.

"Ah," Grimur would respond, half distracted. "And the drilling?"

"They haven't come across anything yet," said Orvar.

Only then might a shadow flicker across Grimur's face. Orvar did not know what sort of involvement his superior had had in choosing the site, what he was likely to lose if the site proved nonproductive. But he could tell he would lose something.

At least the rock they were boring into was igneous and solid—they had gotten that right, even if the site wasn't proving productive. No dust coming out of the shaft. The dust had seeped in, instead, drifting into the shaft through the filtration system. The men had noticed this. It seemed to be everywhere now, a little thicker every second. It hung in the air, a delicate haze that gave a blur to the lights.

Moving about the complex, dragging a finger against the wall, Orvar began to think of himself as being underwater. It was as if he were walking along the ocean floor and had come upon the remnants of a city, flooded somehow and forgotten, never meant to be found again.

And yet, he thought, *this is where I live.*

The men were huddled together talking, but fell silent as he came farther down the shaft. All of the men were present, not just the extractors—the testers were there as well.

"Everything all right?" he asked.

"Just taking a break," one of them said. Lewis.

"Find anything yet?" he asked. Another of the men, Yaeger, he thought, kept brushing off his arms, over and over again. A sort of nervous tic.

"What do you mean?" asked Gordon.

Orvar stared. "What do I mean? The same thing I meant yesterday."

"The site's not going to be productive," said Gordon. "If it was, it would have happened already."

"Shut up, Gordon," said Durham. "Don't harass Orvar."

Orvar shrugged. He was trying not to pay attention to Yaeger, to the restless, endless movement of his hands, brushing, brushing.

"Maybe they made a mistake," he said. "We knew that was a possibility. That's why they send a skeleton crew first. We could still find something."

Gordon shook his head. He was one of the extractors, Orvar remembered. An experienced one.

"I've been on a project that folded," the man said. "By now, we should be packing up."

"Maybe Grimur thinks there's still a chance," said Orvar.

But Gordon did not want to be appeased. "No," he said. "Something's going on."

"Don't be paranoid," said Lee.

"I don't know what it is," said Gordon, "but it's something."

"Gordon," said Orvar, looking him steadily in the face. "There's no hidden project. I promise."

"You trust Orvar, don't you?" Durham said to Gordon. "You can see he's telling the truth."

Gordon reluctantly nodded. "Maybe Grimur just hasn't told him."

"No," said Orvar. "I know Grimur. He'd tell me. Do you want me to ask him?"

"He'll probably lie," mumbled Gordon.

"I'll ask him," said Orvar. "I'll know if he's lying."

"And you'll tell us," prompted Jansen.

Orvar reached out and touched Gordon on the shoulder. The man flinched.

"I'll tell you," said Orvar. "I promise."

*　　*　　*

The shaft seemed longer on the way back. He was out of breath by the time he'd gotten within the complex walls again. He was having trouble gathering his thoughts. *What's wrong with me?* he wondered, but shook it off. No sense letting Gordon's paranoia infect him. Still, what if Gordon was right? What if there was a hidden project? But Grimur would have told him. As security officer, it made sense that he would be told. Didn't it?

Even if he hadn't been told, Grimur wouldn't be able to hide it from him. He was sure, or almost sure, that that was true.

He started toward the office but then, reconsidering, doubled back to check the filters.

When he held his hand up to the vent opening, there was a slight trickle of air, but only very slight. He turned off the system, opened the baffles, removed the filters. Before he could start cleaning, Wilkinson was there, next to him.

"What's wrong?" asked Wilkinson. "Broken?"

"Routine cleaning," said Orvar. "I do this every day."

Wilkinson narrowed his eyes. "But you already did it once today," he said.

Orvar hesitated. Then, slowly, he explained that yes, he had already done it once today, but most days he did it several times, just to be safe. All the while he was thinking, *Wilkinson has been watching me. Why?* Wilkinson was doing the same thing with his arms that Yaeger had been doing earlier, brushing at them again and again, though not quite as frequently. *What's wrong with Wilkinson?*

He watched the man's eyes flit hurriedly about their sockets. *Maybe it's nothing,* he thought. *We'll all be a little nervous, until the site proves productive.* He tried to remember what it was that Wilkinson actually did.

"Which team are you on?" he asked.

"Team?" said Wilkinson, surprised. His hands stopped in midbrush. He squinted. "Are there teams? I thought we were all in this together."

"No," said Orvar. "Where do you work, I mean. The drill or testing the samples?"

Relief washed over the man's face, but was quickly lacquered over by a gnarled layer of suspicion. "Why do you want to know?"

Orvar spread his hands in front of him. "It's just a question, Wilkinson," he said. "Nothing to worry about."

Wilkinson thought about this for a moment, then finally said, "The drill?"

"And you're on break now?" asked Orvar. "Is this how you usually spend your break?"

"I should be getting back," Wilkinson said. A moment later he was retreating, casting nervous glances over his shoulder.

Grimur was hunched over his computer. He barely glanced up as Orvar entered and took a seat.

Orvar waited, his gaze wandering around the room. Nothing to look at, really: Grimur's crumpled bedclothes just visible around the desk's corner, the monitoring panel lit up with green and amber lights, the computer's lid. Past which he could see Grimur's haggard-looking face. He hadn't shaved. His eyes were bloodshot.

Finally Grimur closed the computer, leaned back. Over tented fingers he stared at Orvar.

"Well?" he said.

"They still haven't found anything."

"Then they should keep digging," Grimur said. "They haven't stopped, have they?"

Orvar shook his head. "They're still digging," he said. He hesitated. He was turning the question over in his head, trying to decide how best to phrase it. Whether to phrase it at all. Now that he was here, sitting across from Grimur, it seemed ludicrous. There was no conspiracy, he told himself, only Grimur still doggedly hoping to find something. The simplest explanations were usually correct.

Grimur gestured to the monitoring panel. "You see the amber lights?" he asked.

"Yes," said Orvar. "What about them?"

"Air quality," he said. "You need to clean the filters."

"I just cleaned them," Orvar said.

Grimur shook his head. "As time goes on and the dust builds up, you'll have to clean them more often."

"I've been cleaning them at least twice a day."

"Ah," said Grimur. "I see."

"Shall I clean them again?"

"No, no," said Grimur, absently. "Maybe the monitoring system hasn't caught up." But then he said, "You know, on second thought, it can't hurt. Clean them again."

He stood, moved around to sit on the front edge of his desk. He was brushing his arms, Orvar noticed. Not exactly in the way that either Wilkinson or Yaeger had done it, but still. *Am I doing it too?* wondered Orvar. He glanced down at his hands. For a moment they seemed like someone else's.

"What do you think it's doing to us?" asked Orvar.

"What?"

"This dust," he said. "If it's building up like this in the ventilator, what's it doing inside our bodies?"

Grimur was staring at him, frowning. "What makes you think it's doing anything?"

"Maybe it's not," said Orvar, suddenly cautious.

"The body metabolizes it," said Grimur. "It isn't hurting us. The company wouldn't send us out here if it was."

"You know that for a fact?" asked Orvar.

Grimur didn't answer. Instead he stopped brushing his arms and sat back down. "Clean the filters," he said. "Make sure there's air coming out of the vents afterward."

But Orvar didn't stand. "Some of the men are worried," he said.

Grimur shrugged. "There's always a chance a site won't be productive," he said. "They know that. They get paid either way."

Orvar shook his head. "No," he said. "It's more than that. They think that we're here for some other reason."

"Like what?"

"They don't know," Orvar admitted. "A hidden project."

Grimur guffawed, spread his hands. "Out here? What could it possibly be? Don't be ridiculous."

Orvar watched the man's face as he said this. It was calm, relaxed, giving nothing away. There was no reason not to believe him. But no reason to believe him either.

"They think there's a conspiracy," Orvar said. "They think you're part of it."

Grimur gestured to the computer, to the control panel. "I have enough to worry about without their paranoia," he said. He leaned forward, the corners of his mouth turning down. "Who's the security officer here?"

"Me," said Orvar.

"Then it's your worry."

There was no reason to distrust Grimur. No, the men were simply restless, dissatisfied that the site wasn't productive. They couldn't understand why Grimur kept them working. But Orvar understood. At the very least it kept them busy, stopped them from having any more fights. And yet he understood something else: there would come a time when everything tilted the other way, and the paranoia caused by fruitlessly continuing to dig would do greater damage than shuttering the site.

All this dust, he thought, knocking the filters clean again. Or not clean, exactly—they weren't coming close to clean now. *Maybe the dust is the problem.* He'd felt dizzy ever since they'd landed. The air tasted strange, and he could feel the particles on his skin, clogging his pores, in his throat, thickening. Wasn't it possible that the dust was clogging not only the vents but him? Wouldn't it be in their lungs? Their blood?

And what if the dust wasn't just dust, but something else entirely? *Like what?*

He didn't know. Something organic, something alive.

He shook his head and forced a laugh. *Now who's paranoid?* He was the security officer. He was supposed to be keeping things stable. How could he do that if he started to think such things?

He raised his hand and held it just below the vent. No air coming out, none at all.

For a moment his heart caught in his throat: sheer blind panic. And then he realized he'd simply forgotten to turn the system back on.

When he checked again, there was a little current of air. Nothing substantial, but it was there, a little air, definitely flowing. He wondered if the lights in Grimur's office would be green now.

He wondered, too, how worried he should be.

Halfway to the shaft he realized someone was following him. At first, he thought he was imagining it, the dust-ridden air echoing his own foot-falls back at him, but then he tripped, and for a moment, he heard the sounds behind him separate from his own.

He turned quickly and looked back down the hall. He would have thought less of it if he'd been anywhere else, but there should have been no surprises here. Nothing alive for tens of thousands of miles except for himself and the others. There was only the corridor, ill-lit, littered with boxes and stacked paneling and various supplies. Plenty of places for someone to hide.

He considered retracing his steps, going after them, but instead he kept going. He undid the fastener of his holster, holding his hand loose and ready just above the pistol's butt. *Probably nothing*, he told himself. But he still had to force himself not to hurry.

He turned into the bunkroom and flattened himself against the wall, gun drawn now. He held his breath and waited.

For a long moment, nothing happened, and then he heard the quiet scraping of shoes in the hall. Once they'd gone past the door, he risked a look out. Gordon, at a little distance, just turning down the mouth of the shaft.

Probably nothing, he told himself. *Probably Gordon wasn't following me. Or if he was, it was just to prove to himself that I was on his side.*

Am I? he wondered.

The men were disturbed, upset. And as Grimur had reminded him, it was his responsibility to handle them.

At the mouth of the shaft, he met Yaeger. The man jumped, startled. *Startled because I surprised him, or for some other reason?* wondered Orvar.

"All well?" asked Orvar, trying to render his voice hearty, reassuring.

"Yeah, sure," said Yaeger, not quite willing to meet his eye. But he lingered.

He was rubbing his arms again, a little more quickly now.

"I spoke to Grimur," said Orvar.

"Yeah?" said Yaeger. "So what is it?"

"What's what?"

"Why are we really here?"

Orvar shook his head. "No," he said. "I was right. It's business as usual."

"But you heard Gordon," said Yaeger. "If the site was productive it already would have happened. How's that business as usual?"

"No," said Orvar. "Gordon was on a very different site on a very different planet. He doesn't know."

"If you say so," Yaeger said.

"I do say so," Orvar said. "I'm not lying, Yaeger."

"I'm not Yaeger," said Yaeger. "I'm Lee."

This threw him. "You're Lee?" Orvar said. "I could have sworn you were Yaeger."

"Yeah, well," said the man Orvar couldn't help but think of as Yaeger. "I'm Lee."

"Okay," he said, and the ersatz Yaeger twitched and brushed his arms again. Was he really called Lee? It was impossible for Orvar to believe he'd been wrong all this time. But why would he lie?

"What's wrong with you?" he asked, before starting down the shaft. "Can you stop doing that?"

"Doing what?" asked Yaeger or Lee. When Orvar mimicked him, he folded his arms.

"It's this dust," he said. "It's everywhere."

II

A few days later, the ventilation machinery began to rattle. At first it was hardly noticeable. Had Orvar not been standing there silently, holding his hand to the vent to feel if the air was flowing, he might not have noticed. But it was a little louder every time he went back, after that. He was cleaning the filters four times a day now. Soon he would have no time to do anything but clean filters.

By the time he informed Grimur, the rattle had become a grinding. They both stood beside the ventilator, staring.

"How long has it been doing this?" asked Grimur.

"Not long," said Orvar, evasively. Yes, in hindsight, he should have told Grimur earlier. "How are the readings?"

"Always amber now," Grimur said. "You're cleaning the filters diligently?"

Orvar nodded.

"Then we have a problem," said Grimur.

They stopped the machine and opened the access panel. On their knees, they stared through the narrow opening and up at the engine, Grimur shining his penlight at it. The whole thing was coated with dust, thick with it. Dust stuck to the engine like mold.

"Wipe it off as best you can," said Grimur. "They'll be here in less than a month."

"It's not going to do much good," said Orvar. He gently appropriated the penlight and shined it through the holes in the housing. Inside, the armature was thick with dust.

"You can vacuum it," said Grimur.

"With what?"

"They'll have something with the drilling equipment," the man said. "I think something was on the manifest. If not a vacuum then some kind of a blower."

And indeed, they did have a vacuum, Lee admitted a few minutes later. A small, handheld thing that they kept on the sample table.

"Only there's a problem," Lee added.

"Problem?"

"It stopped working."

Together they unscrewed it, only to find the whole casing packed with the powdery, polleny dust. The motor was burnt out, the circuitry shot.

"How did it get so bad?" Orvar asked.

Lee shrugged. "There's a lot of dust," he said. "It destroys everything."

*　　*　　*

When he returned to close the panel, Gordon was on his back staring up into the machine.

"What are you doing?" Orvar asked.

"What's wrong with it?" asked Gordon.

"Nothing's wrong," claimed Orvar. "I'm just cleaning it. Move over." He fell to his knees and wiped at the machinery as well as he could with a rag.

"That's not going to help any," said Gordon.

Orvar ignored him.

"What's wrong with it?" asked Gordon again, but Orvar chose not to answer.

He closed the cover and stood, brushing the dust off his pantlegs, his arms. He opened the baffles, shook the filters out, slid them back in place. Gordon just watched.

"Nothing to worry about," Orvar claimed again.

But when he started it up, it made a grinding noise.

Orvar, not knowing what else to do, shrugged and left. Gordon stayed near the machine, listening.

Later, when it began to smoke, Gordon was still there. By the time Orvar had been called and managed to open the access panel, the motor was dead.

Grimur, when Orvar finally went to him, looked even more haggard than usual. He already knew something was wrong: behind him, the entire control panel was winking red.

"Any chance of fixing it?" Grimur asked.

"I don't know," said Orvar. "Jansen and Lewis both have mechanical experience, but neither seem to be getting anywhere."

Grimur sighed. "I've sent a message. Or tried to. Communications have been intermittent at best."

"What do we do?" asked Orvar.

"We wait until the full crew arrives. They either repair the ventilation system or carry us out of here."

"We can't wait that long," Orvar said. "There's not enough air. We'll suffocate."

"No," said Grimur. He brandished a crumpled stack of paper, then handed it to Orvar. Orvar took it, looked through it. Measurements, computations of volume, followed by pages of equations. At the end, on the final page, was a single circled number, 24, drawn awkwardly—the 2 a quick single stroke, the 4 itself traced over several times.

"That's the number of days," said Grimur. "That's how long we'll last without ventilation, assuming that I've properly calculated the cubic footage of the structure and figured the current oxygen mixture correctly, and assuming that the oxygen spreads evenly and that everybody's oxygen consumption is a quarter liter per minute. No exercise, no strenuous activity, and we should be fine."

"When are they coming for us?"

"Twenty-one days, nine hours, fifty-two minutes," Grimur said. "We should be fine," he repeated. "We'll have air to spare."

"All right," said Orvar.

"Still, we should fix the ventilator if we can," said Grimur. "Just in case."

"We'll keep trying," said Orvar. He handed the bundle back. "Why paper?" he asked.

"Excuse me?"

"Why do the calculations on paper? Why not the computer?"

"I started them on the computer," Grimur said. "But then the computer started to act strangely. Eventually it died. Too much dust," he said.

"All right," said Orvar. "Let's stay positive. We have enough air.

That's a good thing. What are you going to tell the others?"

"Nothing," said Grimur.

"Nothing?"

"No point in upsetting them."

"You have to tell them something," said Orvar.

"Why?"

"Even if there's enough oxygen, they'll feel worse as it diminishes. They'll experience hypoxia. So will we. Headaches, fatigue, shortness of breath, nausea. We'll stop thinking clearly. If it gets bad enough, we'll hallucinate—we'll fade in and out of consciousness. If they don't understand what's happening, it'll be all the worse."

"How do you know so much about it?" asked Grimur.

"I've been through it before," said Orvar. He didn't volunteer more. "You need to tell them, Grimur," he said again.

Grimur just shook his head. "No," he said.

"If you won't tell them," said Orvar, "I will. They have to know."

"All right," said Grimur. "Tell them. But I won't be responsible for what happens.

He entered the shaft, told the men to turn off the rock drill.

"Orders from on high?" asked Gordon eagerly. "We're giving up?"

"Not exactly on high," he said. "But the drill is off for good."

Together they all went to the testing area. He stopped the tests there, too.

Leaning against the table, he told them what was happening.

"I knew it," said Yaeger, or perhaps Lee, brushing his arms more frantically now. "I knew the dust would be the death of us."

"Ashes to ashes, dust to dust," said Wilkinson, smiling wryly.

"Shut up," said Lewis. He turned to Orvar. "What are we supposed to do?"

"We'll keep trying to fix the ventilation system," he said. "Maybe we'll get somewhere. We'll take apart the drill and scavenge it."

Lewis shook his head. "Nothing doing," he said. "The company makes them vandal-proof. We'd need some serious equipment to open it up."

"Well, do what you can," said Orvar.

"When do we run out of air?"

"We don't," said Orvar. "They're scheduled to arrive long before that. We won't have much oxygen, but we'll have enough to survive."

"You've been told to say that," said Gordon. " Grimur doesn't want us to know we're all going to die."

"No," said Orvar. "I've seen the equations. We're going to be okay."

"Then why bother trying to restart the ventilation system?" asked Jansen. "There's something you're not telling us."

"I'm telling you everything I know," said Orvar.

"Then why bother with the ventilation system?"

"Just in case," said Lee, or perhaps Yaeger. They did, in fact, Orvar noticed, look somewhat alike. "Just in case the pickup is late. Just in case we end up using more air than they've calculated we should. There's no conspiracy, Gordon," he said. "Orvar's our friend."

III

He left the others to talk among themselves, giving them time to get their heads around it. It was only then, once he had fulfilled what he saw as his responsibility, that he had a moment himself to reflect on what was happening.

He lay there on his bunk, staring up at the unfinished ceiling, the flimsy metal panels, the sealant binding their edges, the snarl of electric wire and exposed ductwork. Had Grimur taken into account that the ceiling was exposed, that that might give them just slightly more oxygen? If so, had he taken into account that a good part of that space was occupied with wires and other infrastructure? For that matter, how had Grimur accounted for the boxes and other items scattered down the hall, each of them a place where oxygen could not be? What about the men's bodies, the space they occupied?

It made him nervous. So many variables. Despite the pages and pages of equations, what if Grimur had gotten something wrong? Even a small error, at the wrong place in the equation, could mean that they wouldn't have enough oxygen.

And what about the shaft? That was space that Grimur probably hadn't considered. It was fairly long now, probably several thousand cubic feet of air. If Grimur hadn't taken that into account, then they had a great deal more oxygen than he believed. Perhaps even enough that they would be saved well before the hallucinations started.

No, on second thought, he shouldn't ask if Grimur had considered the shaft. It would only make things worse if it turned out that he had. Better not to know. Better to hope.

The last time this had happened to him he had, by the end of it, been mad enough that he thought he might never come back from it. Just three of them, alone on a free-floating craft, waiting for help to come— it had been all he could do to stop himself from opening the hatch and letting the little air that remained rush out. Not because he had wanted to kill himself, or the other two, but because with the way his mind had begun to work, the way it had gnarled itself, the void beyond the hatch had seemed like salvation. How would his mind respond this time? Would he survive it?

Neither of the other two men had survived. He couldn't remember their names—or rather he could, but wished he couldn't. One had gotten his throat cut, though Orvar was never quite sure whether the man had done it to himself or if their other shipmate had done it. Orvar was certain, or fairly certain, that he hadn't slit the man's throat himself. But after they'd rescued Orvar, they'd refused to answer any of his questions about what had happened. Probably understandable, considering the state he was in. But surely they could have answered them later, once he was himself again.

The other man had gotten it into his head that he'd have a better chance of surviving if he was the only one breathing a particular stretch of air. He'd forced his way into the hold and then disabled the lock. But the hold was quite a bit smaller than the rest of the ship, which meant the majority of the oxygen was out with Orvar rather than in with the other man. This was probably the only thing that saved Orvar. Again, he was sure, or almost sure, that he hadn't forced the other man into the hold and disabled the lock. Though he had to admit it was difficult to remember.

The thing he remembered best was this: the man's hand pressed against the reinforced glass of the door panel once he stopped trying to get out. The hand just resting there, seemingly ordinary, and then shriveling, just a little. First the tips of the fingers, then, gradually, the rest of the hand, turning blue, until Orvar himself was raving and couldn't pay attention to anything, let alone that.

He was talking to Grimur, trying to be helpful. *Properly administered synthetic morphine*, he was suggesting. Grimur shook his head.

"No, just listen," said Orvar. "We sedate them, make them breathe shallowly. They'd use less oxygen. We're all sedated except for one of us, who keeps the others under."

Grimur shook his head. "We have enough oxygen to survive," he insisted.

"But what if your calculations are wrong?"

"They're not wrong," said Grimur.

"But what if—"

"It's all useless speculation anyway," he said. "We don't have any morphine, synthetic or otherwise."

He insisted on examining the medical kit himself—he was the security officer, after all, that gave him the right—but yes, Grimur was right, there was nothing there. Had there never been any morphine in the kit, or had someone filched it, either on this project or on some project before? Didn't matter really. Not now, anyway.

There were still other things, other ways to ensure that they would survive. There must be. All he had to do was think of what they were.

Jansen and Lewis by turns worked on the generator motor, cleaning it as they went. Yaeger and Gordon and Durham spent most of their time at the rock drill, trying to break apart the housing in a way that would leave the motor useful and intact. Nobody was getting anywhere.

What am I doing? wondered Orvar. *Wandering a little, stumbling a little.*

Where are Wilkinson and Lee? he wondered, and a moment later came across them around the turn of a hallway, sitting cross-legged. They were whispering back and forth, taking turns brushing each other's arms, face, hands.

"Orvar, Orvar!" hissed Lee. "Come here," he said.

"What is it?" said Orvar. He approached them cautiously, hands loose and ready, just in case.

"Can we trust you?" asked Wilkinson.

"Sure," said Orvar.

"No, I mean really," said Lee. "Can we really trust you?"

Orvar shrugged. "I don't know," he said. "Can you?"

The pair locked gazes until, finally, Wilkinson nodded slightly. "Yeah, we can," Lee said. "It's just this," he said, and then, irritated, gestured again. "Come closer," he whispered, "closer."

Orvar stooped, brought his ear close to their bearded faces, their cracked and quivering lips. "What is it?" he asked again.

"Just this," said Lee. "You know the air?"

"The air?"

"Air's not the problem," said Lee.

"What's the problem then?"

"Dust," said Wilkinson.

Lee patted Orvar on the shoulder. "Yes," he said, "dust."

"It's everywhere," said Orvar. "Yes, you already told me."

"But that's only part of the problem," said Lee.

"Only the start of the problem," said Wilkinson.

"And what's the rest of it, you ask?" said Lee.

"I don't—" said Orvar.

"The rest," said Lee, his fingernails digging into Orvar's shoulders, "is that the dust is one."

"One," said Orvar, keeping his voice level.

Wilkinson nodded. "You know how we keep all our cells inside our bodies, carrying ourselves around like a sack? The dust is what happens if you don't have a sack. It's still all one thing, but spread everywhere."

The conversation left him strangely unsettled. They were paranoid, nervous, maybe delusional. *But what*, a very small part of him asked, *if they were right?* What if there was something about the dust? What if it wasn't just bad luck that the generator had failed? That Grimur's computer had failed? That the communications system, as Grimur now admitted, had failed? A slow, invisible, systematic destruction of all their equipment. By what? By dust. If humans had managed to incorporate colonies of bacteria into every part of their organism, into their very cells, who was to say that the reverse might not also be true—that a certain sort of consciousness did not necessarily need a body to contain it? Hadn't he believed during his last oxygen shortage that consciousness was not something that resided deep within the body but, rather, something that hovered on his skin's surface, like sweat? What happened if something flicked the sweat off? Where did it go?

He shook his head. No, he didn't believe it. He was just looking for something to distract him.

IV

Three days after the ventilation failed, Orvar had a dream. He was trapped in a pressurized metal sphere, surrounded by water. He was alone, having trouble breathing. He knew there was a rebreather system, with a soda lime scrubber, but when he turned it on, water began to seep in—he felt the pressure building within his ears. Hurriedly he turned it off. He checked the circuit, checked the tubing, but could find nothing wrong. But when he turned it back on, out came water, not air.

He turned it off, but it was too late. The metal of the sphere groaned around him. One side of the sphere dimpled, and a drop of water formed at the top of the porthole, slowly rolling down. There was a sharp pain in his head and a wetness in his ears and down his neck. When he touched the wetness with his hand, he found that it was blood. Another thump, another dent, then another, until the crumpled sphere was hardly bigger than his body, the pressure still building in his head.

He awoke to find Yaeger kneeling beside him in the darkness, shaking him. He pushed the man back, heart thudding.

"Jesus, Yaeger," he whispered, "you scared the shit out of me."

Yaeger lifted his finger to his lips. "They're dead," he said. "You have to come."

"Who's dead?" he asked.

"Come on," Yaeger whispered. And then he wandered out.

Hurriedly Orvar pulled his clothing on. Someone was sitting up in one of the other bunks, watching him, but the light coming through the entranceway was not enough for Orvar to know who it was.

He reached for his holster but found it empty, his gun missing. He cursed. A voice asked him something, but he didn't quite hear what it was. He looked under the pillow, then fell to his knees, looked under the bed. The gun was definitely gone. Nothing to be done now. He made his way quickly through the doorway and out.

Yaeger was halfway down the hall, abeyant. Catching sight of Orvar, he continued forward, picking his way through the boxes.

What the hell? wondered Orvar.

He watched Yaeger turn a corner, and followed in his wake.

About halfway to the corner, he began to wake up, to think more clearly.

Yaeger's hardly the most stable of us, he was thinking. What was he doing following him down a corridor while everybody else slept? Where was the man taking him? What had Yaeger done? Who was dead? Why?

Am I in danger? he wondered.

Hypoxia, he thought. And then repeated, like a mantra: *headache, fatigue, shortness of breath, nausea, elation.*

Hallucinations? What about paranoia? They were part of it too.

He shook his head, dismissed the thought, continued on. Still, he was careful going around the corner, just in case. Yaeger was already at the next turn, waiting. He waved frantically at Orvar and then disappeared around it.

Right, then right again. He's taking me in a circle, thought Orvar.

He began to look around for a weapon. Scooped a length of pipe off the floor, hefted it in his hand. It would do.

He turned right, expecting to see Yaeger at the next corner. Instead the man stood hesitating at the mouth of the shaft. When he saw Orvar, he just nodded, and then stared pointedly at the opening.

When Orvar approached, Yaeger pushed a flashlight at him. "Down there," he said.

"Who is it?" he asked.

But Yaeger just shook his head.

Orvar hesitated a moment, then took the flashlight. He started down. When he turned and looked back, he could see Yaeger standing there, leaning against the wall of the entrance, waiting, motionless for once.

He moved forward, throwing the flashbeam just a little way in front of him. There was only rock, slightly discolored from the dust, shiny in some places from some vagaries in the stone or due to the way the drill bit had slipped. As his eyes adjusted, he could see a gleam that solidified to become the curve of the drill. Besides that, it was just the shaft, nothing else, nothing out of the ordinary.

At least not at first. As he went farther, he began to see a discoloration streaked along the tunnel floor. It was hard to make sense of, initially. But then suddenly he knew it was blood.

He reached down and ran his fingers through it where it was shiniest. Wet still, but tacky. It had begun to dry. Moving farther into the tunnel, he could see the swath of it curving around the front of the rock drill. There was more and more blood, enough that he was certain that whoever it came from was dead.

He moved forward on the balls of his feet, pipe raised.

Halfway around the drill he saw the man's feet. One foot was still shod, the other bare. They rested at very different angles, as if not belonging to the same body. He went farther and saw the legs, then the man's gashed chest. He crouched beside him, steadying himself against the drill with one hand. He could smell blood and the rubber of the rock drill's tire and the dust. All three together were somehow much worse than the smell of blood alone. The throat had been slit ear to ear, the cut very deep and vicious, almost severing the head. The head, too, had been bashed in on one side, beaten until it was pulpy, bits and pieces of bone mingling with the dust. It was hard for Orvar to think of it as human, though he knew it must be. It took him some time to recognize who it was. Wilkinson.

He felt himself growing dizzy. He stood and took a few steps back. He closed his eyes. He only opened them upon hearing the soft footsteps behind him. He turned and saw Yaeger there, a dim ghost.

"Did you kill him?" Orvar asked.

Yaeger shook his head. His eyes in the darkness looked glassy, vacant. *If he did kill him*, thought Orvar, *why would he have guided me to the body?* He would have only done so if he was very clever, or quite mad.

He cleared his throat. "There's only one body here," he said. "But you said 'they.'"

Yaeger nodded. He turned and started back up the shaft.

This time Orvar kept pace. Yaeger did not have to turn and wait and coax him forward. He led him to the end of the shaft and then down the hall, back to the ventilation system. There, he stopped.

For a moment Orvar didn't see him. Or, rather, it. Yaeger was not in the right position, had stopped too soon. Orvar stood there, waiting for Yaeger to continue forward, and when he didn't, he came a little farther forward himself and saw the open access panel, the interior wet with blood.

He crouched and looked in. The body had been forced clumsily up past the motor housing in such a way that it was clear its back had been broken. The throat was cut again, more jaggedly this time and not as deep. The legs seemed intact, unbroken, and the head had not been beaten. Both the eyes had been cut out. It was, he was pretty sure, Lee, the man's gaunt face even more gaunt now that the blood had started to pool lower in the body.

Orvar reached out and touched the body's cheek. It felt waxy. He wasn't sure what that told him. He reached through the access panel and took hold of the arm, bent it at the elbow. It resisted a little, and once bent stayed in the new position. That, he knew, should tell him something about how long the body had been dead.

"Aren't you contaminating the evidence?" asked Yaeger from behind him. It was hard not to flinch.

"I'm trying to figure out how long he's been dead," he said.

"Ah," said Yaeger. And then, as Orvar continued to manipulate Lee's arm, "How long *has* he been dead?"

"I don't know," Orvar admitted reluctantly.

He let go of the arm and worked his head inside the housing. With his face that close to the body the smell was intense. He shined the flash-beam around, trying to decide if he should drag the body out and get a closer look at it.

"Is it the same killer?" asked Yaeger.

"Why wouldn't it be?" asked Orvar. And then he added, "How do you expect me to know?"

"You're in charge of security," said Yaeger, simply. "You're the one who should know."

I'm the one who should know, he thought. *If that's the case, then we're in trouble, because I don't know anything.*

"Wait here," he told Yaeger. "I'll be right back."

It took a while for Grimur to open the door. When he did he was wrapped in a blanket, his hair mussed.

"Do you know what time it is?" asked Grimur, irritated.

"No," said Orvar. "Do you?"

"Not exactly," Grimur admitted, "but I'm certain that we both should be asleep."

"We have a problem," said Orvar.

"Besides the ventilator?"

Orvar nodded. "Two men are dead," he said. "Wilkinson and Lee."

"Of what? Suicide?"

"Someone killed them."

For a moment Grimur just stared at him. And then he slowly began to close the door.

"Wait," said Orvar, blocking the door with his foot. "Didn't you hear what I said?"

"I told you not to tell the men," said Grimur. "But did you listen? No, you didn't."

"This isn't my fault," said Orvar.

"You're security," Grimur said. "It's your fault."

"What should I do?"

Grimur sighed. "Make sure nobody else gets killed."

"But how does that fix anything?" asked Orvar, confused.

"What's wrong with you?" asked Grimur. "We're still days away from running out of oxygen. You should be thinking more clearly."

But maybe Grimur was the one not thinking clearly, thought Orvar. "We need to solve the murders," he said. "They were both obsessed with the dust."

"The dust?" said Grimur. "What does that have to do with anything?"

"They thought the dust could think."

Grimur shook his head. "That's ridiculous. How can dust think?"

"I'm not saying it can," said Orvar. "I'm just saying what they thought."

Grimur sighed, rubbed his face. "Don't try to solve anything. You'll just make it worse. You're not a policeman. You're just a glorified security guard."

Orvar sighed and took his foot out of the door.

"On the plus side," said Grimur, "whether my calculations were right or not, now we have plenty of air." He shut the door.

Yes, thought Orvar on his way back, *there was that.* Two people dead meant enough air. They had nothing to worry about now. They would reach the stage where they had headaches, perhaps, but surely they would be rescued before they started hallucinating. Or before the worst hallucinations, anyway.

Sometimes it felt like he was living through something he had lived through before. What kind of luck did you have to have to twice end up in a situation where there wasn't enough oxygen to go around? What was wrong with him?

He was still puzzling out that question when he reached the entrance to the sleeping quarters. Yaeger was waiting there for him.

"Do you know who did it?" he asked.

Orvar shook his head. "I thought I told you to wait with Lee."

"You need help to sort it all out," said Yaeger.

"I'm not supposed to sort it out."

Yaeger's arms suddenly stopped moving. "Why not?"

"They'll be here soon," he said. "When they arrive they'll have someone trained to do that sort of thing. A proper investigator."

"Will they?" asked Yaeger. "In my experience they don't."

Orvar shrugged. "That's what Grimur claims."

Yaeger nodded. "Won't the evidence be lost by then?"

I don't know," said Orvar. "Maybe."

"There's a killer here. Right now. What about that?"

"I'll keep there from being more killings," said Orvar. "That's something I'm supposed to do."

Yaeger opened his mouth and then closed it. Finally he opened it again.

"Don't you think," he said, "that the only way to stop the killings is to catch the killer?"

The remaining men were huddled inside, talking. When he came in they stopped and then, tentatively, began asking the same questions as Yaeger. Who had done it? Why? How did he plan to catch them? He answered evasively. There was, he realized now, no advantage to suggesting that he would not even try to solve the murders.

"Shouldn't we move the bodies?" asked Jansen.

Orvar shook his head. "Not until they've been thoroughly investigated."

"When will that be?" asked Jansen.

Orvar shrugged. "When the ship gets here."

"And how do you advise us to avoid being killed?" asked Gordon.

"Stick together," Orvar said. "Always be in a group. That's the only way to be sure to stay alive."

V

And yet Orvar was one of the first to break that advice, choosing to patrol the halls alone before returning to bed. What did he hope to find? There was only Grimur plus the five men plus himself—he wasn't going to suddenly discover a new person he could blame the killings on. No, it had to be one of them. Everyone was a suspect. The only thing he knew was that it wasn't him.

Even Yaeger, despite the fact that he'd drawn Orvar's attention to the murders, could have done it. Showing him the bodies could have been a ploy.

So, paranoia after all, whether the oxygen was depleting or no. And of course to the others *he* was a suspect. Perhaps they would believe that was why he wasn't investigating the murders: because he had committed them.

It would make for a difficult few weeks. But there was nothing to be done. They just had to hold on until they were rescued.

*　*　*

He reached the shaft, paused, then followed it down, despite knowing what he would see. It was strange to move down past the drill, with the body already looming up in his mind before it began to actually appear. He saw at first the spattering of blood, dry now, duller than before. The body was just a little farther in than he remembered. He shone the light on it, regarded it. It looked just like it had before. *Why am I here?* he wondered. *What am I hoping to accomplish?*

He didn't know. He stared at the body for some time, trying to fix it in his mind. Did that qualify as evidence? Did it preserve anything? Would it be useful to whoever actually did try to solve the crime?

He didn't know.

He examined the other body again too, the way it was crammed up along the housing of the ventilator motor. It must have been hard to get it up there, he thought, must have required a certain amount of strength. Who was strong enough? Again, he didn't know. Maybe any of them. But maybe not. Likely the men working in the shaft—they were used to physical labor. The men testing the samples: maybe, maybe not.

He had to aim the flashlight at just the right angle to get a clear view. Again he tried to fix the body in his mind. Again, he wasn't sure what he was accomplishing, but it felt better to be doing something.

He expected to see Yaeger in the halls but didn't. He wasn't in the bunk-room either. Orvar went around a second time looking for him, but still didn't find him. Perhaps they just kept on missing each other. Or maybe he was talking to Grimur, or deliberately hiding. He didn't know what, if anything, he should do to find him, and so he ended up doing nothing.

Back in the bunkroom, the remaining men had left their huddle and moved back to their own beds. They were either asleep or pretending to be. He made sure they were all there: Jansen, Lewis, Durham, Gordon. Still no Yaeger.

Jansen's eyes were slightly open; Orvar could see them shining in the darkness.

"Seen Yaeger?" whispered Orvar.

Jansen propped himself up in his bed, shook his head. "He wasn't with you?" he whispered.

Orvar shook his head, drifted back to his own bunk. He stood there for a moment, hesitating, and then sat down. He considered his mental pictures of the bodies. Something was troubling him about one of them, but before he could determine which one, Jansen was there beside him.

"Shouldn't you be out looking for him?" he asked.

"I've already looked," Orvar said.

"Did Yaeger do it?"

"Do what?"

"Kill them," said Durham. "Lee and Wilkinson."

"Yaeger?" said Orvar, surprised. "No, I don't think so."

"He has an alibi?"

"An alibi? No, not exactly."

"Then you can't rule him out?"

"No," said Orvar, slowly. "I can't rule him out. To be honest, I can't rule anybody out."

"Not even me?"

"Not even you."

"I didn't do it," said Durham.

"Go to sleep, Durham," said Orvar.

"If I do," asked Durham, "how do I know I'm going to wake up alive?"

*   *   *

The air felt close, too tight in Orvar's throat. In the dark he listened to the sound of his own breathing, imagining his lungs filling with dust. Perhaps Yaeger *was* the killer. Or perhaps it was one of the others. Or perhaps, somehow, the dust itself. He had a vague sense of being on the verge of choking. Falling asleep felt a little like drowning.

VI

He awoke feeling he had heard something but not quite sure what. His head ached, flaring a bright line of pain. Some of the others were stirring as well. Gordon's bed was empty.

He sat up and pulled his boots on.

"What is it?" asked one of the dark shapes around him. Jansen, probably.

"I don't know," said Orvar. "I thought I heard something."

"Wait," said Lewis, a little panicked. "We'll come with you."

But he was already in the hall. A noise, a loud one: that was what had woken him up. Unless he'd dreamed it.

Out in the hall, he began to faintly smell cordite. So, not a dream. He made his way down the hall in one direction until he realized the smell seemed to be growing fainter, then backtracked. The others were now clustered in the doorway.

"What is it?" Jansen asked again.

"Gunshot," he said simply, and kept going.

Gordon or Yaeger, he thought. Those were the only options. All the others had been in the bunkroom. Either Yaeger shooting Gordon or Gordon killing Yaeger. Or one or the other of them killing Grimur.

He took a turning and threaded his way through a stack of boxes. Had they been arranged like that before? He was already past them when he realized what he'd glimpsed and went back. There, stuffed upright in the middle, was a body. Its face was pushed against the wall; he couldn't see clearly who it was.

"Hello?" he heard a voice call from down the hall. "Who's there?"

He pulled himself back behind a box, heart pounding. "Gordon?" he called out. "Is that you?"

"Orvar?" said the voice. "Is that you?"

He heard the sound of approaching footsteps. He tensed, waiting.

"I thought I heard a shot," said the voice, closer now. "Where are you? It's me. Grimur."

And yes, he realized, it was Grimur—he should have recognized the voice right away. He stepped out to meet him.

"Did you fire a shot?" asked Grimur.

"Somebody did," said Orvar.

"It wasn't you? You're the only one with a gun."

Orvar shook his head. "My gun's missing," he said.

Grimur frowned. "Some security officer you are," he said. "Who has it?"

"I don't know," Orvar admitted. "Yaeger, probably. Unless that's Yaeger there." He gestured between the boxes where the body was. "If so, then it'd be Gordon."

Grimur came closer, squinted. "Shit," he said. "Is that a corpse?"

Instead of answering, Orvar started moving boxes. For a moment the corpse balanced there, leaning against the wall, then it slowly spun and toppled, fell to the floor. There was no gun in the gap, despite the blood spatter against the wall. Definitely not a suicide.

"That's Gordon," said Grimur.

"Then Yaeger has my gun," said Orvar.

"How the hell did you let Yaeger get hold of your gun?"

"He took it, somehow. Without me realizing," said Orvar.

"Why are you brushing your arms like that?" asked Grimur.

"What?" said Orvar. Surprised, he looked down at his moving hands. "It's this goddamn dust, it sticks to everything," he said. "It's like it's alive."

Grimur shook his head. "It's just dust," he said.

"How do you know?" asked Orvar. His voice was getting louder. He was helpless to stop it. "How can you be sure it's not doing something to us?"

"Because it's just dust," said Grimur simply. "I'm going to go back to my room. Try not to let anybody else die."

Back with the others he explained that Gordon was dead and Yaeger nowhere to be found. There was every indication that Yaeger had killed Gordon and the other two as well.

"So you solved it," said Jansen. "That was quick. Yaeger's our killer."

"Yaeger wouldn't do that," said Lewis.

"It's Yaeger," Orvar said.

"Then where is he?" said Lewis.

Orvar shrugged. "Hiding," he said.

"Hiding where?" asked Lewis.

"Why are you brushing your arms?" asked Jansen. "Are you cold?"

Only with an enormous effort was Orvar able to stop. "I don't know where," he said. "I'm searching for him."

"How do we know that you didn't kill them?" asked Durham.

"Why would I do that?" asked Orvar.

"Why would Yaeger?" asked Lewis.

"No," said Jansen slowly. "You heard the shot, Durham. Orvar was here when Gordon was killed."

"He could have set something up," said Durham. "Some sort of trap to make the gun go off automatically. And then as long as he's the first one to the body he could hide the trap."

"Don't be paranoid," said Jansen.

"There are three dead bodies," said Durham. "We'd be fools not to be paranoid."

"Be careful," said Orvar. "Stick together. That's the best thing you can do. That's what will keep you alive." He moved toward the doorway.

"Where are you going?" asked Jansen.

"To find Yaeger."

He looked through the halls and down the shaft and then started poking through boxes, but there was no sign of him. He couldn't find Yaeger anywhere. How was it possible? He had to be somewhere. Eventually he went back to the bunkroom. Everybody was pretending to be sleeping.

"Has Yaeger come back?" he asked.

Nobody responded. Taking that as a no, he went back out again.

He leaned against the samples table in the research area, thinking. Where could Yaeger be? There was a chance he was hiding undetected in one of the boxes, that he hadn't checked thoroughly enough. Or that Yaeger had simply been circling through the halls in a way that deliberately avoided their meeting. It would have been difficult, but it was possible.

Or he could be in Grimur's room.

Yaeger could have snuck in when Grimur came out after hearing the gunshot. Perhaps he was still there, hidden.

But no, thought Orvar, picturing the room in his head, there was nowhere to hide. If he was there, either he was holding Grimur hostage at gunpoint or Grimur was dead.

What was the best way to go about it? He stood outside Grimur's door, hesitating, and then finally knocked lightly. There was no answer. He pressed his ear to the door. No indication of movement inside. Perhaps Yaeger was lying low. Or perhaps he'd left. Orvar knocked again, louder this time. When there was still no answer, he slowly pushed down the door's handle, opened the door, and slipped inside.

The room was dark. He let the flashlight play slowly along the walls. Nobody there, nobody standing anyway. He moved a few steps in and pointed the light down and saw, behind the desk, Grimur's makeshift bed. In it was a human shape, mostly covered in blankets, facing the wall.

Very slowly he approached, keeping the light mostly covered, just enough to make out vague outlines. He moved closer and finally fell to his knees, crawling the rest of the way until he was very close, close enough to be fairly certain that it wasn't Yaeger. It must be Grimur.

Yaeger had already killed him, Orvar thought. He couldn't tell if the sounds he was hearing were the body's breathing or his own. He held his breath, but it didn't help.

He reached out and softly touched the neck. Warm. Still alive. He pulled his hand back but already the body was moving, a blur in the half dark. Something struck him hard in the face and he fell to one side, the flashlight clattering away. Two heavy blows to his ribs and suddenly he couldn't breathe and then the body had clambered on top of him and had its hands wrapped around his throat. Everything went darker still, and then the world seemed to stutter and stop entirely.

A light. Slowly, his eyes began to focus. Grimur was crouching over him, watching him closely, a disgusted expression on his face.

"Coming around?" he asked.

Orvar just groaned.

"I could have killed you," Grimur said. "What were you thinking?" He reached out and helped Orvar sit. Orvar groaned again, his head throbbing. "You can't do that," Grimur explained. "I thought you were trying to kill me."

"I thought you might be dead."

"And that's how you figure out if I am?" he said. "What were you thinking? Do you know how much oxygen we must have wasted, struggling like that?"

"I was looking for Yaeger," said Orvar.

"Yaeger? Why would he be here?"

"We can't find him."

"You must not be looking in the right places," said Grimur.

"We've looked everywhere."

"Obviously not," said Grimur. He helped Orvar to his feet. "Go look somewhere where he might actually be," he said. "Do your fucking job."

Do my job, thought Orvar, a little dizzy, confused. *Do my job.* He made his way back to the bunkroom and lay down. The others were in the beds, dark motionless shapes. They were probably alive. There was no reason to assume they were not. As long as he didn't know they were dead he could think of them as alive.

He stared into the semidarkness, thinking. *Do you know how much oxygen we must have wasted struggling like that?* he heard Grimur say again in his head, saw again his look of mingled concern and disgust. He thought of the diminishing oxygen, the air thick with dust, and through those little twisty mental passages scrabbled his way back to the other time he had been trapped without air. What had gone on exactly? How culpable was he? He hadn't killed the others; he was sure, or almost sure, he hadn't slit the first man's throat. And the man who died in the hold, that had been his own fault. But Orvar hadn't tried to get him out.

He took a deep breath and let it out. A little more oxygen gone.

He shook his head. No, he couldn't think like that. They were still days away from running out of air. It wasn't going to be like last time: they had enough oxygen to last until the company came to get him.

But then he found Grimur's words rising again in his mind. Why had he said that? Now that three people were dead, there was no danger: they had extra air.

So why would Grimur be worried?

He kept thinking too of the ventilator, and of the body stuffed in it. Or not thinking of it, exactly. Just *seeing* it over and over again in his mind. Each time it felt just a little off, as if his mind was revising it.

What did it all mean, all these various things cycling through his mind? How did it all come together? He didn't know. He stared into the dark, willing himself to see a pattern. But he didn't see anything.

Until, suddenly, he did.

VII

He got up and pulled his boots on. He made no effort to hide what he was doing, but he wasn't noisy either. He grabbed the flashlight. If the others were going to say something, then let them say it. If they were not, if they were just going to pretend to be asleep, then so be it.

He went down the hall, to the ventilator. Once there, he fell to his knees and stared up into the housing. There was the body, just as it had been before—or almost. Yes, that's what he'd been trying to understand: it was a body, but it wasn't the body he'd first seen there. The head was twisted away from him, but it wasn't hard to stick his hand up into the housing and wrap it in the hair and tug hard. With a crinkling sound the head came around to reveal Yaeger's face.

He worried the body back and forth until it came loose and spilled out onto the floor. His gun clattered out with it. Back in the housing, pushed farther up, was the other body, the one missing its eyes. The killer had been smart: he'd hidden Yaeger's body so that Orvar would think it was Lee's. But he'd been careless, too. If he'd taken out Lee's body and put Yaeger's above it, Orvar would never have realized it. He would have gone for days thinking that Yaeger was on the loose, when it fact the killer was someone else.

He examined Yaeger's corpse. It hadn't been shot. One side of Yaeger's head was soft. There were marks, too, around the neck, the bruises of fingers. He'd been strangled, probably shoved up into the housing long before Gordon was killed. Someone had killed Yaeger, forced Lee's body up higher, pushed Yaeger in, and then gone after Gordon.

Orvar checked the gun's chamber. Five shots left. He holstered it. *And now*, he thought, *my turn to go after the killer.*

A few moments later he was knocking on Grimur's door. What time was it? Early? Late? He didn't know anymore.

He heard a voice rumbling inside but not what it said. He tried the door's handle, but it was locked. He knocked again.

He heard slow, patient movement within. He tried to imagine Grimur rubbing his eyes, getting up, getting dressed, approaching the door.

"Who is it?" Grimur's voice asked from just inside.

"Orvar," said Orvar.

"What do you want?"

"To come in."

For a moment there was only silence. "What is it this time?" Grimur finally said.

"Somebody else is dead," Orvar said.

At first nothing happened, and then the lock clicked and the door slid open.

"Who?" asked Grimur. His eyes, Orvar saw, were curious, but when Orvar said *Yaeger* something changed.

"Ah," Grimur said. "I see." He waved Orvar into the room. "You haven't done your job very well, have you?" he said.

"On the contrary," said Orvar. "I figured out who killed them."

Grimur stopped. He turned around. His surprise, when he saw that Orvar was pointing the gun at him, seemed genuine.

"You're the killer?" said Grimur.

"Me?" said Orvar. "No, of course not. It's you."

Grimur slowly shook his head. "You're mad," he said. "You're getting confused."

"Don't try to confuse me," said Orvar. "It has to be you."

"Does it?" said Grimur. "Why?"

"No," said Orvar, waving the gun. "Let me explain it to you. We were all in the bunkroom when Gordon was killed. Except for you."

"What about Yaeger? Was Yaeger in the bunkroom?"

"No," Orvar admitted. "He wasn't. But he was already dead."

Grimur swallowed. "Are you sure he was dead by the time Gordon was killed?"

"What?"

"How do you know there aren't two killers? Maybe Yaeger killed Gordon and then someone killed Yaeger."

"Who would the other killer be?"

Grimur shrugged. "Who knows? It could be anybody. Did you watch everybody? Did you have your eye on them all the time?"

"You're trying to confuse me," said Orvar. He licked his lips. His mouth felt too dry.

"No," claimed Grimur. "I'm trying to make you think straight."

"Why would any of them want to kill Yaeger?"

"Why would I want to?"

"No," said Orvar. "You said it. I heard you."

"What did I say?"

"Do you know how much oxygen we must have wasted?"

"So?" said Grimur.

"Why would you care?"

"Why would I care?"

"With the other two dead we have more than enough oxygen to survive. It doesn't matter how much oxygen we wasted."

Grimur once again looked genuinely shocked. "That's your evidence?"

"You lied," Orvar insisted. "You told us there was more oxygen than there was, but knew some of us would have to die if the rest were to survive. You knew that you could kill them and that I, because of what had happened at my last posting, would be blamed."

"What happened at your last posting?"

"You know," said Orvar. "Oxygen shortage. Everybody died but me."

Grimur shook his head. "This is all news to me."

Orvar tried to think back. How much had he told him? He couldn't remember exactly.

"How long has it been since you slept?" asked Grimur.

"That doesn't matter," said Orvar.

"It does matter," said Grimur, firmly. "You're panicked. You've become paranoid. There's something wrong with the air. The dust in it. You're letting it get to you."

Was he? He shook his head. It ached.

"Orvar," said Grimur gently. "Don't you see? I've spent days figuring out how much oxygen we have and how long it will last us. Doesn't it make sense—*even if I know we have enough to survive*—that the first thing I would think of is oxygen?"

Orvar looked at him. The gun shook in his hand. He had been so sure when he had found Yaeger. Wasn't he sure now?

"This has all been a misunderstanding," said Grimur. "I understand why you thought it was me, but surely you see now that you were wrong?"

Orvar didn't answer. *Yes, what if you're wrong?* a part of him was thinking. Alone, in his head, it had all made sense, but now, with Grimur calmly talking, he wasn't sure anymore.

But if it wasn't Grimur, who was it?

No, it had to be Grimur. It had to be.

"Orvar," Grimur said, his voice serene. "Put down the gun."

"No," said Orvar.

Grimur spread his arms slowly. "You're going to kill me over a slip of the tongue?"

"It wasn't a slip."

"Are you crazy? Is that proof? Is it really enough?"

"It's all I have," said Orvar desperately. And when he saw that Grimur, confident now, was going to continue talking, was going to talk him out of killing him, he pulled the trigger.

VIII

He holstered the gun. The shot was still ringing in his ears, and the room reeked of cordite. *Maybe I should have waited*, thought Orvar. *Maybe I should have just immobilized him somehow, tied him up.* But if he'd done that, Grimur would have convinced the others that Orvar was mad, and before he knew it Grimur would be free and Orvar himself tied up.

There was blood all over his shoes, glistening and then slowly growing dull as the dust began to adhere to it. Blood had spattered onto the wall, and there was a swath of it across the floor. There was no point trying to clean up. It was too much to hide.

And it doesn't matter, he told himself. *I didn't do anything wrong. I just killed a killer.*

There was blood on his sleeve. He would have to change his shirt before the others saw. If he didn't, they would think he was the killer. *But I'm not the killer*, he told himself. *Grimur was.* He was almost certain that that was the case. All but certain. Less so, admittedly, than before Grimur had started talking, but still. He looked once around the room and then went out, closing the door behind him. *At least now*, he told himself, *it's over.*

*　　*　　*

But is it really over? his mind was already asking only halfway down the hall. What if he'd gotten it wrong, taking what was plausible for what was actual? What if he'd killed an innocent man? Was there any way to be sure that the killer wasn't still on the loose?

No, he told himself just outside the bunkroom, *there's no way to be sure.* What, really, did he know? One, that the ventilators were broken. Two, they were running out of air. Three, someone, eventually, would rescue them. Four, that he wasn't the killer.

Anything else, everything else, was speculation. He needed to stay aware and alert. He needed to remember that perhaps it wasn't over. If it wasn't, any of the remaining three might be the killer. He had to watch them carefully, keeping his gun within reach.

In the bunkroom, the lights were on, dimly, each of them taking on a strange halo from the dust. All three still-living men were there. Gordon sat on the edge of his bed. Lewis was at the desk and seemed to be writing. Jansen just stood there, arms loose, pretending to do nothing.

Suspicious, Orvar thought.

"Where've you been?" asked Gordon.

"Nowhere," said Orvar.

He moved slowly toward his bunk. How could it already be time to wake up?

Where had the night gone?

"What's on your sleeve?" asked Jansen.

Blood, thought Orvar, but said, "Nothing."

He unbuttoned the shirt, slowly stripped it off, draped it on the post of the bed. *It had to be Grimur*, he thought. *It had to be.* But each time he thought it, he felt less sure.

He kept his movements succinct, steady, trying to give the others no sense of what he was thinking. He took off his gun belt, laid it flat on the bed. He shucked his boots. *Don't be paranoid*, he told himself. *You're not thinking right. It's the lack of oxygen. The dust.* He pushed the gun belt over and sat down. *A little sleep and you'll see things more clearly.*

But he was not given a chance to sleep.

"You found your gun," said Lewis.

He could tell by the way Lewis said it that that wasn't all he meant. In a brief flash he saw it all: he had no choice. In a few hours there would be three more corpses, followed by days of him wandering the complex alone, slowly going mad, head filling with dust, oxygen slowly draining away. In the end, with a little luck, Grimur's calculations would be correct, and the ship would arrive well before he ran out of air. And then he would explain. *It was Grimur, not me. It was the dust, not me. I'm no killer, I swear. I'm just a man lucky to still be alive.*

He blinked. The other three were watching him, frozen, waiting. Jansen was poised, on the balls of his feet, tense. He would probably give Orvar the most trouble, and should be taken care of first. Gordon was standing now. He could be easy or hard, too early to say. Lewis, clueless, was still in the chair. He would be the easiest.

It wasn't me, he told himself again. He reached casually over, pulled the gun belt into his lap. "Yes, Lewis," he said. "I found my gun." *It was the dust*, he practiced, and tried to make himself believe it. And then he smiled and drew his weapon.

THE ENORMOUS RADIO

JOHN CHEEVER

{SELECTED BY RAY BRADBURY}

Jim and Irene Westcott were the kind of people who seem to strike that satisfactory average of income, endeavor, and respectability that is reached by the statistical reports in college alumni bulletins. They were the parents of two young children, they had been married nine years, they lived on the twelfth floor of an apartment house in the East Seventies between Fifth and Madison avenues, they went to the theater on an average of 10.3 times a year, and they hoped someday to live in Westchester. Irene Westcott was a pleasant, rather plain girl with soft brown hair and a wide, fine forehead upon which nothing at all had been written, and in the cold weather she wore a coat of fitch skins dyed to resemble mink. You could not say that Jim Westcott, at thirty-seven, looked younger than he was, but you could at least say of him that he seemed to feel younger. He wore his graying hair cut very short, he dressed in the kind of clothes his class had worn at Andover, and his manner was earnest, vehement, and intentionally naïve. The Westcotts differed from their friends, their classmates, and their neighbors only in an interest they shared in serious music. They went to a great many concerts—although they seldom mentioned this to anyone—and they spent a good deal of time listening to music on the radio.

Their radio was an old instrument, sensitive, unpredictable, and beyond repair. Neither of them understood the mechanics of radio—or of any of the other appliances that surrounded them—and when the instrument faltered, Jim would strike the side of the cabinet with his hand. This sometimes helped. One Sunday afternoon, in the middle of a Schubert quartet, the music faded away altogether. Jim struck the cabinet repeatedly, but there was no response; the Schubert was lost to them forever. He promised to buy Irene a new radio, and on Monday when he came home from work he told her that he had got one. He refused to describe it, and said it would be a surprise for her when it came.

The radio was delivered at the kitchen door the following afternoon, and with the assistance of her maid and the handyman Irene uncrated it and brought it into the living room. She was struck at once with the physical ugliness of the large gumwood cabinet. Irene was proud of her living room, she had chosen its furnishings and colors as carefully as she chose her clothes, and now it seemed to her that the new radio stood among her intimate possessions like an aggressive intruder. She was confounded by the number of dials and switches on the instrument panel, and she studied them thoroughly before she put the plug into a wall socket and turned the radio on. The dials flooded with a malevolent green light, and in the distance she heard the music of a piano quintet. The quintet was in the distance for only an instant; it bore down upon her with a speed greater than light and filled the apartment with the noise of music amplified so mightily that it knocked a china ornament from a table to the floor. She rushed to the instrument and reduced the volume. The violent forces that were snared in the ugly gumwood cabinet made her uneasy. Her children came home from school then, and she took them to the park. It was not until later in the afternoon that she was able to return to the radio.

The maid had given the children their suppers and was supervising their baths when Irene turned on the radio, reduced the volume, and sat down to listen to a Mozart quintet that she knew and enjoyed. The music came through clearly. The new instrument had a much purer tone, she thought, than the old one. She decided that tone was most important and that she could conceal the cabinet behind a sofa. But as soon as she had made her peace with the radio, the interference began. A crackling sound like the noise of a burning powder fuse began to accompany the singing of the strings. Beyond the music, there was a rustling that reminded Irene unpleasantly of the sea, and as the quintet progressed, these noises were joined by many others. She tried all the dials and switches but nothing dimmed the interference, and she sat down, disappointed and bewildered, and tried to trace the flight of the melody. The elevator shaft in her building ran beside the living-room wall, and it was the noise of the elevator that gave her a clue to the character of the static. The rattling of the elevator cables and the opening and closing of the elevator doors were reproduced in her loudspeaker, and, realizing that the radio was sensitive to electrical currents of all sorts, she began to discern through the Mozart the ringing of telephone bells, the dialing of phones, and the lamentation of a vacuum cleaner. By listening more carefully, she was able to distinguish doorbells, elevator bells, electric razors, and Waring mixers, whose sounds had been picked up from the apartments that surrounded hers and transmitted through her loudspeaker. The powerful and ugly instrument, with its mistaken sensitivity to discord, was more than she could hope to master, so she turned the thing off and went into the nursery to see her children.

When Jim Westcott came home that night, he went to the radio confidently and worked the controls. He had the same sort of experience Irene had had. A man was speaking on the station Jim had chosen, and his voice swung instantly from the distance into a force so powerful that it shook the apartment. Jim turned the volume control and reduced the voice. Then, a minute or two later, the interference began. The ringing of telephones and doorbells set in, joined by the rasp of the elevator doors and the whir of cooking appliances. The character of the noise had changed since Irene had tried the radio earlier; the last of the electric razors was being unplugged, the vacuum cleaners had all been returned to their closets, and the static reflected that change in pace that overtakes the city after the sun goes down. He fiddled with the knobs but couldn't get rid of the noises, so he turned the radio off and told Irene that in the morning he'd call the people who had sold it to him and give them hell.

The following afternoon, when Irene returned to the apartment from a luncheon date, the maid told her that a man had come and fixed the radio. Irene went into the living room before she took off her hat and her furs and tried the instrument. From the loudspeaker came a recording of the "Missouri Waltz." It reminded her of the thin, scratchy music from an old-fashioned phonograph that she sometimes heard across the lake where she spent her summers. She waited until the waltz had finished, expecting an explanation of the recording, but there was none. The music was followed by silence, and then the plaintive and scratchy record was repeated. She turned the dial and got a satisfactory burst of Caucasian music—the thump of bare feet in the dust and the rattle of coin jewelry—but in the background she could hear the ringing of bells and a confusion of voices. Her children came home from school then, and she turned off the radio and went to the nursery.

When Jim came home that night, he was tired, and he took a bath and changed his clothes. Then he joined Irene in the living room. He had just turned on the radio when the maid announced dinner, so he left it on, and he and Irene went to the table.

Jim was too tired to make even a pretense of sociability, and there was nothing about the dinner to hold Irene's interest, so her attention

wandered from the food to the deposits of silver polish on the candle-
sticks and from there to the music in the other room. She listened for a
few moments to a Chopin prelude and then was surprised to hear a man's
voice break in. "For Christ's sake, Kathy," he said, "do you always have to
play the piano when I get home?" The music stopped abruptly. "It's the
only chance I have," the woman said. "I'm at the office all day." "So am
I," the man said. He added something obscene about an upright piano, and
slammed a door. The passionate and melancholy music began again.

"Did you hear that?" Irene asked.

"What?" Jim was eating his dessert.

"The radio. A man said something while the music was still going
on—something dirty."

"It's probably a play."

"I don't think it *is* a play," Irene said.

They left the table and took their coffee into the living room. Irene
asked Jim to try another station. He turned the knob. "Have you seen
my garters?" a man asked. "Button me up," a woman said. "Have you
seen my garters?" the man said again. "Just button me up and I'll find
your garters," the woman said. Jim shifted to another station. "I wish you
wouldn't leave apple cores in the ashtrays," a man said. "I hate the smell."

"This is strange," Jim said.

"Isn't it?" Irene said.

Jim turned the knob again. "'On the coast of Coromandel where the
early pumpkins blow,'" a woman with a pronounced English accent said,
"'in the middle of the woods lived the Yonghy-Bonghy-Bò. Two old
chairs, and half a candle, one old jug without a handle...'"

"My God!" Irene cried. "That's the Sweeneys' nurse."

"'These were all his worldly goods,'" the British voice continued.

"Turn that thing off," Irene said. "Maybe they can hear *us*." Jim
switched the radio off. "That was Miss Armstrong, the Sweeneys' nurse,"
Irene said. "She must be reading to the little girl. They live in 17-B. I've

talked with Miss Armstrong in the park. I know her voice very well. We must be getting other people's apartments."

"That's impossible," Jim said.

"Well, that was the Sweeneys' nurse," Irene said hotly. "I know her voice. I know it very well. I'm wondering if they can hear us."

Jim turned the switch. First from a distance and then nearer, nearer, as if borne on the wind, came the pure accents of the Sweeneys' nurse again: """Lady Jingly! Lady Jingly!""" she said, """Sitting where the pumpkins blow, will you come and be my wife," said the Yonghy-Bonghy-Bò...'"

Jim went over to the radio and said "Hello" loudly into the speaker.

"""I am tired of living singly,""" the nurse went on, """on this coast so wild and shingly, I'm a-weary of my life; if you'll come and be my wife, quite serene would be my life...""""

"I guess she can't hear us," Irene said. "Try something else."

Jim turned to another station, and the living room was filled with the uproar of a cocktail party that had overshot its mark. Someone was playing the piano, and singing the Whiffenpoof Song, and the voices that surrounded the piano were vehement and happy. "Eat some more sandwiches," a woman shrieked. There were screams of laughter and a dish of some sort crashed to the floor.

"Those must be the Hutchinsons, in 15-B," Irene said. "I knew they were giving a party this afternoon. I saw her in the liquor store. Isn't this too divine? Try something else. See if you can get those people in 18-C."

The Westcotts overheard that evening a monologue on salmon fishing in Canada, a bridge game, running comments on home movies of what had apparently been a fortnight at Sea Island, and a bitter family quarrel about an overdraft at the bank. They turned off their radio at midnight and went to bed, weak with laughter. Sometime in the night their son began to call for a glass of water and Irene got one and took it to his room. It was very early. All the lights in the neighborhood were extinguished, and from the boy's window she could see the empty street. She went into the living room and tried the radio. There was a faint coughing, a moan, and then a man spoke. "Are you all right, darling?" he asked. "Yes," a woman said wearily. "Yes, I'm all right, I guess." And then she added with great feeling, "But, you know, Charlie, I don't feel like myself anymore. Sometimes there are about fifteen or twenty minutes in the week when I feel like myself. I don't like to go to another doctor, because the doctor's bills are so awful already, but I just don't feel like myself, Charlie. I just never feel like myself." They were not young, Irene thought. She guessed from the timbre of their voices that they were middle-aged. The restrained melancholy of the dialogue and the draft from the bedroom window made her shiver, and she went back to bed.

The following morning, Irene cooked breakfast for the family—the maid didn't come up from her room in the basement until ten—braided her daughter's hair, and waited at the door until her children and her husband had been carried away in the elevator. Then she went into the living room and tried the radio. "I don't want to go to school," a child screamed. "I hate school. I won't go to school. I hate school." "You will go to school," an enraged woman said. "We paid eight hundred dollars to get you into that school and you'll go if it kills you." The next number on the dial produced the worn record of the "Missouri Waltz." Irene shifted the control and invaded the privacy of several breakfast tables. She overheard demonstrations of indigestion, carnal love, abysmal vanity, faith, and despair. Irene's life was nearly as simple and sheltered as it appeared to be, and the forthright and sometimes brutal language that came from the loudspeaker that morning astonished and troubled her. She continued to listen until her maid came in. Then she turned off the radio quickly, since this insight, she realized, was a furtive one.

Irene had a luncheon date with a friend that day, and she left her apartment at a little after twelve. There were a number of women in the elevator when it stopped at her floor. She stared at their handsome and impassive faces, their furs, and the cloth flowers in their hats. Which one of them had been to Sea Island, she wondered. Which one had overdrawn her bank account? The elevator stopped at the tenth floor and a woman with a pair of Skye terriers joined them. Her hair was rigged high on her head and she wore a mink cape. She was humming the "Missouri Waltz."

Irene had two martinis at lunch, and she looked searchingly at her friend and wondered what her secrets were. They had intended to go shopping after lunch, but Irene excused herself and went home. She told the maid that she was not to be disturbed; then she went into the living room, closed the doors, and switched on the radio. She heard, in the course of the afternoon, the halting conversation of a woman entertaining her aunt, the hysterical conclusion of a luncheon party, and a hostess briefing her maid about some cocktail guests. "Don't give the best scotch to anyone who hasn't white hair," the hostess said. "See if you can get rid of that liver paste before you pass those hot things, and could you lend me five dollars? I want to tip the elevator man."

As the afternoon waned, the conversations increased in intensity. From where Irene sat, she could see the open sky above Central Park. There were hundreds of clouds in the sky, as though the south wind had broken the winter into pieces and were blowing it north, and on her radio she could hear the arrival of cocktail guests and the return of children and businessmen from their schools and offices. "I found a good-sized diamond on the bathroom floor this morning," a woman said. "It must have fallen out of that bracelet Mrs. Dunston was wearing last night." "We'll sell it," a man said. "Take it down to the jeweler on Madison Avenue and sell it. Mrs. Dunston won't know the difference, and we could use a couple of hundred bucks..." "'Oranges and lemons, say the bells of St. Clement's,'" the Sweeneys' nurse sang. "'Halfpence and farthings, say the bells of St. Martin's. When will you pay me? say the bells at old Bailey...'" "It's not a hat," a woman cried, and at her back roared a cocktail party. "It's not a hat, it's a love affair. That's what Walter Florell said. He said it's not a hat, it's a love affair," and then, in a lower voice, the same woman added, "Talk to somebody, for Christ's sake, honey, talk to somebody. If she catches you standing here not talking to anybody, she'll take us off her invitation list, and I love these parties."

The Westcotts were going out for dinner that night, and when Jim came home, Irene was dressing. She seemed sad and vague, and he brought her a drink. They were dining with friends in the neighborhood, and they walked to where they were going. The sky was broad and filled with light. It was one of those splendid evenings that excite memory and desire, and the air that touched their hands and faces felt very soft. A Salvation Army band was on the corner playing "Jesus Is Sweeter." Irene drew on her husband's arm and held him there for a minute, to hear the music. "They're really such nice people, aren't they?" she said. "They have such nice faces. Actually, they're so much nicer than a lot of the people we know." She took a bill from her purse and walked over and dropped it into the tambourine. There was in her face, when she returned to her husband, a look of radiant melancholy that he was not familiar with. And her conduct at the dinner party that night seemed strange to him, too. She interrupted her hostess rudely and stared at the people across the table from her with an intensity for which she would have punished her children.

It was still mild when they walked home from the party, and Irene looked up at the spring stars. "'How far that little candle throws its beams,'" she exclaimed. "'So shines a good deed in a naughty world.'" She waited that night until Jim had fallen asleep, and then went into the living room and turned on the radio.

Jim came home about six the next night. Emma, the maid, let him in, and he had taken off his hat and was taking off his coat when Irene ran into the hall. Her face was shining with tears and her hair was disordered. "Go up to 16-C, Jim!" she screamed. "Don't take off your coat. Go up to 16-C. Mr. Osborn's beating his wife. They've been quarreling since four o'clock, and now he's hitting her. Go up there and stop him."

From the radio in the living room, Jim heard screams, obscenities, and thuds. "You know you don't have to listen to this sort of thing," he said. He strode into the living room and turned the switch. "It's indecent," he said. "It's like looking in windows. You know you don't have to listen to this sort of thing. You can turn if off."

"Oh, it's so horrible, it's so dreadful," Irene was sobbing. "I've been listening all day, and it's so depressing."

"Well, if it's so depressing, why do you listen to it? I bought this damned radio to give you some pleasure," he said. "I paid a great deal of money for it. I thought it might make you happy. I wanted to make you happy."

"Don't, don't, don't, don't quarrel with me," she moaned, and laid her head on his shoulder. "All the others have been quarreling all day. Everybody's been quarreling. They're all worried about money. Mrs. Hutchinson's mother is dying of cancer in Florida and they don't have enough money to send her to the Mayo Clinic. At least, Mr. Hutchinson says they don't have enough money. And some woman in this building is having an affair with the superintendent—with that hideous superintendent. It's too disgusting. And Mrs. Melville has heart trouble and Mr. Hendricks is going to lose his job in April and Mrs. Hendricks is horrid about the whole thing and that girl who plays the 'Missouri Waltz' is a whore, a common whore, and the elevator man has tuberculosis and Mr. Osborn has been beating Mrs. Osborn." She wailed, she trembled with grief and checked the stream of tears down her face with the heel of her palm.

"Well, why do you have to listen?" Jim asked again. "Why do you have to listen to this stuff if it makes you so miserable?"

"Oh, don't, don't, don't," she cried. "Life is too terrible, too sordid and awful. But we've never been like that, have we, darling? Have we? I mean we've always been good and decent and loving to one another, haven't we? And we have two children, two beautiful children. Our lives aren't sordid, are they, darling? Are they?" She flung her arms around his neck and drew his face down to hers. "We're happy, aren't we, darling? We are happy, aren't we?"

"Of course we're happy," he said tiredly. He began to surrender his resentment. "Of course we're happy. I'll have that damned radio fixed or taken away tomorrow." He stroked her soft hair. "My poor girl," he said.

"You love me, don't you?" she asked. "And we're not hypercritical or worried about money or dishonest, are we?"

"No, darling," he said.

A man came in the next morning and fixed the radio. Irene turned it on cautiously and was happy to hear a California-wine commercial and a recording of Beethoven's Ninth Symphony, including Schiller's "Ode to Joy." She kept the radio on all day and nothing untoward came from the speaker.

A Spanish suite was being played when Jim came home. "Is everything all right?" he asked. His face was pale, she thought. They had some cocktails and went in to dinner to the "Anvil Chorus" from *Il Trovatore.* This was followed by Debussy's "La Mer."

"I paid the bill for the radio today," Jim said. "It cost four hundred dollars. I hope you'll get some enjoyment out of it."

"Oh, I'm sure I will," Irene said.

"Four hundred dollars is a good deal more than I can afford," he went on. "I wanted to get something that you'd enjoy. It's the last extravagance we'll be able to indulge in this year. I see that you haven't paid your clothing bills yet. I saw them on your dressing table." He looked directly at her. "Why did you tell me you'd paid them? Why did you lie to me?"

"I just didn't want you to worry, Jim," she said. She drank some water. "I'll be able to pay my bills out of this month's allowance. There were the slipcovers last month, and that party."

"You've got to learn to handle the money I give you a little more intelligently, Irene," he said. "You've got to understand that we won't have as much money this year as we had last. I had a very sobering talk with Mitchell today. No one is buying anything. We're spending all our time promoting new issues, and you know how long that takes. I'm not getting any younger, you know. I'm thirty-seven. My hair will be gray next year. I haven't done as well as I'd hoped to do. And I don't suppose things will get any better."

"Yes, dear," she said.

"We've got to start cutting down," Jim said. "We've got to think of the children. To be perfectly frank with you, I worry about money a great deal. I'm not at all sure of the future. No one is. If anything should happen to me, there's the insurance, but that wouldn't go very far today. I've worked awfully hard to give you and the children a comfortable life," he said bitterly. "I don't like to see all of my energies, all of my youth, wasted in fur coats and radios and slipcovers and—"

"Please, Jim," she said. "Please. They'll hear us."

"*Who'll* hear us? Emma can't hear us."

"The radio."

"Oh, I'm sick!" he shouted. "I'm sick to death of your apprehensiveness. The radio can't hear us. Nobody can hear us. And what if they can hear us? Who cares?"

Irene got up from the table and went into the living room. Jim went to the door and shouted at her from there. "Why are you so Christly all of a sudden? What's turned you overnight into a convent girl? You stole your mother's jewelry before they probated her will. You never gave your sister a cent of that money that was intended for her—not even when she needed it. You made Grace Rowland's life miserable, and where was all your piety and your virtue when you went to that abortionist? I'll never forget how cool you were. You packed your bag and went off to have that child murdered as if you were going to Nassau. If you'd had any reasons, if you'd any good reasons—"

Irene stood for a minute before the hideous cabinet, disgraced and sickened, but she held her hand on the switch before she extinguished the music and the voices, hoping that the instrument might speak to her kindly, that she might hear the Sweeneys' nurse. Jim continued to shout at her from the door. The voice on the radio was suave and noncommittal. "An early-morning railroad disaster in Tokyo," the loudspeaker said, "killed twenty-nine people. A fire in a Catholic hospital near Buffalo for the care of blind children was extinguished early this morning by nuns. The temperature is forty-seven. The humidity is eighty-nine."

SAINT KATY THE VIRGIN

JOHN STEINBECK

{SELECTED BY RAY BRADBURY}

n P—— (as the French say), in the year 13—, there lived a bad man who kept a bad pig. He was a bad man because he laughed too much at the wrong times and at the wrong people. He laughed at the good brothers of M—— when they came to the door for a bit of whiskey or a piece of silver, and he laughed at tithe time. When Brother Clement fell in the mill pond and drowned because he would not drop the sack of salt he was carrying, the bad man, Roark, laughed until he had to go to bed for it. When you think of the low, nasty kind of laughter it was, you'll see what a bad man this Roark was, and you'll not be surprised that he didn't pay his tithes and got himself talked about for excommunication. You see, Roark didn't have the proper kind of a face for a laugh to come out of. It was a dark, tight face, and when he laughed it looked as though Roark's leg had just been torn off and his face was getting ready to scream about it. In addition he called people fools, which is unkind and unwise even if they are. Nobody knew what made Roark so bad except that he had been a traveler and seen bad things about the world.

You see the atmosphere the bad pig, Katy, grew up in, and maybe it's no wonder. There are books written about how Katy came from a long line of bad pigs; how Katy's father was a chicken eater and everybody knew it, and how Katy's mother would make a meal out of her own litter if she was let. But that isn't true. Katy's mother and father were good modest pigs insofar as nature has provided pigs with equipment for modesty, which isn't far. But still, they had the spirit of modesty, as a lot of people have.

Katy's mother had litter after litter of nice red hungry pigs, as normal and decent as you could wish. You must see that the badness of Katy wasn't anything she got by inheritance, so she must have picked it up from the man Roark.

There was Katy lying in the straw with her eyes squinted shut and her pink nose wrinkled, as fine and quiet a piglet as you ever saw, until the day when Roark went out to the sty to name the litter. "You'll be Brigid," he said. "And you're Rory and—turn over you little devil!— you're Katy," and from that minute Katy was a bad pig, the worst pig, in fact, that was ever in the County of P———.

She began by stealing most of the milk; what dugs she couldn't suck on, she put her back against, so that poor Rory and Brigid and the rest turned out runts. Pretty soon, Katy was twice as big as her brothers and sisters and twice as strong. And for badness, can you equal this: one at a time, Katy caught Brigid and Rory and the rest and ate them. With such a start, you might expect almost any kind of a sin out of Katy; and sure enough, it wasn't long before she began eating chickens and ducks, until at last Roark interfered. He put her in a strong sty; at least it was strong on his side. After that, what chickens Katy ate she got from the neighbors.

You should have seen the face of Katy. From the beginning it was a wicked face. The evil yellow eyes of her would frighten you even if you had a stick to knock her on the nose with. She became the terror of the neighborhood. At night, Katy would go stealing out of a hole in her sty to raid hen roosts. Now and then even a child disappeared and was heard of no more. And Roark, who should have been ashamed and sad, grew fonder and fonder of Katy. He said she was the best pig he ever owned, and had more sense than any pig in the county.

After a while the whisper went around that it was a were-pig that wandered about in the night and bit people on the legs and rooted in gardens and ate ducks. Some even went so far as to say it was Roark himself who changed into a pig and stole through the hedges at night. That was the kind of reputation Roark had with his neighbors.

Well, Katy was a big pig now, and it came time for her to be bred. The boar was sterile from that day on and went about with a sad suspicious look on his face and was perplexed and distrustful. But Katy swelled up and swelled up until one night she had her litter. She cleaned them all up and licked them off the way you'd think motherhood had changed her ways. When she got them all dry and clean, she placed them in a row and ate every one of them. It was too much even for a bad man like Roark, for as everyone knows, a sow that will eat her own young is depraved beyond human ability to conceive wickedness.

Reluctantly Roark got ready to slaughter Katy. He was just getting the knife ready when along the path came Brother Colin and Brother Paul on their way collecting tithes. They were sent out from the Monastery of M—— and, while they didn't expect to get anything out of Roark, they thought they'd give him a try anyhow, the way a man will. Brother Paul was a thin, strong man, with a thin, strong face and a sharp eye and unconditional piety written all over him, while Brother Colin was a short round man with a wide round face. Brother Paul looked forward to trying the graces of God in Heaven but Brother Colin was all for testing them on earth. The people called Colin a fine man and Paul a good man. They went tithing together, because what Brother Colin couldn't get by persuasion, Brother Paul dug out with threats and descriptions of the fires of Hell.

"Roark!" says Brother Paul, "we're out tithing. You won't go pickling your soul in sulphur the way you've been in the habit, will you?"

Roark stopped whetting the knife, and his eyes for evilness might have been Katy's own eyes. He started out to laugh, and then the beginning of it stuck in his throat. He got a look on his face like the look Katy had when she was for eating her litter. "I have a pig for you," said Roark, and he put the knife away.

The Brothers were amazed, for up to that time they'd get nothing out of Roark except the dog sic'd on them, and Roark laughing at the way they tripped over their skirts getting to the gate. "A pig?" said Brother Colin suspiciously. "What kind of a pig?"

"The pig that's in the sty alone there," said Roark, and his eyes seemed to turn yellow.

The Brothers hurried over to the sty and looked in. They noted the size of Katy and the fat on her, and they stared incredulously. Colin could think of nothing but the great hams she had and the bacon she wore about like a topcoat. "We'll get a sausage for ourselves from this," he whispered. But Brother Paul was thinking of the praise from Father Benedict when he heard they'd got a pig out of Roark. Paul turned away.

"When will you send this pig over?" he asked.

"I'll bring nothing," Roark cried. "It's your pig there. You take her with you or she will stay here."

The Brothers did not argue. They were too glad to get anything. Paul slipped a cord through the nosering of Katy and led her out of the sty; and for a moment Katy followed them as though she were a really good pig. As the three went through the gate, Roark called after them, "Her name is Katy," and the laugh that had been cooped up in his throat so long cackled out.

"It's a fine big sow," Brother Paul remarked uneasily.

Brother Colin was about to answer him when something like a wolf trap caught him by the back of the leg. Colin yelled and spun about. There was Katy contentedly chewing up a piece of the calf of his leg, and the look on her face like the devil's own look. Katy chewed slowly and swallowed; then she started forward to get another piece of Brother Colin, but in that instant Brother Paul stepped forward and landed a fine big kick on the end of her snout. If there had been evil in Katy's face before, there were demons in her eyes then. She braced herself and growled down deep in her throat; she moved forward snorting and clicking her teeth like a bulldog. The Brothers didn't wait for her; they ran to a thorn tree beside the way and up they climbed with grunts and strainings until at last they were out of reach of the terrible Katy.

Roark had come down to his gate to see them off, and he stood there laughing the way they knew they'd get no help from him. Beneath them, on the ground, Katy paced back and forth; she pawed the ground and rooted out great pieces of turf to show her strength; Brother Paul threw a branch at her, and she tore it to pieces and ground the pieces into the earth under her sharp hooves, all the time looking up at them with her slanty yellow eyes and grinning to herself.

The two Brothers seated themselves miserably in the tree, their heads between their shoulders and their robes hugged tight. "Did you give her a good clout on the nose?" Brother Colin asked hopefully.

Brother Paul looked down at his foot and then at the tough leather snout of Katy. "The kick of my foot would knock down any pig but an elephant," he said.

"You cannot argue with a pig," Brother Colin suggested.

Katy strode ferociously about under the tree. For a long time the brothers sat in silence, moodily drawing their robes about their ankles. Brother Paul studied the problem with a disfiguring intensity. At last he observed: "You wouldn't say pigs had much the nature of a lion now, would you?"

"More the nature of the devil," Colin said wearily.

Paul sat straight up and scrutinized Katy with new interest. Then he held his crucifix out before him, and, in a terrible voice cried, "APAGE SATANAS!"

Katy shuddered as though a strong wind had struck her, but still she came on. "APAGE SATANAS!" Paul cried again and Katy was once more buffeted but unbeaten. A third time Brother Paul hurled the exorcism, but Katy had recovered from the first shock now. It had little effect except to singe a few dried leaves on the ground. Brother Paul turned discouraged eyes to Colin. "Nature of the devil," he announced sadly, "but not the devil's own self, else that pig would have exploded."

Katy ground her teeth together with horrible pleasure.

"Before I got that idea about exorcising," Paul mused, "I was wondering about Daniel in the lion's den, and would the same thing work on a pig?"

Brother Colin regarded him apprehensively. "There may be some flaws in the nature of a lion," he argued. "Maybe lions are not so heretic as pigs. Every time there's a tight place for a pious man to get out of, there's a lion in it. Look at Daniel, look at Samson, look at any number of martyrs just to stay in the religious list; and I could name many cases like Androcles that aren't religious at all. No, Brother, the lion is a beast especially made for saintliness and orthodoxy to cope with. If there's a lion in all those stories it must be because of all creatures, the lion is the least impervious to the force of religion. I think the lion must have been created as a kind of object lesson. It is a beast built for parables, surely. But the pig now—there is no record in my memory that a pig recognizes any force but a clout on the nose or a knife in the throat. Pigs in general, and this pig in particular, are the most headstrong and heretic of beasts."

"Still," Brother Paul went on, paying little attention to the lesson, "when you've got ammunition like the church in your hand, it would be a dirty shame not to give it a good try, be it on lion or on pig. The exorcism did not work, and that means nothing." He started to unwind the rope which served him for a girdle. Brother Colin regarded him with horror.

"Paul, lad," he cried, "Brother Paul, for the love of God, do not go down to that pig." But Paul paid him no attention. He unwound his girdle, and to the end of it tied the chain of his crucifix; then, leaning back until he was hanging by his knees, and the skirts of his robe about his head, Paul lowered the girdle like a fishing line and dangled the iron crucifix toward Katy.

As for Katy, she came forward stamping and champing, ready to snatch it and tread it under her feet. The face of Katy was a tiger's face. Just as she reached the cross, the sharp shadow of it fell on her face, and the cross itself was reflected in her yellow eyes. Katy stopped—paralyzed. The air, the tree, the earth shuddered in an expectant silence, while goodness fought with sin.

Then, slowly, two great tears squeezed out of the eyes of Katy, and before you could think, she was stretched prostrate on the ground, making the sign of the cross with her right hoof and mooing softly in anguish at the realization of her crimes.

Brother Paul dangled the cross a full minute before he hoisted himself back on the limb.

All this time Roark had been watching from his gate. From that day on, he was no longer a bad man; his whole life was changed in a moment. Indeed, he told the story over and over to anyone who would listen. Roark said he had never seen anything so grand and inspiring in his life.

Brother Paul rose and stood on the limb. He drew himself to his full height. Then, using his free hand for gestures, Brother Paul delivered the Sermon on the Mount in beautiful Latin to the groveling, moaning Katy under the tree. When he finished, there was complete and holy silence except for the sobs and sniffles of the repentant pig.

It is doubtful whether Brother Colin had the fiber of a true priest-militant in his nature. "Do—do you think it is safe to go down now?" he stammered.

For answer, Brother Paul broke a limb from the thorn tree and threw it at the recumbent sow. Katy sobbed aloud and raised a tear-stained countenance to them, a face from which all evil had departed; the yellow eyes were golden with repentance and the resulting anguish of grace. The Brothers scrambled out of the tree, put the cord through Katy's nose ring again, and down the road they trudged with the redeemed pig trotting docilely behind them.

News that they were bringing home a pig from Roark caused such excitement that, on arriving at the gates of M———, Brothers Paul and Colin found a crowd of monks awaiting them. The Brotherhood squirmed about, feeling the fat sides of Katy and kneading her jowls. Suddenly an opening was broken in the ring, and Father Benedict paced through. His face wore such a smile that Colin was made sure of his sausage and Paul of his praise. Then, to the horror and consternation of everyone present, Katy waddled to a little font beside the chapel door, dipped her right hoof in holy water, and crossed herself. It was a moment before anyone spoke. Then Father Benedict's stern voice rang out in anger. "Who was it converted this pig?"

Brother Paul stepped forward. "I did it, Father."

"You are a fool," said the Abbot.

"A fool? I thought you would be pleased, Father."

"You are a fool," Father Benedict repeated. "We can't slaughter this pig. This pig is a Christian."

"There is more rejoicing in heaven—" Brother Paul began to quote.

"Hush!" said the Abbot. "There are plenty of Christians. This year there's a great shortage of pigs."

It would take a whole volume to tell of the thousands of sickbeds Katy visited, of the comfort she carried into palaces and cottages. She sat by beds of pain and her dear golden eyes brought relief to the sufferers. For a while it was thought that, because of her sex, she should leave the monastery and enter a nunnery, for the usual ribald tongues caused the usual scandal in the county. But, as the Abbot remarked, one need only look at Katy to be convinced of her purity.

The subsequent life of Katy was one long record of good deeds. It was not until one feast-day morning, however, that the Brothers began to suspect that their community harbored a saint. On the morning in question, while hymns of joy and thanksgiving sounded from a hundred pious mouths, Katy rose from her seat, strode to the altar, and, with a look of seraphic transport on her face, spun like a top on the tip of her tail one hour and three quarters. The assembled Brothers looked on with astonishment and admiration. This was a wonderful example of what a saintly life could accomplish.

From that time on M—— became a place of pilgrimage. Long lines of travelers wound into the valley and stopped at the taverns kept by the good Brothers. Daily at four o'clock, Katy emerged from the gates and blessed the multitudes. If any were afflicted with scrofula or trichina, she touched them and they were healed. Fifty years after her death to a day, she was added to the Calendar of the Elect.

The Proposition was put forward that she should be called Saint Katy the Virgin. However, a minority argued that Katy was not a virgin since she had, in her sinful days, produced a litter. The opposing party retorted that it made no difference at all. Very few virgins, so they said, were virgins.

To keep dissension out of the monastery, a committee presented the problem to a fair-minded and vastly learned barber, agreeing beforehand to be guided by his decision.

"It is a delicate question," said the barber. "'You might say there are two kinds of virginity. Some hold that virginity consists in a little bit of tissue. If you have it, you are; if you haven't, you aren't. This definition is a grave danger to the basis of our religion since there is nothing to differentiate between the Grace of God knocking it out from the inside or the wickedness of man from the outside. On the other hand," he continued, "there is virginity by intent, and this definition admits the existence of a great many more virgins than the first does. But here again we get into trouble. When I was a much younger man, I went about in the evenings sometimes with a girl on my arm. Every one of them that ever walked with me was a virgin by intention, and if you take the second definition, you see, they still are."

The committee went away, satisfied. Katy had without doubt been a virgin by intent.

In the chapel at M—— there is a gold-bound, jeweled reliquary, and inside, on a bed of crimson satin, repose the bones of the Saint. People come great distances to kiss the little box, and such as do, go away leaving their troubles behind them. This holy relic has been found to cure female troubles and ringworm. There is a record left by a woman who visited the chapel to be cured of both. She deposes that she rubbed the reliquary against her cheek, and at the moment her face touched the holy object, a hair mole she had possessed from birth immediately vanished and has never returned.

FOR ALL THE RUDE PEOPLE

JACK RITCHIE

{SELECTED BY ALFRED HITCHCOCK}

"**H**ow old are you?" I asked.

His eyes were on the revolver I was holding. "Look, mister, there's not much in the cash register, but take it all. I won't make no trouble."

"I am not interested in your filthy money. How old are you?"

He was puzzled. "Forty-two."

I clicked my tongue. "What a pity. From your point of view, at least. You might have lived another twenty or thirty years if you had just taken the very slight pains to be polite."

He didn't understand.

"I am going to kill you," I said, "because of the four-cent stamp and because of the cherry candy."

He did not know what I meant by the cherry candy, but he did know about the stamp.

Panic raced into his face. "You must be crazy. You can't kill me just because of that."

"But I can."

And I did.

When Dr. Briller told me that I had but four months to live, I was, of course, perturbed. "Are you positive you haven't mixed up the X-rays? I've heard of such things."

"I'm afraid not, Mr. Turner."

I gave it more earnest thought. "The laboratory reports. Perhaps my name was accidentally attached to the wrong..."

He shook his head slowly. "I double-checked. I always do that in cases like these. Sound medical practice, you know."

It was late afternoon and the time when the sun is tired. I rather hoped that when my time came to actually die, it might be in the morning. Certainly more cheerful.

"In cases like this," Dr. Briller said, "a doctor is faced with a dilemma. Shall he or shall he not tell his patient? I always tell mine. That enables them to settle their affairs and to have a fling, so to speak." He pulled a pad of paper toward him. "Also I'm writing a book. What do you intend doing with your remaining time?"

"I really don't know. I've just been thinking about it for a minute or two, you know."

"Of course," Briller said. "No immediate rush. But when you do decide, you will let me know, won't you? My book concerns the things that people do with their remaining time when they know just when they're going to die."

He pushed aside the pad. "See me every two or three weeks. That way we'll be able to measure the progress of your decline."

Briller saw me to the door. "I already have written up twenty-two cases like yours." He seemed to gaze into the future. "Could be a best seller, you know."

*   *   *

I have always lived a bland life. Not an unintelligent one, but bland.

I have contributed nothing to the world—and in that I have much in common with almost every soul on earth—but on the other hand I have not taken away anything either. I have, in short, asked merely to be left alone. Life is difficult enough without undue association with people.

What can one do with the remaining four months of a bland life?

I have no idea how long I walked and thought on that subject, but eventually I found myself on the long curving bridge that sweeps down to join the lake drive. The sounds of mechanical music intruded themselves upon my mind and I looked down.

A circus, or very large carnival, lay below.

It was the world of shabby magic, where the gold is gilt, where the top-hatted ringmaster is as much a gentleman as the medals on his chest are authentic, and where the pink ladies on horseback are hard-faced and narrow-eyed. It was the domain of the harsh-voiced vendors and the shortchange.

I have always felt that the demise of the big circus may be counted as one of the cultural advances of the twentieth century, yet I found myself descending the footbridge and in a few moments I was on the midway between the rows of stands where human mutations are exploited and exhibited for the entertainment of all children.

Eventually, I reached the big top and idly watched the bored ticket-taker in his elevated box at one side of the main entrance.

A pleasant-faced man leading two little girls approached him and presented several cardboard rectangles which appeared to be passes.

The ticket-taker ran his finger down a printed list at his side. His eyes hardened and he scowled down at the man and the children for a moment. Then slowly and deliberately he tore the passes to bits and let the fragments drift to the ground. "These are no damn good," he said.

The man below him flushed. "I don't understand."

"You didn't leave the posters up," the ticket-taker snapped. "Beat it, crumb!"

The children looked up at their father, their faces puzzled. Would he do something about this?

He stood there and the white of anger appeared on his face. He seemed about to say something, but then he looked down at the children. He closed his eyes for a moment as though to control his anger, and then he said, "Come on, kids. Let's go home."

He led them away, down the midway, and the children looked back, bewildered, but saying nothing.

I approached the ticket-taker. "Why did you do that?"

He glanced down. "What's it to you?"

"Perhaps a great deal."

He studied me irritably. "Because he didn't leave up the posters."

"I heard that before. Now explain it."

He exhaled as though it cost him money. "Our advance man goes through a town two weeks before we get there. He leaves posters advertising the show any place he can—grocery stores, shoe shops, meat markets—any place that will paste them in the window and keep them there until the show comes to town. He hands out two or three passes for that. But what some of these jokers don't know is that we check up. If the posters aren't still up when we hit town, the passes are no good."

"I see," I said dryly. "And so you tear up the passes in their faces and in front of their children. Evidently that man removed the posters from the window of his little shop too soon. Or perhaps he had those passes *given* to him by a man who removed the posters from his window."

"What's the difference? The passes are no good."

"Perhaps there is no difference in that respect. But do you realize what you have done?"

His eyes were narrow, trying to estimate me and any power I might have.

"You have committed one of the most cruel of human acts," I said stiffly. "You have humiliated a man before his children. You have inflicted a scar that will remain with him and them as long as they live. He will take those children home and it will be a long, long way. And what can he say to them?"

"Are you a cop?"

"I am not a cop. Children of that age regard their father as the finest man in the world. The kindest, the bravest. And now they will remember that a man had been bad to their father—and he had been unable to do anything about it."

"So I tore up his passes. Why didn't he buy tickets? Are you a city inspector?"

"I am not a city inspector. Did you expect him to *buy* tickets after that humiliation? You left the man with no recourse whatsoever. He could not *buy* tickets and he could not create a well-justified scene because the children were with him. He could do nothing. Nothing at all, but retreat with two children who wanted to see your miserable circus and now they cannot."

I looked down at the foot of his stand. There were the fragments of many more dreams—the debris of other men who had committed the capital crime of not leaving their posters up long enough. "You could at least have said, 'I'm sorry, sir. But your passes are not valid.' And then you could have explained politely and quietly why."

"I'm not paid to be polite." He showed yellow teeth. "And mister, I *like* tearing up passes. It gives me a kick."

And there it was. He was a little man who had been given a little power and he used it like a Caesar.

He half rose. "Now get the hell out of here, *mister*, before I come down there and chase you all over the lot."

Yes. He was a man of cruelty, a two-dimensional animal born without feeling and sensitivity and fated to do harm as long as he existed. He was a creature who should be eliminated from the face of the earth.

If only I had the power to…

I stared up at the twisted face for a moment more and then turned on my heel and left. At the top of the bridge I got a bus and rode to the sports shop at Thirty-seventh. I purchased a .32-caliber revolver and a box of cartridges.

Why do we *not* murder? Is it because we do not feel the moral justification for such a final act? Or is it more because we fear the consequences if we are caught—the cost to us, to our families, to our children?

And so we suffer wrongs with meekness, we endure them because to eliminate them might cause us even more pain than we already have.

But I had no family, no close friends. And four months to live.

The sun had set and the carnival lights were bright when I got off the bus at the bridge. I looked down at the midway and he was still in his box.

How should I do it? I wondered. Just march up to him and shoot him as he sat on his little throne?

The problem was solved for me. I saw him replaced by another man—apparently his relief. He lit a cigarette and strolled off the midway toward the dark lakefront.

I caught up with him around a bend concealed by bushes. It was a lonely place, but close enough to the carnival so that its sounds could still reach me.

He heard my footsteps and turned. A tight smile came to his lips and he rubbed the knuckles of one hand. "You're asking for it, mister."

His eyes widened when he saw my revolver.

"How old are you?" I asked.

"Look, mister," he said swiftly. "I only got a couple of tens in my pocket."

"How old are you?" I repeated.

His eyes flicked nervously. "Thirty-two."

I shook my head sadly. "You could have lived into your seventies.

Perhaps forty more years of life, if only you had taken the simple trouble to act like a human being."

His face whitened. "Are you off your rocker, or something?"

"A possibility."

I pulled the trigger.

The sound of the shot was not as loud as I had expected, or perhaps it was lost against the background of the carnival noises.

He staggered and dropped to the edge of the path and he was quite dead.

I sat down on a nearby park bench and waited.

Five minutes. Ten. Had no one heard the shot?

I became suddenly conscious of hunger. I hadn't eaten since noon. The thought of being taken to a police station and being questioned for any length of time seemed unbearable. And I had a headache, too.

I tore a page from my pocket notebook and began writing:

A careless word may be forgiven. But a lifetime of cruel rudeness cannot. This man deserves to die.

I was about to sign my name, but then I decided that my initials would be sufficient for the time being. I did not want to be apprehended before I had a good meal and some aspirins.

I folded the page and put it into the dead ticket-taker's breast pocket.

I met no one as I returned up the path and ascended the footbridge. I walked to Weschler's, probably the finest restaurant in the city. The prices are, under normal circumstances, beyond me, but I thought that this time I could indulge myself.

After dinner, I decided an evening bus ride might be in order. I rather enjoyed that form of city excursion and, after all, my freedom of movement would soon become restricted.

The driver of the bus was an impatient man and clearly his passengers were his enemies. However, it was a beautiful night and the bus was not crowded.

At Sixty-eighth Street, a fragile white-haired woman with cameo features waited at the curb. The driver grudgingly brought his vehicle to a stop and opened the door.

She smiled and nodded to the passengers as she put her foot on the first step, and one could see that her life was one of gentle happiness and very few bus rides.

"Well!" the driver snapped. "Is it going to take you all day to get in?"

She flushed and stammered. "I'm sorry." She presented him with a five-dollar bill.

He glared. "Don't you have any change?"

The flush deepened. "I don't think so. But I'll look."

The driver was evidently ahead on his schedule and he waited.

And one other thing was clear. He was enjoying this.

She found a quarter and held it up timorously.

"In the box!" he snapped.

She dropped it into the box.

The driver moved his vehicle forward jerkily and she almost fell. Just in time she managed to catch hold of a strap.

Her eyes went to the passengers, as though to apologize for herself— for not having moved faster, for not having immediate change, for almost falling. The smile trembled and she sat down.

At Eighty-second, she pulled the buzzer cord, rose, and made her way forward.

The driver scowled over his shoulder as he came to a stop. "Use the rear door. Don't you people ever learn to use the rear door?"

I am all in favor of using the rear door. Especially when a bus is crowded. But there were only a half a dozen passengers on this bus and they read their newspapers with frightened neutrality.

She turned, her face pale, and left by the rear door.

The evening she had had, or the evening she was going to have, had now been ruined. Perhaps many more evenings, with the thought of it.

I rode the bus to the end of the line.

I was the only passenger when the driver turned it around and parked.

It was a deserted, dimly lit corner, and there were no waiting passengers at the small shelter at the curb. The driver glanced at his watch, lit a cigarette, and then noticed me. "If you're taking the ride back, mister, put another quarter in the box. No free riders here."

I rose from my seat and walked slowly to the front of the bus. "How old are you?"

His eyes narrowed. "That's none of your business."

"About thirty-five, I'd imagine," I said. "You'd have had another thirty years or more ahead of you." I produced the revolver.

He dropped the cigarette. "Take the money," he said.

"I'm not interested in money. I'm thinking about a gentle lady and perhaps the hundreds of other gentle ladies and the kind harmless men and the smiling children. You are a criminal. There is no justification for what you do to them. There is no justification for your existence."

And I killed him.

I sat down and waited.

After ten minutes, I was still alone with the corpse.

I realized that I was sleepy. Incredibly sleepy. It might be better if I turned myself in to the police after a good night's sleep.

I wrote my justification for the driver's demise on a sheet of note paper, added my initials, and put the page in his pocket.

I walked four blocks before I found a taxi and took it to my apartment building.

I slept soundly and perhaps I dreamed. But if I did, my dreams were pleasant and innocuous, and it was almost nine before I woke.

After a shower and a leisurely breakfast, I selected my best suit. I remembered I had not yet paid that month's telephone bill. I made out a check and addressed an envelope. I discovered that I was out of stamps. But no matter, I would get one on the way to the police station.

I was almost there when I remembered the stamp. I stopped in at a corner drugstore. It was a place I had never entered before.

The proprietor, in a semi-medical jacket, sat behind the soda fountain reading a newspaper and a salesman was making notations in a large order book.

The proprietor did not look up when I entered and he spoke to the salesman. "They've got his fingerprints on the notes, they've got this handwriting, and they've got his initials. What's wrong with the police?"

The salesman shrugged. "What good are fingerprints if the murderer doesn't have his in the police files? The same goes for the handwriting if you got nothing to compare it with. And how many thousand people in the city got the initials L. T.?" He closed his book. "I'll be back next week."

When he was gone, the druggist continued reading the newspaper.

I cleared my throat.

He finished reading a long paragraph and then looked up. "Well?"

"I'd like a four-cent stamp, please."

It appeared almost as though I had struck him. He stared at me for fifteen seconds and then he left his stool and slowly made his way to the rear of the store toward a small barred window.

I was about to follow him, but a display of pipes at my elbow caught my attention.

After a while I felt eyes upon me and looked up.

The druggist stood at the far end of the store, one hand on his hip and the other disdainfully holding the single stamp. "Do you expect me to bring it to you?"

And now I remembered a small boy of six who had had five pennies. Not just one this time, but five, and this was in the days of penny candies.

He had been entranced by the display in the showcase—the fifty varieties of sweet things, and his mind had revolved in a pleasant indecision. The red whips? The licorice? The grab bags? But not the candy cherries. He didn't like those.

And then he had become conscious of the druggist standing beside the display case—tapping one foot. The druggist's eyes had smoldered with irritation—no, more than that—with anger. "Are you going to take all day for your lousy nickel?"

He had been a sensitive boy and he had felt as though he had received a blow. His precious five pennies were now nothing. This man despised them. And this man despised him.

He pointed numbly and blindly. "Five cents of that."

When he left the store he had found that he had the candy cherries.

But that didn't really matter. Whatever it had been, he couldn't have eaten it.

Now I stared at the druggist and the four-cent stamp and the narrow hatred for anyone who did not contribute directly to his profits. I had no doubt that he would fawn if I purchased one of his pipes.

But I thought of the four-cent stamp, and the bag of cherry candy I had thrown away so many years ago.

I moved toward the rear of the store and took the revolver out of my pocket. "How old are you?"

When he was dead, I did not wait longer than necessary to write a note. I had killed for myself this time and I felt the need of a drink.

I went several doors down the street and entered a small bar. I ordered a brandy and water.

After ten minutes, I heard the siren of a squad car.

The bartender went to the window. "It's just down the street." He took off his jacket. "Got to see what this is all about. If anybody comes in, tell them I'll be right back." He put the bottle of brandy on the bar. "Help yourself, but tell me how many."

I sipped the brandy slowly and watched the additional squad cars and finally the ambulance appear.

The bartender returned after ten minutes and a customer followed at his heels. "A short beer, Joe."

"This is my second brandy," I said.

Joe collected my change. "The druggist down the street got himself murdered. Looks like it was by the man who kills people because they're not polite."

The customer watched him draw a beer. "How do you figure that? Could have been just a holdup."

Joe shook his head. "No. Fred Masters—he's got the TV shop across the street—found the body and he read the note."

The customer put a dime on the bar. "I'm not going to cry about it. I always took my business someplace else. He acted as though he was doing you a favor every time he waited on you."

Joe nodded. "I don't think anybody in the neighborhood's going to miss him. He always made a lot of trouble."

I had been about to leave and return to the drugstore to give myself up, but now I ordered another brandy and took out my notebook. I began making a list of names.

It was surprising how one followed another. They were bitter memories, some large, some small, some I had experienced and many more that I had witnessed—and perhaps felt more than the victims.

Names. And that warehouseman. I didn't know his name, but I must include him.

I remembered the day and Miss Newman. We were her sixth graders and she had taken us on another one of her excursions—this time to the warehouses along the river, where she was going to show us "how industry works."

She always planned her tours and she always asked permission of the places we visited, but this time she strayed or became lost and we arrived at the warehouse—she and the thirty children who adored her.

And the warehouseman had ordered her out. He had used language which we did not understand, but we sensed its intent, and he had directed it against us and Miss Newman.

She was small and she had been frightened and we retreated. And Miss Newman did not report to school the next day or any day after that and we learned that she had asked for a transfer.

And I, who loved her, too, knew why. She could not face us after that.

Was he still alive? He had been in his twenties then, I imagined.

When I left the bar a half an hour later, I realized I had a great deal of work to do.

The succeeding days were busy ones and, among others, I found the warehouseman. I told him why he was dying, because he did not even remember.

And when that was done, I dropped into a restaurant not far away.

The waitress eventually broke off her conversation with the cashier and strode to my table. "What do you want?"

I ordered a steak and tomatoes.

The steak proved to be just about what one could expect in such a neighborhood. As I reached for my coffee spoon, I accidentally dropped it to the floor. I picked it up. "Waitress, would you mind bringing me another spoon, please?"

She stalked angrily to my table and snatched the spoon from my hand. "You got the shakes, or something?"

She returned in a few moments and was about to deposit a spoon, with considerable emphasis, upon my table.

But then a sudden thought altered the harsh expression of her face. The descent of the arm diminuendoed, and when the spoon touched the tablecloth, it touched gently. Very gently.

She laughed nervously. "I'm sorry if I was sharp, mister."

It was an apology, and so I said, "That's quite all right."

"I mean that you can drop a spoon anytime you want to. I'll be glad to get you another."

"Thank you." I turned to my coffee.

"You're not offended, are you, mister?" she asked eagerly.

"No. Not at all."

She snatched a newspaper from an empty neighboring table. "Here, sir, you can read this while you eat. I mean, it's on the house. Free."

When she left me, the wide-eyed cashier stared at her. "What's with all that, Mable?"

Mable glanced back at me with a trace of uneasiness. "You can never tell who he might be. You better be polite these days."

As I ate I read, and an item caught my eye. A grown man had heated pennies in a frying pan and tossed them out to some children who were making trick-or-treat rounds before Halloween. He had been fined a miserable twenty dollars.

I made a note of his name and address.

Dr. Briller finished his examination. "You can get dressed now, Mr. Turner."

I picked up my shirt. "I don't suppose some new miracle drug has been developed since I was here last?"

He laughed with self-enjoyed good nature. "No, I'm afraid not." He watched me button the shirt. "By the way, have you decided what you're going to do with your remaining time?"

I had, but I thought I'd say, "Not yet."

He was faintly perturbed. "You really should, you know. Only about three months left. And be sure to let me know when you do."

While I finished dressing, he sat down at his desk and glanced at the newspaper lying there. "The killer seems to be rather busy, doesn't he?"

He turned a page. "But really the most surprising thing about the crimes seems to be the public's reaction. Have you read the Letters from the People column recently?"

"No."

"These murders appear to be meeting with almost universal approval. Some of the letter writers even hint that they might be able to supply the murderer with a few choice names themselves."

I would have to get a paper.

"Not only that," Dr. Briller said, "but a wave of politeness has struck the city."

I put on my coat. "Shall I come back in two weeks?"

He put aside the paper. "Yes. And try to look at this whole thing as cheerfully as possible. We all have to go someday."

But his day was indeterminate and presumably in the distant future.

My appointment with Dr. Briller had been in the evening, and it was nearly ten by the time I left my bus and began the short walk to my apartment building.

As I approached the last corner, I heard a shot. I turned into Milding Lane and found a little man with a revolver standing over a newly dead body on the quiet and deserted sidewalk.

I looked down at the corpse. "Goodness. A policeman."

The little man nodded. "Yes, what I've done does seem a little extreme, but you see he was using a variety of language that was entirely unnecessary."

"Ah," I said.

The little man nodded. "I'd parked my car in front of this fire hydrant. Entirely inadvertently, I assure you. And this policeman was waiting when I returned to my car. And also he discovered that I'd forgotten my driver's license. I would not have acted as I did if he had simply written out a ticket—for I was guilty, sir, and I readily admit it—but he was not content with that. He made embarrassing observations concerning my intelligence, my eyesight, the possibility that I'd stolen the car, and finally on the legitimacy of my birth." He blinked at a fond memory. "And my mother was an angel, sir. An angel."

I remembered a time when I'd been apprehended while absentmindedly jaywalking. I would contritely have accepted the customary warning, or even a ticket, but the officer insisted upon a profane lecture before a grinning assemblage of interested pedestrians. Most humiliating.

The little man looked at the gun in his hand. "I bought this just today and actually I'd intended to use it on the superintendent of my apartment building. A bully."

I agreed. "Surly fellows."

He sighed. "But now I suppose I'll have to turn myself over to the police?"

I gave it thought. He watched me.

He cleared his throat. "Or perhaps I should just leave a note? You see I've been reading in the newspapers about…"

I lent him my notebook.

He wrote a few lines, signed his initials, and deposited the slip of paper between two buttons of the dead officer's jacket.

He handed the notebook back to me. "I must remember to get one of these."

He opened the door of his car. "Can I drop you off anywhere?"

"No, thank you," I said. "It's a nice evening. I'd rather walk."

Pleasant fellow, I reflected, as I left him.

Too bad there weren't more like him.

SUICIDE WOODS

BENJAMIN PERCY

At least once a month, we shrug on our backpacks and follow Mr. Engel along the trails stitching the four hundred acres of Forest Park, of firs and spruce and cedars, that everyone calls Suicide Woods. This is not far from Portland, in the Tualatin Mountains, and within its canyons we traverse a series of switchbacks, drop out of sunlight and into shadow. The honk and grumble of the city is replaced by the rush of Balch Creek. The wind never stops blowing here, damp and cool, shivering the branches and hushing our ears. When we talk, we whisper.

At night, some say, ghosts hang like torn rags in the trees. But even in the daytime we find bodies so often that Mr. Engel seems to have them marked on a map. They lie in beds of moss. They dangle from trees like ornaments. We find them alone and together, clothed and naked.

The forest is so thick that weeks can pass before the dead are discovered. We leave the trails and hike ten feet apart, parting the sword ferns with walking sticks, peering into blackberry tangles. When we hear the angry buzz of flies or the crack of a gunshot, when we see vultures roosting in the trees like little men in black cloaks, when we come upon a face as pale as a mushroom gaping from the undergrowth, we clump together; we circle the body and hold hands and cry.

Mr. Engel says it's good to cry. He says it's like lancing a boil, that it gets out the poisons stewing inside us. He says we need to face our emotions, and that's why he takes us here, to share with us the reality of death—the bloated faces, the soiled underwear, the skin the shade of a green-black thunderhead. He tries so hard. He wants to make us better.

There are ten or twelve or fifteen of us, our number ever fluctuating, because one of us might be in the hospital or in rehab or curled up in a corner clutching a tattery doll. Or dead. One of us could very well be dead. Death is always a possibility. That's what unites us. That's what drew us to Mr. Engel's website—and later his home, where he hosts his weekly meetings. In all of us there is a want to drink Drano, to dive in front of a semi, to take power tools to our wrists.

Mr. Engel wears Chuck Taylors, tight black jeans with the hems rolled up, skull T-shirts, thrift-store cardigans. He is in his forties, but looks to be in his sixties. "Sadness ages you," he says, and he is right; though our ages vary from nineteen to seventy-two, we all suffer from the bent faces and collapsed postures of the elderly.

His wrists carry white lines on them. We are all similarly marked. There is Jean, whose neck healed crookedly after she hanged herself. There is Sam, his skull dented and bald-patched from the bullet still seeded deep in his brain. There is Denver, who makes a sound like gargling when she talks, as though she never coughed up all the pond water she tried to drown herself in. Cara has thin, gray teeth from all the times she's puked up pills and Mason looks like many pieces of gum chewed up and spit out from the time he took a gasoline shower and torched himself with a lit cig. It is not as easy to die as you think.

Some of us have jobs—tending bar or shelving books or roasting beans—but many of us do not. We live with our parents or we live with our siblings or we live with our children. They do not trust us to live alone. We fill our days with video games and YouTube clips and television programs that feature people stripping weight or hunting spouses or remodeling kitchens, fabricating a brighter life that seems unavailable to us. Sometimes we go days without talking to anyone except the pizza delivery guy.

We take Xanax. We take Lorazapam. We take Prozac and Paxil and Zoloft. Dozens of little moons dissolve inside us and make our brains deaden and our hearts fizz. Sometimes we are so sad we do not move. We will stare at the floor or the ceiling or the wall for hours, watch the shadows lean, watch a spider spin a ghostly sac around a carpenter ant. We sit so long that when we stand our muscles cramp and ache as if we are already succumbing to rigor mortis.

This is why Mr. Engel forces us to exercise. We take long hikes in Suicide Woods and the Columbia River Gorge and near the base of Mt. Hood. He forces us blinking into the sun, forces our seizing calves and calcified spines into movement. He says that with regular exercise the heart's chambers expand, the muscle thickens. And if there is anything we need, it is more heart.

Sometimes Mr. Engel invites over instructors, yogis or senseis, who tell us how to breathe and bend our bodies. Mr. Engel lives in a bungalow in West Linn; his living room is walled by mirrors, like a dance studio, so that when we attempt a flying crow or take a fist to the temple we can watch ourselves falling a thousand times over.

We are falling when she walks in, when she opens the door without knocking and stands in the blinding rectangle of sunlight and says, "Am I in the right place?"

We fall in love easily. All it takes is a smile at the supermarket register, two hands reaching for the sugar at the coffeehouse, a long look in the rearview mirror, and we're yours. Though you'll never know it. We're too afraid of rejection, Mr. Engel says, so we never take risks. We never talk to the puddle-eyed girl, the shovel-jawed guy—never ask for a number, offer to buy a drink. We watch them sidelong and for a few minutes our hearts grow full with possibility—and then they walk away and the what-ifs and maybes are replaced by should-haves and might-have-beens and shattered bathroom mirrors.

Her name is Tenley. We have never met anyone named Tenley before, but we feel like we should have. The letters sound so right when set next to each other, hard in the front, buoyant in the back. There should be more Tenleys in the world.

Tenley is an art major. A photography student at Portland State. She carries a long-nosed Canon around her neck. Her skin is offset by hair the same nightmare-black as her clothes. A nose ring and eyebrow stud catch the light and shine. She is tattooed with a Chinese character on her wrist, a strawberry ice cream cone on her bicep, a kraken with tentacles trailing up her neck. A blue teardrop drips down her cheek, and when Denver asks about it—with her swampy gurgling voice—when she jokes and says, "Isn't that supposed to mean you killed someone? Have you killed someone?" Tenley says, "Not yet. But I'm going to," and when we say, "Who?" she says, "Me. I'm going to kill me."

* * *

Today, when we hike Suicide Woods, Tenley joins us. She says the moss-furred branches and feathery sword ferns make this place look like some kind of fairy tale; that we ought to sprinkle bread crumbs to find our way back. We picnic on a ridge of basalt knuckling out over the drainage. While we munch our chips and snap our apples and gurgle warm water from canteens, Mr. Engel asks us to imagine our best self.

We ask him what he means and he says, "I mean you at your best. Your ideal self. Dream big. What are you doing?"

Nobody wants to go first. Nobody ever wants to go first. We lower our heads and hide behind our bangs. So he calls on us.

Sam licks the peanut butter off his teeth and says he sees himself doing two girls at once. "And they're loving it."

Mason sees himself eating a steak at a fancy restaurant, but not too fancy, not like wearing a jacket fancy, just fancy enough that the steak is prime and the napkins linen.

Denver says she would be in a library, one with big stained-glass windows with colored light streaming through them, reading leather-bound books in a leather-backed chair, the kind with the gold buttons.

Then Tenley speaks. "I am at Mann's Chinese Theater in Hollywood," she says, "surrounded by movie stars in tuxedos and gowns. Someone tears open an envelope and calls my name and I climb the stairs to the stage in a strapless gold dress. The applause is thunderous. Dozens of cameras are trained on me, and tens of millions of eyes. I accept the statue. I reach into the scoop of my dress, as if to withdraw my acceptance speech, and while everyone's still expecting me to pull out a slip of paper I grab my gun. It's a Derringer. Then I bring it to my mouth and pull the trigger."

No one says anything, not until later, after we pack up our lunches and zip up our backpacks and hike farther into the woods, after we find a body in the creek with the water foaming over it. When Tenley brings her camera to her eye and begins to snap photos, Mr. Engel says, in a shout so different from his usual whispery voice that it startles us, "Why would you say that? Don't ever say that again."

In his living room, Mr. Engel asks us to lie down and close our eyes and imagine we have been diagnosed with cancer. "You have three months to live," he says. "What will you do in that time? How will you fill what remains of your life?"

He walks among us and against the carpet his socks sizzle with electricity.

"Now you have a month. What do you do? Where do you go?"

He waits a long time between his sentences. "Now a week. Now a day. Now ten minutes."

Our eyes are closed, but we see him through the scrim of our eyelashes when he leans over Tenley and says, "Who will you spend your time with?"

He reaches out to touch her cheek and a blue jolt erupts from his finger and makes her gasp.

We begin to watch them more carefully now, Mr. Engel and Tenley. She shows up to meetings early and leaves late. She thumbs a message on her phone and his pocket buzzes and he brings a hand to it and smiles. In his bathroom we discover another toothbrush. The bristles smell like cigarette ash.

She rides shotgun when he drives us to funerals. They sit together in the pews for the man who starved himself down to a bundle of flesh-smeared sticks, for the woman who hanged herself and now wears a turtleneck to conceal her ripped windpipe, her lips superglued shut to contain her distended tongue.

One day, Tenley asks if she can take our photos. We say yes, but only if we can cover our faces, and she says okay and makes us line up. Some of us put our hands to our faces and peek through the fingers, and some of us pull our shirts up so that we appear headless. Tenley snaps and snaps and snaps.

We huddle around her and study the digital display. "You're good," we say when she clicks through the photos, some of us cast in shadow, others in light.

Then an image of Mr. Engel appears. He is sitting in bed, propped up by pillows. Shirtless. A halo of smoke blurs his face. "Oops," she says. "Went too far." She punches a button and the screen goes black.

Mr. Engel has a picture window with a bench beneath it. On the bench stands a life-size doll, a girl of about five or seven. She wears a different outfit every day: overalls, flower skirts, white shorts with yellow tank tops. Her hair is sometimes in a braid and sometimes in pigtails and sometimes parted cleanly down the middle. None of us have ever asked about her.

But Tenley is different from the rest of us. Unafraid. She asks. She asks about the girl in the window and Mr. Engel goes quiet. His face slacks and his body withers and he stares into a middle distance and for a moment he becomes one of us, one of the group, not our leader but our peer.

"My daughter died," he says in a voice we don't recognize, a voice that sounds like something drawn from the bottom of a well. "She died three years ago and that was her doll."

Tenley touches him on the wrist, traces the scars with her fingernail, and as she does, we all feel cut to the bone.

Mr. Engel asks us to leave. He says this so quietly we are not certain he says anything at all.

Then he says it again. "Please please please leave."

We haven't been there more than five minutes. We haven't even eaten the brownies yet. We haven't dimmed the lights and passed the talking rock, an agate the size of a plum, and shared our latest nightmare. We haven't held hands and looked each other in the eye and promised to return next time. We aren't ready. We don't want to go. But we do as he tells us. We stand and file toward the door and let in a painful wedge of light. Everyone except Tenley. She remains at his side, stroking his scars, until he rips away from her and sweeps his hand like a scythe and says, "You too."

A week passes before we hear from Mr. Engel, and when we do, his email is full of exclamation marks. He writes that he has been planning something for us! Something special! And he can't wait to show us! An overnight getaway!

In the past he only used exclamation marks sparingly. We are worried. We go to him, not wanting help, but wanting to help him.

It rains here as many days as it doesn't. The sky is as gray as the pavement. Moss furs roofs. Mold breathes out of basements. We step out of Mr. Engel's van into a spitting mist. We approach the wrought-iron gate that runs along the parking lot. LONE FIR CEMETERY, the sign reads.

Mr. Engel's smile trembles at the edges when he says he has a surprise for us. He says to follow him. We do. We always do. One sleeve of his cardigan is shorter than the other and he keeps pulling at a loose string, unwinding the fabric further, revealing his scars.

A backhoe has carved out thirteen holes. Beside each of them rises a mound of dirt squirming with worms. The headstones are blank. Inside a white tent—the kind you'd see at a catered wedding—sit thirteen coffins with their lids gaping.

"Who died?" we ask.

"You did!" he says, and we see then that the coffins are empty.

He says he will outfit us with an oxygen tank, Clif Bars, a water bottle. We will spend the night six feet under. We will be buried alive. His voice wavers with excitement when he says this will be a kind of final test, and though it will be uncomfortable, we will return from the experience with a better appreciation for life.

He wants so badly for this to be a good idea, and we want to believe in him.

He burrows his hands into the pockets of his sulfur-yellow cardigan. "So who's first?"

Of course Tenley volunteers. Who else among us would be so willing?

She does not smile, but gives us the thumbs-up before we close the lid on her. We shoulder the weight of the coffin and carry it to the grave. With ropes we lower it into the muddy cavity, and with shovels we drop dirt over her until she vanishes. Mr. Engel slips the backhoe driver two twenties and he takes care of the rest.

It is hard to tell, over the noise of the engine, but we think we hear screaming.

Then it is our turn.

One night feels like many. We try to sleep, but in our dreams the walls narrow, the ceilings lower. Every breath is dirt-scented. Our eyes forget color; we do not know whether they are open or closed. There is no clock ticking off the minutes, no street lamp glowing in the window, no sound except our panicked breathing as we imagine the worms tunneling toward us.

Maybe for the first time, we feel afraid to die.

Oxygen hisses through our masks. Whatever you do, Mr. Engel warned us, do not touch the tank. Even if you feel like you're choking, you aren't. Fiddle with the settings, though, and you will run out of air. But with the masks pressed to our mouths and our lungs gulping, we can't help but feel certain he is wrong. He is wrong and we are going to die and this is what awaits us, this is what death is.

We want the backhoe driver to wake up, finish his coffee and cigarette, key the engine. We want Mr. Engel to pull his hands out of his pockets and get to work shoveling. And then, one by one, we hear a scrape, a thud, voices. The sun blinds us and we blink our eyes at shutter-speed. Our muscles cry out with the wonderful pain of movement. We weep and clumsily applaud and strangle each other into hugs. "I'm so happy," we say. "I'm so fucking happy!"

The ground is marshy but the rain has stopped. The sun burns through a hole in the clouds. One more grave remains; the backhoe grumbles and carves up four feet of dirt as black and sticky as a chocolate cake. We drop into the pit and shovel off the rest, our blades sending up sparks when they clash. The coffin takes shape beneath us; we kneel and wipe away the dirt and knock at the lid and say, "Tenley! You did it, Tenley!"

It takes another five minutes to arrange the ropes, to haul the coffin from the hole, and by then we all feel giddy, exhilarated. When we undo the clasp the coffin opens with a sucking sound.

"Oh no," Mr. Engel says. "No, no, no."

The satin is shredded. Her fingernails are broken and rimmed with blood. Her skin is as sepia-toned as an old photo, except for her tattoos, the teardrop on her cheek as blue as a fallen speck of sky. On one side of her sits the oxygen tank—knobbed to its highest setting, emptied too early—and on the other, her camera, its final photo one of darkness.

Mr. Engel keeps saying, "No." But he should be saying, "Yes." Because we look at her and know he was right. His efforts have paid off. We are better. He has made us better. We have never felt more repulsed by death. We have never felt so terribly alive.

IN THE PENAL COLONY

FRANZ KAFKA

{SELECTED BY RAY BRADBURY}

"It's a remarkable piece of apparatus," said the officer to the explorer and surveyed with a certain air of admiration the apparatus which was after all quite familiar to him. The explorer seemed to have accepted merely out of politeness the Commandant's invitation to witness the execution of a soldier condemned to death for disobedience and insulting behavior to a superior. Nor did the colony itself betray much interest in this execution. At least, in the small sandy valley, a deep hollow surrounded on all sides by naked crags, there was no one present save the officer, the explorer, the condemned man, who was a stupid-looking wide-mouthed creature with bewildered hair and face, and the soldier who held the heavy chain controlling the small chains locked on the prisoner's ankles, wrists, and neck, chains which were themselves attached to each other by communicating links. In any case, the condemned man looked so like a submissive dog that one might have thought he could be left to run free on the surrounding hills and would only need to be whistled for when the execution was due to begin.

The explorer did not much care about the apparatus and walked up and down behind the prisoner with almost visible indifference while the officer made the last adjustments, now creeping beneath the structure, which was bedded deep in the earth, now climbing a ladder to inspect its upper parts. These were tasks that might well have been left to a mechanic, but the officer performed them with great zeal, whether because he was a devoted admirer of the apparatus or because of other reasons the work could be entrusted to no one else. "Ready now!" he called at last and climbed down from the ladder. He looked uncommonly limp, breathed with his mouth wide open, and had tucked two fine ladies' handkerchiefs under the collar of his uniform. "These uniforms are too heavy for the tropics, surely," said the explorer instead of making some inquiry about the apparatus, as the officer had expected. "Of course," said the officer, washing his oily and greasy hands in a bucket of water that stood ready, "but they mean home to us; we don't want to forget about home. Now just have a look at this machine," he added at once, simultaneously drying his hands on a towel and indicating the apparatus. "Up till now a few things still had to be set by hand, but from this moment it works all by itself." The explorer nodded and followed him. The officer, anxious to secure himself against all contingencies, said: "Things sometimes go wrong, of course; I hope that nothing goes wrong today, but we have to allow for the possibility. The machinery should go on working continuously for twelve hours. But if anything does go wrong it will only be some small matter that can be set right at once."

"Won't you take a seat?" he asked finally, drawing a cane chair out from among a heap of them and offering it to the explorer, who could not refuse it. He was now sitting at the edge of a pit, into which he glanced for a fleeting moment. It was not very deep. On one side of the pit the excavated soil had been piled up in a rampart, on the other side of it stood the apparatus. "I don't know," said the officer, "if the

Commandant has already explained this apparatus to you." The explorer waved one hand vaguely; the officer asked for nothing better, since now he could explain the apparatus himself. "This apparatus," he said, taking hold of a handle and leaning against it, "was invented by our former Commandant. I assisted at the very earliest experiments and had a share in all the work until its completion. But the credit of inventing it belongs to him alone. Have you ever heard of our former Commandant? No? Well, it isn't saying too much if I tell you that the organization of the whole penal colony is his work. We who were his friends knew even before he died that the organization of the colony was so perfect that his successor, even with a thousand new schemes in his head, would find it impossible to alter anything, at least for many years to come. And our prophecy has come true; the new Commandant has had to acknowledge its truth. A pity you never met the old Commandant!—But," the officer interrupted himself, "I am rambling on, and here stands his apparatus before us. It consists, as you see, of three parts. In the course of time each of these parts has acquired a kind of popular nickname. The lower one is called the 'Bed,' the upper one the 'Designer,' and this one here in the middle that moves up and down is called the 'Harrow.'" "The Harrow?" asked the explorer. He had not been listening very attentively, the glare of the sun in the shadeless valley was altogether too strong, it was difficult to collect one's thoughts. All the more did he admire the officer, who, in spite of his tight-fitting full-dress uniform coat, amply befrogged and weighed down by epaulettes, was pursuing his subject with such enthusiasm and, besides talking, was still tightening a screw here and there with a spanner. As for the soldier, he seemed to be in much the same condition as the explorer. He had wound the prisoner's chain around both his wrists, propped himself on his rifle, let his head hang, and was paying no attention to anything. That did not surprise the explorer, for the officer was speaking French, and certainly neither the soldier nor the prisoner understood a word of French. It was all the more remarkable, therefore, that the prisoner was nonetheless making an effort to follow the officer's explanations. With a kind of drowsy persistence he directed his gaze wherever the officer pointed a finger, and at the interruption of the explorer's question he, too, as well as the officer, looked round.

"Yes, the Harrow," said the officer, "a good name for it. The needles are set in like the teeth of a harrow and the whole thing works something like a harrow, although its action is limited to one place and contrived with much more artistic skill. Anyhow, you'll soon understand it. On the bed here the condemned man is laid—I'm going to describe the apparatus first before I set it in motion. Then you'll be able to follow the proceedings better. Besides, one of the cogwheels in the Designer is badly worn; it creaks a lot when it's working; you can hardly hear yourself speak; spare parts, unfortunately, are difficult to get here.—Well, here is the Bed, as I told you. It is completely covered with a layer of cotton wool; you'll find out why later. On this cotton wool the condemned man is laid, facedown, quite naked, of course; here are straps for the hands, here for the feet, and here for the neck, to bind him fast. Here at the head of the bed, where the man, as I said, first lays down his face, is this little gag of felt, which can be easily regulated to go straight into his mouth. It is meant to keep him from screaming and biting his tongue. Of course the man is forced to take the felt into his mouth, for otherwise his neck would be broken by the strap." "Is that cotton wool?" asked the explorer, bending forward. "Yes, certainly," said the officer, with a smile, "feel it for yourself." He took the explorer's hand and guided it over the bed. "It's specially prepared cotton wool, that's why it looks so different; I'll tell you presently what it's for." The explorer already felt a dawning interest in the apparatus; he sheltered his eyes from the sun with one hand and gazed up at the structure. It was a huge affair. The Bed and the Designer were of the same size and looked like two dark wooden chests. The Designer hung about two meters above the Bed; each of them was bound at the corners with four rods of brass that almost flashed out rays in the sunlight. Between the chests shuttled the Harrow on a ribbon of steel.

The officer had scarcely noticed the explorer's previous indifference, but he was now well aware of his dawning interest; so he stopped explaining in order to leave a space of time for quiet observation. The condemned man imitated the explorer; since he could not use a hand to shelter his eyes he gazed upward without shade.

"Well, the man lies down," said the explorer, leaning back in his chair and crossing his legs.

"Yes," said the officer, pushing his cap back a little and passing one hand over his heated face, "now listen! Both the Bed and the Designer have an electric battery each; the Bed needs one for itself, the Designer for the Harrow. As soon as the man is strapped down, the Bed is set in motion. It quivers in minute, very rapid vibrations, both from side to side and up and down. You will have seen similar apparatus in hospitals; but in our Bed the movements are all precisely calculated; you see, they have to correspond very exactly to the movements of the Harrow. And the Harrow is the instrument for the actual execution of the sentence."

"And how does the sentence run?" asked the explorer.

"You don't know that either?" said the officer in amazement, and bit his lips. "Forgive me if my explanations seem rather incoherent. I do beg your pardon. You see, the Commandant always used to do the explaining; but the new Commandant shirks this duty; yet that such an important visitor"—the explorer tried to deprecate the honor with both hands, the officer, however, insisted—"that such an important visitor should not even be told about the kind of sentence we pass is a new development, which—" He was just on the point of using strong language but checked himself and said only: "I was not informed, it is not my fault. In any case, I am certainly the best person to explain our procedure, since I have here"—he patted his breast pocket—"the relevant drawings made by our former Commandant."

"The Commandant's own drawings?" asked the explorer. "Did he combine everything in himself, then? Was he soldier, judge, mechanic, chemist, and draughtsman?"

"Indeed he was," said the officer, nodding assent, with a remote, glassy look. Then he inspected his hands critically; they did not seem clean enough to him for touching the drawings; so he went over to the bucket and washed them again. Then he drew out a small leather wallet and said: "Our sentence does not sound severe. Whatever commandment the prisoner has disobeyed is written upon his body by the Harrow. This prisoner, for instance"—the officer indicated the man—"will have written on his body: HONOR THY SUPERIORS!"

The explorer glanced at the man; he stood, as the officer pointed him out, with bent head, apparently listening with all his ears in an effort to catch what was being said. Yet the movement of his blubber lips, closely pressed together, showed clearly that he could not understand a word. Many questions were troubling the explorer, but at the sight of the prisoner he asked only: "Does he know his sentence?" "No," said the officer again, eager to go on with his exposition, but the explorer interrupted him: "He doesn't know the sentence that has been passed on him?" "No," said the officer again, pausing a moment as if to let the explorer elaborate his question, and then said: "There would be no point in telling him. He'll learn it on his body." The explorer intended to make no answer, but he felt the prisoner's gaze turned on him; it seemed to ask if he approved such ongoings. So he bent forward again, having already leaned back in his chair, and put another question: "But surely he knows that he has been sentenced?" "Nor that either," said the officer, smiling at the explorer as if expecting him to make further surprising remarks. "No," said the explorer, wiping his forehead, "then he can't know either whether his defense was effective?" "He has had no chance of putting up a defense," said the officer, turning his eyes away as if speaking to himself and so sparing the explorer the shame of hearing self-evident matters explained. "But he must have had some chance of defending himself," said the explorer, and rose from his seat.

The officer realized that he was in danger of having his exposition of the apparatus held up for a long time; so he went up to the explorer, took him by the arm, waved a hand toward the condemned man, who was standing very straight now that he had so obviously become the center of attention—the soldier had also given the chain a jerk—and said: "This is how the matter stands. I have been appointed judge in this penal colony. Despite my youth. For I was the former Commandant's assistant in penal matters and know more about the apparatus than anyone. My guiding principle is this: Guilt is never to be doubted. Other courts cannot follow the principle, for they consist of several opinions and have higher courts to scrutinize them. That is not the case here or at least, it was not the case in the former Commandant's time. The new man has certainly shown some inclination to interfere with my judgment, but so far I have succeeded in fending him off and will go on succeeding. You wanted to have the case explained; it is quite simple, like all of them. A captain reported to me this morning that this man, who had been assigned to him as a servant and sleeps before his door, had been asleep on duty. It is his duty, you see, to get up every time the hour strikes and salute the captain's door. Not an exacting duty, and very necessary, since he has to be a sentry as well as a servant, and must be alert in both functions. Last night the captain wanted to see if the man was doing his duty. He opened the door as the clock struck two and there was his man curled up asleep. He took his riding whip and lashed him across the face. Instead of getting up and begging pardon, the man caught hold of his master's legs, shook him and cried: 'Throw that whip away or I'll eat you alive.'— That's the evidence. The captain came to me an hour ago, I wrote down his statement and appended the sentence to it. Then I had the man put in chains. That was all quite simple. If I had first called the man before me and interrogated him, things would have got into a confused tangle. He would have told lies, and had I exposed these lies he would have backed them up with more lies, and so on and so forth. As it is, I've got him and

I won't let him go.—Is that quite clear now? But we're wasting time, the execution should be beginning and I haven't finished explaining the apparatus yet." He pressed the explorer back into his chair, went up again to the apparatus, and began: "As you see, the shape of the Harrow corresponds to the human form; here is the harrow for the torso, here are the harrows for the legs. For the head there is only this one small spike. Is that quite clear?" He bent amiably forward toward the explorer, eager to provide the most comprehensive explanations.

The explorer considered the Harrow with a frown. The explanation of the judicial procedure had not satisfied him. He had to remind himself that this was in any case a penal colony where extraordinary measures were needed and that military discipline must be enforced to the last. He also felt that some hope might be set on the new Commandant, who was apparently of a mind to bring in, although gradually, a new kind of procedure which the officer's narrow mind was incapable of understanding. This train of thought prompted his next question: "Will the Commandant attend the execution?" "It is not certain," said the officer, wincing at the direct question, and his friendly expression darkened. "That is just why we have to lose no time. Much as I dislike it, I shall have to cut my explanations short. But of course tomorrow, when the apparatus has been cleaned—its one drawback is that it gets so messy—I can recapitulate all the details. For the present, then, only the essentials.— When the man lies down on the Bed and it begins to vibrate, the Harrow is lowered onto his body. It regulates itself automatically so that the needles barely touch his skin; once contact is made the steel ribbon stiffens immediately into a rigid band. And then the performance begins. An ignorant onlooker would see no difference between one punishment and another. The Harrow appears to do its work with uniform regularity. As it quivers, its points pierce the skin of the body which is itself quivering from the vibration of the Bed. So that the actual progress of the sentence can be watched, the Harrow is made of glass. Getting the needles fixed in the glass was a technical problem, but after many experiments we overcame the difficulty. No trouble was too great for us to take, you see. And now anyone can look through the glass and watch the inscription taking form on the body. Wouldn't you care to come a little nearer and have a look at the needles?"

The explorer got up slowly, walked across, and bent over the Harrow. "You'll see," said the officer, "there are two kinds of needles arranged in multiple patterns. Each long needle has a short one beside it. The long needle does the writing, and the short needle sprays a jet of water to wash away the blood and keep the inscription clear. Blood and water together are then conducted here through small runnels into this main runnel and down a waste pipe into the pit." With his finger the officer traced the exact course taken by the blood and water. To make the picture as vivid as possible he held both hands below the outlet of the waste pipe as if to catch the outflow, and when he did this the explorer drew back his head and feeling behind him with one hand sought to return to his chair. To his horror he found that the condemned man too had obeyed the officer's invitation to examine the Harrow at close quarters and had followed him. He had pulled forward the sleepy soldier with the chain and was bending over the glass. One could see that his uncertain eyes were trying to perceive what the two gentlemen had been looking at, but since he had not understood the explanation he could not make head or tail of it. He was peering this way and that way. He kept running his eyes along the glass. The explorer wanted to drive him away, since what he was doing was probably culpable. But the officer firmly restrained the explorer with one hand and with the other took a clod of earth from the rampart and threw it at the soldier. He opened his eyes with a jerk, saw what the condemned man had dared to do, let his rifle fall, dug his heels into the ground, dragged his prisoner back so that he stumbled and fell immediately, and then stood looking down at him, watching him struggling and rattling in his chains. "Set him on his feet!" yelled the officer, for he noticed that the explorer's attention was being too much distracted by the prisoner. In fact he was even leaning right across the Harrow, without taking any notice of it, intent only on finding out what was happening to the prisoner. "Be careful with him!" cried the officer again. He ran round the apparatus, himself caught the condemned man under the shoulders, and with the soldier's help got him up on his feet, which kept slithering from under him.

"Now I know all about it," said the explorer as the officer came back to him. "All except the most important thing," the officer answered, seizing the explorer's arm and pointing upward: "In the Designer are all the cogwheels that control the movements of the Harrow, and this machinery is regulated according to the inscription demanded by the sentence. I am still using the guiding plans drawn by the former Commandant. Here they are"—he extracted some sheets from the leather wallet—"but I'm sorry I can't let you handle them, they are my most precious possessions. Just take a seat and I'll hold them in front of you like this, then you'll be able to see everything quite well." He spread out the first sheet of paper. The explorer would have liked to say something appreciative, but all he could see was a labyrinth of lines crossing and recrossing each other, which covered the paper so thickly it was difficult to discern the blank spaces between them. "Read it," said the officer. "I can't," said the explorer. "Yet it's clear enough," said the officer. "It's very ingenious," said the explorer evasively, "but I can't make it out," "Yes," said the officer with a laugh, putting the paper away again, "it's no calligraphy for schoolchildren. It needs to be studied closely. I'm quite sure that in the end you would understand it too. Of course the script can't be a simple one; it's not supposed to kill a man straight off, but only after an interval of, on an average, twelve hours; the turning point is reckoned to come at the sixth hour. So there have to be lots and lots of flourishes around the actual script; the script itself runs round the body only in a narrow girdle; the rest of the body is reserved for the embellishments. Can you appreciate now the work accomplished by the Harrow and the whole apparatus?—Just watch it!" He ran up the ladder, turned a wheel, called down: "Look out, keep to one side!" and everything started working. If the wheel had not creaked, it would have been marvelous. The officer, as if surprised by the noise of the wheel, shook his fist at it, then spread out his arms in excuse to the explorer and climbed down rapidly to peer at the working of the machine from below. Something perceptible to no one save himself was still not in order; he clambered up again, did something with both his hands in the interior of the Designer, then slid down one of the rods, instead of using the ladder, so as to get down quicker, and with the full force of his lungs, to make himself heard at all in the noise, yelled in the explorer's ear: "Can you follow it? The Harrow is beginning to write; when it finishes the first draft of the inscription on the man's back, the layer of cotton wool begins to roll and slowly turns the body over, to give the Harrow fresh space for writing. Meanwhile the raw part that has been written lies on the cotton wool, which is specially prepared to staunch the bleeding and so makes all ready for a new deepening of the script. Then these teeth at the edge of the Harrow, as the body turns further round, tear the cotton wool away from the wounds, throw it into the pit, and there is more work for the Harrow. So it keeps on writing deeper and deeper for the whole twelve hours. The first six hours the condemned man stays alive almost as before, he suffers only pain. After two hours the felt gag is taken away, for he has no longer strength to scream. Here, into this electrically heated basin at the head of the bed, some warm rice pap is poured, from which the man, if he feels like it, can take as much as his tongue can lap. Not one of them ever misses the chance. I can remember none, and my experience is extensive. Only about the sixth hour does the man lose all desire to eat. I usually kneel down here at that moment and observe what happens. The man rarely swallows his last mouthful, he only rolls it round his mouth and spits it out into the pit. I have to duck just then or he would spit it in my face. But how quiet he grows at just about the sixth hour! Enlightenment comes to the most dull-witted. It begins around the eyes. From there it radiates. A moment that might tempt one to get under the Harrow oneself. Nothing more happens than that the man begins to understand the inscription, he purses his mouth as if he were listening. You have seen how difficult it is to decipher the script with one's eyes; but our man deciphers it with his wounds. To be sure, that is a hard task; he needs six hours to accomplish it. By that time the Harrow has pierced him quite through and casts him into the pit, where he pitches down upon the blood and water and the cotton wool. Then the judgment has been fulfilled, and we, the soldier and I, bury him."

The explorer had inclined his ear to the officer and with his hands in his jacket pockets watched the machine at work. The condemned man watched it too, but uncomprehendingly. He bent forward a little and was intent on the moving needles when the soldier, at a sign from the officer, slashed through his shirt and trousers from behind with a knife, so that they fell off; he tried to catch at his falling clothes to cover his nakedness, but the soldier lifted him into the air and shook the last remnants from him. The officer stopped the machine, and in the sudden silence the condemned man was laid under the Harrow. The chains were loosened and the straps fastened on instead; in the first moment that seemed almost a relief to the prisoner. And now the Harrow was adjusted a little lower, since he was a thin man. When the needle points touched him a shudder ran over his skin; while the soldier was busy strapping his right hand, he flung out his left hand blindly; but it happened to be in the direction toward where the explorer was standing. The officer kept watching the explorer sideways, as if seeking to read from his face the impression made on him by the execution, which had been at least cursorily explained to him.

The wrist strap broke; probably the soldier had drawn it too tight. The officer had to intervene, the soldier held up the broken piece of strap to show him. So the officer went over and said, his face still turned toward the explorer: "This is a very complex machine, it can't be helped that things are breaking or giving way here and there; but one must not thereby allow oneself to be diverted in one's general judgment. In any case, this strap is easily made good; I shall simply use a chain; the delicacy of the vibrations for the right arm will of course be a little impaired." And while he fastened the chains, he added: "The resources for maintaining the machine are now very much reduced. Under the former Commandant I had free access to a sum of money set aside entirely for this purpose. There was a store, too, in which spare parts were kept for repairs of all kinds. I confess I have been almost prodigal with them, I mean in the past, not now as the new Commandant pretends, always looking for an excuse to attack our old way of doing things. Now he has taken charge of the machine money himself, and if I send for a new strap they ask for the broken old strap as evidence, and the new strap takes ten days to appear and then is of shoddy material and not much good. But how I am supposed to work the machine without a strap, that's something nobody bothers about."

The explorer thought to himself: It's always a ticklish matter to intervene decisively in other people's affairs. He was neither a member of the penal colony nor a citizen of the state to which it belonged. Were he to denounce this execution or actually try to stop it, they could say to him: You are a foreigner, mind your own business. He could make no answer to that, unless he were to add that he was amazed at himself in this connection, for he traveled only as an observer with no intention at all of altering other people's methods of administering justice. Yet here he found himself strongly tempted. The injustice of the procedure and the inhumanity of the execution were undeniable. No one could suppose that he had any selfish interest in the matter, for the condemned man was a complete stranger, not a fellow countryman or even at all sympathetic to him. The explorer himself had recommendations from high quarters, had been received here with great courtesy, and the very fact that he had been invited to attend the execution seemed to suggest that his views would be welcome. And this was all the more likely since the Commandant, as he had heard only too plainly, was no upholder of the procedure and maintained an attitude almost of hostility to the officer.

At that moment the explorer heard the officer cry out in rage. He had just, with considerable difficulty, forced the felt gag into the condemned man's mouth when the man in an irresistible access of nausea shut his eyes and vomited. Hastily the officer snatched him away from the gag and tried to hold his head over the pit; but it was too late, the vomit was running all over the machine. "It's all the fault of that Commandant!" cried the officer, senselessly shaking the brass rods in front. "The machine is befouled like a pigsty." With trembling hands he indicated to the explorer what had happened. "Have I not tried for hours at a time to get the Commandant to understand that the prisoner must fast for a whole day before the execution. But our new, mild doctrine thinks otherwise. The Commandant's ladies stuff the man with sugar candy before he's led off. He has lived on stinking fish his whole life long and now he has to eat sugar candy! But it could still be possible, I should have nothing to say against it, but why won't they get me a new felt gag, which I have been begging for the last three months. How should a man not feel sick when he takes a felt gag into his mouth that more than a hundred men have already slobbered and gnawed in their dying moments?"

The condemned man had laid his head down and looked peaceful, the soldier was busy trying to clean the machine with the prisoner's shirt. The officer advanced toward the explorer, who in some vague presentiment fell back a pace, but the officer seized him by the hand, and drew him to one side. "I should like to exchange a few words with you in confidence," he said, "May I?" "Of course," said the explorer, and listened with downcast eyes.

"This procedure and method of execution, which you are now having the opportunity to admire, has at the moment no longer any open adherents in our colony. I am its sole advocate, and at the same time the sole advocate of the old Commandant's tradition. I can no longer reckon on any further extension of the method, it takes all my energy to maintain it as it is. During the old Commandant's lifetime the colony was full of his adherents; his strength of conviction I still have in some measure, but not an atom of his power; consequently the adherents have skulked out of sight, there are still many of them but none of them will admit it. If you were to go into the teahouse today, on execution day, and listen to what is being said, you would perhaps hear only ambiguous remarks. These would all be made by adherents, but under the present Commandant and his present doctrines they are of no use to me. And now I ask you: because of this Commandant and the women who influence him, is such a piece of work, the work of a lifetime"—he pointed to the machine—"to perish? Ought one to let that happen? Even if one has only come as a stranger to our island for a few days? But there's no time to lose, an attack of some kind is impending on my function as judge; conferences are already being held in the Commandant's office from which I am excluded; even your coming here today seems to me a significant move; they are cowards and use you as a screen, you, a stranger.—How different an execution was in the old days! A whole day before the ceremony the valley was packed with people; they all came only to look on; early in the morning the Commandant appeared with his ladies; fanfares roused the whole camp; I reported that everything was in readiness; the assembled company—no high official dared to absent himself—arranged itself round the machine; this pile of cane chairs is a miserable survival from that epoch. The machine was freshly cleaned and glittering, I got new spare parts for almost every execution. Before hundreds of spectators—all of them standing on tiptoe as far as the heights there—the condemned man was laid under the Harrow by the Commandant himself. What is left today for a common soldier to do was then my task, the task of the presiding judge, and was an honor for me. And then the execution began! No discordant noise spoilt the working of the machine. Many did not care to watch it but lay with closed eyes in the sand; they all knew: Now Justice is being done. In the silence one heard nothing but the condemned man's sighs, half muffled by the felt gag. Nowadays the machine can no longer wring from anyone a sigh louder than the felt gag can stifle; but in those days the writing needles let drop an acid fluid, which we're no longer permitted to use. Well, and then came the sixth hour! It was impossible to grant all the requests to be allowed to watch it from nearby. The Commandant in his wisdom ordained that the children should have the preference; I, of course, because of my office had the privilege of always being at hand; often enough I would be squatting there with a small child in either arm. How we all absorbed the look of transfiguration on the face of the sufferer, how we bathed our cheeks in the radiance of that justice, achieved at last and fading so quickly! What times these were, my comrade!" The officer had obviously forgotten whom he was addressing; he had embraced the explorer and laid his head on his shoulder. The explorer was deeply embarrassed, impatiently he stared over the officer's head. The soldier had finished his cleaning job and was now pouring rice pap from a pot into the basin. As soon as the condemned man, who seemed to have recovered entirely, noticed this action he began to reach for the rice with his tongue. The soldier kept pushing him away, since the rice pap was certainly meant for a later hour, yet it was just as unfitting that the soldier himself should thrust his dirty hands into the basin and eat out of it before the other's avid face.

The officer quickly pulled himself together. "I didn't want to upset you," he said. "I know it is impossible to make those days credible now. Anyhow, the machine is still working and it is still effective in itself. It is effective in itself even though it stands alone in this valley. And the corpse still falls at the last into the pit with an incomprehensible gentle wafting motion, even although there are no hundreds of people swarming round like flies as formerly. In those days we had to put a strong fence round the pit, it has long since been torn down."

The explorer wanted to withdraw his face from the officer and looked round him at random. The officer thought he was surveying the valley's desolation; so he seized him by the hands, turned him round to meet his eyes, and asked: "Do you realize the shame of it?"

But the explorer said nothing. The officer left him alone for a little; with legs apart, hands on hips, he stood very still, gazing at the ground. Then he smiled encouragingly at the explorer and said: "I was quite near you yesterday when the Commandant gave you the invitation. I heard him giving it. I know the Commandant. I divined at once what he was after. Although he is powerful enough to take measures against me, he doesn't dare to do it yet, but he certainly means to use your verdict against me, the verdict of an illustrious foreigner. He has calculated it carefully: this is your second day on the island, you did not know the old Commandant and his ways, you are conditioned by European ways of thought, perhaps you object on principle to capital punishment in general and to such mechanical instruments of death in particular, besides you will see that the execution has no support from the public, a shabby ceremony—carried out with a machine already somewhat old and worn—now, taking all that into consideration, would it not be likely (so thinks the Commandant) that you might disapprove of my methods? And if you disapprove, you wouldn't conceal the act (I'm still speaking from the Commandant's point of view), for you are a man to feel confidence in your own well-tried conclusions. True, you have seen and learned to appreciate the peculiarities of many peoples, and so you would not be likely to take a strong line against our proceedings, as you might do in your own country. But the Commandant has no need of that. A casual, even an unguarded remark will be enough. It doesn't even need to represent what you really think, so long as it be used speciously to serve his purpose. He will try to prompt you with sly questions, of that I am certain. And his ladies will sit around you and prick up their ears; you might be saying something like this: 'In our country we have a different criminal procedure,' or 'In our country the prisoner is interrogated before he is sentenced,' or 'We haven't used torture since the Middle Ages.' All these statements are as true as they seem natural to you, harmless remarks that pass no judgment of my methods. But how would the Commandant react to them? I can see him, our good Commandant, pushing his chair away immediately and rushing on to the balcony, I can see his ladies streaming out after him, I can hear his voice—the ladies call it a voice of thunder—well, and this is what he says: 'A famous Western investigator, sent out to study criminal procedure in all the countries of the world, has just said that our old tradition of administering justice is inhumane. Such a verdict from such a personality makes it impossible for me to countenance these methods any longer. Therefore from this very day I ordain...' and so on. You may want to interpose that you never said any such thing, that you never called my methods inhumane, on the contrary your profound experience leads you to believe they are most humane and most in consonance with human dignity, and you admire the machine greatly—but it will be too late; you won't even get onto the balcony, crowded as it will be with ladies; you may try to draw attention to yourself, you may want to scream out; but a lady's hand will close your lips—and I and the work of the old Commandant will be done for."

The explorer had to suppress a smile; so easy, then, was the task he had felt to be so difficult. He said evasively: "You overestimate my influence; the Commandant has read my letters of recommendation, he knows that I am no expert in criminal procedure. If I were to give an opinion, it would be as a private individual, an opinion no more influential than that of any ordinary person, and in any case much less influential than that of the Commandant, who, I am given to understand, has very extensive powers in this penal colony. If this attitude to your procedure is as definitely hostile as you believe, then I fear the end of your tradition is at hand, even without any humble assistance from me."

Had it dawned on the officer at last? No, he still did not understand. He shook his head emphatically, glanced briefly round at the condemned man and the soldier, who both flinched away from the rice, came close up to the explorer, and without looking at his face but fixing his eye on some spot on his coat said in a lower voice than before: "You don't know the Commandant; you feel yourself—forgive the expression—a kind of outsider so far as all of us are concerned; yet, believe me, your influence cannot be rated too highly. I was simply delighted when I heard that you were to attend the execution all by yourself. The Commandant arranged it to aim a blow at me, but I shall turn it to my advantage. Without being distracted by lying whispers and contemptuous glances—which could not have been avoided had a crowd of people attended the execution—you have heard my explanations, seen the machine, and are now about to watch the execution. You have doubtless already formed your own judgment; if you still have some small uncertainties the sight of the execution will resolve them. And now I make this request to you: help me against the Commandant!"

The explorer would not let him go on. "How could I do that?" he cried. "It's quite impossible. I can neither help nor hinder you."

"Yes, you can," the officer said. The explorer saw with a certain apprehension that the officer had clenched his fists. "Yes, you can," repeated the officer, still more insistently. "I have a plan that is bound to succeed. You believe your influence is insufficient. I know that it is sufficient. But even granted that you are right, is it not necessary, for the sake of preserving this tradition, to try even what might prove insufficient? Listen to my plan, then. The first thing necessary for you to carry it out is to be as reticent as possible today regarding your verdict on these proceedings. Unless you are asked a direct question you must say nothing at all; but what you do say must be brief and general; let it be remarked that you would prefer not to discuss the matter, that you are out of patience with it, that if you are to let yourself go you would use strong language. I don't ask you to tell any lies; by no means; you should only give curt answers, such as: 'Yes, I saw the execution,' or 'Yes, I had it explained to me.' Just that, nothing more. There are grounds enough for any impatience you betray, although not such as will occur to the Commandant. Of course, he will mistake your meaning and interpret it to please himself. That's what my plan depends on. Tomorrow in the Commandant's office there is to be a large conference of all the high administrative officials, the Commandant presiding. Of course the Commandant is the kind of man to have turned these conferences into public spectacles. He has had a gallery built that is always packed with spectators. I am compelled to take part in the conferences, but they make me sick with disgust. Now, whatever happens, you will certainly be invited to this conference; if you behave today as I suggest, the invitation will become an urgent request. But if for some mysterious reason you're not invited, you'll have to ask for an invitation; there's no doubt of your getting it then. So tomorrow you're sitting in the Commandant's box with the ladies. He keeps looking up to make sure you're there. After various trivial ridiculous matters, brought in merely to impress the audience—mostly harbor works, nothing but harbor works!—our judicial procedure comes up for discussion too. If the Commandant doesn't introduce it, or not soon enough, I'll see that it's mentioned. I'll stand up and report that today's execution has taken place. Quite briefly, only a statement. Such a statement is not usual, but I shall make it. The Commandant thanks me, as always, with an amiable smile, and then he can't restrain himself, he seizes the excellent opportunity. 'It has just been reported,' he will say, or words to that effect, 'that an execution was witnessed by the famous explorer who has, as you all know, honored our colony so greatly by his visit to us. His presence at today's session of our conference also contributes to the importance of this occasion. Should we not now ask the famous explorer to give us his verdict on our traditional mode of execution and the procedure that leads up to it?' Of course there is loud applause, general agreement, I am more insistent than anyone. The Commandant bows to you and says: 'Then in the name of the assembled company, I put the question to you.' And now you advance to the front of the box. Lay your hands where everyone can see them, or the ladies will catch them and press your fingers.—And then at last you can speak out. I don't know how I'm going to endure the tension of waiting for that moment. Don't put any restraint on yourself when you make your speech, publish the truth aloud, lean over the front of the box, shout, yes indeed, shout your verdict, your unshakable conviction, at the Commandant. Yet perhaps you wouldn't dare to do that, it's not in keeping with your character, in your country perhaps people do these things differently, well, that's all right too, that will be quite as effective, don't even stand up, just say a few words, even in a whisper, so that only the officials beneath you will hear them, that will be quite enough, you don't even need to mention the lack of public support for the execution, the creaking wheel, the broken strap, the filthy gag of felt, no, I'll take all that upon me, and, believe me, if my indictment doesn't drive him out of the conference hall, it will force him to his knees to make the acknowledgment: Old Commandant, I humble myself before you.—That is my plan; will you help me to carry it out? But of course you are willing, what is more, you must." And the officer seized the explorer by both arms and gazed, breathing heavily, into his face. He had shouted the last sentence so loudly that even the soldier and the condemned man were startled into attending; they had not understood a word but they stopped eating and looked over at the explorer, chewing their previous mouthfuls.

From the very beginning the explorer had no doubt about what answer he must give; in his lifetime he had experienced too much to have any uncertainty here; he was fundamentally honorable and unafraid. And yet now, facing the soldier and the condemned man, he did hesitate, for as long as it took to draw one breath. At last, however, he said, as he had to: "No." The officer blinked several times but did not turn his eyes away. "Would you like me to explain?" asked the explorer. The officer nodded wordlessly. "I do not approve of your procedure," said the explorer then, "even before you took me into your confidence—of course I shall never in any circumstances betray your confidence—I was already wondering whether it would be my duty to intervene and whether my intervention would have the slightest chance of success. I realized to whom I ought to turn: to the Commandant, of course. You have made that fact even clearer, but without having strengthened my resolution, on the contrary, your sincere conviction has touched me, even though it cannot influence my judgment."

The officer remained mute, turned to the machine, caught hold of a brass rod, and then, leaning back a little, gazed at the Designer as if to assure himself that it was all in order. The soldier and the condemned man seemed to have come to some understanding; the condemned man was making signs to the soldier, difficult though his movements were because of the tight straps; the soldier was bending down to him; the condemned man whispered something and the soldier nodded.

The explorer followed the officer and said: "You don't know yet what I mean to do. I shall tell the Commandant what I think of the procedure, certainly, but not at a public conference, only in private; nor shall I stay here long enough to attend any conference; I am going away early tomorrow morning, or at least embarking on my ship."

It did not look as if the officer had been listening. "So you did not find the procedure convincing," he said to himself and smiled, as an old man smiles at childish nonsense and yet pursues his own meditations behind the smile.

"Then the time has come," he said at last, and suddenly looked at the explorer with bright eyes that held some challenge, some appeal for cooperation. "The time for what?" asked the explorer uneasily, but got no answer.

"You are free," said the officer to the condemned man in the native tongue. The man did not believe it at first. "Yes, you are set free," said the officer. For the first time the condemned man's face woke to real animation. Was it true? Was it only a caprice of the officer's, that might change again? Had the foreign explorer begged him off? What was it? One could read these questions on his face. But not for long. Whatever it might be, he wanted to be really free if he might, and he began to struggle so far as the Harrow permitted him.

"You'll burst my straps," cried the officer, "lie still! We'll soon loosen them." And signing the soldier to help him, he set about doing so. The condemned man laughed wordlessly to himself, now he turned his face left toward the officer, now right toward the soldier, nor did he forget the explorer.

"Draw him out," ordered the officer. Because of the Harrow this had to be done with some care. The condemned man had already torn himself a little in the back through his impatience.

From now on, however, the officer paid hardly any attention to him. He went up to the explorer, pulled out the small leather wallet again, turned over the papers in it, found the one he wanted, and showed it to the explorer. "Read it," he said. "I can't," said the explorer. "I told you before that I can't make out these scripts." "Try taking a close look at it," said the officer and came quite near to the explorer so that they might read it together. But when even that proved useless, he outlined the script with his little finger, holding it high above the paper as if the surface dared not be sullied by touch, in order to help the explorer to follow the script in that way. The explorer did make an effort, meaning to please the officer in this respect at least, but he was quite unable to follow. Now the officer began to spell it, letter by letter, and then read out the words. "'BE JUST!' is what is written here," he said. "Surely you can read it now." The explorer bent so close to the paper that the officer feared he might touch it and drew it farther away; the explorer made no remark, yet it was clear that he still could not decipher it. "'BE JUST!' is what is written there," said the officer once more. "Maybe," said the explorer. "I am prepared to believe you." "Well, then," said the officer, at least partly satisfied, and climbed up the ladder with the paper; very carefully he laid it inside the Designer and seemed to be changing the disposition of all the cogwheels; it was a troublesome piece of work and must have involved wheels that were extremely small, for sometimes the officer's head vanished altogether from sight inside the Designer, so precisely did he have to regulate the machinery.

The explorer, down below, watched the labor uninterruptedly, his neck grew stiff and his eyes smarted from the glare of sunshine over the sky. The soldier and the condemned man were now busy together. The man's shirt and trousers, which were already lying in the pit, were fished out by the point of the soldier's bayonet. The shirt was abominably dirty and its owner washed it in the bucket of water. When he put on the shirt and trousers both he and the soldier could not help guffawing, for the garments were of course slit up behind. Perhaps the condemned man felt it incumbent on him to amuse the soldier, he turned around and around in his slashed garments before the soldier, who squatted on the ground beating his knees with mirth. All the same, they presently controlled their mirth out of respect for the gentlemen.

When the officer had at length finished his task aloft, he surveyed the machinery in all its details once more, with a smile, but this time shut the lid of the Designer, which had stayed open till now, climbed down, looked into the pit and then at the condemned man, noting with satisfaction that the clothing had been taken out, then went over to wash his hands in the water bucket, perceived too late that it was disgustingly dirty, was unhappy because he could not wash his hands, in the end thrust them into the sand—this alternative did not please him, but he had to put up with it—then stood upright and began to unbutton his uniform jacket. As he did this, the two ladies' handkerchiefs he tucked under his collar fell into his hands. "Here are your handkerchiefs," he said, and threw them to the condemned man. And to the explorer he said in explanation: "A gift from the ladies."

In spite of the obvious haste with which he was discarding first his uniform jacket and then all his clothing, he handled each garment with loving care, he even ran his fingers caressingly over the silver lace on the jacket and shook a tassel into place. This loving care was out of keeping with the fact that as soon as he had a garment off he flung it at once with a kind of unwilling jerk into the pit. The last thing left to him was his short sword with the sword belt. He drew it out of the scabbard, broke it, then gathered all together, the bits of the sword, the scabbard, and the belt, and flung them so violently down that they clattered into the pit.

Now he stood naked there. The explorer bit his lips and said nothing. He knew very well what was going to happen, but he had no right to obstruct the officer in anything. If the judicial procedure the officer cherished were really so near its end—possibly as a result of his own intervention, as to which he felt himself pledged—then the officer was doing the right thing; in his place the explorer would not have acted otherwise.

The soldier and the condemned man did not understand at first what was happening, at first they were not even looking on. The condemned man was gleeful at having got the handkerchiefs back, but he was not allowed to enjoy them for long, since the soldier snatched them with a sudden, unexpected grab. Now the condemned man in turn was trying to twitch them from under the belt where the soldier had tucked them, but the soldier was on his guard. So they were wrestling, half in jest. Only when the officer stood quite naked was their attention caught. The condemned man especially seemed struck with the notion that some great change was impending. What had happened to him was now going to happen to the officer. Perhaps even to the very end. Apparently the foreign explorer had given the order for it. So this was revenge. Although he himself had not suffered to the end, he was to be revenged to the end. A broad, silent grin now appeared on his face and stayed there all the rest of the time.

The officer, however, had turned to the machine. It had been clear enough previously that he understood the machine well, but now it was almost staggering to see how he managed it and how it obeyed him. His hand had only to approach the Harrow for it to rise and sink several times till it was adjusted to the right position for receiving him; he touched only the edge of the Bed and already it was vibrating; the felt gag came to meet his mouth, one could see that the officer was really reluctant to take it but he shrank from it only a moment, soon he submitted and received it. Everything was ready, only the straps hung down at the sides, yet they were obviously unnecessary, the officer did not need to be fastened down. Then the condemned man noticed the loose straps, in his opinion the execution was incomplete unless the straps were buckled, he gestured eagerly to the soldier and they ran together to strap the officer down. The latter had already stretched out one foot to push the lever that started the Designer; he saw the two men coming up; so he drew his foot back and let himself be buckled in. But now he could not reach the lever; neither the soldier nor the condemned man would be able to find it, and the explorer was determined not to lift a finger. It was not necessary; as soon as the straps were fastened the machine began to work; the Bed vibrated, the needles flickered above the skin, the Harrow rose and fell. The explorer had been staring at it quite a while before he remembered that a wheel in the Designer should have been creaking; but everything was quiet, not even the slightest hum could be heard.

Because it was working so silently the machine simply escaped one's attention. The explorer observed the soldier and the condemned man. The latter was the more animated of the two, everything in the machine interested him, now he was bending down and now stretching up on tiptoe, his forefinger was extended all the time pointing out details to the soldier. This annoyed the explorer. He was resolved to stay till the end, but he could not bear the sight of these two. "Go back home," he said. The soldier would have been willing enough, but the condemned man took the order as a punishment. With clasped hands he implored to be allowed to stay, and when the explorer shook his head and would not relent, he even went down on his knees. The explorer saw that it was no use merely giving orders, he was on the point of going over and driving them away. At that moment he heard a noise above him in the Designer. He looked up. Was the cogwheel going to make trouble after all? But it was something quite different. Slowly the lid of the Designer rose up and then clicked wide open. The teeth of a cogwheel showed themselves and rose higher, soon the whole wheel was visible, it was as if some enormous force were squeezing the Designer so that there was no longer room for the wheel, the wheel moved up till it came to the very edge of the Designer, fell down, rolled along the sand a little on its rim and then lay flat. But a second wheel was already rising after it, followed by many others, large and small and indistinguishably minute, the same thing happened to all of them, at every moment one imagined the Designer must now really be empty, but another complex of numerous wheels was already rising into sight, falling down, trundling along the sand, and lying flat. This phenomenon made the condemned man completely forget the explorer's command, the cogwheels fascinated him, he was always trying to catch one and at the same time urging the soldier to help, but always drew back his hand in alarm, for another wheel always came hopping along which, at least on its first advance, scared him off.

The explorer, on the other hand, felt greatly troubled; the machine was obviously going to pieces; its silent working was a delusion; he had a feeling that he must now stand by the officer, since the officer was no longer able to look after himself. But while the tumbling cogwheels absorbed his whole attention he had forgotten to keep an eye on the rest of the machine; now that the last cogwheel had left the Designer, however, he bent over the Harrow and had a new and still more unpleasant surprise. The Harrow was not writing, it was only jabbing, and the Bed was not turning the body over but only bringing it up quivering against the needles. The explorer wanted to do something, if possible, to bring the whole machine to a standstill, for this was no exquisite torture such as the officer desired, this was plain murder. He stretched out his hands. But at that moment the Harrow rose with the body spitted on it and moved to the side, as it usually did only when the twelfth hour had come. Blood was flowing in a hundred streams, not mingled with water, the water jets too had failed to function. And now the last action failed to fulfill itself, the body did not drop off the long needles, streaming with blood it went on hanging over the pit without falling into it. The Harrow tried to move back to its old position, but as if it had itself noticed that it had not yet got rid of its burden it stuck after all where it was, over the pit. "Come and help!" cried the explorer to the other two, and himself seized the officer's feet. He wanted to push against the feet while the others seized the head from the opposite side so the officer might be slowly eased off the needles. But the other two could not make up their minds to come; the condemned man actually turned away; the explorer had to go over to them and force them into position at the officer's head. And here, almost against his will, he had to look at the face of the corpse. It was as it had been in life; no sign was visible of the promised redemption; what the others had found in the machine the officer had not found; the lips were firmly pressed together, the eyes were open with the same expression as in life, the look was calm and convinced, through the forehead went the point of the great iron spike.

As the explorer, with the soldier and the condemned man behind him, reached the first houses of the colony, the soldier pointed to one of them and said: "There is the teahouse."

In the ground floor of the house was a deep, low, cavernous space, its walls and ceiling blackened with smoke. It was open to the road all along its length. Although this teahouse was very little different from the other houses of the colony, which were all very dilapidated, even up to the Commandant's palatial headquarters, it made on the explorer the impression of a historic tradition of some kind, and he felt the power of past days. He went near to it, followed by his companions, right up between the empty tables that stood in the street before it, and breathed the cool, heavy air that came from the interior. "The old man's buried here," said the soldier. "The priest wouldn't let him lie in the church-yard. Nobody knew where to bury him for a while, but in the end they buried him here. The officer never told you about that, for sure, because of course that's what he was most ashamed of. He even tried several times to dig the old man up by night, but he was always chased away." "Where is the grave?" asked the explorer, who found it impossible to believe the soldier. At once both of them, the soldier and the condemned man, ran before him pointing with outstretched hands in the direction where the grave should be. They led the explorer right up to the back wall, where guests were sitting at a few tables. They were apparently dock laborers, strong men with short, glistening, full black beards. None had a jacket, their shirts were torn, they were poor, humble creatures. As the explorer drew near, some of them got up, pressed close to the wall, and stared at him. "It's a foreigner," ran the whisper around him, "he wants to see the grave." They pushed one of the tables aside, and under it there was really a gravestone. It was a simple stone, low enough to be covered by a table. There was an inscription on it in very small letters, the explorer had to kneel down to read it. This was what it said: *Here rests the old Commandant. His adherents, who now must be nameless, have dug this grave and set up this stone. There is a prophecy that after a certain number of years the Commandant will rise again and lead his adherents from the house to recover the colony. Have faith and wait!* When the explorer had read this and risen to his feet he saw all the bystanders around him smiling, as if they too had read the inscription, had found it ridiculous, and were expecting him to agree with them. The explorer ignored this, distributed a few coins among them, waiting till the table was pushed over the grave again, quitted the teahouse, and made for the harbor.

The soldier and the condemned man had found some acquaintances in the teahouse, who detained them. But they must have soon shaken them off, for the explorer was only halfway down the long flight of steps leading to the boats when they came rushing after him. Probably they wanted to force him at the last minute to take them with him. While he was bargaining below with a ferryman to row him to the steamer, the two of them came headlong down the steps, in silence, for they did not dare to shout. But by the time they reached the foot of the steps the explorer was already in the boat, and the ferryman was just casting off from the shore. They could have jumped into the boat, but the explorer lifted a heavy knotted rope from the floorboards, threatened them with it, and so kept them from attempting the leap.

THE PILGRIM AND THE ANGEL

E. LILY YU

Three days before Mr. Fareed Halawani was washed and turned to face the northeast, a beatific smile on his face, he had the unusual distinction of entertaining the angel Gabriel at the coffee shop he operated in the unfashionable district of Moqattam in Cairo. Fareed was tipped back in his monobloc chair, watching the soccer game on television. The cigarette between his lips wobbled with disapproval at the referee's calls. Above him on the wall hung a photograph of a young man, barely eighteen, bleached to pale blue. His rolled-up prayer mat rested below. It was a quiet hour before lunch, and the coffee shop was empty. Right as the referee held up a yellow card, a scrub-bearded man strode in.

"Peace to you, Fareed," the stranger boomed. "Arise!"

Fareed laughed and tapped out a grub of ash. "Peace to you. New to the neighborhood?"

"Not at all. I know you, Fareed," the stranger said. "You pray with devotion and give generously to the poor."

"So does my neighbor," said Fareed, "though that hasn't helped him find a husband for his big-nosed daughter. Can I get you a glass of tea?"

"The one thing you lack to perfect your faith is the hajj."

"Well, with business as slow as it is, and one thing and another..." Fareed coughed. "Truth is, may God forgive me, I'm saving up to visit my son. He's an electrician in Miami. Doesn't call home. What would you like to drink?"

"I have come to take you on hajj."

"I've got too much to do without that," Fareed said. He had quarreled half the night with Umm Ahmed over their son, whose lengthening silence his wife interpreted as pneumonia or incarceration or death, though Fareed supposed it was simply the cheerful thoughtlessness of the young. He had washed six stacks of brown glasses caked and swirled with tea dust, his joints sour from four hours' sleep, before unrolling his shirtsleeves and sitting down to his soccer match. But for the rigorous sense of hospitality that his own father had drummed into him, nothing could have stirred him from his chair, his chewed cigarette, and the goals that Al-Ahly was piling up over Zamalek. His bones clicked as he stood. He reached for a clean glass.

But the angel spread his stippled peacock-colored wings, which trembled like paper and made the room run with light, and said again, simply, "I am taking you on hajj."

Fareed choked on his cigarette. "Now? Me? Are you crazy? I have customers to care for!"

Gabriel glanced around the deserted shop and shrugged, his wings dipping and prisming the walls. Then he vanished. The prayer mat propped against the wall fluttered open and enfolded Fareed. While he kicked and expostulated, it carried him headfirst out the door and into the clear hard sky, to the astonishment of a motorcyclist sputtering past.

"Sir! Sayyid! Are you djinn or demon?" Fareed called out. "Where are you taking me? What have I done?"

"I am taking you on hajj!" the angel said joyfully from within the rug, his voice muffled, as if by a mouthful of wool.

"If you are taking me anywhere," Fareed said, struggling against the tightening mat, "make it Miami. And you have to get me home by midnight. Umm Ahmed will worry, and I have to shut up the shop." He finally freed his arms from the grapple of the prayer mat. Below them, the countryside zoomed by, green and very distant. Fareed blanched.

"I can circle the globe as fast as thought," said Gabriel. "Of course we'll have you home by then."

"Perhaps a little slower, I have a heart condition," Fareed said, but they whistled up like a rocket, and the wind hammered the next words back into his throat.

When he dared to look again, the silver trickle of the Delta flared below them. Then they were gliding over the shark tooth of the Sinai and the crinkling, inscrutable sea.

"This is really not necessary," Fareed shouted. "If I sell my shop I can buy an economy-class Emirates ticket to Jeddah tomorrow. You can send me home now."

"No need to sell your shop!" the angel said. "No need to wrestle suitcases through the airport and sit for hours with someone's knees in the small of your back. No need to worry."

"Right," Fareed said miserably.

By the time they reached the Arabian Peninsula, the dry, scouring wind had become unbearable. "Water," Fareed croaked. "Please, water."

"So spoke Ishmael in Hagar's lap," Gabriel said within the mat. "She had nothing to give him but prayers and tears. But I heard her crying out. I struck the ground with the tip of my wing, and water poured forth."

"Water!"

"Yes, water as clear and cool as glass. That was the well Zamzam. I shall take you to drink from it."

Fareed groaned a sand-scratched groan, then shut his eyes and muttered over and over the suras of the dying.

"Here we are," Gabriel said, what felt like hours later, lofting a red-faced Fareed onto a heap of sand. "That's Juhfa in the distance. Come, put on your ihram."

"What ihram?" Fareed said.

But as he spoke, a bright, cold stream boiled up from the ground, and the prayer mat unraveled and wove itself into two soft white rectangles, which settled like tame doves at his feet.

Fareed gulped the sweet water, washed himself as well as he could, then peeled off his shirt and trousers and wound the white cloths about himself. The stream receded as silently as it had sprung up, the dark stain it had made in the sand drying at once to nothing.

He had barely caught his breath when his white drapes shut like a fist and lifted him high into the air.

Wonders upon wonders, Fareed thought. But why him? Why an indulgent father, an inattentive husband, whose kindnesses were small and tea-glass sized? Why would any angel bother himself with someone so unworthy?

Guilt niggled at him like a pebble in his shoe. He could see Umm Ahmed rolling her eyes and shaking her head, hands on hips. *Angels? You say angels took you to Mecca? This is why you left the shop unlocked and unwatched? What kind of a layabout husband did I marry? You want me to call you Hajji now? Are you kidding me?* It filled him with a terrified kind of love.

"What am I going to tell Umm Ahmed?" he moaned.

"The truth! That your piety and prayers have been recognized. That Gabriel himself has led you on pilgrimage."

"She will throw shoes at me," Fareed sighed.

"Look," the angel said, as if he had not heard. They were descending through glittering skyscrapers and moon-tipped minarets. The Grand Mosque loomed before them, a wedding cake of marble that stunned Fareed to speechlessness.

He had always imagined making the pilgrimage as a fat and successful old man, cushioned by Umm Ahmed's sarcastic good humor and Ahmed's bright chatter. Now he had neither. Loneliness shivered and rang in him like a note struck from a bell.

Fareed barely had time to stammer the talbiyah through parched lips as they flew around the Kaaba, once, twice, seven times, his body cradled in the unseen angel's arms. His mumble was swallowed up in the susurrus of prayer rising from the slow white foam of pilgrims below. Fareed knew he was in the presence of the divine. He was humbled.

"Here is your Zamzam water," the angel said. A plastic pitcher ascended to them, revolving slowly. Fareed grasped it and drank.

"Now hold tight," the angel said, although Fareed had nothing to hold on to. The pitcher tumbled away like a meteor. "Over there is the path between Safa and Marwa, paved, enclosed, and air-conditioned now. Very comfortable and convenient."

"I don't suppose—"

"No! We shall take the path as Hagar found it. Think: your child dying in exile, the hot noonday sun beating upon your head. Think: how strong her faith, how deep her despair."

Fareed and the angel swooped seven times over the crenellations and cascades of white marble. As they hurtled over the walkway, dry air whipping their faces, Fareed imagined the rubble and grit below the elaborate masonry. He saw in his mind a thin dark woman plunging barefoot over the stones, tearing her black hair, her child left beneath a thornbush to suck thirstily at shadows. He thought of Umm Ahmed's reddened eyes and weary, dismissive waving—*leave me alone, my son is gone*—and of the phone that shrilled and yammered all day but rarely spoke with his son's voice. The image he held of his son was the photograph of Ahmed in uniform, taken during his mandatory service, when he was still a boy and anxious to please.

"Now—" the angel began, but Fareed spoke first, flapping his arms as he hung in the air.

"Enough! Enough!"

"But you haven't—"

"Give me my clothes and my shoes."

"Your faith is incomplete without the hajj," Gabriel remonstrated. "What answer will you give the other angels when they question you?"

Fareed felt cold despite the thick sunlight. His chest tightened. "Where are you taking me?"

"On hajj."

"No. Take me to my clothes."

The angel swerved out of the mosque. They returned to the desert place where his shirt and trousers lay folded beside his shoes. Only a little sand had accumulated in the heels. As Fareed stooped for them, his ihram fell away and became once more his threadbare prayer mat.

Beside him, the angel coalesced into a bluish glow containing edges and angles and complex, intersecting wings. Only the vaguest suggestion of a face shimmered in the chaos. He was painful to behold.

"Shall I bring you home?"

Fareed straightened, dust swirling and settling in his damp garments and sweat-sticky hair. A decision crystallized on his tongue. "If this is real and true, and I am not dreaming—if you are truly an angel and no evil spirit—then you will please take me to see my son."

"After all of this? After I brought you in my arms to the Honored City, to Masjid al-Haram itself—you want to go to America?"

"Especially after all of this," Fareed said. "If you are capable of these marvels, you can transport me to Florida as well."

The angel extruded a finger from chaos and curled it around his chin.

Fareed said, "Hagar burned and tore her feet as she ran in search of water for her son. Did you not hear her weeping?"

"That I did."

"And out of pity for her and her child you caused water to flow from barren rock."

"That is true."

"Then perhaps pity will move you to carry me to Miami," said Fareed. "I have not seen my son in three years." He folded his arms. "I did not ask you to come. I did not ask to be taken on hajj. I did not ask to be hauled out of my shop without so much as a note to my wife."

"Also true."

Fareed put one hand over his breast, where a dull ache was growing. "So take me to see my son. This once. It's the least you could do for me. Considering."

Deep inside the blue matrix of the angel, polygons meshed and disentangled with a sound like silver bells.

"All right, enough, let's go," Gabriel said, dissolving. "Back on the prayer mat with you." The rug rose from the sand and hovered an inch above the ground, undulating smoothly.

Fareed looked at it and made a small, quiet, unhappy noise. He resolved that if he ever made it home, he would buy a new, less willful prayer mat, perhaps one of the cheap ones with a pattern of combs and pitchers, made on Chinese looms.

Rolled up in his prayer mat, Mr. Fareed Halawani of Moqattam, coffee shop owner and pilgrim, came to an abrupt halt in front of the Chelsea Hotel in Miami. The carpet snapped straight, and Fareed spun once in the air before hitting the manicured lawn.

His son turned away from his pickup, shouldering a wreath of wires. He wiped sweat and wet hair out of his eyes, blinking against the sunlight and the mirages wavering out of the pavement.

"Dad?" he said, surprised.

Fareed stared up at the blue sky, bottomless as the one over Cairo, and listened to the strange, extravagant hiss of the lawn sprinkler. A single defiant dandelion bobbed above his nose, drifting in and out of focus. His stomach was still roiling from the rough flight across the Atlantic.

"That's it," Ahmed said, putting the back of his hand to his forehead. "I'm seeing things. I'm going crazy."

"You could pretend to be happy to see me," Fareed said.

"You can't possibly be here. You can't. I must have heatstroke."

"Go drink some water. I'll still be here when you get back."

His son extended a browned, broad hand and flinched when Fareed grasped it. But he helped his father to his feet.

"Do you believe me now?" Fareed said.

"What are you doing here?"

"Visiting you. You don't call home often enough."

"How did you get here?"

The prayer mat lay meekly upon the grass.

"An angel brought me, I think."

"An angel."

"Maybe an ifrit, it was horrible enough. We went to Mecca first, then came here. I insisted."

Ahmed stared. "Are you all right?"

"Of course I'm all right."

"Did you hit your head? Do you feel feverish?"

Fareed frowned. "You think I'm lying."

"No, I—" Ahmed shook his head. "I've got a job to finish here, okay? You can come with me while I do it, then we'll take you home and I'll— we'll figure out what to do with you." He picked up his black toolbox in one hand and offered the other to his father.

"I don't need to be supported," Fareed said. "I feel fine."

*   *   *

The truck's tires squealed as they pulled off the highway onto a narrow, shaded road. Beards of gray moss trailed from the trees and brushed the top of the truck. Ahmed lived in a pleasant white box, its postage-stamp lawn planted with crimson creepers and edged with large, smooth stones.

"No visa, right?" Ahmed said, unlocking the door. "No passport?"

"Nothing. Very unofficial, this visit. But I don't think you have to worry about getting me home," Fareed said. He felt the rug twitch in his arms.

His son's house contained only things that were bright and new: chairs and tables in colorful plastics or upholstered in triangle prints, a glass bookcase stuffed with calendars and phone books, two photos in chromium frames on the wall. One of the photos was of Fareed, his wife, and Ahmed, taken seven years ago in Alexandria. The other photograph—

"Who is she?" Fareed said, nudging the frame so it hung askew.

His son flushed. "She's, I met her, ah, a few months ago—"

"I see."

"A year, actually," Ahmed said, looking away. "She's really nice. Very sweet. Really."

"Does she cook well? Is she a believer? Are you engaged?" Fareed stared at the picture. "Does she have a name?"

"Rosa." Ahmed shifted from one foot to another. "What do you want for dinner? I could make some fuul—"

"You do know your mother and I have been trying to find you a good Egyptian girl? Aisha's a sensible woman, thirty-six, steady job at the bank—"

"That isn't necessary."

"Apparently not." Fareed raised an eyebrow at Rosa, who beamed innocently from the frame. "You might have told us."

"I was going to."

"When was the last time you called, anyway?"

"I've been busy," Ahmed mumbled.

"I can see that."

"Business has been good."

"I'm—glad," Fareed said, glancing around the small room. The odor of newness filled his nose and made his chest twinge.

"Midnight," the angel whispered in his ear, faint as a breeze. "Five hours. You'll make a mess if you stay, you know. Hospital bills, no identification, no papers."

Fareed clasped his hands stiffly behind his back. "So, Rosa. Do I get to meet this woman?"

His son's silence hurt more than he expected.

"Is it my clothes? I'll change—"

"No."

"You can translate for me. Shouldn't she meet her fiancé's parents?"

"Fiancé? She's not—" Ahmed flung up his hands. "It's too complicated, Dad. Listen. If you paid someone, to bring you here—"

"I didn't," Fareed said quietly. "You have nothing to worry about. I'll be gone soon." He paused, studying his son. "If I let you do what you wanted when you were younger, it was out of love. Not wanting to see you caged up. I wonder if that was wrong of me."

"It was fine." Ahmed began to open and shut the cabinets.

Fareed sighed. "Do this for me," he said. He had spotted the black telephone on the counter, winking with unspoken messages, and now he lifted up the handset and held it out to his son. "Call your mother tonight. Just one phone call. Just one. She misses you. She needs you."

Ahmed hesitated, then nodded reluctantly.

"Don't worry about dinner. I should go."

"No, stay, please. I'll cook for you. You'll be impressed."

His son was different and strange in this house, taller and stronger than the boy Fareed remembered. He had worked confidently at the hotel, snipping, stripping, splicing, and now he conjured up knives, pans, chopping boards, a blue gas flame with the casual swiftness of experience.

To Fareed's surprise, Ahmed, who had never cooked or lifted a finger at home, made fuul with eggs and lemon-sauced lamb on rice. After cleaning the last crisp speck from his bowl, Fareed wiped his mouth on the back of his hand and pushed back from the table.

"It is very good."

Ahmed fixed his eyes on the floor, embarrassed.

"Two daughters," the angel said. "Three years apart. One will have your strong chin. One will have Umm Ahmed's singing voice."

"Call your mother," Fareed said. "And give Rosa my regards. I should be going." He glanced toward the sofa, over whose arm he had draped the prayer mat. A corner of the cloth fluttered, although there was no breeze in the room.

In their small flat in Moqattam, in the hours before dawn, Umm Ahmed rubbed a track in the floor with her pacing. Dinner had gone cold on the stove and moved uneaten into the fridge. The coffee shop had been empty and unlocked. She had groped blindly over the lintel for the spare key and found it untouched, checked the register and found it still full. A thoughtful patron had turned off the television on his way out, though the ashtrays and water pipes still trailed gray ribbons in the air. Through the dimness of the shop the picture of Ahmed in fatigues, long faded to blue ghostliness, gazed down on her.

No one knew where her husband was. No one had seen him since morning. No one knew what had happened. She dropped into a kitchen chair, exhausted, and put her head in her arms. Stars and green neon lights glowed outside the window. Automobile engines roared through the night. She had the sinking sensation of being perfectly alone.

Then, on its cream-colored cradle, the phone rang and trembled, rang and trembled.

"Hello? Ahmed? Habibi, it's been so long—how could you—how are you—?"

Outside, like a scrap of burnt paper, her husband's prayer mat, wrapped around a dark, heavy form, drifted down to their doorstep.

HOUSING PROBLEM

HENRY KUTTNER

{SELECTED BY RAY BRADBURY}

Jacqueline said it was a canary, but I contended that there were a couple of lovebirds in the covered cage. One canary could never make that much fuss. Besides, I liked to think of crusty old Mr. Henchard keeping lovebirds; it was so completely inappropriate. But whatever our roomer kept in that cage by his window, he shielded it—or them—jealously from prying eyes. All we had to go by were the noises.

And they weren't too simple to figure out. From under the cretonne cloth came shufflings, rustlings, occasional faint and inexplicable pops, and once or twice a tiny thump that made the whole hidden cage shake on its redwood pedestal-stand. Mr. Henchard must have known that we were curious. But all he said, when Jackie remarked that birds were nice to have around, was "Claptrap! Leave that cage alone, d'ya hear?"

That made us a little mad. We're not snoopers, and after that brush-off, we coldly refused to even look at the shrouded cretonne shape. We didn't want to lose Mr. Henchard, either. Roomers were surprisingly hard to get. Our little house was on the coast highway; the town was a couple of dozen homes, a grocery, a liquor store, the post office, and Terry's restaurant. That was about all. Every morning Jackie and I hopped the bus and rode in to the factory, an hour away. By the time we got home we were pretty tired. We couldn't get any household help—war jobs paid a lot better—so we both pitched in and cleaned. As for cooking, we were Terry's best customers.

The wages were good, but before the war we'd run up too many debts, so we needed extra dough. And that's why we rented a room to Mr. Henchard. Off the beaten track with transportation difficult, and with the coast dimout every night, it wasn't too easy to get a roomer. Mr. Henchard looked like a natural. He was, we figured, too old to get into mischief.

One day he wandered in, paid a deposit; presently he showed up with a huge Gladstone and a square canvas grip with leather handles. He was a creaking little old man with a bristling tonsure of stiff white hair and a face like Popeye's father, only more human. He wasn't sour; he was just crusty. I had a feeling he'd spent most of his life in furnished rooms, minding his own business and puffing innumerable cigarettes through a long black holder. But he wasn't one of those lonely old men you could safely feel sorry for—far from it! He wasn't poor and he was completely self-sufficient. We loved him. I called him grandpa once, in an outburst of affection, and my skin blistered at the resultant remarks.

Some people are born under lucky stars. Mr. Henchard was like that. He was always finding money in the street. The few times we shot craps or played poker, he made passes and held straights without even trying. No question of sharp dealing—he was just lucky.

I remember the time we were all going down the long wooden stairway that leads from the cliff top to the beach. Mr. Henchard kicked at a pretty big rock that was on one of the steps. The stone bounced down a little way, and then went right through one of the treads. The wood was completely rotten. We felt fairly certain that if Mr. Henchard, who was leading, had stepped on that rotten section, the whole thing would have collapsed.

And then there was the time I was riding up with him in the bus. The motor stopped a few minutes after we'd boarded the bus; the driver pulled over. A car was coming toward us along the highway and, as we stopped, one of its front tires blew out. It skidded into the ditch. If we hadn't stopped when we did, there would have been a head-on collision. Not a soul was hurt.

Mr. Henchard wasn't lonely; he went out by day, I think, and at night he sat in his room near the window most of the time. We knocked, of course, before coming in to clean, and sometimes he'd say, "Wait a minute." There'd be a hasty rustling and the sound of that cretonne cover going on his birdcage. We wondered what sort of bird he had, and theorized on the possibility of a phoenix. The creature never sang. It made noises. Soft, odd, not-always-birdlike noises. By the time we got home from work, Mr. Henchard was always in his room. He stayed there while we cleaned. On weekends, he never went out.

As for the cage…

One night Mr. Henchard came out, stuffing a cigarette into his holder, and looked us over.

"Mph," said Mr. Henchard. "Listen, I've got some property to tend to up north, and I'll be away for a week or so. I'll still pay the rent."

"Oh, well," Jackie said. "We can—"

"Claptrap," he growled. "It's my room. I'll keep it if I like. How about that, hey?"

We agreed, and he smoked half his cigarette in one gasp. "Mm-m. Well, look here, now. Always before I've had my own car. So I've taken my birdcage with me. This time I've got to travel on the bus, so I can't take it. You've been pretty nice—not peepers or pryers. You got sense. I'm going to leave my birdcage here, but *don't you touch that cover!*"

"The canary—" Jackie gulped. "It'll starve."

"Canary, hmm?" Mr. Henchard said, fixing her with a beady, wicked eye. "Never you mind. I left plenty o' food *and* water. You just keep your hands off. Clean my room when it needs it, if you want, but don't you dare touch the birdcage. What do you say?"

"Okay with us," I said.

"Well, you mind what I say," he snapped.

That next night, when we got home, Mr. Henchard was gone. We went into his room and there was a note pinned to the cretonne cover. It said, MIND, NOW! Inside the cage something went *rustle-whirr.* And then there was a faint pop.

"Hell with it," I said. "Want the shower first?"

"Yes," Jackie said.

Whirr-r went the cage. But it wasn't wings. *Thump!*

The next night I said, "Maybe he left enough food, but I bet the water's getting low."

"Eddie!" Jackie remarked.

"All right, I'm curious. But I don't like the idea of birds dying of thirst, either."

"Mr. Henchard said—"

"All right, again. Let's go down to Terry's and see what the lamb chop situation is."

The next night—Oh, well. We lifted the cretonne. I still think we were less curious than worried. Jackie said she once knew somebody who used to beat his canary.

"We'll find the poor beast cowering in chains," she remarked, flicking her dust cloth at the windowsill behind the cage. I turned off the vacuum. *Whish—trot-trot-trot* went something under the cretonne.

"Yeah—" I said. "Listen, Jackie. Mr. Henchard's all right, but he's a crackpot. That bird or birds may be thirsty now. I'm going to take a look."

"No. Uh—yes. We both will, Eddie. We'll split the responsibility."

I reached for the cover, and Jackie ducked under my arm and put her hand over mine.

Then we lifted a corner of the cloth. Something had been rustling around inside, but the instant we touched the cretonne, the sound stopped. I meant to take only one swift glance. My hand continued to lift the cover, though. I could see my arm moving and I couldn't stop it. I was too busy looking.

Inside the cage was a—well, a little house. It seemed complete in every detail. A tiny house painted white, with green shutters—ornamental, not meant to close—for the cottage was strictly modern. It was the sort of comfortable, well-built house you see all the time in the suburbs. The tiny windows had chintz curtains; they were lighted up, on the ground floor. The moment we lifted the cloth, each window suddenly blacked out. The lights didn't go off, but shades snapped down with an irritated jerk. It happened fast. Neither of us saw who or what pulled down those shades.

I let go of the cover and stepped back, pulling Jackie with me.

"A d-dollhouse, Eddie!"

"With dolls in it?"

I stared past her at the hooded cage. "Could you, maybe, do you think, perhaps, train a canary to pull down shades?"

"Oh, my! Eddie, listen."

Faint sounds were coming from the cage. Rustles, and an almost inaudible pop. Then a scraping.

I went over and took the cretonne cloth clear off. This time I was ready; I watched the windows. But the shades flicked down as I blinked.

Jackie touched my arm and pointed. On the sloping roof was a miniature brick chimney; a wisp of pale smoke was rising from it. The smoke kept coming up, but it was so thin I couldn't even smell it.

"The c-canaries are c-cooking," Jackie gurgled.

We stood there for a while, expecting almost anything. If a little green man had popped out of the front door and offered us three wishes, we shouldn't have been much surprised. Only nothing happened.

There wasn't a sound, now, from the wee house in the birdcage.

And the blinds were down. I could see that the whole affair was a masterpiece of detail. The little front porch had a tiny mat on it. There was a doorbell, too.

Most cages have removable bottoms. This one didn't. Resin stains and dull gray metal showed where soldering had been done. The door was soldered shut, too. I could put my forefinger between the bars, but my thumb was too thick.

"It's a nice little cottage, isn't it?" Jackie said, her voice quavering. "They must be such *little* guys—"

"Guys?"

"Birds. Eddie, who lives in that house?"

"Well," I said. I took out my automatic pencil, gently inserted it between the bars of the cage, and poked at an open window, where the shade snapped up. From within the house something like the needle beam of a miniature flashlight shot into my eye, blinding me with its brilliance. As I grunted and jerked back, I heard a window slam and the shade come down again.

"Did you see what happened?"

"No, your head was in the way. But—"

As we looked, the lights went out. Only the thin smoke curling from the chimney indicated that anything was going on.

"Mr. Henchard's a mad scientist," Jackie muttered. "He shrinks people."

"Not without an atom smasher," I said. "Every mad scientist's got to have an atom smasher to make artificial lightning."

I put my pencil between the bars again. I aimed carefully, pressed the point against the doorbell, and rang. A thin shrilling was heard.

The shade at one of the windows by the door was twitched aside hastily, and something probably looked at me. I don't know. I wasn't quick enough to see it. The shade fell back in place, and there was no more movement. I rang the bell till I got tired of it. Then I stopped.

"I could take the cage apart," I said.

"Oh *no*! Mr. Henchard—"

"Well," I said, "when he comes back, I'm going to ask him what the hell. He can't keep pixies. It isn't in the lease."

"He doesn't have a lease," Jackie countered.

I examined the little house in the birdcage. No sound, no movement. Smoke coming from the chimney.

After all, we had no right to break into the cage. Housebreaking? I had visions of a little green man with wings flourishing a nightstick, arresting me for burglary. Did pixies have cops? What sort of crimes...

I put the cover back on the cage. After a while, vague noises emerged. *Scrape. Thump. Rustle, rustle, rustle. Pop.* And an unbirdlike trilling that broke off short.

"Oh, my," Jackie said. "Let's go away quick."

We went right to bed. I dreamed of a horde of little green guys in Mack Sennett cop uniforms, dancing on a bilious rainbow and singing gaily.

The alarm clock woke me. I showered, shaved, and dressed, thinking of the same thing Jackie was thinking of. As we put on our coats, I met her eyes and said, "Shall we?"

"Yes. Oh, golly, Eddie! D-do you suppose they'll be leaving for work, too?"

"What sort of work?" I inquired angrily. "Painting buttercups?"

There wasn't a sound from beneath the cretonne when we tiptoed into Mr. Henchard's room. Morning sunlight blazed through the window. I jerked the cover off. There was the house. One of the blinds was up; all the rest were tightly firm. I put my head close to the cage and stared through the bars into the open window, where scraps of chintz curtains were blowing in the breeze.

I saw a great big eye looking back at me.

This time Jackie was certain I'd got my mortal wound. The breath went out of her with a whoosh as I caromed back, yelling about a horrible bloodshot eye that wasn't human. We clutched each other for a while and then I looked again.

"Oh," I said, rather faintly. "It's a mirror."

"A *mirror?*" she gasped.

"Yeah, a big one, on the opposite wall. That's all I can see. I can't get close enough to the window."

"Look on the porch," Jackie said.

I looked. There was a milk bottle standing by the door—you can guess the size of it. It was purple. Beside it was a folded postage stamp.

"Purple milk?" I said.

"From a purple cow. Or else the bottle's colored. Eddie, is that a newspaper?"

It was. I strained my eyes to read the headlines. EXTRA was splashed redly across the sheet, in huge letters nearly a sixteenth of an inch high. EXTRA — FOTZPA MOVES ON TUR! That was all we could make out.

I put the cretonne gently back over the cage. We went down to Terry's for breakfast while we waited for the bus.

When we rode home that night, we knew what our first job would be. We let ourselves into the house, discovered that Mr. Henchard hadn't come back yet, switched on the light in his room, and listened to the noises from the birdcage.

"Music," Jackie said.

It was so faint I scarcely heard it, and, in any case, it wasn't real music. I can't begin to describe it. And it died away immediately. *Thump, scrape, pop, buzz.* Then silence, and I pulled off the cover.

The house was dark, the windows were shut, the blinds were down.

Paper and milk bottle were gone from the porch. On the front door was a sign that said—after I used a magnifying glass: QUARANTINE! SCOPPY FEVER!

"Why, the little liars," I said. "I bet they haven't got scoppy fever at all."

Jackie giggled wildly. "You only get scoppy fever in April, don't you?"

"April and Christmas. That's when the bread-and-butter flies carry it. Where's my pencil?"

I rang the bell. A shade twitched aside, flipped back; neither of us had seen the—hand?—that moved it. Silence; no smoke coming out of the chimney.

"Scared?" I asked.

"No. It's funny, but I'm not. They're such standoffish little guys. The Cabots speak only to—"

"Where the pixies speak only to goblins, you mean," I said. "They can't snoot us this way. It's our house their house is in, if you follow me."

"What can we do?"

I manipulated the pencil, and, with considerable difficulty, wrote LET US IN on the white panel of the door. There wasn't room for more than that. Jackie tsked.

"Maybe you shouldn't have written that. We don't want to get *in*. We just want to see them."

"Too late now. Besides, they'll know what we mean."

We stood watching the house in the birdcage, and it watched us, in a sullen and faintly annoyed fashion. SCOPPY FEVER, indeed!

That was all that happened that night.

The next morning we found that the tiny front door had been scrubbed clean of my pencil marks, that the quarantine sign was still there, and that there was a bottle of green milk and another paper on the porch. This time the headline said: EXTRA—FOTZPA OVERSHOOTS TUR!

Smoke was idling from the chimney. I rang the bell again. No answer. I noticed a domino of a mailbox by the door, chiefly because I could see through the slot that there were letters inside. But the thing was locked.

"If we could see whom they were addressed to—" Jackie suggested.

"Or whom they're from. That's what interests me."

Finally, we went to work. I was preoccupied all day, and nearly welded my thumb onto a boogie-arm. When I met Jackie that night, I could see that she'd been bothered, too.

"Let's ignore them," she said as we bounced home on the bus. "We know when we're not wanted, don't we?"

"I'm not going to be high-hatted by a—by a critter. Besides, we'll both go quietly nuts if we don't find out what's inside that house. Do you suppose Mr. Henchard's a wizard?"

"He's a louse," Jackie said bitterly. "Going off and leaving ambiguous pixies on our hands!"

When we got home, the little house in the birdcage took alarm, as usual, and by the time we'd yanked off the cover, the distant, soft noises had faded into silence. Lights shone through the drawn blinds. The porch had only the mat on it. In the mailbox we could see the yellow envelope of a telegram.

Jackie turned pale. "It's the last straw," she insisted. "A telegram!"

"It may not be."

"It is, it is, I know it is. Aunt Tinker Bell's dead. Or Iolanthe's coming for a visit."

"The quarantine sign's off the door," I said. "There's a new one. It says WET PAINT."

"Well, you will scribble all over their nice clean door."

I put the cretonne back, turned off the light switch, and took Jackie's hand. We stood waiting. After a time something went *bump-bump-bump*, and then there was a singing, like a teakettle. I heard a tiny clatter.

Next morning there were twenty-six bottles of yellow milk—bright yellow—on the tiny porch, and the Lilliputian headline announced: EXTRA—TUR SLIDES TOWARD FOTZPA! There was mail in the box, too, but the telegram was gone.

That night things continued much as before. When I pulled the cloth off there was a sudden, furious silence. We felt that we were being watched around the corners of the miniature shades. We finally went to bed, but in the middle of the night I got up and took another look at our mysterious tenants. Not that I saw *them*, of course. But they must have been throwing a party, for bizarre, small music and wild thumps and pops died into silence as I peeked.

In the morning there was a red bottle and a newspaper on the little porch. The headline said: EXTRA—FOTZPA GOES UP!

"My work's going to the dogs," I said. "I can't concentrate for thinking about this business—and wondering…"

"Me, too. We've *got* to find out somehow."

I peeked. A shade came down so sharply that it almost tore free from its roller.

"Do you think they're mad?" I asked.

"Yes," Jackie said, "I do. We must be bothering the very devil out of 'em. Look—I'll bet they're sitting inside by the windows, boiling mad, waiting for us to go away. Maybe we'd better go. It's time for the bus anyway."

I looked at the house, and the house, I felt, looked at me with an air of irritated and resentful fury. Oh, well. We went to work.

We were tired and hungry when we got back that night, but even before removing our coats we went into Mr. Henchard's room. Silence. I switched on the light while Jackie pulled off the cretonne cover from the cage.

I heard her gasp. Instantly I jumped forward, expecting to see a little green guy on that absurd porch—or anything, for that matter. I saw nothing unusual. There was no smoke coming from the chimney.

But Jackie was pointing to the front door. There was a neat, painted sign tacked to the panel. It said, very sedately, simply, and finally: TO LET.

"Oh, oh, oh!" Jackie said.

I gulped. All the shades were up in the tiny windows and the chintz curtains were gone. We could see into the house for the first time. It was completely and awfully empty.

No furniture, anywhere. Nothing at all but a few scrapes and scratches on the polished hardwood floor. The wallpaper was scrupulously clean; the patterns, in the various rooms, were subdued in good taste. The tenants had left their house in order.

"They moved," I said.

"Yes," Jackie murmured. "They moved out."

All of a sudden I felt lousy. The house—not the tiny one in the cage, but our own—was awfully empty. You know how it is when you've been on a visit, and come home into a place that's full of nothing and nobody?

I grabbed Jackie and held her tight. She felt pretty bad, too. You wouldn't think that a tiny TO LET sign could make so much difference.

"What'll Mr. Henchard say?" Jackie asked, watching me with big eyes.

Mr. Henchard came home two nights later. We were sitting by the fire when he walked in, his Gladstone swinging, the black cigarette holder jutting from below his beak. "Mph," he greeted us.

"Hello," I said weakly, "glad you're back."

"Claptrap!" said Mr. Henchard firmly as he headed for his room. Jackie and I looked at one another.

Mr. Henchard squalled in sheer fury. His twisted face appeared around the door.

"Busybodies!" he snarled. "I *told* you—"

"Wait a minute," I said.

"I'm moving out!" Mr. Henchard barked. "Now!" His head popped back out of sight; the door slammed and locked. Jackie and I waited, half expecting to be spanked.

Mr. Henchard bounced out of his room, Gladstone suspended from one hand. He whirled past us toward the door. I tried to stop him. "Mr. Henchard—"

"Claptrap!"

Jackie pulled one arm, I got a grip on the other. Between us, we managed to bring him to a stop.

"Wait," I said. "You've forgotten your—uh—birdcage."

"That's what you think," he snarled at me. "You can have it. Meddlers! It took me months to build that little house just right, and months more to coax 'em to live in it. Now you've spoiled it. They won't be back."

"Who?" Jackie gulped.

His beady eyes were fixed malignantly on us. "My tenants. I'll have to build a new house now—ha! But this time I won't leave it within reach of meddlers."

"Wait," I said. "Are—are you a m-magician?"

Mr. Henchard snorted. "I'm a good craftsman. That's all it takes. You treat them right, and they'll treat you right. Still—" And he gleamed a bit with pride. "—it isn't everybody who knows how to build the right sort of house for *them!*"

He seemed to be softening, but my next question aroused him again.

"What were they?" he snapped. "The Little Folk, of course. Call 'em what you like. Nixie, pixie, leprechaun, brownie—they've had lots of names. But they want a quiet, respectable neighborhood to live in, not a lot of peeping and prying. Gives the property a bad name. No wonder they moved out! And—mph!—they paid their rent on time, too. Still, the Little Folk always do," he added.

"Rent?" Jackie said faintly.

"Luck," Mr. Henchard said. "Good luck. What did you expect they'd pay in—money? Now I'll have to build another house to get my special luck back."

He gave us one parting glare, jerked open the door, and stamped out. We stood looking after him. The bus was pulling into the gas station down the slope, and Mr. Henchard broke into a run.

He caught the bus, all right, but only after he'd fallen flat on his face. I put my arm around Jackie.

"Oh, gosh," she said. "His bad luck's working already."

"Not *bad*," I pointed out. "Just normal. When you rent a little house to pixies, you get a lot of extra good luck."

We sat in silence, watching each other. Finally without saying a word, we went into Mr. Henchard's vacated room. The birdcage was still there. So was the house. So was the TO LET sign.

"Let's go to Terry's," I said.

We stayed later than usual. Anybody would have thought we didn't want to go home because we lived in a haunted house. Except that in our case the exact opposite was true. Our house wasn't haunted anymore. It was horribly, desolately, coldly vacant.

I didn't say anything till we'd crossed the highway, climbed the slope, and unlocked our front door. We went, I don't know why, for a final look at the empty house. The cover was back on the cage, where I'd replaced it, but *thump, rustle, pop*! The house was tenanted again!

We backed out and closed the door before we breathed.

"No," Jackie said. "We mustn't look. We mustn't ever, *ever*, look under that cover."

"Never," I said. "Who do you suppose..."

We caught a very faint murmur of what seemed to be boisterous singing. That was fine. The happier they were, the longer they'd stay. When we went to bed, I dreamed that I was drinking beer with Rip Van Winkle and the dwarfs. I drank 'em all under the table.

It was unimportant that the next morning was rainy. We were convinced that bright yellow sunlight was blazing in through the windows. I sang under the shower. Jackie burbled inarticulately and joyously. We didn't open Mr. Henchard's door.

"Maybe they want to sleep late," I said.

It's always noisy in the machine shop, and a hand truck load of rough cylinder casings going past doesn't increase the din noticeably. At three o'clock that afternoon, one of the boys was rolling the stuff along toward the storeroom and I didn't hear it or see it until I'd stepped back from my planer, cocking my eye at its adjustment.

Those big planers are minor juggernauts. They have to be bedded in concrete, in heavy thigh-high cradles on which a heavily weighted metal monster—the planer itself—slides back and forth.

I stepped back, saw the hand truck coming, and made a neat waltz turn to get out of its way. The boy with the hand truck swerved, the cylinders began to fall out, and I took an unbalanced waltz step that ended with my smacking my thighs against the edge of the cradle and doing a neat, suicidal half somersault. When I landed, I was jammed into the metal cradle, looking at the planer as it zoomed down on me. I've never in my life seen anything move so fast.

It was all over before I knew it. I was struggling to bounce myself out, men were yelling, the planer was bellowing with bloodthirsty triumph, and the cylinder heads were rolling around underfoot all over the place. Then there was the crackling, tortured crash of gears and cams going to pieces. The planer stopped. My heart started.

After I'd changed my clothes, I waited for Jackie to knock off. Rolling home on the bus, I told her about it. "Pure dumb luck. Or else a miracle. One of those cylinders bounced into the planer in just the right place. The planer's a mess, but I'm not. I think we ought to write a note of thanks to our—uh—tenants."

Jackie nodded with profound conviction. "It's the luck they pay their rent in, Eddie. I'm glad they paid in advance, too!"

"Except that I'm off the payroll till the planer's fixed," I said.

We went home through a storm. We could hear a banging in Mr.

Henchard's room, louder than any noise that had ever come from the birdcage. We rushed upstairs and found the casement windows had come open. I closed them. The cretonne cover had been half blown off the cage, and I started to pull it back in place. Jackie was beside me. We looked at the tiny house; my hand didn't complete its gesture. The TO LET sign had been removed from the door. The chimney was smoking greasily. The blinds were tightly down, as usual, but there were other changes.

There was a small smell of cooking—scorned beef and skunk cabbage, I thought wildly. Unmistakably it came from the pixie house. On the formerly immaculate porch was a slopping-over garbage can, and a minuscule orange crate with unwashed, atom-sized tin cans and what were indubitably empty liquor bottles. There was a milk bottle by the door, too, filled with biliously lavender liquid. It hadn't been taken in yet, nor had the morning paper. It was certainly a different paper. The lurid size of the headlines indicated that it was a yellow tabloid.

A clothesline, without any clothes hanging on it at the moment, had been tacked up from one pillar of the porch to a corner of the house.

I jerked down the cover, and fled after Jackie into the kitchen. "My God!" I said.

"We should have asked for references," she gasped. "Those aren't *our* tenants!"

"Not the tenants we used to have," I agreed. "I mean the ones Mr. Henchard used to have. Did you see that garbage pail on the porch!"

"And the clothesline," Jackie added. "How—how sloppy."

"Jukes, Kallikaks, and Jeeter Lesters. This isn't Tobacco Road."

Jackie gulped. "Mr. Henchard said they wouldn't be back, you know."

"Yeah, but, well—"

She nodded slowly, as though beginning to understand. I said, "Give."

"I don't know. Only Mr. Henchard said the Little Folk wanted a quiet, respectable neighborhood. And we drove them out. I'll bet we gave the birdcage—the location—a bad reputation. The better-class pixies won't live there. It's—oh, dear—maybe it's a slum."

"You're very nuts," I said.

"I'm not. It must be that. Mr. Henchard said as much. He told us he'd have to build a new house. Desirable tenants won't move into a bad neighborhood. We've got sloppy pixies, that's all."

My mouth opened. I stared at her.

"Uh-huh. The tenement type. I'll bet they keep a pixilated goat in the kitchen," Jackie babbled.

"Well," I said, "we're not going to stand for it. I'll evict 'em. I—I'll pour water down their chimney. Where's the teakettle?"

Jackie grabbed me. "No, don't! We can't evict them, Eddie. We mustn't. They pay their rent," she said.

And then I remembered. "The planer—"

"Just that," Jackie emphasized, digging her fingers into my biceps. "You'd have been killed today if you hadn't had some extra good luck. Those pixies may be sloppy, but they pay their rent."

I got the angle. "Mr. Henchard's luck worked differently, though. Remember when he kicked that rock down the beach steps, and they started to cave in? Me, I do it the hard way. I fall in the planer, sure, and a cylinder bounces after me and stops the machine, but I'll be out of a job till the planer's fixed. Nothing like that ever happened to Mr. Henchard."

"He had a better class of tenant," Jackie explained, with a wild gleam in her eye. "If Mr. Henchard had fallen in the planer, a fuse would have blown, I'll bet. Our tenants are sloppy pixies, so we get sloppy luck."

"They stay," I said. "We own a slum. Let's get out of here and go down to Terry's for a drink."

We buttoned our raincoats and departed, breathing the fresh, wet air. The storm was slashing down as furiously as ever. I'd forgotten my flashlight, but I didn't want to go back for it. We headed down the slope, toward Terry's faintly visible lights.

It was dark. We couldn't see much through the storm. Probably that was why we didn't notice the bus until it was bearing down on us, head-lights almost invisible in the dimout.

I started to pull Jackie aside, out of the way, but my foot slipped on the wet concrete, and we took a nosedive. I felt Jackie's body hurtle against me, and the next moment we were floundering in the muddy ditch beside the highway while the bus roared past us and was gone.

We crawled out and made for Terry's. The barman stared at us, said, "Whew!" and set up drinks without being asked.

"Unquestionably," I said, "our lives have just been saved."

"Yes," Jackie agreed, scraping mud from her ears. "But it wouldn't have happened this way to Mr. Henchard."

The barman shook his head. "Fall in the ditch, Eddie? And you too? Bad luck!"

"Not bad," Jackie told him feebly. "Good. But sloppy." She lifted her drink and eyed me with muddy misery. I chinked my glass against hers.

"Well," I said. "Here's luck."

NONE BEFORE ME

SIDNEY CARROLL

{SELECTED BY RAY BRADBURY}

John Olney Gresham had time, inclination, and money enough to be a connoisseur. He also had the correct instinct: He was a born miser. What he kept, he kept to himself alone. The privacy of property was his first passion and possibly his last. His earliest memories did not include a mother, father, sisters, brothers, nor even relatives of any proximity whatsoever. He had never had a sweetheart. Now in his last lonely days, he had neither wife nor kin. He had only his collection, his large house (somewhat on the baroque brownstone side), and servants. These were old and quiet and capable, never offering—never daring—to speak one unnecessary word to the master. Gresham timed his movement to the heavy gold watch in his pocket—a time for waking, a time for eating, a time for stepping from the dusty tranquility of his den into the abominable traffic of the world and thence to the little shops where he did his trading, and a time for spending endless hours with his collection.

Gresham was a man who had improvised the main strategy of his life and then stuck ponderously to the stratagem. Connoisseurship had been a whim with him back in the long ago, and he had devoted his life to it. One nameless day in his monotone life he had seen an ivory figurine in a store window. Its simple symmetry had appealed to him. He had haggled over the price, bought the figurine, taken it home to study it, and he had suddenly become a collector of ivory. That had been the first whim. It had taken him for the first time out of the aimless rich young man's existence into the shops of the town. But once he invaded the shops he discovered a world far beyond the one he had bargained for. He discovered that ivory is a world unto itself, that as it gets more and more expensive it gets better and better. Immediately, therefore, Gresham acquired the most expensive piece of ivory carving in the world. Then he discovered that bagging the fox in the first five minutes destroys the very purpose—the thrill of the hunt. So the second whim seized him, in the form of the one inspiration of his life. Why not (it was such a simple notion after all—why had it never occurred to anybody else?) why not acquire the best single piece of anything in *any* line? Ivory was simply one kind of hunting; he had conquered it with one bold stroke. There were still diamonds to collect, and coral, and paintings, and tapestries, and—*pah!* there must be many things. So Gresham started to collect the best of anything in any line. His life was consecrated to it.

Thus it was that a certain Mr. Pegerine felt safe in his own mind one day when he called Gresham at the one time of the day when the servants were allowed to answer the phone. "I would like to speak to Mr. Gresham," said Pegerine, who was master of, among other things, the archaic speech of his calling. "Whom shall I say is on the telephone?" asked the servant. "Mr. Pegerine, dealer in Unusual Antiquities." Gresham came to the phone. "Yes? What is it?"

"Mr. Gresham, I have for you—something—the rarest, the most unusual. There is nothing like it in the entire world."

"What is it?"

"Mr. Gresham, I would really and truly prefer not to say. An item like this—it requires an effect of surprise. It must not be described beforehand."

"Bring it up. Tomorrow at four."

"Mr. Gresham, for this one time, you must come to my place. It is a large item. It is delicate. It is not possible to transport it indiscriminately. If it were not necessary, I would not—"

"Very well. Tomorrow at four. I'll be at your place."

"Thank you, Mr. Gresham."

When Gresham got to Pegerine's the next day, promptly, of course, on the stroke of four, old Pegerine led him into the back room. There it was. On an Empire table at which six people could eat with comfort, it stood.

It was the most magnificent doll's house in the world.

It was slightly under five feet high. Even to an innocent eye it was obviously perfect, marvelously perfect in every detail. It was an old European sort of house, almost square, with four floors and a gable of roof covered with chimneys. A stork in a nest snuggled against one of the chimneys. The entire facade of the house had been swung open on hinges. Eighteen rooms were thus exposed, and the effect, on the closest scrutiny, was almost frightening, in its perfection of detail. The tiny pictures on the walls, the silver service in the dining room, the linens in the closets, the rugs, the mullioned windows, the doors and doorknobs—all these seemed to mock the perfection of the life-size world.

"The rugs were made by Aubusson," said Pegerine. "The little paintings"—he pointed at them with a slender gold pencil—"are miniatures by Fragonard, Greuze, Watteau... and here—just here—one by Vigée-Lebrun, the only miniature she ever painted. Worth a fortune in itself. Signed. The scale is actually one-twelfth actual size, one inch equals one foot. The house in reality would be approximately fifty feet high, ten feet to each floor and another ten for the roof. Each pane of glass in each window is beveled, every mirror is in a solid gold frame, every gold frame is set with precious stones. Notice, please, where I point the pencil—the detail in the wallpaper. It should be examined with a glass. Now take the glassware. Crystal, every piece of it. The dishes were made originally for the second child of Marie Antoinette. I have the papers. Now notice the people..."

And truly the little people in these little rooms were the most astonishing of all.

It is a perverse fact that of all the images man continues to make of man, the one which resembles him the least is the one which is intended to resemble him the most—namely, the doll. Nobody can make a doll that looks as if it breathes. But the artisan who had fashioned the tiny inhabitants of this extraordinary house had come close to the secret, small as his creatures were. In the living room on the ground floor, an aged grandmother sat in a rocking chair, with four children seated at her feet. The skin of the grandmother's face was veined at the temples. The wrinkles at her eyes had flickering shadows. She held a piece of knitting. Her hands were brown and waxen and bony, and the flesh and the grace of old fingers had been so scrupulously copied that they looked remarkably nimble; you would expect to hear, momentarily, the clicking of the knitting needles. The children around the grandmother, gazing up at her with loving admiration, were unique personalities, each with a different expression on his half-inch face. In an upstairs room an infant slept in a cradle shaped like a swan. The child slept; it truly slept. Flights of angels were painted on the walls of the room.

"Notice the wood paneling," said Pegerine, bending over. But by that time Pegerine knew there was really no need for him to play the guide on a conducted tour any longer. He had seen the expression on Gresham's face. He knew he had made the sale.

"Tell me," said Gresham, trying to stifle his excitement, "this sort of thing—I mean now—dollhouses..."

"One of the oldest of the arts, Mr. Gresham. One of the most respected. Archeology shows that in the oldest civilizations the inhabitants of the earth built dollhouses. Toys! This is the ultimate in toy making! Is there anyone who doubts that toy making is a major art?"

"I wouldn't know," Gresham snapped.

"It is true, sir. One of the oldest of the arts, and here, before you, the finest specimen ever made. Not the largest, that is obvious. Not the most ornate—there are complete models of Fontainebleau in existence. But the finest, beyond any doubt the finest."

"How would I know that?"

"I will guarantee it. Written down."

"All right, I'll buy it."

"Very good, Mr. Gresham."

"On one condition."

"Yes, Mr. Gresham?"

"If I ever find a better one I want my money back."

"With pleasure, Mr. Gresham."

It was transported, with infinite pains, to Gresham's house. He had it placed in the den, in the very center of the room.

The den was a museum to shame museums. It is unfortunate that after Gresham's death the room was disassembled piece by piece and raffled off to the bidders. The two hundred pieces it once contained now grace some two hundred dens and museums in two hundred parts of the world; the monstrous luxuriance of that room is lost forever. In its original entirety it was fantastic. Gresham had the world's most expensive pieces of ivory, a diamond the peer of the Koh-i-noor, an emerald statuette four inches high, a Da Vinci madonna, a Shakespeare quarto, and so forth and so forth. The priceless et cetera of Gresham's life was arranged in glass cases, or leather boxes, or under lock and key, and Gresham fondled each object, one by one, every day of his life. He was everything the ideal connoisseur must be—rich man, miser, haggler. He was also (and this is important) a great lover. He fondled his pieces with his eyes, his hands, even his lips. Every morning he had flowers distributed through the den. The diamond, the emerald, the ivory gave him all the ecstasy of the blood his fat body could stand. Into the very middle of this inanimate harem Gresham placed the wonderful doll's house.

It was placed upon a sturdy table, so that anybody sitting in front of it had an excellent eye-level view of most of it. Its position in the center of the den was, in its singular way, symbolic. In very little time the doll's house became the center of Gresham's life.

He started by devoting the better part of a whole day to it. He sat in a chair with his hands clasped over his capacious middle, staring at the little objects one by one with placid and puffy eyes. The eyes moved slowly behind the eyeglasses, selecting the single objects to study, then focusing. He sat in the chair until he had memorized the position, the appearance, the personality of every object in every room. He did not touch a thing.

On the second day he began to touch. His short heavy fingers were not skillful in the ordinary uses of fingers. In a word, he was clumsy. Fortunately, he knew it. He was careful. Delicately, as delicately as he could, he reached out and felt the texture of the rugs, the surface of the wood paneling on the library walls, the silken edge of a fringe on a beautiful lamp. His pudgy fingers floated through the exquisite rooms like pink balloons. It was enough to frighten the little people. He did not touch *them.* He did not dare. They were so fragile and so perfect. He shrank from the terrible prospect of harming them in the least degree.

On the third day he began to touch the little people.

Now Pegerine counted it the finest day's work of his career when he sold the doll's house. His profit from the deal was enormous. He had wild thoughts that night. Gresham was his client now, his friend. He could sell the absurd old fat man many things now. All a man like Pegerine needs is one such client. Now he could comb the cellars and the collections of the city, the world, and pick the finest and the best—and he could sell it all to Gresham. A man who would spend that kind of money for a doll's house would spend money for anything. Pegerine's dreams ran high that night. He had no inkling that he had lost for all time the best customer he had ever had.

None of the dealers in the city ever knew what happened, least of all Pegerine. Mr. Gresham suddenly stopped buying. Whenever the dealers called the house at the appointed hour they were politely informed that Mr. Gresham was "not in the market for things, not anymore, thank you." Did that mean forever? Yes, thank you, it meant forever. No, Mr. Gresham was not ill. No, he was not planning a trip. Nobody could understand it, least of all Pegerine. None of them ever had the slightest suspicion of the fact that it was Pegerine who had slain the goose.

For the truth of the matter is that when Gresham began to play with his doll's house, he found what he had been looking for all his life. The search of the old orphan was over. Here it was—a real home, and family, and children to do his bidding. The more he played with the doll's house, that fat, ungenerous, niggardly old man, the more he reverted to childhood.

He locked the doors of his den, for he wanted no intruding servants to discover him at the game. If a servant happened to discover him fondling a precious stone it would have caused him no embarrassment, but to have somebody find him playing with dolls would have thrown him into a fit. So he would have his breakfast early, then go upstairs to the den, lock the door, pull the chair up to the doll's house, and begin to play. At first he did it only in the mornings. In the afternoons, after lunch, he would devote himself to the other parts of his collection. But the doll's house drew him more and more, and he became impatient with everything else, like a child who cannot eat lunch in the intensity of his desire to have done and get back to his toys, and soon he gave up the rest of the collection altogether. He now devoted himself, morning, noon, and night, to the doll's house. The diamond lay forgotten in its velvet bed, there were no more caresses for the ivory. Gresham's whole life was in the doll's house.

When his fingers became more accustomed to the little things, he let his fancy roam. For the first time in his life, Gresham played games. He began to rearrange the furniture, to rehang the pictures, to move the tiny rugs about. He exchanged andirons from the fireplace on the fourth floor with those from a fireplace on the second. But most of all and best of all he played with the little people. He moved the children in the parlor so that they all surrounded the grandmother instead of facing her. He liked it that way for a week, then he put them back again. In the kitchen a tiny buxom servant, all in white, stood bending over the woodstove. Gresham moved her so that she stood over the sink instead. He kept her there. The baby in the swan bed he did not touch at all. He liked it where it was, under the lovely flight of angels. There were other people in the other rooms, men and women and children. These he deployed and maneuvered. He became the ultimate in interior decorators: he could arrange the inhabitants of the house, put them and keep them where they looked best to him.

In a short time Gresham began to talk to himself. At least, the servants passing in the hall, passing swiftly and discreetly past the den, hearing his voice making an unaccustomed cooing sound, assumed he was talking to himself. This they did not take amiss. Anything might be expected from Mr. Gresham. Talking to himself in the privacy of his most private chamber was quickly and tacitly accepted as simply one more eccentricity. But the truth of the matter was that Gresham was not talking to himself. He was conversing with the little people.

"Now," he said, as he tipped the grandmother lightly back in her rocker and made her swing back and forth. "Isn't that comfy?" He sat there, tipping the rocker every time it gave signs of stopping in its arc. Slyly, swiftly, he would lift his eyes from the grandmother in the parlor, and aim his glance at the master bedroom. "What! Johnny, Mary—*kissing!* Soon as my back is turned?" With admonishments he would turn John and Mary back to back. "Don't want anybody hurt around here," he would say, slyly.

With the children he was just as solicitous. He soon gave names to each one of them, and he coddled them until they might have been the most spoiled brats in Christendom. "Emma," he would say, "did you enjoy your lunch today?" For he had gotten into the habit of moving the children and their elders into the dining room at meal hours, sitting them in their proper places, and changing the plates and removing the silver for every pretended course. He stopped short only at serving them food. He preserved his sanity to that extent. At night, however, he moved every one of the little people into beds in the various bedrooms, and in the morning he awakened them with a cheery "Gooood morning!"

Seven weeks of this and Gresham began to evolve his theory.

It was a simple theory. When one comes to examine it in the light of all pertinent facts, it was almost a natural theory. Gresham began to figure that he was God.

Why not? He had purchased, for an exorbitant fee, a world of his own. The creatures in it he owned body and soul. Over these creatures he exercised an authority complete, unquestioned, irrevocable. His hand moving among these walls was—why not?—the hand of Destiny.

What is the meaning of Destiny? Whatever the words that describe it, in whatever definition, it always has some secret concern with the future. Then the hand that controls the futures—is it not the very hand of Destiny? Only in Gresham's brain, only on Gresham's sufferance, did the future of the little people exist. Gresham's pudgy fingers moved through the rooms, arranging furniture, and liaisons, and lives, with the tender mercy of a benevolent god. What *was* he, then, but God Almighty to this household, this world, this universe of his very own?

Thus the theory took shape, thus it rolled around in his brain, gathering momentum. He drew a picture for himself: he conceived of the world as a series of worlds one within the other, each with its own god, and the gods growing progressively larger, and interlocking, like one of those astounding Oriental balls within balls. Gresham was god of the doll's house, another was god of Gresham's world, and another was god of that god. No—it wasn't so much like an Oriental ball; it was more like a telescope. As he sat in his chair moving his little people backward and forward, upstairs and downstairs, controlling the present and the future of everything and everybody in that house, that world, that universe, he, Gresham, knew that he was God. It added a ticklish pleasure to the game. Now he had a divine scheme.

Now he created such a rigid routine for his people that he could not leave the room anymore, except to retire to his bedroom for sleep. He dressed and undressed his creatures twice a day, read solemn bedtime stories to the children, and conversed long hours with the adults. Now Gresham had all his meals sent to the den, and he was impatient with the servants when they took too long laying out the tray for him, or picking up the empty dishes after he had hurriedly dined. The moments were precious to him; he had so many things to do for his people.

Up to that point, up to the moment of the formation of his theory, Gresham had been a benevolent god. Now, with his catechism set, he began to ponder the ways of all gods, and that started him exercising some of the little extra privileges of his class. After all, a god has to tinker. He began by inflicting certain discomforts, even pain, upon his creatures. One day he tipped the little grandmother so far back in her chair she fell out and lay in a heap on the floor. "See!" Gresham told her. "Life isn't *all* comfy!" Now, whenever one of the children was a little perverse in his movements, refusing to stand or sit in quite the manner Gresham had in mind, he took to spanking it. "Let that teach you a lesson!" he shouted. "Do as you're told! Conform!"

The change from benevolent to vindictive god grew with his growing realization of the absolute power he possessed. Up till now he had been charmed by his playthings and had acted like a father to an adopted family. Now, when the father became the heavenly father, he indulged himself in his omniscience. When the children weren't looking he stole toys from the playroom. He hid them in the kitchen. One day he took the knitting needles from the grandmother's hands. "Enough damn knitting!" he stormed at her. "Try working for a living! Sweat of your brow!" He took her, rocking chair and all, and dumped her in the kitchen. He even attacked the swan crib and the sleeping infant. He knocked the crib over and the infant came tumbling out, rolling over and over on the floor. "Train 'em young," said Gresham. "Teach 'em life's full of hard knocks." He let the infant lie on the floor for two days. He pretended to pay no attention to the wailing sound he heard.

They found Gresham later in a pool of blood, his head cracked in places like an egg tapped with a spoon. The glass of the window in the den had been smashed to bits.

The theory of the police was that Gresham had climbed to the windowsill in order to throw himself out the window. That, being a fat and awkward man, he had bumped into the glass, shattering it. That he had then suffered some sort of attack, or had tripped, and had fallen over backward on his head. That was the way the police figured it out. But Gresham himself would have told them a different story about what happened that night.

He could have told them that he had had an extremely trying day with his flock. Nobody would stand up correctly. The furniture didn't look right. The baby wouldn't go to sleep. "Damn it!" he had screamed. "Shut up! All of you! Do as I say or—or—damn it, you'll roast in hell!" In his anger he kept moving things about with clumsy impatience—beds, chairs, rugs, pictures, people—and the index finger of his right hand, probing into the far corners of the infant's nursery, felt something it had never felt before. It was high up toward the ceiling in the room, which is why Gresham's eyes and fingers had never found it before. He had never stooped low enough to see the ceilings of the second floor. Now he bent over to look, and when he saw it he growled. He ripped it from a triangular shelf high up in the corner. It was a tiny religious figure. It might have been a madonna. He held it in the palm of his hand. It was all green and gold paint over plaster, and there was flowerlike calligraphy on the folds of its cloak and a benign expression upon a face as large as the head of a hatpin. He held it in his hand for some minutes. Then he had to loosen his tie. Then he held the thing between thumb and index finger and with one powerful squeeze he crushed it to powder. He flicked it from his fingertips.

"Fools!"

He rose from his chair and stood face-to-face with the house. He lifted his right hand clear over his left shoulder. His eyes were terrible. With one stroke of the arm he could end existence for all of them, then and there. He shuddered, a wrathful god. "No other gods before Me—!" he began. "No—" But the arm came slowly down to his side again. He quivered a little, but he did not stroke. He subsided, a forgiving god.

That was the night Gresham could not sleep. Jealousy tore at his eyelids, gnawed inside of him. An ancient dyspepsia crept back in and gave him twinges, until he knew he could lie there no longer and simply stare at the ceiling.

"Idols," he murmured, "heathen idols!"

His pajamas were wet with sweat; jealousy seeped through his pores. He tossed on the damp sheets until he could stand it no more. He rose from the bed and strode with mighty steps out of the bedroom, into the hallway, into the den.

It was a dark night. No moonlight came through the windows. It was late, the blackest late part of night. He wanted no light for what he was about to do, so he did not turn on the switch. It took him minutes for his eyes to see through the darkness. The first thing they saw, of course, was the doll's house. He walked noiselessly, with a fat man's grace, up to it.

"I gave you life," he said in an even voice. "Now..."

Once more he raised his heavy right arm over his left shoulder. He raised himself on his toes. This time he brought the back of his hand down against the house with all his strength, and what occurred first was the splintering of the wood where his hand hit—a split-second sound of splintering. The blow swept the whole marvelous house off the table, and it fell to the floor with a great crash. It was no sturdy framework that held that house together—too precise it was, and too delicate to be that strong. The framework caved in like glass. In a heap then, at Gresham's feet, lay a shattered mass of splinters, and bits of glass, and the irreplaceable furniture, and the little people, and torn pieces of the incomparable wallpaper, all in a rubble, like the rubble after a bombing.

"You fools!" Gresham shouted.

It was the back of Gresham's hand that had smote the building. Now the knuckles were bleeding. The hand was at his side and the blood dripped to the floor. "You fools," he shouted. "Never heard of a Day of Judgment? Wouldn't believe me when I warned you? The power of life is the power of death! I warned you—"

He raised the wounded hand and looked at it. The blood ran down his forearm. "Wash you in the blood—I'll wash you in the blood—you stupid, selfish, disobedient—*people*!"

He stood over the rubble and shouted, and exulted, and sweated. God—even a god—cannot be entirely calm after producing an earthquake. Gresham could not keep his arms from shaking. But he knew he could go to sleep now. The evildoers had been slaughtered, vengeance had been wrought.

But first he walked to the window—first he wanted, for some strange reason, a look at the night sky. He walked to the window and leaned heavily upon the sill. He was still breathing hard, his throat and his brain felt curiously congested. He climbed on the broad sill, as if, by getting closer to the window, he could suck in more air. He stood there on the sill, leaning his full weight against the window, panting hard. He looked up at the sky. It was the faintest pale blue of the very early dawn. Not a single cloud floated up there—nothing… till Gresham saw. From the immense void, covering half the shoulder of the sky, the back of an enormous Hand was coming down at him—swiftly, powerfully, vengefully.

RAY BRADBURY was the author of more than three dozen books, including *Fahrenheit 451, The Martian Chronicles, The Illustrated Man*, and *Something Wicked This Way Comes*, as well as hundreds of short stories. He wrote for the theater, cinema, and TV, including the screenplay for John Huston's *Moby Dick* and the Emmy Award–winning teleplay *The Halloween Tree*, and adapted for television sixty-five of his stories for the Ray Bradbury Theater. He was the recipient of the 2000 National Book Foundation's Medal for Distinguished Contribution to American Letters, the 2007 Pulitzer Prize Special Citation, and numerous other honors.

FREDRIC BROWN was born in Cincinnati, Ohio, in 1906. He is perhaps best known for his use of humor in science fiction writing and for his mastery of the "short short" form: many of his stories were intricately plotted but less than a thousand words long. He wrote three science fiction novels and many mystery novels, including *The Fabulous Clipjoint* (1947), which won the Edgar Award for outstanding first mystery novel. His story "Arena" was among the twenty science fiction stories selected by the Science Fiction Writers of America for inclusion in *The Science Fiction Hall of Fame* (1970), and writers such as Philip K. Dick, Robert A. Heinlein, Ayn Rand, and Mickey Spillane have cited him as a direct influence. He died on March 11, 1972, at the age of sixty-five.

SIDNEY CARROLL was born in Brooklyn in 1913. Though he wrote most frequently for television, he is perhaps best remembered for writing the screenplay for *The Hustler* (1963), for which he was nominated for an Academy Award. In 1957, he won an Edgar Award for "The Fine Art of Murder," an installment of the ABC program *Omnibus*. He also won Emmy Awards for *China and the Forbidden City* (1963) and *The Louvre* (1978). Carroll was married to Broadway lyricist June Carroll from 1940 until his death in 1988. He is the father of the novelist Jonathan Carroll.

JOHN CHEEVER was born in 1912, in Quincy, Massachusetts. He left Thayer Academy at age seventeen; the experience served as the nucleus of his first published story, "Expelled" (1930), which was bought by the *New Republic* and immediately established the mode of keen, often critical observation of everyday, middle-class American lives that he would refine over the ensuing five decades. Cheever spent the summer of 1933 at the Yaddo artists' colony in Saratoga Springs, New York, and settled in New York City in the mid-1930s. There he began a lifelong association with the *New Yorker*, which ultimately published 119 of his stories. In 1942, Cheever enlisted in the army. He was transferred by an officer who had read his first story collection to a post in Astoria, Queens. Most of his former infantry company would be killed in the D-Day invasion. He was made a Guggenheim Fellow in 1951, and was elected to the National Institute of Arts and Letters in 1957. Though primarily remembered for his short stories, Cheever also wrote four novels: *The Wapshot Chronicle*, his first, won the National Book Award in 1958, and *Falconer* (1977), his last, was a best seller. *The Stories of John Cheever*, a comprehensive collection, won the 1979 Pulitzer Prize for Fiction. He died of cancer on June 18, 1982, in Ossining, New York.

The best-selling author of classics such as *Charlie and the Chocolate Factory*, *The BFG*, and *Matilda*, **ROALD DAHL** has many times been voted children's all-time favorite author and was described by the London *Times* on his death as "one of the most widely read and influential writers of our generation." His writing career began with articles for magazines such as the *New Yorker* and he wrote successful novellas and short stories for adults before concentrating on his outstanding children's stories. A selection of his adult stories was dramatized for television under the title *Tales of the Unexpected* and many of his children's books have been adapted for film and the stage, including the phenomenally successful Broadway musical of *Matilda*. His books are translated into more than fifty languages and have sold two hundred million copies worldwide.

BRIAN EVENSON is the author of twelve books of fiction, most recently the novel *Immobility* and the story collection *Windeye*. Next year will see the publication of a book he wrote on Chester Brown's graphic novel *Ed the Happy Clown*. He is the recipient of three O. Henry Awards for his short fiction, an IHG Award for his collection *The Wavering Knife*, an ALA-RUSA Award for his novel *Last Days*, and he was also a finalist for an Edgar Award for his novel *The Open Curtain*. He lives with his wife, Kristen Tracy, and their son, Max, in Providence, Rhode Island, where he teaches in the Literary Arts Program of the college that was the basis for H. P. Lovecraft's Miskatonic University.

LUCILLE FLETCHER was born in Brooklyn in 1912. She graduated from Vassar College in 1933, and worked throughout the 1930s as a music librarian, copyright clerk, and publicity writer at CBS, where she met her first husband, composer Bernard Herrmann. A magazine story she wrote, "My Client Curly," was adapted first for radio and later for the film *Once Upon a Time* (1944). Her radio play *Sorry, Wrong Number* premiered in 1943 to great critical acclaim and popularity; it was reprised in several later radio productions, adapted for an eponymous 1948 film directed by Anatole Litvak and starring Barbara Stanwyck, and adapted by Allan Ullman into a 1948 "novelette." Fletcher's radio play *The Hitch-Hiker* was presented on the Orson Welles Show in 1941, and adapted for an episode of *The Twilight Zone* in 1960. In total she wrote fourteen radio plays and nine novels, as well as the libretto of Herrmann's 1951 opera version of Emily Brontë's *Wuthering Heights*. She was married to her second husband, the novelist and playwright Douglas Wallop, for thirty-six years. She died in 2000.

JOSEPH CHAMBERLAIN FURNAS was born in Indianapolis in 1906. He attended Harvard University, where he wrote for many college publications. Furnas was perhaps best known for a 1935 article "...And Sudden Death!," which *Reader's Digest* reprinted eight million times. The article chronicled grisly car accidents and was credited with inspiring the automobile industry and the federal Transportation Department to enhance safety measures for motorists. He was a longtime contributor to the *American Scholar* and wrote prolifically for newspapers such as the *New York Times* and magazines such as the *Saturday Evening Post*, *Collier's*, *Look*, and *Reader's Digest*. He also wrote an informal three-volume social history of the American colonies and the United States; a "wet" history of the temperance movement; biographies of Fanny Kemble and Robert Louis Stevenson; several novels; and an autobiography, *My Life in Writing: Memoirs of a Maverick*. He died in 2001 in Stanton, New Jersey.

JOSEPHINE W. JOHNSON was born in May 1910 on the family farm in Kirkwood, Missouri, and grew up in nearby Webster Groves. She attended Washington University in St. Louis but left in 1932 without a degree to go home and write. She set up in her mother's attic where, with light from a dormer spilling across her desk, she wrote and wrote. Stories from the attic began appearing in national magazines and a New York editor asked if she was considering a novel. She wrote *Now in November* and was at home one spring day when a reporter rang up to tell her that she had won the 1935 Pulitzer Prize for fiction. She was twenty-four. Josephine would go on to publish three more novels, dozens of short stories (including two collections), a book of poetry, many essays, a children's book, a picture-book text, a memoir, and *The Inland Island*, a nonfiction blend of nature journal, ecological manifesto, and walk in the woods. In 1969, it became an unlikely best seller, hailed by critics and widely read by the growing environmental movement. The loves of her life were her husband, Grant Cannon, her three children, Terry, Annie, and Carol, and the thirty-seven acres of "island" near Cincinnati that she watched run wild at the uneasy border of outer suburb and inner country. She died in February 1990.

FRANZ KAFKA was born on July 3, 1883, in Prague, to a family of middle-class Ashkenazi Jews. He obtained a doctorate in law at the German Karl-Ferdinands-Universität of Prague, where he met his lifelong friend Max Brod. Kafka found employment with the Worker's Accident Insurance Institute, but wrote often of his boredom at his *Brotberuf*, or day job, and preferred to spend time writing stories and letters. His political views, his Judaism, and his possibly schizoid personality all remain subjects of debate. He was diagnosed with tuberculosis in 1917, and spent most of the rest of his life in sanatoriums, dying in Vienna on June 3, 1924. Only a few of Kafka's literary works, all of which were written in German, were published during his lifetime: the story collections *Betrachtung* (*Contemplation*) and *Ein Landarzt* (*A Country Doctor*), and individual stories, such as "Die Verwandlung" ("The Metamorphosis"). Kafka's unfinished works, including his novels *Der Process*, *Das Schloss*, and *Amerika*, were published posthumously, mostly by Brod, who ignored Kafka's wish to have the manuscripts destroyed. Appreciation for Kafka's work increased after his death and, today, he is widely regarded as one of the most important writers of the twentieth century.

HENRY KUTTNER was born in Los Angeles in 1915. He was raised in relative poverty after the death of his father and, as a young man, he worked for the literary agency of his uncle, Laurence D'Orsay. In 1936, Kuttner sold the story "The Graveyard Rats" to the pulp magazine *Weird Tales*. Writing for *Weird Tales* brought him into direct correspondence with that magazine's premier contributor, H.P. Lovecraft; he set several stories in Lovecraft's Cthulhu Mythos and, through Lovecraft, met fellow writer Catherine L. Moore, whom he married in 1940. Though he continued to write and publish on his own, he also frequently collaborated with Moore, publishing several cowritten novels and stories (often under the joint pseudonym Lewis Padgett, a combination of their mothers' maiden names). Many authors have cited Kuttner as an important influence, including Richard Matheson, who dedicated his acclaimed novel *I Am Legend* to Kuttner. In his introduction to *The Best of Henry Kuttner*, Ray Bradbury called Kuttner a "pomegranate writer: popping with seeds—full of ideas." Kuttner died of a heart attack in Los Angeles in 1958.

JULIAN MAY was born in Chicago in 1931. As a teenager she published the science fiction fanzine *Interim Newsletter* and, in 1950, she sold her first science fiction short story, "Dune Roller," to *Astounding Science Fiction*. In 1952, after chairing the Tenth World Science Fiction Convention and selling one other story, she left the science fiction field and spent the next twenty-six years writing thousands of science encyclopedia articles and hundreds of scientific and historical books for children and young adults. During this time she also ran an editorial service for small publishers with her husband, the editor and anthologist T.E. Dikty. In the mid-1970s, she rekindled her interest in science fiction, and has since published twenty science fiction novels.

CHINA MIÉVILLE is the author of nine novels, including *The City & the City*, *Embassytown*, and *Railsea*, and of a collection of short stories, *Looking for Jake*. His nonfiction includes *London's Overthrow* and *Between Equal Rights*. He has won the Hugo, World Fantasy, and Arthur C. Clarke Awards. He lives and works in London.

BENJAMIN PERCY is the author of two novels, *Red Moon* and *The Wilding*, as well as two short-story collections, *Refresh, Refresh* and *The Language of Elk*. His fiction and nonfiction have been read on National Public Radio and published by *Esquire* (where he is a contributing editor), *GQ*, *Time*, *Men's Journal*, *Outside*, the *Wall Street Journal*, the *Paris Review*, and *Tin House*. His honors include an NEA fellowship, the Whiting Writers' Award, the Plimpton Prize, two Pushcart Prizes, and inclusion in *Best American Short Stories* and *Best American Comics*. His next novel, *The Dead Lands*, a postapocalyptic reimagining of the Lewis and Clark saga, is forthcoming from Grand Central/ Hachette in 2014.

JOHN GEORGE REITCI, who wrote under the name Jack Ritchie, was born in 1922 in Milwaukee, Wisconsin. He served in the army in the Central Pacific during World War II and, when he returned home to Milwaukee, he began writing mystery stories. He wrote prolifically over the next four decades; his stories appeared in a diverse array of publications including *Manhunt* magazine, *Stag* magazine, *Smashing Detective Stories*, the *Philadelphia Inquirer*, the *New York Daily Mirror*, and *Good Housekeeping*. His story "The Green Heart" was adapted into the movie *A New Leaf* (1971), directed by Elaine May, and his story "The Absence of Emily" won an Edgar Award in 1981. Reitci completed one novel, *Tiger Island*, shortly before his death in 1983.

JOHN STEINBECK was born in 1902 in Salinas, California. As a teenager, he spent summers working on ranches alongside migrant workers. He attended Stanford University but left without a degree. He first achieved critical success in 1935 with the novel *Tortilla Flat*. Soon thereafter he wrote a series of novels concerning the travails of common people during the Great Depression, including *Of Mice and Men* (1937) and *The Grapes of Wrath*, which won the National Book Award and the Pulitzer Prize for Fiction in 1939. Steinbeck was strongly influenced by his friendship with the ecologist and philosopher Edward Ricketts, with whom he wrote

The Log from the Sea of Cortez, an account of an expedition to the Gulf of California. In 1943, he traveled to Europe as a war correspondent for the *New York Herald Tribune* and worked with the Office of Strategic Services, the predecessor of the CIA. A few years later, he made the first of many trips to the Soviet Union, chronicling his trip in *A Russian Journal*. In 1952, he published *East of Eden*, which he considered his magnum opus. He was elected to the American Academy of Arts and Letters in 1948, won the Nobel Prize for literature in 1962, and received a Presidential Medal of Freedom from Lyndon B. Johnson in 1964.

ALLAN ULLMAN was born in 1908. He graduated from the Wharton School of the University of Pennsylvania in 1929. He worked as a book advertising salesman for the *New York Times*, as promotion director of Random House Inc., as an executive of the Book of the Month Club, and finally as the head of the *Times* book and education division. He also wrote several thriller novelizations of radio plays and screenplays, including Lucille Fletcher's *Night Man* and *Sorry, Wrong Number.* He died in 1982 in Southampton, New York.

E. LILY YU received the 2012 John W. Campbell Award for Best New Writer, as well as nominations for the 2012 Hugo, Nebula, and World Fantasy Awards. Her fiction has appeared in *Boston Review*, *Clarkesworld*, *Apex* magazine, and *The Best Science Fiction and Fantasy of the Year*. Once upon a time, she was a volunteer at the Egyptian Museum in Cairo. She is currently working on a novel, a video game for Tale of Tales, and a PhD.

THE BEST OF McSWEENEY'S

Edited by Dave Eggers and Jordan Bass

To commemorate the fifteenth anniversary of the journal called "a key barometer of the literary climate" by the *New York Times* and twice honored with a National Magazine Award for fiction, here is *The Best of McSweeney's*—a comprehensive collection of some of the magazine's most remarkable work. Drawing on the full range of the journal thus far—from the very earliest volumes to the Chris Ware–edited graphic novel issue to the full-on Sunday-newspaper issue known as the *San Francisco Panorama*, *The Best of McSweeney's* is a fascinating glimpse into recent literary history.

Featuring Wells Tower, David Foster Wallace, Andrew Sean Greer, Nicholson Baker, Zadie Smith, Peter Orner, Simon Rich, Mary Miller, Ellie Kemper, John Hodgman, Sam Lipsyte, Lydia Millet, Deb Olin Unferth, Adam Levin, George Saunders, Clancy Martin, Daniel Alarcón, Sarah Vowell, Arthur Bradford, Todd Pruzan, Jonathan Lethem, Kevin Moffett, Sean Wilsey, Kevin Brockmeier, Roddy Doyle, Jess Walter, Steven Millhauser, A.M. Homes, Chris Ware, Adrian Tomine, Daniel G. Clowes, Joe Sacco, Chris Adrian, Julie Hecht, Lydia Davis, Michael Chabon, Dan Chaon, Jonathan Ames, Sheila Heti, Rick Moody, Jennie Erin Smith, Michelle Orange, Lawrence Weschler, Breyten Breytenbach, Gunnhild Øyehaug, Nyuol Lueth Tong, Ellen van Neerven-Currie, Edwin Rozic, Laird Hunt, Glen David Gold, Jennifer Egan, Jennifer Michael Hecht, Mike Sacks, John Moe, Steve Delahoyde, Amy Fusselman, Colleen Werthmann, Tom O'Donnell, Bill Tarlin, and Ben Jahn.

Available at store.mcsweeneys.net and your local independent bookstore.

DON'T LOOK BEHIND YOU

FREDRIC BROWN

{SELECTED BY ALFRED HITCHCOCK}

Just sit back and relax, now. Try to enjoy this; it's going to be the last story you ever read, or nearly the last. After you finish it you can sit there and stall a while, you can find excuses to hang around your house, or your room, or your office, wherever you're reading this; but sooner or later you're going to have to get up and go out. That's where I'm waiting for you: outside. Or maybe closer than that. Maybe in this room.

You think that's a joke of course. You think this is just a story in a book, and that I don't really mean you. Keep right on thinking so. But be fair; admit that I'm giving you fair warning.

Harley bet me I couldn't do it. He bet me a diamond he's told me about, a diamond as big as his head. So you see why I've got to kill you. And why I've got to tell you how and why and all about it first. That's part of the bet. It's just the kind of idea Harley would have.

I'll tell you about Harley first. He's tall and handsome, and suave and cosmopolitan. He looks something like Ronald Coleman, only he's taller. He dresses like a million dollars, but it wouldn't matter if he didn't; I mean that he'd look distinguished in overalls. There's a sort of magic about Harley, a mocking magic in the way he looks at you; it makes you think of palaces and far-off countries and bright music.

It was in Springfield, Ohio, that he met Justin Dean. Justin was a funny-looking little runt who was just a printer. He worked for the Atlas Printing & Engraving Company. He was a very ordinary little guy, just about as different as possible from Harley; you couldn't pick two men more different. He was only thirty-five, but he was mostly bald already, and he had to wear thick glasses because he'd worn out his eyes doing fine printing and engraving. He was a good printer and engraver; I'll say that for him.

I never asked Harley how he happened to come to Springfield, but the day he got there, after he'd checked in at the Castle Hotel, he stopped in at Atlas to have some calling cards made. It happened that Justin Dean was alone in the shop at the time, and he took Harley's order for the cards; Harley wanted engraved ones, the best. Harley always wants the best of everything.

Harley probably didn't even notice Justin; there was no reason why he should have. But Justin noticed Harley all right, and in him he saw everything that he himself would like to be, and never would be, because most of the things Harley has, you have to be born with.

And Justin made the plates for the cards himself and printed them himself, and he did a wonderful job—something he thought would be worthy of a man like Harley Prentice. That was the name engraved on the card, just that and nothing else, as all really important people have their cards engraved.

He did fine-line work on it, freehand cursive style, and used all the skill he had. It wasn't wasted, because the next day when Harley called to get the cards he held one and stared at it for a while, and then he looked at Justin, seeing him for the first time. He asked, "Who did this?"

And little Justin told him proudly who had done it, and Harley smiled at him and told him it was the work of an artist, and he asked Justin to have dinner with him that evening after work, in the Blue Room of the Castle Hotel.

That's how Harley and Justin got together, but Harley was careful. He waited until he'd known Justin a while before he asked him whether or not he could make plates for five- and ten-dollar bills. Harley had the contacts; he could market the bills in quantity with men who specialized in passing them, and—most important—he knew where he could get paper with the silk threads in it, paper that wasn't quite the genuine thing, but was close enough to pass inspection by anyone but an expert.

So Justin quit his job at Atlas and he and Harley went to New York, and they set up a little printing shop as a blind, on Amsterdam Avenue south of Sherman Square, and they worked at the bills. Justin worked hard, harder than he had ever worked in his life, because besides working on the plates for the bills, he helped meet expenses by handling what legitimate printing work came into the shop.

He worked day and night for almost a year, making plate after plate, and each one was a little better than the last, and finally he had plates that Harley said were good enough. That night they had dinner at the Waldorf-Astoria to celebrate and after dinner they went the rounds of the best night clubs, and it cost Harley a small fortune, but that didn't matter because they were going to get rich.

They drank champagne, and it was the first time Justin ever drank champagne and he got disgustingly drunk and must have made quite a fool of himself. Harley told him about it afterwards, but Harley wasn't mad at him. He took him back to his room at the hotel and put him to bed, and Justin was pretty sick for a couple of days. But that didn't matter, either, because they were going to get rich.

Then Justin started printing bills from the plates, and they got rich.

After that, Justin didn't have to work so hard, either, because he turned down most jobs that came into the print shop, told them he was behind schedule and couldn't handle any more. He took just a little work, to keep up a front. And behind the front, he made five- and ten-dollar bills, and he and Harley got rich.

He got to know other people whom Harley knew. He met Bull Mallon, who handled the distribution end. Bull Mallon was built like a bull, that was why they called him that. He had a face that never smiled or changed expression at all except when he was holding burning matches to the soles of Justin's bare feet. But that wasn't then; that was later, when he wanted Justin to tell him where the plates were.

And he got to know Captain John Willys of the Police Department, who was a friend of Harley's, to whom Harley gave quite a bit of the money they made, but that didn't matter either, because there was plenty left and they all got rich. He met a friend of Harley's who was a big star of the stage, and one who owned a big New York newspaper. He got to know other people equally important, but in less respectable ways.

Harley, Justin knew, had a hand in lots of other enterprises besides the little mint on Amsterdam Avenue. Some of these ventures took him out of town, usually over weekends. And the weekend that Harley was murdered Justin never found out what really happened, except that Harley went away and didn't come back. Oh, he knew that he was murdered, all right, because the police found his body—with three bullet holes in his chest—in the most expensive suite of the best hotel in Albany. Even for a place to be found dead in, Harley Prentice had chosen the best.

All Justin ever knew about it was that a long distance call came to him at the hotel where he was staying, the night that Harley was murdered—it must have been a matter of minutes, in fact, before the time the newspapers said Harley was killed.

It was Harley's voice on the phone, and his voice was debonair and unexcited as ever. But he said, "Justin? Get to the shop and get rid of the plates, the paper, everything. Right away. I'll explain when I see you." He waited only until Justin said, "Sure, Harley," and then he said, "Attaboy," and hung up.

Justin hurried around to the printing shop and got the plates and the paper and a few thousand dollars' worth of counterfeit bills that were on hand. He made the paper and bills into one bundle and the copper plates into another, smaller one, and he left the shop with no evidence that it had ever been a mint in miniature.

He was very careful and very clever in disposing of both bundles. He got rid of the big one first by checking in at a big hotel, not one he or Harley ever stayed at, under a false name, just to have a chance to put the big bundle in the incinerator there. It was paper and it would burn. And he made sure there was a fire in the incinerator before he dropped it down the chute.

The plates were different. They wouldn't burn, he knew, so he took a trip to Staten Island and back on the ferry and, somewhere out in the middle of the bay, he dropped the bundle over the side into the water.

Then, having done what Harley had told him to do, and having done it well and thoroughly, he went back to the hotel—his own hotel, not the one where he had dumped the paper and the bills—and went to sleep.

In the morning he read in the newspapers that Harley had been killed, and he was stunned. It didn't seem possible. He couldn't believe it; it was a joke someone was playing on him. Harley would come back to him, he knew. And he was right; Harley did, but that was later, in the swamp.

But anyway, Justin had to know, so he took the very next train for Albany. He must have been on the train when the police went to his hotel, and at the hotel they must have learned he'd asked at the desk about trains for Albany, because they were waiting for him when he got off the train there.

They took him to a station and they kept him there a long long time, days and days, asking him questions. They found out, after a while, that he couldn't have killed Harley because he'd been in New York City at the time Harley was killed in Albany, but they knew also that he and Harley had been operating the little mint, and they thought that might be a lead to who killed Harley, and they were interested in the counterfeiting, too, maybe even more than in the murder. They asked Justin Dean questions, over and over and over, and he couldn't answer them, so he didn't. They kept him awake for days at a time, asking him questions over and over. Most of all they wanted to know where the plates were. He wished he could tell them that the plates were safe where nobody could ever get them again, but he couldn't tell them that without admitting that he and Harley had been counterfeiting, so he couldn't tell them.

They located the Amsterdam shop, but they didn't find any evidence there, and they really had no evidence to hold Justin on at all, but he didn't know that, and it never occurred to him to get a lawyer.

He kept wanting to see Harley, and they wouldn't let him; then, when they learned he really didn't believe Harley could be dead, they made him look at a dead man they said was Harley, and he guessed it was, although Harley looked different dead.

He didn't look magnificent, dead. And Justin believed, then, but still didn't believe. And after that he just went silent and wouldn't say a word, even when they kept him awake for days and days with a bright light in his eyes, and kept slapping him to keep him awake. They didn't use clubs or rubber hoses, but they slapped him a million times and wouldn't let him sleep. And after a while he lost track of things and couldn't have answered their questions even if he'd wanted to.

For a while after that, he was in a bed in a white room, and all he remembers about that are nightmares he had, and calling for Harley and an awful confusion as to whether Harley was dead or not, and then things came back to him gradually and he knew he didn't want to stay in the white room; he wanted to get out so he could hunt for Harley. And if

Harley was dead, he wanted to kill whoever had killed Harley, because Harley would have done the same for him.

So he began pretending, and acting, very cleverly, the way the doctors and nurses seemed to want him to act, and after a while they gave him his clothes and let him go.

He was becoming cleverer now. He thought, What would Harley tell me to do? And he knew they'd try to follow him because they'd think he might lead them to the plates, which they didn't know were at the bottom of the bay, and he gave them the slip before he left Albany, and he went first to Boston, and from there by boat to New York, instead of going direct.

He went first to the print shop, and went in the back way after watching the alley for a long time to be sure the place wasn't guarded. It was a mess; they must have searched it very thoroughly for the plates.

Harley wasn't there, of course. Justin left and from a phone booth in a drugstore he telephoned their hotel and asked for Harley and was told Harley no longer lived there; and to be clever and not let them guess who he was, he asked for Justin Dean, and they said Justin Dean didn't live there anymore either.

Then he moved to a different drugstore and from there he decided to call up some friends of Harley's, and he phoned Bull Mallon first and because Bull was a friend, he told him who he was and asked if he knew where Harley was.

Bull Mallon didn't pay any attention to that; he sounded excited, a little, and he asked, "Did the cops get the plates, Dean?" and Justin said they didn't, that he wouldn't tell them, and he asked again about Harley.

Bull asked, "Are you nuts, or kidding?" And Justin just asked him again, and Bull's voice changed and he said, "Where are you?" and Justin told him. Bull said, "Harley's here. He's staying undercover, but it's all right if you know, Dean. You wait right there at the drugstore, and we'll come and get you."

They came and got Justin, Bull Mallon and two other men in a car, and they told him Harley was hiding out way deep in New Jersey and that they were going to drive there now. So he went along and sat in the back seat between two men he didn't know, while Bull Mallon drove.

It was late afternoon then, when they picked him up, and Bull drove all evening and most of the night and he drove fast, so he must have gone farther than New Jersey, at least into Virginia or maybe farther, into the Carolinas.

The sky was getting faintly gray with first dawn when they stopped at a rustic cabin that looked like it had been used as a hunting lodge. It was miles from anywhere, there wasn't even a road leading to it, just a trail that was level enough for the car to be able to make it.

They took Justin into the cabin and tied him to a chair, and they told him Harley wasn't there, but Harley had told them that Justin would tell them where the plates were, and he couldn't leave until he did tell.

Justin didn't believe them; he knew then that they'd tricked him about Harley, but it didn't matter, as far as the plates were concerned. It didn't matter if he told them what he'd done with the plates, because they couldn't get them again, and they wouldn't tell the police. So he told them, quite willingly.

But they didn't believe him. They said he'd hidden the plates and was lying. They tortured him to make him tell. They beat him, and they cut him with knives, and they held burning matches and lighted cigars to the soles of his feet, and they pushed needles under his fingernails. Then they'd rest and ask him questions and if he could talk, he'd tell them the truth, and after a while they'd start to torture him again.

It went on for days and weeks—Justin doesn't know how long, but it was a long time. Once they went away for several days and left him tied up with nothing to eat or drink. They came back and started in all over again. And all the time he hoped Harley would come to help him, but Harley didn't come, not then.

After a while what was happening in the cabin ended, or anyway he didn't know any more about it. They must have thought he was dead; maybe they were right, or anyway not far from wrong.

The next thing he knows was the swamp. He was lying in shallow water at the edge of deeper water. His face was out of the water; it woke him when he turned a little and his face went under. They must have thought him dead and thrown him into the water, but he had floated into the shallow part before he had drowned, and a last flicker of consciousness had turned him over on his back with his face out.

I don't remember much about Justin in the swamp; it was a long time, but I just remember flashes of it. I couldn't move at first; I just lay there in the shallow water with my face out. It got dark and it got cold, I remember, and finally my arms would move a little and I got farther out of the water, lying in the mud with only my feet in the water. I slept or was unconscious again and when I woke up it was getting gray dawn, and that was when Harley came. I think I'd been calling him, and he must have heard.

He stood there, dressed as immaculately and perfectly as ever, right in the swamp, and he was laughing at me for being so weak and lying there like a log, half in the dirty water and half in the mud, and I got up and nothing hurt anymore.

We shook hands and he said, "Come on, Justin, let's get you out of here," and I was so glad he'd come that I cried a little. He laughed at me for that and said I should lean on him and he'd help me walk, but I wouldn't do that, because I was coated with mud and filth of the swamp and he was so clean and perfect in a white linen suit, like an ad in a magazine. And all the way out of that swamp, all the days and nights we spent there, he never even got mud on his trouser cuffs, nor his hair mussed.

I told him just to lead the way, and he did, walking just ahead of me, sometimes turning around, laughing and talking to me and cheering me up. Sometimes I'd fall but I wouldn't let him come back and help me.

But he'd wait patiently until I could get up. Sometimes I'd crawl instead when I couldn't stand up anymore. Sometimes I'd have to swim streams that he'd leap lightly across.

And it was day and night and day and night, and sometimes I'd sleep, and things would crawl across me. And some of them I caught and ate, or maybe I dreamed that. I remember other things, in that swamp, like an organ that played a lot of the time, and sometimes angels in the air and devils in the water, but those were delirium, I guess.

Harley would say, "A little farther, Justin; we'll make it. And we'll get back at them, at all of them."

And we made it. We came to dry fields, cultivated fields with waist-high corn, but there weren't ears on the cob for me to eat. And then there was a stream, a clear stream that wasn't stinking water like the swamp, and Harley told me to wash myself and my clothes and I did, although I wanted to hurry on to where I could get food.

I still looked pretty bad; my clothes were clean of mud and filth but they were mere rags and wet, because I couldn't wait for them to dry, and I had a ragged beard and I was barefoot.

But we went on and came to a little farm building, just a two-room shack, and there was a smell of fresh bread just out of an oven, and I ran the last few yards to knock on the door. A woman, an ugly woman, opened the door and when she saw me she slammed it again before I could say a word.

Strength came to me from somewhere, maybe from Harley, although I can't remember him being there just then. There was a pile of kindling logs beside the door. I picked one of them up as though it were no heavier than a broomstick, and I broke down the door and killed the woman. She screamed a lot, but I killed her. Then I ate the hot fresh bread.

I watched from the window as I ate, and saw a man running across the field toward the house. I found a knife, and I killed him as he came in at the door. It was much better, killing with the knife; I liked it that way.

I ate more bread, and kept watching from all the windows, but no one else came. Then my stomach hurt from the hot bread I'd eaten and I had to lie down, doubled up, and when the hurting quit, I slept.

Harley woke me up, and it was dark. He said, "Let's get going; you should be far away from here before it's daylight."

I knew he was right, but I didn't hurry away. I was becoming, as you see, very clever now. I knew there were things to do first. I found matches and a lamp, and lighted the lamp. Then I hunted through the shack for everything I could use. I found clothes of the man, and they fitted me not too badly except that I had to turn up the cuffs of the trousers and the shirt. His shoes were big, but that was good because my feet were so swollen. I found a razor and shaved; it took a long time because my hand wasn't steady, but I was very careful and didn't cut myself much.

I had to hunt hardest for their money, but I found it finally. It was sixty dollars.

And I took the knife, after I had sharpened it. It isn't fancy; just a bone-handled carving knife, but it's good steel. I'll show it to you, pretty soon now. It's had a lot of use.

Then we left and it was Harley who told me to stay away from the roads, and find railroad tracks. That was easy because we heard a train whistle far off in the night and knew which direction the tracks lay. From then on, with Harley helping, it's been easy.

You won't need the details from here. I mean, about the brakeman, and about the tramp we found asleep in the empty reefer, and about the near thing I had with the police in Richmond. I learned from that; I learned I mustn't talk to Harley when anybody else was around to hear. He hides himself from them; he's got a trick and they don't know he's there, and they think I'm funny in the head if I talk to him. But in Richmond I bought better clothes and got a haircut and a man I killed in an alley had forty dollars on him, so I had money again. I've done a lot of traveling since then. If you stop to think you'll know where I am right now.

I'm looking for Bull Mallon and the two men who helped him. Their names are Harry and Carl. I'm going to kill them when I find them. Harley keeps telling me that those fellows are big-time and that I'm not ready for them yet. But I can be looking while I'm getting ready so I keep moving around. Sometimes I stay in one place long enough to hold a job as a printer for a while. I've learned a lot of things. I can hold a job and people don't think I'm too strange; they don't get scared when I look at them like they sometimes did a few months ago. And I've learned not to talk to Harley except in our own room and then only very quietly so people in the next room won't think I'm talking to myself.

And I've kept in practice with the knife. I've killed lots of people with it, mostly on the streets at night. Sometimes because they look like they might have money on them, but mostly just for practice and because I've come to like doing it. I'm really good with the knife by now. You'll hardly feel it.

But Harley tells me that kind of killing is easy and that it's something else to kill a person who's on guard, as Bull and Harry and Carl will be.

And that's the conversation that led to the bet I mentioned. I told Harley that I'd bet him that, right now, I could warn a man I was going to use the knife on him and even tell him why and approximately when, and that I could still kill him. And he bet me that I couldn't and he's going to lose that bet.

He's going to lose it because I'm warning you right now and you're not going to believe me. I'm betting that you're going to believe that this is just another story in a book! That you won't believe that this is the *only* copy of this book that contains this story and that this story is true. Even when I tell you how it was done, I don't think you'll really believe me.

You see I'm putting it over on Harley, winning the bet, by putting it over on you. He never thought, and you won't realize how easy it is for a good printer, who's been a counterfeiter too, to counterfeit one story in a book. Nothing like as hard as counterfeiting a five-dollar bill.

I had to pick a book of short stories and I picked this one because I happened to notice that the last story in the book was titled "Don't Look Behind You" and that was going to be a good title for this. You'll see what I mean in a few minutes.

I'm lucky that the printing shop I'm working for now does book work and had a typeface that matches the rest of this book. I had a little trouble matching the paper exactly, but I finally did and I've got it ready while I'm writing this. I'm writing this directly on a linotype, late at night in the shop where I'm working days. I even have the boss's permission, told him I was going to set up and print a story that a friend of mine had written, as a surprise for him, and that I'd melt the type metal back as soon as I'd printed one good copy.

When I finish writing this I'll make up the type in pages to match the rest of the book and I'll print it on the matching paper I have ready. I'll cut the new pages to fit and bind them in; you won't be able to tell the difference, even if a faint suspicion may cause you to look at it. Don't forget I made five- and ten-dollar bills you couldn't have told from the original, and this is kindergarten stuff compared to that job. And I've done enough bookbinding that I'll be able to take the last story out of the book and bind this one in instead of it and you won't be able to tell the difference no matter how closely you look. I'm going to do a perfect job of it if it takes me all night.

And tomorrow I'll go to some bookstore, or maybe a newsstand or even a drugstore that sells books and has other copies of this book, ordinary copies, and I'll plant this one there. I'll find myself a good place to watch from, and I'll be watching when you buy it.

The rest I can't tell you yet because it depends a lot on circumstances, whether you went right home with the book or what you did. I won't know till I follow you and keep watch till you read it—and I see that you're reading the last story in the book.

If you're home while you're reading this, maybe I'm in the house with you right now. Maybe I'm in this very room, hidden, waiting for you to finish the story. Maybe I'm watching through a window. Or maybe I'm sitting near you on the streetcar or train, if you're reading it there. Maybe I'm on the fire escape outside your hotel room. But wherever you're reading it, I'm near you, watching and waiting for you to finish. You can count on that.

You're pretty near the end now. You'll be finished in seconds and you'll close the book, still not believing. Or, if you haven't read the stories in order, maybe you'll turn back to start another story. If you do, you'll never finish it.

But don't look around; you'll be happier if you don't know, if you don't see the knife coming. When I kill people from behind they don't seem to mind so much.

Go on, just a few seconds or minutes, thinking this is just another story. Don't look behind you. Don't believe this—*until you feel the knife.*